The Economics of Keynes in Historical Context

By the same author:

New Perspectives on Keynes (edited with Allin F. Cottrell)

The Causes and Costs of Depository Institution Failures (edited with Allin F. Cottrell and John H. Wood)

The Economics of Keynes in Historical Context

An Intellectual History of the *General Theory*

Michael S. Lawlor
Wake Forest University, USA

330.156
L418ℓ

First published 2006 by
PALGRAVE MACMILLAN
Houndmills, Basingstoke, Hampshire RG21 6XS and
175 Fifth Avenue, New York, N.Y. 10010
Companies and representatives throughout the world

PALGRAVE MACMILLAN is the global academic imprint of the Palgrave
Macmillan division of St. Martin's Press, LLC and of Palgrave Macmillan Ltd.
Macmillan® is a registered trademark in the United States, United Kingdom
and other countries. Palgrave is a registered trademark in the European
Union and other countries.

ISBN-13: 978-0-333-97717-0 hardback
ISBN-10: 0-333-97717-3   hardback

This book is printed on paper suitable for recycling and made from fully
managed and sustained forest sources.

A catalogue record for this book is available from the British Library.

Library of Congress Cataloging-in-Publication Data

Lawlor, Michael S.
    The economics of Keynes in historical context: an intellectual history
    of the General Theory/Michael S. Lawlor.
        p. cm.
    Includes bibliographical references and index.
    ISBN 0-333-97717-3
        1. Keynesian economics. 2. Keynes, John Maynard, 1883–1946. General
    theory of employment, interest and money. I. Keynes, John Maynard,
    1883–1946. General theory of employment, interest and money. II. Title.

HB99.7.L36 2006
330.15'6–dc22
                                                                2006045341

10   9   8   7   6   5   4   3   2   1
15   14   13   12   11   10   09   08   07   06

Printed and bound in Great Britain by
Antony Rowe Ltd, Chippenham and Eastbourne

For my family

Contents

List of Figures   xii

Acknowledgments   xiii

Preface   xv

Introductory Material: Motivation, Methodology and Overview   1

Chapter 1   Motivation: Approaching the *General Theory*   3
Historically

    I. A "history" of a book   3

    II. Keynes's question   4

    III. The Keynes literature   7

Chapter 2   Methodological Stance: The Marshallian   16
Structure of the *General Theory*

    I. The Marshallian method   16

    II. Keynes's treatment of time   18

    III. Keynes's use of equilibrium   22

Chapter 3   Overview   25

Part I Keynes, Cambridge and the Economics   33
of Employment

Chapter 4   Introduction: Keynes, the *General Theory* and   35
the Labor Market

    I. Unemployment and the *General Theory*   35

    II. Labor markets in the *General Theory*   36

Chapter 5   The "Late Victorian" Intellectual Context of   40
Marshall's Labor Market Views

    I. Unemployment to the Victorians: The Background   40
      to Marshallianism

    II. Marshall and the late Victorian labor question   44

Chapter 6 The Treatment of Labor Markets in Marshallian   53
Economics

    I. Marshall's method and his treatment of distribution   53
       in the *Principles of Economics*

    II. Marshall's marginal product of labor, efficiency   56
        wages and the national dividend

    III. Dobb: Labor market orthodoxy in interwar Cambridge   63

    IV. Pigou: Mechanical Marshallianism   66

Chapter 7 Keynes and the Labor Market   71

    I. Keynes as a Marshallian   71

    II. Keynes as a young don   75

    III. Keynes in the twenties: An emerging social   79
        theory of wages

    IV. Conclusion: The labor market in the   86
        General Theory in Historical Context

Part II A Philosopher and a Speculator   **93**

Chapter 8 Looking Backward from the *General Theory:*   95
On the Historical Origins of Keynes's Financial Market Views

    I. Introduction to Part II   95

    II. Two problems of later Marshallian economics: 96
        "The Representative Firm" and the joint-stock
        company

    III. Looking backward from the *General Theory*   103

Chapter 9 Stock Equilibrium in Asset Markets and   107
"The Folly of Amateur Speculators": The Marshallian Setting

    I. Introduction   107

    II. Marshall's 1871 essay "Money"   108

    III. Marshall on speculation   111

    IV. H. C. Emery: *Speculation on the Stock and Produce*   116
        Exchanges of the United States

V. The historical record and Keynes's developing views   123
of speculation

Chapter 10   The Evolution of Keynes's Views on Asset Markets   126
and Speculation

    I. The young don as philosopher of speculation, 1909–14   126

    II. The philosopher starts speculating, 1919–23   132

    III. Speculation and the credit cycle, 1923–30   139

    IV. Conclusion: "Faithful" investing and speculative   147
    economics, 1931–36

Part III "Shifting Equilibria" in a Monetary Economy   **153**

Chapter 11   The Development of Cambridge Monetary   155
Thought 1870–1935

    I. Introduction   155

    II. Early twentieth century monetary and business   158
    cycle theory

    III. Specific Marshallian monetary antecedents   160

    IV. Marshallian monetary and cycle theory as a precursor   165
    to the *General Theory*

    V. Marshall's pupils   168

    VI. Keynes and Marshallian monetary economics   176

Chapter 12   Keynes's Development as a Cambridge Monetary   178
Theorist

    I. Introduction   178

    II. The historical context for Keynes as a monetary economist   179

    III. Pre-war lectures: "The Theory of Money"   181

    IV. Debates with Dennis Robertson and "Forced savings"   183

    V. The *Tract*: Portrait of a monetary society in crisis   188

    VI. "A Piece of Financial Machinery"   195

VII. From the *Tract* to the *Treatise*   201

VIII. *A Treatise on Money*   203

Chapter 13   Sraffa and Hayek on "Own Rates of Interest"   213

    I. Introduction   213

    II. Setting the stage   215

    III. "Assuming Away the Object"   218

    IV. "Incantations and a Little Poison"   221

    V. "Essential Confusion"   224

    VI. Curtain Call: The method of neutral money once again   227

    VII. The goals of monetary theory   229

Chapter 14   Keynes: "The Essential Properties of Interest   237
and Money"

    I. Introduction   237

    II. From Sraffa to Keynes: The state of monetary theory, 1935   240

    III. Keynes: The theory of interest and the theory of   243
employment

    IV. The essential properties of interest: Own-rates in   244
a monetary economy

    V. The Structure of own-rates in asset market equilibrium   249

    VI. Stocks of assets and flows of activity: The *General*   259
Theory viewed through the own-rates equilibrium
construct

    VII. Keynes's views of capital   264

    VIII. The essential properties of money   268

    IX. Money, prices and conventions: The social context   272
for monetary analysis

    X. The "Keynes Connection" versus the "Wicksell Connection"   275

    XI. Conclusion   278

Conclusion: A Theory of a Monetary Economy   **281**

Chapter 15   "Natural Rate" Mutations: Keynes, Leijonhufvud and   283
the Wicksell Connection

    I. Introduction   283

   II. "The Wicksell Connection"   284

  III. Leijonhufvud and Keynes on liquidity preference   285

  IV. Chapter 17: Stock equilibrium and "own-rates" of interest   288

   V. Liquidity preference, saving, and investment   292

  VI. Conclusion: Wicksell revisited   298

Notes   301

Sources and Bibliography   333

Author Index   345

Subject Index   348

List of Figures

15.1   The interest rate and the amount of loanable funds

15.2   A bond price and time

15.3   IS/LM with Keynes's marginal efficiency of capital

Acknowledgments

In the course of writing a book over a long period I have discussed its contents with many people who have contributed to my thinking in various ways. None is responsible for what follows, but each had a part in the form it has taken for which I thank them. They include the following: Peter Alexander, Bruce Allen, David Anderson, Philip Arestis, Bradley Bateman, John Burger, Matt Burns, Simone Caron, Victoria Chick, Robert Clower, A. W. Coats, Neil De Marchi, Robert Dimand, Ethan Dougherty, John Duca, Steve Fleetwood, Don Frey, Craufurd Goodwin, Peter Groenewegen, Malachi Hachoen, Harold Hageman, Geoff Hodgson, Robert Hollinger, Kevin Hoover, Peter Howitt, Elias Kahlil, David Laidler, Clive Lawson, Tony Lawson, Axel Leijonhufvud, Greg Lilly, Charlie Meyer, Cortney Midla, Hyman Minsky, Candace Modlin, Donald Moggridge, Gary Mongiovi, Don Patinkin, Ray Petridis, Steve Pratten, Rod O'Donnell, Gerald O'Driscoll, Christopher Ryan, Jochen Runde, Dennis Starleaf, Ian Taplin, Jim Tomlinson and E. Roy Weintraub.

Support for this project was provided by the following: a Southern Regional Education Board grant, a Wake Forest University Archie Fund summer grant, a Wake Forest University Saguiv Hadari sabbatical grant, a Clare Hall College visiting fellowship, a Cambridge University Faculty of Economics visiting appointment, and a Wake Forest University Reynolds faculty improvement leave. The generosity of each organization is gratefully acknowledged.

Permission for quotation is provided as follows. In Chapters 7 and 10, to quote from the Unpublished writings of J. M. Keynes copyright the Provost and Scholars of King's College Cambridge 2006, permission is kindly provided by King's College, Cambridge. These writings are deposited at the King's College Library, Cambridge. I thank Professor Peter Jones, Librarian of King's College, for arranging this permission.

Permission for extensive use or reproduction of parts of the following is also authorized.

In Chapters 6 and 7, with the kind permission of Springer Science and Business Media, parts of Michael S. Lawlor, 1993, "Keynes, Cambridge and the New Keynesian Economics." *Labor Economics: Problems in Analyzing Labor Markets* (W. A. Darity, ed., pp. 11–58). Boston: Kluwer Academic Press.

In Chapter 9, with the kind permission of Duke University Press, Michael S. Lawlor, 1994, "On The Historical Origin of Keynes's Views on Financial Markets." *Higgling: Transactors and Their Markets in the History of Economics* (N. De Marchi and M. Morgan, eds., *History of Political Economy*, Volume 26, supplement, pp. 184–225). Durham: Duke University Press.

In Chapter 10, with the kind permission of Routledge Publishers, Michael S. Lawlor, 1997, "Keynes and Financial Market Processes in Historical Context: From the *Treatise* to the *General Theory." Capital Controversy, Post-Keynesian Economics and the History of Economics: Essays in Honour of Geoff Harcourt* (P. Arestis and M. Sawyer, eds., pp. 233–48). London: Routledge.

In Chapter 13, with the kind permission of Taylor and Francis Publisher (http://www.tandf.co.uk), M. Lawlor, M. and B. Horn, 1992. "Notes on the Sraffa-Hayek Exchange." *Review of Political Economy* (Volume 4, pp. 317–340).

In Chapter 14, with the kind permission of Springer Science and Business Media, parts of Michael S. Lawlor, 1994, "The Own Rates Framework as an Interpretation of the *General Theory*: A Suggestion for Complicating the Keynesian Theory of Money." *Keynes: The State of the Debate* (John Davis, ed., pp. 39–102). London: Routledge.

In Chapter 15, with kind permission of Duke University Press, Allin C. Cottrell and Michael S. Lawlor, 1991, "'Natural Rate' Mutations: Keynes, Leijonhufvud and the 'Wicksell Connection.'" *History of Political Economy* (Volume 23, pp. 625–43).

Preface

I first became interested in Keynes's economics during my undergraduate education. The major influence on me at this period was Bobbie Horn. I thank Bobbie both for firing my enthusiasm for the history of economics and holding out such a high standard of scholarship to follow. I continue to be guided by his example.

In graduate school, under the indulgent supervision of Dudley Luckett, I was given free rein to write part of my dissertation on an aspect of Keynesian monetary theory. He also provided me with valuable discussions of the history of economics and of monetary theory. Part of the present study is founded on the work I did in that dissertation. Also during my graduate career, Karl Fox should be acknowledged for his influence. At a critical time in my education, he showed me what a life of scholarship can be.

Since the time I became professionally interested in the Keynes literature, I have had a number of sources of advice and stimulation. First I feel fortunate to have formed a close friendship and a working relationship with Sandy Darity. His intelligence, creativity and work ethic are constant inspirations.

The same holds for the interaction I have enjoyed with John H. Wood over the years. I am particularly grateful for the generosity he has provided in reading a number of the chapters of this book in draft form and providing valuable comments. We have not always agreed upon economic matters, but his questioning nature and willingness to explore ideas have made me a better economist.

I have been fortunate to spend time at Cambridge University, both as a guest of the Economics Faculty and as a visiting fellow of Clare Hall. The research, writing and interaction with scholars there substantially deepened my conception of Keynes's economics. None of that would have been possible without the generous welcome, and later invitation for a longer stay, that was offered by Geoff Harcourt. I have had the pleasure of his friendship and collegiality ever since. He has been a continuing and large influence on the direction that the research for this book has taken.

Another strong influence from my experience in Cambridge was T. K. Rymes. Tom is an economist possessing the rare combination of a deep interest in both modern economic theory and the history of economic thought. He brought home to me the value of Alfred Marshall in understanding Keynes. Tom's questions and his own work have spurred me to dig deeper into the historical record and to look further at the theoretical meaning of Keynes's position on fundamental questions of monetary economics.

I would also like to acknowledge the constant stimulus that my work in the history of monetary economics, and indeed in economics in general, has received over a number of years from my friend and co-worker Allin Cottrell. He is truly an excellent critic and a generous colleague. He personally read in draft all of the versions of this book. His comments and suggestions have been invaluable. Chapter 15 is from an article that Allin and I wrote together. Allin also kindly created the diagrams in Chapter 15.

Other people contributed to this work more indirectly, perhaps without realizing having done so. Very significant stimulus in this regard has been due to the many long conversations I have had over a number of years, in England and elsewhere, with my good friends John Davis and Zohreh Emami. I count the meeting of their family and my own as one of the happiest results of my stay in Cambridge.

The same good fortune resulted in my meeting Jacqueline Cox, now of the University of Cambridge Archives. She was then the Modern Archivist at King's College and, as such, my source for installments of the Keynes papers for daily reading. She has grown into a treasured family friend.

Finally, I wish to record my greatest debt to my wife, Jan, and my daughters, Emma and Moria, without whose great love and many sacrifices this book would not have been possible.

M.S.L.
Winston-Salem, North Carolina
February 2006

Introductory Material: Motivation, Method and Overview

A study of the history of opinion is a necessary preliminary to the emancipation of the mind.

J. M. Keynes (*CW* 9)

Professor Johnson reproaches Keynes for the influence that Marshall had upon him, for he does not appreciate Marshall's good points. Marshall inherited from Ricardo two qualities which are lacking in the branch of the neo-classical school that derives from Walras. He had (though confusedly) a sense of time. The short period is here and now, with concrete stocks of means of production in existence. Incompatibilities in the situation – in particular between the capacity of equipment and expected demand for output – will determine what happens next. Long-period equilibrium is not at some date in the future; it is an imaginary state of affairs in which there are no incompatibilities with the existing situation, here and now. Secondly, Marshall had a sense of the structure of society. His world is peopled with types (though idealized in a way that nowadays sometimes seems comical) who have different parts to play – the business-man, the worker, the householder – each with his own characteristic motives and problems.

Joan Robinson (1962)

1
Motivation: Approaching the *General Theory* Historically

I. A "history" of a book

This is a book about a book. It takes as its task the exploration of the development of the economic ideas that came to fruition in John Maynard Keynes's *General Theory of Employment, Interest and Money*, published in 1936. My purpose is to suggest some novel ways in which that book can be seen as a development of Keynes's intellectual history and context. I take as a starting point, the object of my analysis, the text of the *General Theory* along with the original supporting documents assembled by the editors of Keynes's *Collected Works*. Of particular importance in the *Collected Works* are the supporting documents that surround the *General Theory* – drafts, correspondences and related publications from Keynes's papers. They are organized into three volumes. The first two (*CW* 13 and 14) correspond to Keynes's pre-publication "Preparation," and his post-publication (but pre-World War II) "Defense and Development," of the *General Theory*. The last (*CW* 29), the contents of the now famous laundry basket later found in Keynes's country home, supplement the earlier volumes with private papers from both periods. The form and novelty of the theoretical interpretation of the *General Theory* that emerges from my study is the result of historical research into the origins and development of the ideas found in these materials.

Thus this is a reading of the *General Theory* that looks exclusively *backwards* from 1936 for its inspiration. It also only *selectively* uses the pre-1936 literature by limiting discussion to those sources that appear to me to have been most influential in pushing Keynes's own thinking forward. The emphasis is on the dynamic development of Keynes' ideas and on those of his close intellectual influences concerning the *General Theory*'s main themes of employment, interest and money. My research is mainly based on material drawn from the *Collected Works*, the Keynes Archive at King's College, Cambridge, and the surrounding economics literature that these sources point to as influential on Keynes. My major concern was to find what Keynes's teachers, intellectual influences, business activities and public policy involvements, along with his own previous writings, had to say on the cognate topics of employment, interest and money. Yet, though the research was largely conducted by reading back from 1936, the study that follows was then written mostly forward, starting from points in Victorian-era economics that this research suggests as the earliest origins or background to Keynes's thinking. From these beginning points, I have constructed a series of intertwined historical narratives, each following a thread of Keynes's developing ideas from his formative influences, through his own earlier writings and related activities, up to an endpoint in an aspect of the *General Theory*.

Part I treats the development of views on the operation of labor markets from Marshall to the *General Theory*, with an emphasis on English (and especially, Cambridge) economics. Part II then returns to the Victorian age and follows the evolution of Keynes's understanding of money, asset markets and speculation, again culminating in the *General Theory*. Finally, Part III examines the antecedents of Keynes's most developed commentary on the essential properties of interest and money, particularly in the context of interwar business cycle theory. In so doing, the last section also offers an alternative framework for capturing a whole picture of the theoretical development that ended in the *General Theory*: a general analysis of how employment and output interact with money, interest and speculation. By "alternative," I mean an alternative to the more conventional method of expressing Keynes's message in the *General Theory* that was adopted by the mainstream of the economics profession in the postwar era: the IS/LM model.

Thus, as is inevitable in discussing Keynes, even this largely historical exercise also contains a theoretical viewpoint on macroeconomics. I make no claim to be instructing modern economic theorists on Keynesian fundamentalism. Instead I hope to offer some interesting, and little noticed, aspects of macroeconomics that were unearthed by seriously following Keynes's trials and tribulations in formulating the *General Theory*. I can hope that they might be useful to macroeconomists as well as to Keynes scholars and historians of economics. Yet, as a truth in advertising clause for a contentious age of economics, when labels often seem more important than they ought to be, let me state plainly, at the most general level, the theoretical view of the *General Theory* that will emerge and will be emphasized in different ways in what follows.

II. Keynes's question

The central theoretical question addressed in the *General Theory* concerns the nature of the self-adjusting properties of a monetary economy. What was new or revolutionary in Keynes's argument of 1936 was his claim that modern competitive systems, naturally and without policy interference, need not – note I do not say could not or will not – equilibrate efficiently at full employment. I do not believe that Keynes's subtle and multifaceted forays into this question are captured by a particular "model," so much as by a theoretical attitude which takes this question seriously by, for instance, not starting with the presumption that such an adjustment must take place. It is obvious by this criterion that such a theory may give rise to whole classes of models in the spirit of the *General Theory*, each exhibiting different facets of the question. It is clear to me now, after much study of Keynes, that the *General Theory* itself suggests a *variety* of suggestions of such models. Indeed, this is not surprising given Keynes's own view of economics. Consider, for instance, the following comment he wrote to Roy Harrod in 1938 (*CW* 14, pp. 296–7):

> Economics is a science of thinking in terms of models joined to the art of choosing models which are relevant to the contemporary world. It is compelled to be this, because, unlike the typical natural science, the material to which it is applied is, in too many respects, not homogeneous through time. The object of a model is to segregate the semi-permanent or relatively constant factors from those which are transitory or fluctuating so as to develop a logical way of thinking about the latter, and of understanding the time sequences to which they give rise in particular cases.

I hope to show in this book that those models that emphasize the uncertainty that Keynes found so pervasive and influential an aspect of investing and asset holding, and so of capital and money markets, will be those most in the spirit of Keynes's own ideas. But other attempts to model macroeconomic self-adjustment from other standpoints could just as legitimately be seen as in the tradition of Keynes's work in 1936, if they were to honestly confront Keynes's question. By the same criteria, if one is interested in investigating Keynes's question – even if just to refute it as potted textbook treatments so often do – there is no theoretical (as opposed to polemical) sense in purporting to do so by adopting frameworks, so fashionable of late, which assume such efficient equilibration to be the natural outcome of the unfettered operation of the system.

Thus if I have to be labeled here, for the tastes of modern theoretical debates, I would have to say that my reading of Keynes manifestly does find him to be a variety of what I suppose is now called "Post Keynesian." Accepting that label, I would hasten to add that the real story in what follows might be described as "How Keynes Came to Be a Post Keynesian." It is in this spirit that I offer at the end of the book a simple version of his argument based on the *General Theory*'s Chapter 17 analysis of what Keynes saw as the essential properties of interest and money.[1] In this sense the last section will serve as an endpoint at which the previous historical narratives will coalesce. I am not claiming that this is the only or best model of Keynes. It does not rule out, nor does it necessarily conflict with models that follow more faithfully the interdependent-market-multiplier interpretations that are more common in textbook depictions of Keynes. In this book, it will serve the useful purpose of illustrating how the previous chapters' narrative threads can be tied together. It is also – happily for the historians – in keeping with what I see as the trend of thought suggested by the historical context in which my reading finds the *General Theory* to be embedded.

One more truth in advertising clause should be put forward here. This reading of the development of the economics of Keynes is not an encyclopedic treatment of the historical origins of each chapter of the *General Theory*, or even all of its major themes. I am conscious of many more such topics that could be treated similarly, for instance, Keynes's views on the army of heretics, or his last chapter on social philosophy, to name just two topics I leave unexplored. Nor do I treat the work of Hawtrey and Robertson in as much detail as they merit.[2] More glaringly, for some readers, I have not treated the history of the consumption function and multiplier or the mechanical form of the marginal efficiency of capital in any detail. Thus this book is only a partial study in the development of Keynes's economics through the *General Theory*. It is not meant to be the last word on the *General Theory*, just a different and, I hope, interesting perspective.

Partly, this selective coverage is due to my own interests, talents and time constraints. Partly it is driven by my intent to offer a history of what many commentators have suggested are the most theoretically radical themes that Keynes put forward in 1936, those elements of the *General Theory* that could not easily fit into the standard IS/LM interpretation. For me these are the themes of how the interaction of investment under uncertainty combined with modern financial markets might sometimes drive employment changes independently of what we economists have come to call "the supply and demand for labor." But this intent itself is reinforced by the fact that these elements of the *General Theory* are, on my reading, essential elements of what is new and interesting there.

While I do not deny that the general outline of the IS/LM approach is indeed present in the *General Theory*, nor do I claim that as a first approximation to macroeconomics for undergraduates the IS/LM model would be inappropriate, one clear fact that should be apparent in Keynes scholarship by now is that the standard "Keynesian" view it enshrines is insufficient to capture the complexity of Keynes's thinking. Crucially important though the message was in 1936 (and today), there is just so much more to the *General Theory* than a model in which aggregate demand determines output via a consumption function and multiplier combined with investment decisions made simultaneously with money market equilibrium. Also, much of the history of these standard Keynesian themes has already been covered well, for instance in Shackle (1967) and Patinkin (1976 and 1982). The premise that there is more than this to Keynes's message in 1936 serves as the justification for another book on the subject.

III. The Keynes literature

There is a huge literature devoted to the interpretation of Keynes's intellectual life and his *General Theory*. How is this book then different and worth the reader's attention? In answering that question let me start by suggesting a view of the state of scholarship on Keynes at the turn of the new millennium. Since the publication of Keynes's *Collected Writings* (finished in 1989) and the opening of the complete unpublished archive of his papers at King's College, Cambridge University (in 1989), it has become clear that the standard reading of his work in the postwar era was seriously misleading. Earlier interpretations of Keynes, with some notable exceptions such as Timlin (1942), Klein (1947), Dillard (1948), Harrod (1951), Shackle (1967), Leijonhufvud (1968) and Chick (1983), were written by economists with little or no interest in the historical record.[3] In fact, until very recently, economists have been content to interpret Keynes's work almost exclusively from the standpoint of contemporary macroeconomic theory and policy, thus neglecting not only the tremendous variety of his other work (including even his other work in economics besides the *General Theory*), but also the extent to which the concerns of his intellectual setting were not those of modern economics.[4] To date, this narrow view has been enlarged by pioneering work in the analysis of Keynes's philosophical writings (O'Donnell, 1989; Davis, 1994; Coates, 1996) and Keynes's work as a policy advisor (Clarke, 1988; Bateman, 1996), as well as the appearance of large-scale biographies (Hession, 1981; Skidelsky, 1983; 1992, 2000; Moggridge, 1992).[5] In terms of his economic theory proper, much journal ink has been expended in the last 20 years in pursuit of the historical Keynes, too much to be recorded here. Again, most often, this had been written within the context of contemporary theoretical debates, but its historical richness has grown with time.

Looking back, the most influential pioneers in unearthing the historical Keynes-qua-economic-theorist were Axel Leijonhufvud and G. L. S. Shackle. Leijonhufvud's (1968) call to differentiate Keynesian economics from the historical writings of Keynes himself, what he called the "Economics of Keynes," caused a stir by suggesting that there was more to Keynes than postwar macroeconomists had acknowledged. Working at the time when the vast materials of the Keynes archive were yet to be available, Leijonhufvud's major contribution was to recognize the value of reading both the text of the *General Theory* and Keynes's previous books, especially *A Treatise on Money* (1930). It is fair to say, however, that his work was as much creative new theorizing about macroeconomics[6] as it was a historical account. Professor Leijonhufvud's other outstanding contribution was to attempt (particularly in Leijonhufvud, 1981) to situate Keynes of both the *Treatise* and the *General Theory* in the context of interwar business cycle theory. It will appear in this book, especially in Part III, how great a debt I owe to Leijonhufvud's pioneering work in this area, and at the same time how much I disagree with his interpretation.

G. L. S. Shackle was also an early exponent of the value of Keynes scholarship for understanding Keynes' economics. In fact, it is hard to disentangle much of what Shackle wrote on economic theory from what he wrote on the history of economics; the two activities being a unique and fascinating joint product in his hands. He did not ever really attempt a deep search of more than the published record of economic debate and thus missed much of the richness of material now available on Keynes. Nevertheless, along the way, he produced some intriguing historical accounts, particularly of the critical ferment in economic theory that took place in the years between the great wars.

Shackle's view of Keynes is dominated by his own concerns with radical uncertainty and the consequent role that liquidity plays in investors' decisions. I happen to share Shackle's interest in this aspect of Keynes, as will be seen in Parts II and III, and was profoundly impressed with his work very early in my education on Keynes. In some ways what is offered in this book is an alternative historical narrative of many of the same themes in Keynes's work that Shackle wrestled with in his career.

Where I have come to depart from Shackle concerns two interrelated matters. First, I think he very much overrated the connection between Keynes and the Stockholm School of Macroeconomics, particularly in his preoccupation with the notion that the *General Theory* is only logically saved by adoption of the *ex ante-ex post* distinction (Shackle, 1967, Chapters 9–15).[7] Second, I disagree with Shackle's view that Keynes's emphasis on the precariousness of expectations ultimately must lead to an almost nihilistic attitude toward constructing useful macroeconomics models.

Lurking in the background of both of these aspects of his Keynes's scholarship is Shackle's extreme distaste for *equilibrium* notions, which he thought violated the world that economic theory was trying to describe so much as to make such concepts useless. He clearly realized that Keynes did not feel the same way[8] and this fact is at the heart of the difference between what follows and a more Shackleian interpretation of Keynes. Particularly in Parts II and III, I will argue that Keynes, as any good Marshallian would, was trying, even in his most extended forays into the role of uncertainty and expectations, to formulate an equilibrium account of the operation of these forces – which in Part III, following Keynes, I call a system of "shifting equilibria."

Other efforts to study the historical background to the *General Theory* that have been most influential in the literature were those of Patinkin (1976, 1982), Meltzer (1988), and most recently, Laidler (1991, 1999). To differentiate these books it is perhaps best to try to summarize their purposes. Allan Meltzer's *Keynes: A Different Interpretation* (1988), sets out to defend a particular model – his "Different Interpretation" of the macroeconomics of the *General Theory* set forth in an earlier journal article (Meltzer, 1981). By recourse to a study of a selected number of Keynes's earlier works in economics, Meltzer explores ways in which the postwar interpretation was seriously out of line with Keynes's own writings. He stresses that Keynes was interested in the depiction of a system by which equilibrium levels of involuntary unemployment can be studied adequately. Further, Meltzer notes Keynes's emphasis on the role of uncertainty about long-term investment decisions as the major source of persistently less than optimum output and employment. In short, Meltzer's basic view of the theoretical message of the *General Theory* is very close to my own.

However, I would not want to endorse Meltzer's view of Keynes as an advocate of fixed monetary rules nor attempt to describe him as mainly being concerned with the divergence between private and social cost of the optimum capital. I judge these stances on Meltzer's part as ahistorical anachronisms, stemming from his self-conscious attempt to stuff Keynes into a modern theoretical framework. Overall, though our views of Keynes's theoretical question form a common ground, there is not much overlap between this work and Meltzer's. Primarily this is because Meltzers's use of Keynes's texts is so unrelentingly motivated by the desire to show how they validate his own particular "model" of the *General Theory*. No disparagement is intended in noting that Meltzer's book is best viewed not as a historical exercise at all, so much as an example of a theoretical modeler rummaging in the Keynesian attic for spare parts out of which to build an engine of appropriately modern vintage. My purpose is, instead, to explore the historically rich vein of the intellectual context for Keynes's developing economic ideas over his lifetime. One example of the distinction is evident in the very truncated pre-history to the *General Theory* that Meltzer utilized. His interest extends only back to the twenties, and only to Keynes's major works in that period. One of Meltzer's primary points is that Keynes had already adopted a policy stance in line with the *General Theory* in the twenties: skepticism of a purely monetary response to serious downturns and advocacy of state directed policies to increase investment directly, and indirectly, by reducing long-term uncertainty over prospective financial returns. The *General Theory* was thus something of a closing of the intellectual circle by which a theoretical framework for these policies was provided. I agree in broad outline with this view but want to look back to the origins of both these policy stances and his theoretical forays to explore the associated economic theory. This will take us far earlier into Keynes's intellectual development and will involve us far more broadly in his intellectual context than the few sources that Meltzer relies upon from the twenties.

Don Patinkin was, like Meltzer, an economic theorist of note. His early work (1948, 1956) on monetary theory stressed the role of the real-balance effect, by which changes in prices are supposed, after some initial disturbing demand shock, to reestablish macroeconomic equilibrium at full employment. In the most commonly discussed scenario (originally due to Pigou, 1943, 1947), a recession will set off a deflation, which would tend to raise the real value of household money balances and so spur enough spending out of this increasing wealth to push output and employment back toward their original, full employment values. Though theoretically contentious and empirically little supported, I would contend that the outlook of this variant of Keynesianism – particularly its emphasis on the strictly *disequilibrium* nature of unemployment and its grafting of a Keynesian aggregate demand onto an otherwise classically determined supply side – is also at the root of much of Patinkin's historical scholarship on Keynes. It should immediately be added, however, that Patinkin spent much more of his intellectual energy than Meltzer on tracing historical precedents for his interpretation of Keynes's work. Even his early theoretical work (1948, 1956), for example, was replete with rather voluminous historical appendices. Nevertheless there is some commonality in the style of work of both of these esteemed theorists on the pre-history of the *General Theory*.[9] Thus when Patinkin later set out to describe Keynes's development as a monetary theorist (1976) and to look for "anticipations of the *General Theory*" (1982), it is not surprising that he concentrated on the development and anticipations of those distinctly postwar Keynesian themes to which his own theoretical work made such a contribution.

It is not my purpose here to enter into an extended critique of Patinkin's monetary theory (which for that matter would involve a critique of a good part of neoclassical synthesis monetary theory; see Rogers, 1989, Chapters 3 and 4 and Appendix 4 for a good account of this) or his resulting interpretation of Keynes. To some extent this whole book implicitly serves that purpose. But for the sake of many readers whose background in macroeconomics and Keynes scholarship was shaped by Patinkin's substantial contributions, a few brief remarks will suffice to make my point that Patinkin and I have a different message to deliver with respect to the intellectual history of Keynes's economics.

Patinkin saw the essence of the *General Theory* in the 45° diagrams familiar to introductory macroeconomic texts (Patinkin, 1976, p. 88, 1982, p. 10). Harking back to his own real-balance effect monetary theory (1956 [1965], p. 323–4) he interprets the central theoretical issue Keynes raised to be the reconciliation of this diagram's emphasis on the role of aggregate demand-driven adjustment in the quantity of output with a Walrasian notion of general equilibrium (1976, Chapter 10). Patinkin creates such a reconciliation by interpreting Keynesian economics as the full general equilibrium system in a state of *dynamic disequilibrium*. He states, for instance, ". . . I have interpreted the *General Theory* not as a static theory of unemployment equilibrium, but as a dynamic theory of unemployment *dis*equilibrium (Patinkin, 1976, p. 113, emphasis in original)." This disequilibrium state is set off by a fall in investment and consequent decline in output. What delays the recovery to full employment equilibrium is the presumed high interest elasticity of money demand and low interest elasticity of investment demand, standard workhorses of IS/LM Keynesianism (see Patinkin, 1976, pp. 102–4, for example). Also characteristic of this view is the casting of Keynes's concept of involuntary unemployment as a disequilibrium in the labor market because of a (variously explained) rigid nominal wage. Correspondingly, Keynes's emphasis on the influence of expectations and their liability to sudden change, leading to shifts in the whole money demand and investment demand schedules (as opposed to elasticity along a given curve), is played down by Patinkin (1976, pp. 103–6, 141–2).

My general remarks above on the central theoretical problem addressed in the *General Theory* should already mark off my theoretical interests from those of Patinkin's. The parallel follows in terms of the historical issues raised in his *Keynes's Monetary Thought: A Study of its Development* (1976) and *Anticipations of the General Theory* (1982). There is much of lasting value in both books concerning aspects of the pre-history of the *General Theory*. But I hope to provide in what follows an alternative history that was left unexplored by Patinkin in his search for a "Keynesian" Keynes.

The first (Patinkin, 1976) is a purposeful listing of commonalities and differences in Keynes's "trilogy" of monetary theory, the *Tract*, the *Treatise* and the *General Theory*. I would call it the search for the development of Patinkin's preferred Keynesian model. He explicitly claims (p. 10) little novelty from the "traditional" view of these works in his interpretation of them, which I take to mean from the orthodoxy of postwar neoclassical synthesis monetary theory, as exemplified by Patinkin's own *Money, Interest and Prices* (1956). What follows is a modeling exercise, searching for the evolution of the Keynesian model, as Patinkin sees it, in those texts. Unlike Meltzer's case, however, his is scrupulously cast in the scant equations and diagrams that Keynes himself used in those texts. Overall the picture is Patinkin's dynamic disequilibria view I have just outlined, supplemented by extensive quotations from Keynes.

The second, less focused set of essays (Patinkin, 1982), variously details what I would call the pre-history of some of the component parts of the Keynesian model. What ties the essays together is an underlying unity of purpose, to investigate the possibility of antecedents or multiple discoveries in the literature for what Patinkin sees as Keynes's central message that aggregate demand determines output. In Part I of Patinkin's book, the Swedes and Kalecki are both vetted in detail and found wanting. Part II critiques Post Keynesian interpretations of Book I of the *General Theory*, particularly those of Weintraub (1958) and of Davidson and Smolensky (1964) that emphasize Keynes's Marshallian roots and the importance of his unique conception of aggregate demand and supply. Patinkin expresses no interest in the context or background of these parts of the *General Theory*. Instead, his goal is the reconstruction of these arguments in more modern dress, based on the proposition that Keynes himself was confused, and Wientraub, Davidson and Smolensky even more so. Part III is on the history of Keynesian monetary theory and that of the pre-Keynes Cambridge school. It is motivated by the claims of monetarism to have discovered a wholly separate tradition of "Chicago School" monetary theory. Its main conclusions are that there was no separate school prior to the *General Theory* (both Irving Fisher's American line and the Marshall–Pigou line were substantively similar); and that neither contained the conceptual framework of Keynes in the *General Theory*.

The latter point turns for Patinkin on the contention that the Cambridge school prior to Keynes did not have a theory of "the effects on the equilibrium rate of interest of a shift in the tastes of the individual with reference to the desired asset-composition of his portfolio" (1982, p. 179). Thus, again fitting into the traditional monetary theory of Patinkin's day, it was the contribution of liquidity preference theory to have done so. Part IV, "Keynes and Econometrics," is concerned with the role played by Clark and Kuznets' revolution in national accounting in the thirties, in the effort by Keynes to work out the *General Theory*.

The reader looking for the most direct comparison of the present book with Patinkin's work will find it in Patinkin's downplaying of the influence of Marshall on Keynes's economics and his attribution to the *General Theory* of a Walrasian style of analysis, associated with Patinkin's persistent notion that unemployment must be a dynamic disequilibrium phenomenon.[10] In my view, there is no influence on Keynes of Walrasianism. It is true that this style of theorizing was characteristic of "Keynesian" monetary theory in the postwar era, with its preoccupation with the proper accounting of simultaneous market clearing prices, its concern with correct numbers of equations for equilibrium and so on. This interpretation of Keynes is also built into the IS/LM tradition, and, when wedded to a classical supply side, quite naturally leads to the typical "Keynesian" emphasis on impediments to adjustment (such as rigid wages) that Keynes himself never relied upon to explain unemployment. Primarily, I believe this theoretical trajectory is preordained by the reliance on Walrasian styles of analysis that define the putative full equilibrium of the system as "market clearing." Thus Marshall figures in this view almost negatively. He was insufficiently Walrasian himself and his monetary theory, Patinkin holds, did not contain a serious theory of portfolio choice in the face of changing interest rates.

In this book I will emphasize an alternative view of Marshall's influence on Keynes. In Part I, I will investigate the Marshallian tradition of labor market analysis. I will show how distorted a view of Keynes's labor market analysis results from such "Keynesian" (I will call them "Pigovian") conceptions as that unemployment is solely and everywhere caused by rigid wages. We will see that Marshall himself was very suspicious of the traditional supply and demand depiction of the labor market. So too was much of interwar Cambridge economics, as increasingly was Keynes. I also believe that Patinkin's restricted view of the Marshallian influence on Keynes's monetary theory is (relatedly) flawed. In Part II, I emphasize that there *was*, contra

Patinkin, a rich tradition of Marshallian analysis of the demand for assets by an individual, with reference to costs and opportunities at the margin. I argue that this conception formed a sort of meta-theoretical framework for monetary work that dominates all of Keynes's monetary theory from the *Tract* to the *General Theory*. Moreover, there was also a rich tradition, ignored in Patinkin's view, but well known to Marshall and Keynes, of analysis of the more realistic features of asset market trading, particularly speculation. I spend considerable time in Part II developing the history of these traditions, describing how it influenced Keynes and how he built upon it. What I conclude, again contrary to Patinkin, is that it was Keynes's achievement in monetary theory to combine these aspects of his Marshallian inheritance – a general portfolio choice theory of asset holding and a realistic theory of spec-ulation in organized asset markets – always building upon both his unique philosophical outlook and his practical investment experience. Significantly, this leads me to reverse Patinkin's negative evaluation of the lack of influence on the *General Theory* from Keynes's views on the pervasive role of uncer-tainty in the operation asset markets. On the contrary, uncertainty is insep-arable from Keynes's attempts to investigate the problem of monetary economies getting stuck in high unemployment equilibria.

Finally, in Part III, I show that there is an aspect of the *General Theory* that provides a mechanism for expressing this confluence of themes from Keynes's intellectual development and that it was a common element of much of Marshallian monetary theory. This is the theoretical framework of simultaneous asset market equilibrium, famously used by Keynes to suggest that while all assets have a unique real "own" rate of interest, markets will drive them all to equilibrate in money terms. In this part of his thinking, where (as I will emphasize) he is also reacting to the business cycle theories of Marshall, Wicksell, Hawtrey, Robertson and Hayek, we see Keynes's most general conception of asset market equilibrium, put forth in Chapter 17 of the *General Theory*. This equilibrium conception, which I suggest in Part III as an alternative way of conceptualizing the central vision of the *General Theory*, was developed, after much intellectual effort by Keynes, from Marshallian roots, not Walrasian ones.

As a final comment on this book's relationship to the modern secondary literature, I must recognize that there is a degree of overlap in the history covered here, and what David Laidler covers in his two magnificent works of scholarship on the history of monetary theory, *The Golden Age of the Quantity Theory* (1991) and *Fabricating the Keynesian Revolution* (1999). Yet the questions I pose and, consequently, the story I tell is very different from Laidler's. The main difference is that my narrative is designed to follow the personal twists and turns of Keynes's own theoretical development toward the *General Theory*. Both of Laidler's books, on the other hand, are painted on a much more panoramic scale, and concern the evolution of the think-ing of the whole economic profession about monetary and macroeconomic matters. The most telling contrast is with Laidler's (1999) treatment of the discussion of monetary theory between the end of World War I and the beginning of World War II.

His concern is to debunk the historical accuracy of a standard potted text-book view of the origins and history of macroeconomics. According to this view macroeconomics was born of a clash between Keynes, the lone revolu-tionary, and the old and sclerotic classical camp that was unresponsive to the economic crisis of the 1930s. Laidler argues that the 1930s was rather a theoretically vibrant period of many contributions of which Keynes's was just one among many, and moreover the profession was already much in favor of most of the counter-cyclical policies later associated with Keynes. Similarly, it is in this eclectic period that the roots of the IS/LM's dominance were set.

For IS/LM, Laidler argues, was a properly synthetic mix, agreeable to most of the profession, of certain elements from Keynes's *General Theory* (though not its most radical and unique aspects) and those of other interwar contrib-utors to the macroeconomic debates of the thirties. That model also provided a conveniently expressed and teachable way of framing the historically myth-ical Keynesian versus the classics dichotomy, in its ability to express both the purportedly "old" and the "new" views as variations on the assumed slopes of these two curves. Thus, the Keynesian Revolution was neither uniquely Keynesian nor particularly revolutionary.

Now there are many detailed points I could make about Laidler's argu-ment. For instance, like Laidler, as already indicated, I also see much more value in the classical Marshallian tradition than the potted Keynesian his-tory does. But I mine a few select veins of this historical context that appear from my reading to have been crucial in moving Keynes's thinking forward in his progression to the *General Theory*. I also, however, view Keynes's advances within this tradition as much more progressive than Laidler allows. Alternatively, I think it is a far stretch to argue, as Laidler does, that all of the most valuable of Keynes's insights (along with the rest of the best of interwar monetary theory) was distilled by the profession into the post-war IS/LM tradition. But my larger point here is that I could in principle agree with all of Laidler's thesis about the history of the IS/LM consensus, and still not view it as more than tangential to my theme. For Laidler is not concerned with the particulars of Keynes's own theoretical development. His treatment of Keynes and the *General Theory* is driven by, first, a search for commonalities between Keynes and other interwar monetary and busi-ness cycle theorists and, second, an accounting of the elements of the *General Theory* in terms of whether they will, or will not, eventually find a place in the IS/LM model, the endpoint of his story.

Another way of comparing our respective visions is by reference to the fact that Laidler also offers, almost as an aside, the view that the most radical ele-ments of Keynes's *General Theory* were not taken up by the mainstream of the profession in the IS/LM synthesis (which Laidler thinks is altogether proper). Our projects intersect at this point. Perpendicular to Laidler's project what most interests me are those very elements that, on his reading, were properly lost from view in the rush to incorporate Keynes's message in the conventional macroeconomic wisdom of the postwar era. I therefore do not spend much time on the development of the multiplier or the marginal efficiency of capital and have little interest in tracing those parts of the *General Theory* that make up the basis for the IS/LM framework. But I do have much to offer that is new, and not present in Laidler's more expansive survey, about how Keynes came to suggest his radical theoretical vision in 1936. I am unearthing a history that was made invisible by the establishment of the IS/LM consensus.

2
Methodological Stance: The Marshallian Structure of the *General Theory*

I. The Marshallian method

Ever since Hicks's (1937) pioneering interpretation of the *General Theory*, traditional Keynesian macroeconomics has been expressed in terms of a vision of interconnected sets of aggregated markets. Thus it has become commonplace for economists to speak of "the" markets for goods, labor, money and bonds, and of the simultaneous equilibrium solution of them considered as a system, when discussing various theoretical or applied macroeconomic issues. In fact, a case can be made that in the postwar era this became the basic meta-theory of macroeconomics *and* that it is Walrasian in origin and outlook (Weintraub, 1979). It is also true that a textual basis for the interconnectedness of the decisions of consumers, investors and asset holders is clearly present in the *General Theory* of 1936. Since Walrasian conceptions and mathematical treatments of economic theory were rapidly gaining ground at just the juncture at which Keynes's book was published, it is not surprising that many young, mathematically trained interpreters "naturally" cast its central message in the form of simultaneous equilibrium equations in the spirit of Walras (Young, 1987; Laidler 1999, Chapters 11 and 12). But this interpretation, so widely accepted to the profession now, is not so natural an interpretation from the alternative perspective of looking backwards from the *General Theory* in 1936.

For one thing, the text itself is not so organized. The *General Theory* consists of 24 chapters grouped into 6 books. Of these, we can safely exclude from relevance to Keynes's main theoretical argument the last three chapters that make up Book VI, "Short Notes Suggested by the General Theory." These "notes" on the trade cycle, the history of aggregate demand, and the social philosophy suggested to Keynes by his new theory are clearly afterthoughts. It is an irony of the book's fortunes that a quote from the last of these chapters, devoted by Keynes to "madmen in authority," is probably the passage most remembered by economists today. Book I, titled "Introduction," contains three chapters. The first is not really a chapter at all, but an amazingly haughty one-page taunt to the profession in telegraphed form. Here is my more general theory of your special case – full stop. No one ever accused Keynes of a lacking in self-confidence!

Chapter 2, one of only two places (the other being Chapter 19, "Changes in Money Wages") where a serious discussion of the labor market is offered, is, of course, titled "The Postulates of the Classical Economics." It is not titled "My Theory of the Labor Market," though it does introduce what he considers the crucial new category of "involuntary unemployment." It ends, after having cast much theoretical and observational doubt on the classical supply and demand theory of employment, not with another labor market analysis, but with a discussion of Mill and Marshall on Say's Law. Keynes's implied suggestion is that the discussion of involuntary unemployment requires a change in focus from the labor market to aggregate demand. Chapter 3, "The Principle of Effective Demand," is more properly considered the earliest overview offered by Keynes of his argument in its most general form. In essence, here we see Keynes proposing that employment is not a function of "the labor market" at all, but rather of the interaction of aggregate supply and (his innovation) aggregate demand (it is also a "model" designed as a preliminary that does not reappear often later in the book).

Many modern readers skip Book II, which concerns Keynes's "definitions and ideas." It is worth noting, however, that there is no definition or idea expressed there that looks Walrasian in character. No strictures on counting equations and unknowns, or discussions of the existence of equilibrium prices and so on, are in sight. Rather, the most important issue, besides definitions and choices of units, in the whole of Book II is an entire chapter (Chapter 5) devoted to the subject of "Expectation as Determining Output and Employment." Again, this is hardly a Walrasian idea. Closer perusal of this chapter suggests that it should be seen as Keynes's explanation of the new method of the theory to be offered. What he offers here is a unique twist on the Marshallian distinction of the short and the long period. In the process of Keynes's recasting of this distinction, we can see the emergence of his vision of macroeconomics. Although it has not been sufficiently appreciated in the historical literature, this theoretical vision is unequivocally set up as an equilibrium state that occurs in the chronological present – the short term considered in calendar time – but not as one that will naturally be overcome by forces which will eventually find their full expression in the hypothetical long-term future. Thus analytically he is not interested in the states of long-period equilibrium set out by Marshall as an object of analysis appropriate to relative price determination.[1] This is because Keynes thought that his problem – determining output of the whole system in the short term – called for a different approach compared to Marshall's long-period equilibrium in the following sense.

Two types of expectations form the crucial building blocks of Keynes's method. "Long-term expectations" govern "what the entrepreneur can hope to earn in the shape of future returns if he purchases (or, perhaps, manufactures) 'finished' output as an addition to his capital equipment." Short-term expectations, on the other hand, are concerned "with the price which a manufacturer can expect to get for his 'finished' output at the time when he commits himself to starting the process which will produce it" (*GT*, pp. 46–47). Firms will revise short-term expectations continuously as they are checked by realized results from the market for their output. Alternatively, the long planning horizon, construction and life of a capital investment make long-term expectations incapable of the same information feedback. Consequently, though changeable, the short-period expectations are in a sense assumed always to be in equilibrium for Keynes.[2] Like Marshall's higgling of the market, which is always going on but assumed to be completed for the definition of equilibrium supply and demand, short-period expectations are not an important issue for Keynes. The issue of paramount theoretical importance in the *General Theory* is how the changes in long term expectations, and therefore in investment demand, alter the equilibrium output in the short term.

A result of this theoretical framework is an upending of Marshall's vision. No longer are Marshall's long-period forces preeminent in the sense that all short-period phenomena are expected always to accommodate to them. I will argue in Section II that Keynes eventually came to consider long-run normal values, for instance those associated with marginal rates of return to capital investment, as having lost, in the context of macroeconomic equilibrium, the role they play in Marshall's schema as fundamental attractors to which the system gravitates. Mostly this development in Keynes's thinking, I will argue, came from his philosophically analyzing his own practical experience in actual asset markets and trying to reconcile that view with economic theory. Consequently, Keynes's theory, as he shows in this chapter, is an expectational story about the short period, or as he put it later in the book, "the theory of a system in which changing views about the future are capable of influencing the present situation" (*GT*, p. 293). In a manner, Keynes foreshortens Marshall's basic view of the role of time in economics. Equilibrium occurs today in the contemplation of a long term that is actually never realized. Marshall, alternatively, set his analysis in a long period that has already been realized and which is not expected to change. In so doing, Keynes elevates *the state of long-term expectations* to a fundamental force, on par with those of productivity and preferences, but by channeling all these forces onto the present situation. Importantly, we will see in the coming chapters, Marshall and Keynes eventually saw that important aspects of modern financial trading suggested such a treatment of these fundamental forces.

II. Keynes's treatment of time

In my view it is thus correct to say that the *General Theory* is focused on the short run. Yet contrary to arguments sometimes made in the secondary literature on Keynes (Rogers, 1994, 1997), I do not believe that this necessarily means that his conception of the determinants of output and employment thereby represent only passing transitional phenomena that will eventually be dominated by more fundamental long-run forces. This is to say that those traditional conceptions of long-run forces are not more fundamental if one believes – as I think there is good reason to believe – that Keynes's own conception of macroeconomics has any relevance to the actual determinants of output and employment. As I hope to show, there *is* no more long period in the macroeconomic world envisioned in Keynes's *General Theory*, just a succession of changing regimes of long-period expectation. Another way to put this would be to say that while such factors as changing technology and population are perhaps two very important long-run determinants of *potential* output, Keynes is claiming that they actually exert an influence over *actual* output only as they influence the *current* long-period expectations of investors.

This would not seem so radical an idea on the face of it, if it were not the case that so much of macroeconomic theory seems designed to deny it. One could always argue, as modern macroeconomics often does, that it would be better to conduct our analysis as if we were discussing long-period positions. In doing so, modern theorists are assuming away the very issue that Keynes wanted to investigate. Take for instance, the paradigmatic macro situation, where the demand for investment goods suddenly changes. Many modern theorists stage such discussion against the backdrop of a long-run supply and demand framework, in which it is assumed that a smooth fall in the rate of interest will result and that a new long-period position of lower investment (and savings) and more consumption will emerge. Macroeconomics then becomes the story of how such a smooth, otherwise "natural," transition might be temporarily slowed. Thus "short run," in this vision, is equivalent to temporary and passing disequilibria, set against a long-period equilibrium of seeming inevitability. Nevertheless, this would not be a discussion of the theory Keynes is presenting. Keynes's overall view, I hope to show, is that such assumed transitions are, for perfectly natural and endogenous reasons, in fact rare and unlikely, *but not impossible*.

It is the nature of long-term expectations, and the difficulty of assuming that changing regimes of such expectations are likely to be driven only by the productivity of capital, as they would be in Marshall's long period, that drives Keynes to see such transitions as so unlikely. Moreover, for Keynes the real task of a theory of output and employment ("as a whole," in his language) is to show why it may in many circumstances be so natural that the smooth transition does not occur – and also why there is possibly no offsetting tendency for an automatic movement toward full employment. In seeking to answer this question he replaces, rather than just mucks up with frictions, the Marshallian theory of the long period. Since, for Keynes, inherently incorrigible long-term expectations are the motive force of investment decisions, it is their nature and effects that his fundamental methodological framework is designed to elucidate. Thus, theorizing about such presumed fundamentals, as the traditional long-run standpoint emphasizes, must distort the message of the *General Theory*. More importantly, if Keynes's view of the nature and importance of long-term expectations is tenable as a description of reality, systematically ignoring that rather radical view of investment demand (by modern standards), robs our analysis of involuntary unemployment, deficient output and so on of one of the essential aspects of the reality of a modern economy's "output as a whole."

The argument that Keynes meant to provide a "long-period" theory of employment is often built on his discussion in Chapter 5 of what, in his schema of expectation-determined employment, the logical characteristics of an associated long-period position would be. Alternatively, Keynes's claim is that *if* a given set of long-term expectations were ever to last long enough for all of its effects to work themselves out, then the resulting capital stock would consist entirely of investments, and the resulting total employment would consist entirely of jobs, due entirely to this original, unchanging set of long-period expectations. I should quickly add, to prevent misunderstanding, that Keynes does not require that this set of long-term expectations implies a stationary state. Rather, it could be an expectation relevant for investment purposes of, for example, "a steady increase in wealth or population." The requirement in his framework, analogous to an assumption of constant technology in the Marshallian long period, is that these expectations be "unchanging" (*GT*, p. 48, n. 1). The only conception analogous to the Marshallian long-period state in Keynes's scheme, then, would be an economy where a steady state of expectations would combine with a steady state of capital accumulation to produce a steady level of output growth corresponding to that state of expectation (*GT*, p. 48).

But even then (as opposed to the case in Marshall's long period), there is no reason, in the *General Theory*, why such a long-period position should necessarily correspond to full employment. This will depend, to put it crudely, on how bullish the current expectations are in relation to the level of investment that would be consistent with full employment. But having established the logical possibility of such an extended regime of unchanging expectations, Keynes stresses that this state is unlikely to ever be obtained due to the fact that "the state of [long-term] expectation is liable to constant change, a new expectation being super-imposed long before the previous change has fully worked itself out" (*GT*, p. 50). This means that actual short-run positions will typically consist of a series of different vintages of capital, each the result of the different past regimes of long-period expectations that had originally prompted the investment in them.

We cannot ignore this "fact" by a retreat into "long-period" effects, of the kind Marshall often assumed, where, for instance, the stock of capital would be fully adjusted to a regime of technology and tastes. For Keynes immediately follows this formal definition of his expectational long period by a consideration of the "relevance of this discussion for our present purpose" (*GT*, p. 50) in which he dismisses the relevance of even the expectational sense of the long period for his purposes. It is not just that changing events always outpace the move to such a long period. Truthfully, we often fall back on this argument when explaining to undergraduates how a Marshallian analysis can be relevant to microeconomics. Equally important for macroeconomics, the effects of such past transitions in long-term expectations for the state of employment today can be ignored because they are already embodied in one of Keynes's "given" conditions, the current capital stock:

> It follows, therefore, that, in spite of the above [discussion of long-period expectations and the complications of transitions between them], to-day's employment can be correctly described as being governed by to-day's expectations taken in conjunction with to-day's capital equipment.
>
> (*GT*, p. 50)

Finally, notice that this also means that a preoccupation with the long run is not only idle with respect to the determination of current output and employment, it is counterproductive. We never can expect to get to a macroeconomic long period, so if our theory is assuming we are already there, it has assumed away the question under consideration. Keynes's realization of this early in his attempt at framing his new theory of employment is suggested by his correspondence with Bertil Ohlin (*CW* 14, pp. 184–201) and his subsequent published comments (Keynes 1937c, *CW* 14, pp. 215–23) on why he had abandoned any type of "period analysis."

The relevant point for our discussion from these writings is that Keynes appeared to have given much thought to the logical architecture of his theory and in so doing he must have found the treatment of expectations the most difficult ingredient to accommodate. His solution was to be the very "method" of "expectation as determining output and employment" from Chapter 5 that we are reviewing here. To Ohlin, for instance, we find Keynes rejecting the Swedish *ex ante-ex post* method as follows.[3]

> This is in fact almost precisely on the lines that I was thinking and lecturing somewhere about 1931 and 1932, and subsequently abandoned. My reason for giving it up was owing to my failure to establish any definite unit of time, and I found that that made very artificial any attempt to state the theory precisely. So, after writing out many chapters along what were evidently the Swedish lines, I scrapped the lot and felt that my new treatment was much safer and sounder from a logical point of view.
>
> (*CW* 14, p. 184)

In other words, it is not logically possible to treat current expectations as theoretically comparable to past expectations. What are relevant to decisions (and effective demand) only are the current (long-period) expectations and current capital stock. Alternatively,

... when one comes to prove something truly logical and properly watertight, then I believe there are advantages in my method and that the *ex post* and *ex ante* device cannot be precisely stated without very cumbrous devices. I used to speak of "funnels of process," but the fact that the funnels are all of different lengths and overlap on another meant that at any given time there was no aggregate realized result capable of being compared with some aggregate expectation at some earlier period.

(*CW* 14, p. 185)

What *can* be compared usefully, however, are past and present capital stocks. Given these, the decision to offer employment will be based on current long-period expectations. States of the capital stock, in conjunction with expectations then, replace in the *General Theory* the overlapping funnels of the results of past expectations. What is relevant for today's employment of past regimes of expectations is all embodied for Keynes in the existing capital equipment those past expectations caused to be built. Thus the existing capital stock embodies the history of long-term expectations.

III. Keynes's use of equilibrium

Returning to the organization of the *General Theory*, the parts of the text which offer perhaps the most grist for an enterprising Walrasian looking to mill a new simultaneous equilibrium theory would be in Book III, "The Propensity to Consume," and Book IV, "The Inducement to Invest."[4] Here, again, though certain individual level and aggregate level relationships between consumers, investors and asset holders are clearly explored, nowhere do we find them depicted in Walrasian terms as identifiable supplies and demands for which we should seek a set of simultaneous market clearing prices. Instead, the functional forms he proposes are propounded as shorthand depictions, for which, in every case, there immediately follows a more subtle investigation of the subjective psychological, historical and institutional factors these functional representations attempt to capture.

Nevertheless, it is also true that Keynes is continually discussing the issue of *equilibrium* outcomes for employment and income. This is the difficulty that seems to have so puzzled Don Patinkin and G. L. S. Shackle. Patinkin's solution was to interpolate a Walrasian approach for Keynes, whereby his equilibrium notions become disequilibria. In the process he also was led logically to downplay the extensive role that expectations and uncertainty play in Keynes's discussion. Shackle's diametrically opposed reaction was to reject the validity of any type of equilibrium method for discussing the monetary and expectational themes that he saw as integral to Keynes's vision. Alternatively, another brilliant theorist of the Keynesian era, Robert Clower, also grappled his whole career with the construction of a proper equilibrium framework in which to both understand Keynes and put the discussion of Keynes's questions on a proper logical footing. It is thus interesting to note that Clower's later writings[5] have tended to focus on the distinctly Marshallian character of Keynes's method of theorizing. Clower remarks:

> Keynes did not become an economist in a vacuum; he lived at a time when economics was dominated by the teaching of Alfred Marshall. Keynes was not ignorant of the work of Walras (see Hicks 1982; Edgeworth, 1925); but his family background, education and life as a Fellow of King's College added strength to other influences conducive to Marshallian habits of thought. (Clower, 1997, p. 36)

Here is a useful hint pointing to the depiction of Keynes-contra-Walras that we are suggesting. Tellingly constructing a "Marshallesque" version of Keynes, Clower (1997) arrives at the same general methodological point *analytically* that we are proposing to establish *historically*: there is an alternative meta-theoretical tradition, derived from Marshall, of theorizing about the economy that is distinct from the Walrasian tradition, and that forms the basis for the most general method pursued by Keynes in constructing the *General Theory*.

What are the elements of this method and its distinctive differences from the Walrasian tradition?[6] In the hands of Marshall of the *Principles*, this method is dominated by the dictates of applied partial analysis, the method of *ceteris paribus* and comparative statics and by the distinction between the short and the long period and their interaction. It is also dominated by a flexible attitude to formal expression, which favors a sort of "portmanteau" approach to general theoretical statements. Theories so constructed are designed to be usefully general, in the sense that they are intended to be filled in by the economist's judgment of the important historical and institutional factors that arise in particular applications.[7]

Marshall's theory, as has often been observed, has a less abstract flavor than Walrasian theorizing, where in favor of abstract completeness no bow to empirical implementation is even contemplated. The apparent applications of the Marshallian method of theorizing in the *General Theory* are manifold. They include what Clower (1997, p. 40) calls "Keynes's partial equilibrium model of aggregate demand and supply"[8] in Chapter 3 of the *General Theory*. Here is a clear example of how Keynes could adapt the old Marshallian style of theorizing to his new expectation-based "short period" setting. To begin the investigation of employment-as-determined-by-expectation, and to isolate the relevant forces at work, all of aggregate demand and supply are packed into just two portmanteau functions: the Z and D curves. With a temporary *ceteris paribus* assumption of a fixed money wage (to be relaxed later in Chapter 19), and ignoring for now the later complicated breakdown of investment and consumer behavior, the aggregate demand and supply expectations of entrepreneurs are all that determine output and employment. Analytically and rhetorically, this sketch is offered as a sort of prop, a demonstration of where the argument is headed. The rest of the book then unfolds as the D relation, in particular, is broken down successively into the narrower portmanteau relationships of the consumption function, the multiplier and the marginal efficiency of capital schedule, and from there into their more fundamental psychological, historical and institutional determinants. Neither the consumption function, the multiplier nor the marginal efficiency of capital has an exact analog in a Walrasian decomposition of the economy into market supply and demand relations.

Yet it is important to realize that Keynes changed the metaphysics of his treatment from that of Marshall's individual market or industry setting. In the *General Theory* Keynes is continually suggesting the inadequacy of microeconomic theorizing at the macroeconomic level, where various fallacies of composition call into question easy analogies from individual, or industry, level equilibrium to equilibrium of "output as a whole." Notice, as Clower points out, that this is not only a matter of quantity adjustment versus price adjustment – the usual Marshallian/Walrasian distinction. Both Marshall and Keynes saw the short-period adjustment of goods markets primarily in terms of quantity adjustments (we will see in Part II that this was reversed in the case of asset markets for both of them). Thus the two end points of the multiplier process are properly seen as an example of how different static equilibria, all of which would meet Marshall's criteria for individual market clearing, shift under the force of changing long-term expectations and the resulting macro-level propensities to invest.

Similarly, Keynes's objection to the standard view whereby equilibrium savings and investment determine the interest rate is that it neglects the fact that the scale of macro activity is assumed in such microeconomic equilibria. Thus his recourse to the one diagram in the book (*GT*, p. 180) is to demonstrate the classical theory of interest, in which an intersecting set of supply and demand functions are shown to be internally, on their own criteria, unable to satisfy equilibrium. The microeconomic market rate of interest, Keynes is arguing, will only be determinate once we know the macroeconomic scale of output. Keynes clearly was thinking of these issues in terms of using Marshall's style of theorizing for his own purposes of determining output as a whole – even if ultimately for the subversive purpose of exploding the more tranquil message Marshall had used his theorizing to convey.

3
Overview

The foregoing chapter is what might be termed a methodological critique of the Walrasian interpretation of the *General Theory*. Some readers will recognize that others have made somewhat similar arguments in other contexts (Kregel, 1976, is perhaps the most extensive treatment). It is a critique of Keynesianism that is completely consistent with my historical work, and which represents a crucial step on the scholarly road to reconstructing Keynes's argument in the *General Theory*.

My goal in this book goes further. In trying to reconstruct a historical/theoretical context for the development of Keynes's economics, I hope to deepen and strengthen the view of Keynes as a Marshallian. First, I provide an extensive documentary account of what Marshall, the Marshallians and Keynes actually did write concerning the cognate topics of employment, interest and money. Second, I construct a coherent narrative of Keynes's own theoretical development as a creative Marshallian theorist with regard to these themes. Finally, I end by trying to tie these historical themes together with a theoretical interpretation of the *General Theory* that stresses both Keynes's Marshallian roots and his creative development from those roots.

In Part I, "Keynes, Cambridge and Unemployment," I trace the trajectory in Cambridge economics from Marshall to the *General Theory* with respect to the question of labor market analysis and unemployment. We begin in Chapter 4 by very briefly highlighting what Keynes did and did not discuss concerning the labor market in the *General Theory*. That treatment forces the conclusion that his comments there were to negatively evaluate the ability of what he saw as inherited labor market analysis to explain mass unemployment. Thus we are led to investigate the Cambridge economics tradition that he broadly characterized as "classical" and which sends us back to this tradition's source in Alfred Marshall. Chapter 5 involves an attempt to characterize the "Late Victorian" social theory context for Marshall's work. Situating Marshall in this social context makes sense of his attempt to weld his theory of economic markets with a program of improving the condition of the working classes. It also suggests that his labor market analysis will have to confront the eradication of poverty – what he considered the "high theme" and the end and purpose of economics. Thus the Marshallian strand of "classical" economics – that which influenced Keynes – already by 1870 had a substantial anti-*laissez faire* component.

That is followed in Chapter 6 with a detailed look at Marshall's and his immediate students' analysis of the labor market. There we find a rich theoretical tradition emanating from the *Principles* that I characterize as having split into two distinct visions by the interwar period when Keynes was writing the *General Theory*. In one, best represented by the Cambridge Economic Handbook *Wages* (1928), by Maurice Dobb, Marshall's own skepticism about the use of supply and demand in questions related to distribution has become paramount. In Dobb's hands the determination of wages becomes theoretically indeterminate in traditional supply and demand treatments, without the closure given by labor market institutions and conventions, such as work practices and collective bargaining. Moreover, his extensive discussion of these institutions makes it clear that Dobb and Keynes (the Handbook series editor) were well-versed in the sort of labor market characteristics that nowadays go by the historically inaccurate title of "New Keynesian" economics. Interestingly, however, neither of them considered such characteristics as an explanation of the problem of unemployment.

The other strand of Cambridge labor market analysis is represented by the work of A. C. Pigou, who I argue developed a distinctly non-Marshallian, *mechanical* schema by which wages and employment are solely a function of supply and demand strictly interpreted. It is to Pigou's conception, going back to the first decade of the twentieth century, that we can trace the now traditionally misnamed (New and Old) "Keynesian" explanation of unemployment as due always and everywhere to labor market rigidities, such as an inflexible money wage.

Keynes's development in this context is then traced in Chapter 7. He is first seen, based on archival evidence, starting in his earliest lectures at Cambridge as a slavish Marshallian. Yet as he turned to independent thinking on the topic in the 1920s, we find his policy-oriented writings developing what I call a "social justice" view of the operation of labor markets – whereby relative money wages are given analytic force in determining wages (as well as moral urgency). This view arose in the context of a monetary argument that the nominal wage-level was seen by Keynes as crucial to the distributional effects of monetary policy. The culmination of this sociological theory of the labor market can be seen in Keynes's "Economic Consequences of Mr. Churchill" (1925). It is also later offered as part of his critique of the classical theory in Chapter 2 of the *General Theory*.

At the end of Chapter 7, we show that this is a view that fits well within Marshall's and Dobb's labor market schema. From its standpoint we are able to make historical sense of Keynes's contention – aimed at Pigou in Chapter 19 of the *General Theory* – that flexible money wages would increase the instability of employment, rather than the reverse. On the basis of this evidence, I further argue that the discussion of the *General Theory* is an example of the flexibility of the original Marshallian framework, as extended by Dobb, to investigate a question that Marshall himself never tackled, unemployment. In this sense it is perfectly natural to argue, as Keynes does in the *General Theory*, that labor market practices (such as resistance to flexible money wages) are not malfunctions of the system, as Pigou would have it, but are in fact important sources of stability for the economic system. In so arguing Keynes was merely riding Marshall's method into new fields.

This forms the basis for the argument that the role of Keynes's discussion of the "postulates of the classical economists" in Chapter 2 of the *General Theory*, is properly seen as almost entirely a negative one – a theoretical clearing of the decks. In keeping with the Cambridge insularity to which Keynes was particularly prone, Chapter 2 thus can also be seen as a negative verdict by one student of Marshall (Keynes) on the work of another (Pigou). The result for our overall view of the *General Theory* is the clear conclusion that the labor market plays a very minor role there. I will thus argue that Keynes's economics is not the economics of wage and price inflexibility, such as the New Keynesian viewpoint enshrines. For Keynes, involuntary unemployment is not caused in the labor market at all and cannot be cured there by wage flexibility. Theoretically we are forced to look elsewhere. Historically and textually this leads us to our second large topic, where most of the action does take place in the *General Theory*, in the fascinating discussions of the interplay between financial markets, expectations and spending on new capital goods in Book IV of the *General Theory*, "The Inducement to Invest."

Part II, "A Philosopher and a Speculator," therefore, traverses a similar time period as Part I does, looking for the background to Keynes's views on the economics of financial markets. Here the record also begins with Marshall. As an introduction, Chapter 8 argues for recognition of the now forgotten context for Keynes's financial market views. This context is both theoretical and institutional. For one there were developing aspects of modern capitalist economies and of related financial transactions that did not accord well with the Marshallian system as set out in the *Principles*. Thus we must delve into the exploration of how public corporations, large-scale production and speculation were viewed by Marshall both early and late in his career. We find the monetary aspects of this problem, though recognized by Marshall, were left particularly undeveloped in his later works. We also argue that Keynes's "other lives" (Skidelsky, 1992) as a philosopher and a speculator had real and lasting import for his theoretical attempts to fill this developing challenge to the Marshallian theoretical program.

In Chapter 9 we thus go back to explore two important aspects of Marshall's views. First, using the now available early writings – which in Keynes's time were part of the much discussed oral, unpublished, tradition in Cambridge monetary theory – we find a strong theoretical statement by Marshall from an 1871 essay on "Money" where he lays out a general framework for asset market equilibrium. It is both an individual level analysis of portfolio choices based on balancing rates of return against the "conveniences" various assets offer, and a market level general equilibrium construct by which implicit rates of return on all assets are equalized by trading.[1] We claim that this framework became Keynes's basic supply and demand meta-theory for asset markets – extending even to the construction of the *General Theory*.

Second, we also find in Marshall's unpublished writings an extremely interesting discussion of actual asset market practices and institutions, recently brought to light by Dardi and Gallegati (1992), titled "The Folly of Amateur Speculators Makes the Fortunes of Professionals. The Wiles of Some Professionals" (Marshall, 1899). In the latter we find Marshall seriously considering the possible destabilizing effects of modern financial trading practices. In the end, though Marshall here flirts with how such practices may constitute possible alterations to his basic asset market equilibrium view of financial markets as efficient mechanisms for transmitting "fundamentals," he leaves these two notions unreconciled.

Yet the following out of the full ramifications of this intellectual conflict in the Marshallian literature may be thought of as the basis for all of Keynes's own later work in monetary theory. Before proceeding to chronicle this development of Keynes's thinking, though, we pause to consider the contents of a remarkable and forgotten classic, H. C. Emery's *Speculation on the Stock and Produce Exchanges of the United States* (1896). It is to Emery that we can trace the Anglo-American profession's understanding of how organized exchanges, especially in America after 1870, altered the behavior and opportunities of financial market participants and created new forms of speculation – with potentially system-changing consequences.

What is particularly interesting about Emery is his detailed discussions of the role of professional traders, and the circumstances under which their practices might fuel what we would today call speculative bubbles. Many of the details of financial market practices that Keynes would later incorporate into his discussion of long-term expectations in Chapter 12 of the *General Theory* can be found in Emery. The path of this influence is complex. Marshall was a close student of Emery. His 1899 essay lists it as his main source on modern practices. Moreover, as I document from archival evidence, Keynes used Emery as a text in his early lectures to two courses at Cambridge titled "Modern Business Methods" and "The Stock Exchange and the Money Market," given between 1909 and 1914.

This background prepares us to develop in Chapter 10 Keynes's own thinking on the operation and effect of financial markets over his career. Three identifiable strands of this development intertwine and inform our narrative.

In one sense Keynes's development as an economist is a story of a philosopher of probability, which Keynes was more deeply than he was an economist before the 1920s, philosophically interpreting Emery's description of the trading that is characteristic of modern financial markets. Thus, for instance, from the earliest stage of his career from 1909 to 1914, we see Keynes taking a unique, philosophically informed, stance on the basis of expectations that define *speculation* in Emery's work.

In a second sense, there is a continual growth in Keynes's awareness of and insight into these very practices, as he gains personal and professional experience in actual trading activity. This phase of growth is particularly evident in the period after the Great War, 1919–24, when he begins to speculate on currency and commodities. One other closely related documentary source that we examine in this regard is the record of Keynes's personal trading, and especially the content of his professional advice and memoranda – to his College, investment partners and friends – about his views of proper investment strategy.

Thus the third aspect of his financial market views concerns an interesting feedback loop that develops between his theoretical work in economics and his investment activity and advice. Three periods of the simultaneous evolution of Keynes's personal and theoretical activity are identified. From 1909 to 1923, drawing on his then current view that speculators are merely possessors of superior information, Keynes tries to bring his war-finance experience to bear on his own account, so to speak. After several financial setbacks, he sets out in the mid-1920s to develop a model of the "credit cycle" that would both solve the enigma of business cycles, then so pressing in economic theory, and inform his second strategy of "timing" the market to match this cycle. This effort culminates in his *Treatise on Money* (1930). Amid other more external influences, it was the recognition of the failure of both the business cycle theory of the *Treatise*, and its application as a trading strategy, that sent Keynes back to the drawing board in the 1930s. This third, and final, evolution of his stance toward financial markets is evident in documents he wrote from 1931–36. In these documents the influence of speculation, particularly in trading of "liquid" assets, is dethroned from being largely a corrective device for the smoothing out of the effects on markets of supply fluctuations, as it had been in his writings of the twenties. Instead, speculation assumes what is now considered its characteristic Keynesian aspect as a possible threat to the system as a whole, in its possible exacerbating effect on fluctuations in the rate of new capital formation.

Correspondingly, we find in his private memoranda from the 1930s the emergence of a policy Keynes calls "faithful" investing. The latter implies an informed "buy and hold" strategy focused on selected stocks. In terms of his philosophical view of the basis of speculation, Keynes had come to conclude by the 1930s that neither superior knowledge nor a superior timing strategy were practicable solutions to "the dark forces of time and ignorance" that could envelop financial markets. The theoretical outcome of this – sometimes rude – education in practical trading activity for Keynes was a revision of

Marshall's belief that the forces of productivity and thrift were not the only fundamental forces determining equilibrium asset prices. Now, in response to the uncertainty modern trading practices present to participants, he suggests adding the preference for liquidity to the fundamental forces determining equilibrium.

Part II ends with a discussion in Chapter 10 of how the *General Theory*, in its integration of speculative financial activity into a theory of output as a whole, can be seen as Keynes's final answer to the unresolved dichotomy presented by Marshall's monetary work. What Marshall had seen as the minor, but worrisome, "folly of amateur speculators," is transformed in the *General Theory*. After much practical experience of speculation, and using the foundations of asset market analysis that Marshall had laid, the philosopher of speculation had created a generalized theory of a speculating economy.

This last point concerns another aspect of Part II, one that is more analytically developed in Section III. The framework for theorizing asset market equilibrium that serves as the bedrock of all of Keynes's evolving theories of financial markets is from the first to the last Marshallian in origin. Yet Keynes used this framework in ways that Marshall probably never even contemplated. Thus a continual aspect of the narrative of Part II leads naturally to Part III. In both we are concerned to emphasize the influence on Keynes of Marshall's 1871 essay on "Money" – with its view of both individual portfolio choice and general asset market equilibrium. In his immediate post-*General Theory* defense and development writings, where he debated the critics of his interest rate theory, Keynes relies almost exclusively on this framework. He does so both by framing his own theory *and* that of his critics in terms of Marshall's meta-theory for asset market equilibrium. Thus we conclude Section II by arguing that if any general equilibrium framework is to be seen as the bedrock of Keynes's economics, it should be this Marshallian-style of theorizing, not a Walrasian approach.

In Part III, "Shifting Equilibrium in a Monetary Economy," we chronicle the development of this Marshallian "model" for monetary analysis, to argue that one way of viewing the *General Theory* is through the most extended use Keynes made of Marshall's vision for monetary theory, in the own-rates discussion of Chapter 17 of the *General Theory*.

Historically, we begin the development of this theme by documenting in Chapter 11 the concerns and analyses of the Cambridge monetary tradition. We first analyze the cycle work of Marshall and his most faithful, but less creative, followers A. C. Pigou and Frederick Lavington. Principally this concerns specification of the demand for money and the analysis of savings and investment. We then go on to document the creative work done in this tradition by Ralph Hawtrey and D. H. Robertson. A strong interest in distributional effects of monetary policy is evident as well as a thorough understanding of the issues that later were to go by the term "forced savings." Recent uncovering by analysts of a clear discussion by these "interwar cycle theorists" of the adjustment of output over the cycle is noted. Despite this, however, we find that the hold over the whole Marshallian school – including the pre-*General Theory* Keynes – of the attraction of long-period theorizing relegated this to a passing, cyclical influence.

Chapter 12 recovers this ground, from pre-World War I through the composition of *A Treatise on Money* in 1930, in terms of Keynes's development as a Cambridge monetary theorist. We find that Keynes differed from his contemporary colleagues in two aspects of his work that would bear fruit in the *General Theory*. One is his ability to bring true institutional and practical experience to his theoretical work on monetary theory. This is evident especially in his treatment of the "theory of the forward markets" in *A Tract on Monetary Reform* in 1923 and in his grafting of this insight into a theory of the cycle in *A Treatise on Money* in 1930. The other aspect of his work that is unusual for its time and place is an emphasis on the fundamental ways that a monetary economy differs from a non-monetary one. Both of these elements of his thought reach a culmination in his discussion of "The Essential Properties of Interest and Money" in the *General Theory*.

But before detailing that analysis, we detour from our main argument to review his involvement with the Wicksellian and related Austrian traditions of business cycle analysis in Chapter 13. Here we see a challenge to the Cambridge Marshallians' view of the crisis of the thirties within the economics profession mounted by F. A. Hayek. Though we detail how Piero Sraffa's review of Hayek's *Prices and Production* (1931) was devastating to this challenge, the lasting import for economic theory concerns the validity and usefulness of the Wicksellian framework for monetary theory. Sraffa's review of Hayek in 1932 provides us with insight into the essentially non-monetary, barter, quality of the Wicksellian tradition. It also suggests reasons why it alone is insufficient to analyze a true monetary economy. Thus this interlude presents us with a picture of a clash between Marshallian theory, particularly as developed to that point by Keynes, and Hayek's unique interpretation of Wicksell whereby the use of money to conduct savings and investment become the *sine qua non* of the business cycle. It also provided some sort of spark to Keynes's own thinking about the essential properties of a monetary economy during this period, when Sraffa was also a member of Keynes's "Circus" discussion group of the *Treatise*.

Hence this motivates my argument that this 1932 clash of frameworks between a Marshallian style of theorizing by Sraffa and one from the Wicksellian tradition, represented by Hayek, can usefully be viewed as a debate over the fundamental aims of monetary analysis.[2] Consequently, it reduces to a discussion of how to best characterize the "essential properties of interest and money" – the title of our final historical Chapter 14. Of course, this is also the title of Keynes's Chapter 17 in the *General Theory*. I will argue that in that chapter we see Keynes making constructive use of Sraffa's more critically considered commodity rates in an attempt to sum up the *General Theory* on a different analytical plane than the more traditional ones that become popular in the postwar era. Interestingly, Keynes does so in combination with that long established tradition in monetary analysis we traced to Marshall in our previous studies.

In keeping with Keynes's claim to have presented a generalization of his predecessors, we argue that Chapter 17 of the *General Theory* is thus at once both traditional and innovative. It is traditional in its attempts to answer the most long-established questions of monetary theory: Why does a positive interest rate exist? What determines its level? What is especially monetary about it? Its innovation, and Keynes's claim for a theoretical breakthrough of the first magnitude, is to link these questions with the issue of the level of employment and output. He does so, it turns out, by modeling financial expectations and asset holding behavior under uncertainty with real investment activity in an integral way. Chapter 17 thus encapsulates at the most fundamental level of abstraction that Keynes ever used in dealing with these topics, an integrated theory of the equilibrium level of *employment, interest and money*.

We finish the book with Chapter 15. Instead of a formal concluding chapter we offer another angle on the meaning of Keynes's economics by presenting a more theoretical critique of an influential view of the analytical issues at stake in the interwar period: Axel Leijonhufvud's "Wicksell Connection." Here we depart from historical exegesis and try to show the theoretical usefulness of Keynes's essential properties of interest and money for exploring Keynes's question of involuntary unemployment.

Part I Keynes, Cambridge and the Economics of Employment

Marshall, who was more alive than many economists to the complexity of the economic world, where all things are subject to 'mutual interaction,' attempted to provide a synthetic view, in which the forces which affected the supply of labour and the forces which affected the demand for labour were combined. On the whole, the theory which he reached was less rigidly deterministic than the traditional doctrines: for example, it allowed scope to the influence of collective bargaining by trade unions on wages, through its effect not only on the efficiency, but also on the "supply price" of labour.

M. Dobb (1928)

Keynes . . . drank Marshall with his mother's milk.

J. Robinson, (1953)

This Marshallian methodological legacy is visible in the *General Theory*, which uses important parts of Marshall's analytic engine. One of these is Marshall's limited emphasis on the virtues of market clearing as compared with Pigou, and his hesitancy in applying the supply and demand apparatus to the labor market.

P. Groenewegen (1995b)

Part 1 Keynes, Cambridge and the Economics of Employment

4
Introduction: Keynes, the *General Theory* and the Labor Market

I. Unemployment and the *General Theory*

Mass and lingering unemployment – "the intractable million," to use Pigou's (1947, p. 43)[1] apt term – was clearly the overriding social concern behind Keynes's *General Theory of Employment, Interest and Money*.[2] It is a peculiarity of that book, though, that much less of its space is given over to an analysis of the labor market than to almost any other aspect of Keynes's argument. The essence of explicit treatment comes in the form of the critique of the "classical postulates" in Chapter 2 of the book, in the justly infamous definitions of involuntary unemployment in both Chapters 2 and 3, and in the more interesting (and unfortunately less read) discussion of "changes in money wages" in Chapter 19 and its appendix (on Pigou's theory of unemployment). At a stretch, we might add to this list Chapter 20, "The Employment Function," but in reality it is nothing but an attempt at a formal summation of his theory, which had been much better summarized in words in Chapter 18, "The General Theory Re-Stated."

The point to stress is the fact that so much more space and effort is devoted to output, money and interest in the *General Theory*, than to *employment in the sense of the functioning of labor market supply and demand*. This is significant. In chapters to follow we will argue that Keynes's book is best thought of as a theory of output driven by investment and conditioned by a thorough and realistic awareness of financial market processes.[3]

In the broadest sense, Keynes is arguing that, outside of full employment (where the labor market can act as an upward bound on employment), the labor market is essentially a passive derivative of the rate of output.

Yet it is not thereby appropriate to ignore the treatment of labor markets that does exist in the book in the pursuit of these greater concerns. After all, the definitions that self-consciously proclaim a theoretical revolution in revealing what is claimed as the previously neglected category of "involuntary unemployment" were meant to define the terms of Keynes's achievement. They have also been the subject of interminable debate by theorists ever since.[4] Hence, Part I intends to investigate the historical origins, development and content of Keynes's views on the operation of labor markets.

My intended contribution to this debate is to show that an understanding of the intellectual context in which Keynes developed his ideas will help to explain both what Keynes was driving at in the scant treatment of the labor market in the *General Theory*, and why it became so difficult to interpret after the *General Theory*. I shall argue that the structure of Keynes's argument and the sources for labor market behavior and analysis that he had to draw upon in writing the *General Theory* shed new light on the old and continuing problem of the place of the labor market in macroeconomics. Two major issues will be shown to be important to such a contextual understanding.

One is the nature and use of supply and demand for the analysis of labor markets by Marshall and his immediate successors. This tradition, which peaked in Maurice Dobb's Cambridge Economic Handbook *Wages* (1928), should be seen as the background to Keynes's theoretical forays in understanding the labor market. Second, we will detail how Keynes took this Marshallian tradition, with its tendency toward theoretical "indeterminacy" in the labor market, and combined it with his observation of events and policy advisory activities to explain the growing crises of the twenties and thirties. In the process we will argue that the "facts," as he was wont to call them, caused him severe doubts about a rigid wage explanation of unemployment. Fittingly, for a man whose greatest gift was to rapidly interpolate between policy needs and theoretical work, a survey of his more popular writings of this period will reveal Keynes to be developing what we will term his "social justice" theory of wages. This loosely sociological analysis of what Keynes saw as the "facts" of labor markets argued that, in conditions of mass unemployment, relative money wages are as important as the traditional notions of supply and demand theory for the determination of labor market outcomes. Both of these strands of thought make unreferenced appearances in, and aid an understanding of, his argument concerning the labor market in the *General Theory*.

II. Labor markets in the *General Theory*

As a preface to our look backward from the *General Theory*, we wish to erect some signposts emanating from the text itself. Without trying to push a particular theoretical agenda at this point, I wish merely to establish the existence of the two elements of our argument stated above so that sufficient reason is created in the reader's mind for an extensive foray into the pre-*General Theory* labor market literature that we will develop in Chapters 5 and 6. This is much trodden ground for the Keynes scholar so I will be at pains to be brief.

Keynes's argument in Chapter 2 against the classical theory of employment is explicitly twofold. The first critique of the classical postulates of employment that he offers is judged "not theoretically fundamental" and is based not on theory, but on "the actual attitude of workers toward real wages and money-wages respectively" (*GT*, p. 8). Basically it questions the form of the classical labor supply function. This follows from Keynes's observation that workers do not object to the lowering of the real wage consequent upon a general price rise, but they do object to an equivalent lowering of the money wage. His argument, previously forged in the intense labor struggles of the twenties, we shall see, is that this means that over certain ranges workers are interested in relative *money* wages. Thus he concludes that the existing level of real wages does not adequately measure the marginal disutility of labor (*GT*, p. 8). The importance of this to Keynes is that it reveals the absurdity of a labor market analysis that would explain mass unemployment as the result of downwardly rigid money wages:

> Moreover, the contention that the unemployment which characterizes a depression is due to a refusal by labour to accept a reduction of money wages is not clearly supported by the facts. It is not very plausible to assert that unemployment in the United States in 1932 was due either to labour obstinately refusing to accept a reduction of money-wages or to its obstinately demanding a real wage beyond what the productivity of the economic machine was capable of furnishing. Wide variations are experienced in the volume of employment without any apparent change either in the minimum real demand of labour or in its productivity. Labour is not more truculent in the depression than in the boom – far from it. Nor is its physical productivity less. These facts from experience are *prima facie* ground for questioning the adequacy of the classical analysis.
>
> (*GT*, p. 9)

In Chapter 7, I will show that this sociological observation of fact was fully worked out by Keynes in his policy testimony and writings on the growing problem of unemployment from the mid-twenties onward.

Keynes's second critical attack on the classical theory of employment in Chapter 2 of the *General Theory* was the part he considered the most theoretically "fundamental." It involves what I think could be a fairly simple argument, but which the standards of interwar verbal theorizing, a forgotten type of "rigor" that Keynes aspired to, forced into tortuous definitional expressions. Simply put, it said that in the presence of involuntary unemployment, the classical postulates defining the supply and demand for labor as functions of the real wage are indeterminate on their own terms – that is, they cannot alone determine the real wage and level of employment. Hence, if so, and if we are interested in the question of what does determine the volume of employment in states of high unemployment, the labor market alone is apparently insufficient to the issue. We are forced to another theoretical plane. This argument in a sense clears the ground for the Principle of

Effective Demand to be introduced in Chapter 3. Two quotations will give the essence of his view:

> The traditional theory maintains, in short, *that the wage bargains between the entrepreneurs and the workers determine the real wage.*
>
> (*GT*, p. 11, emphasis in original)

> But the other, more fundamental objection, which we shall develop in the ensuing chapters, flows from our disputing the assumptions that the general level of real wages is directly determined by the character of the wage bargain. In assuming that the wage bargain determines the real wage the classical school have slipt in an illicit assumption. For there may be *no* method available to labour as a whole whereby it can bring the wage-goods equivalent of the general level of money-wages into conformity with the marginal disutility of the current volume of employment. There may exist no expedient by which labour as a whole can reduce its real wage to a given figure by making revised money bargains with the entrepreneurs. This will be our contention. We shall endeavor to show that primarily it is certain other forces which determine the general level of real wages. The attempt to elucidate this problem will be one of our main themes. We shall argue that there has been a fundamental misunderstanding of how in this respect the economy in which we live actually works.
>
> (*GT*, p. 13, emphasis in original)

This element of indeterminacy in the labor market was also a prominent part of the pre-*General Theory* theoretical tradition at Cambridge. What I hope to show in what follows is that Keynes had good reason to doubt that the labor market alone, including its institutions, legal framework and traditional and trade-union practices, would be able to provide an explanation of mass unemployment. His education and work in the Marshallian labor market tradition was replete with awareness and subtle analyses of these issues – the same issues which figure so prominently in the continuing postwar attempts to theorize rigid wage explanations of unemployment. Significantly, it is not to Keynes but to Pigou, who becomes Keynes's major oppositional foil on matters concerning the labor market, that we must go to unearth the origins of the tradition of using these institutional rigidities of the labor market to explain unemployment.[5]

Thus, as we look back at the intellectual setting of Keynes's views in pre-War Cambridge economics we will find that the complexity of our story grows. Marshallianism is the major influence, of course, but we shall see that its legacy is ambiguous. Marshall not only spawned Pigou's (1933) amazingly out-of-touch treatment, *The Theory of Unemployment*, but also Dobb's subtle and historically informed view of labor markets in his Cambridge Economic

Handbook *Wages* (1928). Our reading of this context will thus support the view that there was more than one way to be a Marshallian (although to be fair to the master, one might say Cambridge economists at this period tended to be either "Marshallians" or "Pigovians"). Thus Keynes's reaction against his upbringing in 1936 coupled with his obvious retention of Marshallian habits of thought becomes more understandable. Our reading of the work of Marshall, Dobb, the early Keynes, and even the *early* Pigou will reveal a subtle and sophisticated microeconomic labor market analysis. In fact, most of the issues now being raised by modern unemployment theorists (such as the New Keynesians) were treated by these authors going back as far as before World War I. Interestingly, though, Marshall, Keynes and Dobb did not see such institutional realism as necessarily relevant to unemployment. Pigou, however, clearly did, and thus becomes the logical direct opposition to Keynes's views in the *General Theory.*

We will argue that there is enough commonality of outlook on labor markets in this literature that we can posit a pre-*General Theory* Cambridge Orthodoxy in the form of Dobb's *Wages*. But it was only the mechanical Pigovian form of labor analysis that saw this recognition as an adequate explanation of unemployment. Thus when Keynes came to part with this Pigovian tradition of labor market theory, as he did in his pursuit of the question of mass unemployment, he was simultaneously departing from a view in many important aspects like that of modern (New and Old) Keynesian analysts. For this reason, our final argument will be that Keynes's view of involuntary unemployment, while it does not deny the welcome realism of sophisticated labor market analysis such as Dobb's or the New Keynesian Economics, is in fact a metaphysical category distinct from the usual categories then and now current in the literature.

We now turn to that Victorian world of which Marshall was so much a part. We wish in particular to delve into the Victorian and Marshallian views on labor and unemployment. Our later task will be to show that Keynes took a large, ultimately transforming, step out of this context in writing the *General Theory.* Nevertheless, he never completely lost touch with some of its characteristic methods and concerns.

5
The "Late Victorian" Intellectual Context of Marshall's Labor Market Views

I. Unemployment to the Victorians: The background to Marshallianism

One of the most striking things about the history of economists' treatment of unemployment is the comparatively late stage at which it was even considered a problem worthy of attention (see Garraty, 1978). In the texts of the period of classical political economy the issue was not widely discussed, it generally being considered part and parcel of poverty and the conditions of the working class.

Thus in Adam Smith (1776), while wage theory and the issue of labor mobility is clearly discussed, what we might today recognize as unemployment rarely shows its head. After the incorporation of the Malthusian doctrine by Ricardo, and the growing influence of Benthamite utilitarianism (Dicey, 1905, Chapter 6) the general tone of the discussion of labor by economists became the "dismal" outlook of legend. In the context of the English classical system, what discussion of unemployment there was would generally have been understood as part of the Poor Law Debates. Here the issue was not so much why people did not have jobs as the proper public management of the poor, the vagrant and the beggar. Under the influence of the Malthusian theory and the wages fund doctrine economists like Nassau Senior – whose views were instrumental in the drafting of the New Poor Law in 1834 – displayed much more of a moral than an analytical tone. As an example the poor law reform, which introduced the workhouse to England, was largely an attempt to avoid encouraging slothful beggars from easily becoming wards of the state. The exception in this, of course, is the work of Marx (1867), where a reserve army of the unemployed becomes a natural feature of a capitalist system. Be that as it may, it is noteworthy in analytical terms that the classicals did not conceptualize the analysis of labor issues in terms of the market supply and demand approach that would later dominate discussion.

With the advent of neo-classical marginalism the attention of economics shifted from the broad classical themes of growth and distribution to the narrow ones of individual motivation in economic decisions and the operation of markets. It took the second generation of marginalists to extend this method to the issues of labor and wages with the rise to dominance of marginal productivity analysis in the 1890s. Henceforward and to the present day, the marginalist supply and demand approach would dominate mainstream discussion of labor issues. The labor market was to be taken as a special instance of the general laws of markets. This set the theoretical stage for the treatment of unemployment that Keynes, in an entirely ahistorical homogenization of seemingly every author before 1936, would later characterize as "classical." To just mention one case of violence Keynes thereby did to the historical record, an argument of our next chapter will be that his real "classical" opponent on labor market analysis, Pigou, is clearly distinguishable from his contemporaries and his predecessors. Especially important is the fact that he stands out all the more when considered as part of the Cambridge tradition. Marshall, we will see, cannot be painted with the same brush.[1]

But the use of this theoretical framework, it must be said, was not immediately taken up by economists in the pursuit of the question of unemployment. Just how this happened is a complicated issue involving the concrete historical events of the late nineteenth and early twentieth centuries, the simultaneous drive to professionalize economics and the enterprising work of various outsiders to the emerging "professional" clique.

As industrialization advanced, the "problem of the unemployed" became a progressively larger issue in British society. Initially its explanation centered on the low morality attributed to the unemployed. Over time, however, its treatment came also to be tied to the issue of the trade cycle. Actual documentation and analysis of unemployment was originally spurred by social inquiries conducted by non-economists, particularly those associated with the Fabians and Edwardian "problem-centered social investigators."[2] Most notable in this regard was the work of Charles Booth (1902), who conducted an influential statistical account of the extent of poverty and unemployment in London in the 1880s; Benjamin Seebohm Rowntree (1902), who conducted a similar study in York; and William Beveridge (1909), whose book marked out unemployment as a "problem of industry" and became a rallying point for Fabian reformers at the turn of the century.

Booth and Rowntree tended to focus on the squalidness of working-class living and working conditions and to ascribe much of it to related evidence of workers' depraved habits with regard to overcrowding, drink, sexual deviancy, prostitution and child abandonment. This behavior was then often traced to moral failings, especially with regard to the inherent laziness of workers. Laziness fit nicely with the older notion, from the classical writers on the Poor Laws for instance, of the "deserving poor" versus the "undeserving poor." The latter were considered to be of such low morality that they could not be helped and in fact wasted resources better spent on the improvable workers, those who would respond to opportunities for betterment. A good example was the cooperative movement, an effort to organize workers into organizations to purchase goods together and pool savings and collectively provide insurance. Labor reformers, Alfred Marshall enthusiastically among them, saw cooperation in consumption[3] as a way of raising workers' standard of living while also building their moral character. Working cooperatively would allow workers to move up the ranks of humanity by self-help, through the pooling of resources and the consequent "group morality" it depended upon and engendered, as well as through the experience in management it offered. But if workers had no innate moral faculties – as was variously described to be the case in Irishmen, Jews, non-rural urban degenerates (that is, not the superior recent immigrants from the countryside, who could be depended upon to understand common decency) and others – then improvement was impossible.

It was these latter, "degenerate" poor who were most often described by social investigators as likely to be unemployed in the later Victorian period, after 1870. Thus unemployment came to be considered a problem of the "casual" attachment to hard work and regular employment that certain demoralized classes of workers exhibited. "Casual labor" was epitomized for Victorian Britain by the example of the poor of inner city London, and especially by the East London dockworkers (Jones, 1971). Stedman Jones recounts how the 1840s through 1870s were years when redevelopment, industrial expansion and public infrastructure projects, particularly the clearing of land and building of great railroad and dock projects, had crowded London's poor into ever more scarce, more subdivided and more dear quarters[4] of slum housing in central and east London ("the rookeries"). These became the horrendous precincts described in such shocking detail by Booth and others.

Meanwhile, cheaper public transport allowed the more prosperous classes to flee to the suburbs. This was an outlet, which for reasons of proximity to work, insufficient income and preferential transport and house building patterns, was out of reach to the poor. Adding strain to this situation, trade cyclicality increased after 1880, worsening the poverty of these bare subsistence workers. Thus their situation was made more desperate just as their political power was being unleashed by the expanded enfranchisement, and by the trade union movement. A result was a large upswing in urban unrest. So much unrest occurred that it led to calls for Royal Commissions of inquiry, some of which Alfred Marshall participated in. Unrest also created a palpable sense of fear among the middle classes, largely directed at London's casual labor population, or the "residuum" of the working class as it came to be called. Fear reached a fever pitch of crisis in the mid-1880s as increasing strikes, demonstrations and growing political activity by workers called for a "major re-orientation" of social policy toward the poor:

> The social crisis of London in the mid-1880s engendered a major re-orientation of middle-class attitudes towards the casual poor. In conjunction with growing anxiety about the decline of Britain's industrial supremacy, apprehensions about the depopulation of the countryside and uncertainty about the future political role of the working class, fear of the casual residuum played a significant part in provoking the intellectual assault which began to be mounted against *laissez faire* both from the right and left in the 1880s.
>
> (Jones, 1971, pp. 296–7)

William Beveridge, who eventually became the mainstream spokesman of this "re-formulation," was also primarily motivated by the plight of the casual poor of London, the dockworkers in particular. His aim was to minimize casual labor and provide a way out of poverty for hard workers. His diagnosis was not that the morality of all unemployed workers was at fault, but that the structure of the labor market was. Specifically, Beveridge (1909) saw unemployment as a "problem of industry" that could be solved by more efficient exchanges of information about labor supply and demand, coupled with an effective government removal, to a sort of permanent dole, of those incorrigible casual laborers who did not want more stable employment.[5] Later, in our section of the next chapter on Pigou, we will see how nicely this fits in with a microeconomic theoretical view of labor. But Beveridge's contribution to the economic *theory* of unemployment was negligible. He was important in a wider sense of bringing the issue of unemployment into such prominence that the economics profession felt required to comment. Also, Beveridge explicitly tried to bring the latest economic theory to bear upon the problem to the extent that he proposed solving unemployment by reforming labor markets to more closely resemble the market model provided by economic theory – by, for instance, replacing the employer-dominated daily (spot) auctioning of dock workers with a government-run labor exchange that would offer, he hoped, longer term employment opportunities.

Finally, the most important direct challenge to the dominant economic *theory* of unemployment at the time was presented in the voluminous output of the self-confessed "economic heretic," J. A. Hobson. It was Hobson's role to challenge the Victorian complacency regarding unemployment and to pin much of the blame on the irrelevance of then orthodox economics, with its presumption of automatic adjustments via Say's Law, and what he saw as its apologetic outlook. This combined with his underconsumptionist attack on the great Victorian belief in the virtue of thrift clearly made a marked man of Hobson, and he never gained status within economics. It is also true that his formulations were often lacking in clearness. That his popular appeal was great, however, is attested by the frequency with which orthodox economists (of which Pigou is the most prominent) went out of their way to refute him. Although mostly known for the many versions of his business cycle work,[6] *Problem of the Unemployed* (Hobson, 1896) is Hobson's most interesting direct commentary on the issues of concern here. In reading the book today, one is struck by the extent to which Hobson uses such "Keynesian" terminology as "aggregate supply" and "aggregated demand (p. 117),"and his clear identification of unemployment with "all forms of *involuntary* leisure (p. 9, emphasis added)." In retrospect, considering Keynes's claims of novelty for the "comparatively simple ideas" of his *General Theory* four decades later, what is most modern about Hobson's treatment is his strong disassociation of unemployment from the *individual* "morality" of the unemployed as opposed to the *social* causes at work:

> A depression of the staple trade in a town throws out of employment 10 per cent. of those who are normally employed. The charity organizer with his individual scrutiny sets to work, and a close investigation of each "case" discloses in most of this 10 per cent. some moral or economic defect: there is drink, laziness, inefficiency, or some other personal fault discernible in, or imputed to, most of these "unemployed." Our "thorough" investigator, having, as he thinks, found a sufficient reason why each man should be unemployed, reaches the conclusion that "unemployment" is due to individual causes. Such conclusion is, of course, wholly fallacious. Personal causes, no doubt, explain in a large measure who are the individuals that shall represent the 10 per cent. "unemployed," but they are in no true sense even contributory causes of the "unemployment." When economic causes lower the demand for labour, competition will tend to squeeze out of employment those individuals who, for reasons, sometimes moral, sometimes industrial, are less valuable workers than their fellows. If these individuals had not been morally or industrially defective they would have kept their work, but necessarily by pushing out another 10 per cent.
>
> (Hobson, 1896, p. 47)

II. Marshall and the late Victorian labor question

> Marshall's ultimate aim in both writing and teaching economics was the hope that the economic knowledge his wider audience gained from his work would assist in the elevation of character by lifting society's standard of life.
>
> Groenewegen (1995a)

The explanation for the fact that the English economists had so little to say about unemployment in the Victorian era, when it gained such prominence outside the profession, probably rests, as with much of that group's strengths and weaknesses, with the work and attitudes of Alfred Marshall. Yet Marshall was a complicated personality and his economics was dense and sometimes beclouding (as some of his Cambridge successors, such as Joan Robinson, were later inclined to say). Consequently, it is perhaps no surprise that we can trace to Marshall's influence *both* the extreme neglect and misrepresentation Keynes would accuse economic theoreticians of concerning unemployment, *and* also the roots of Keynes's own later revolutionary outlook.

In this and the following two chapters, I will employ a series of circling attacks on the vast and important question of Marshall's thought on labor – his social and intellectual motivations, the form of his economic theory and the wide and varied impact he had on economics in general, and that of Keynes in particular. Hopefully this will provide, in a comparatively short space, a kaleidoscopic vision of the immense range and complexity of Marshall's thought.

In the rest of this chapter I will link Marshall's social and political outlook, his education and his biography to the Victorian labor reform context we just surveyed. We will then turn to the treatment of labor and wages in Marshallian economics proper in Chapter 6. First we will investigate the labor aspects of his *Principles of Economics*. This will be followed by two sections on the influence of Marshall's ideas on the economic theory of the Cambridge school. Chapter 7 will then be devoted to the career-long development of Keynes's views on labor, unemployment and wages.

The underlying motivation for Marshall's theoretical treatment of labor markets in the *Principles* is difficult to divine from that text alone. Marshall scholarship, however, provides us with many resources with which to fill this gap. Hints as to Marshall's earliest intellectual motivations were long ago offered by Keynes's (1925) famous biographical sketch, which we use below in our attempt to more explicitly link these two thinkers. Viner's (1941) insightful, if impressionistic, note on the personal and social aspects of Marshall's work is another useful early source. Unpublished writings by Marshall have long been recognized for their historical value, and were often cited by his students and colleagues as extremely influential in the form of "private circulations." Thus the collections issued immediately upon his death by former students and colleagues (Pigou, 1925; Keynes, 1926) as well as later additions by modern Marshall scholars (Whitaker, 1975; Groenewegen, 1996) offer interesting and useful material on his wider social views and earliest work and influences. This is especially the case on two cognate topics which strongly link Marshall's and Keynes's work: labor market issues (treated in Part I of this book) and financial market analysis (analyzed in Part II). Finally, an especially useful source for understanding Marshall's complete intellectual life is Peter Groenewegen's (1995a) recent biography. Coming surprisingly late for the first full-length life of a figure as significant as Marshall, and obviously exhaustively researched, Groenewegen's book provides a new wealth of extensive evidence and valuable commentary on Marshall's social philosophy and wider intellectual life.[7]

The now legendary story of the young Alfred Marshall fixing a portrait of a "working man" over his mantle, to keep him focused on the fact that his more esoteric work in economic theory was ultimately aimed as bettering such men's lives, highlights a real, lasting and important aspect of his intellectual makeup, brought out well in Groenewegen's book.[8] Marshall, starting from mathematics, became an economist in an attempt to find an answer to the miseries of poverty in his day. Moreover, as is attested by his later frequent calls for an economics that would enable workers to live a "higher" life, he never really lost this motivation.[9] He was a product of the secular, but still almost evangelical, reformism of the Victorian era, perhaps best exemplified by Marshall's early mentor on ethical values, Henry Sidgwick. These earnest "unbelievers" (Cockshut, 1964) were men of a post-religious zeal whose interest was to do good, but to do so rationally and thoughtfully. Suffused with this spirit, Marshall originally felt that poverty and the problems of the working classes could be alleviated by the proper inculcation of moral and ethical behavior in workers. However he was soon struck by a conviction, stressed in most of his works in the 1870s (see Whitaker, 1975, Volume 2, pp. 341–95; Groenewegen, 1995a, pp. 174–9), that behavior was largely determined by the *conditions* of work, the wages it paid and the consequent state of children's early family life.[10] It could be said that it was this postgraduate realization, coupled with his simultaneous loss of religious faith, that set him off on a seven-year search for a new vocation in life (Groenewegen, 1995a, Chapter 5). This search traversed metaphysical philosophy, including deep detours into Sidgwick's moral science and Kant, took a short side-trip into the then emerging field of psychology and landed, finally, in economics. Marshall found economics both ripe for a systematization that would yield to his mathematical talents and morally utilitarian in his pursuit of the riddle of poverty.

His conviction that the moral degradation of poverty was at bottom work-related, in the special social sense of depending on how work was organized and paid – a view he called "ethology" and seems to have first encountered in reading John Stuart Mill – was also driven home by his numerous "educational" trips, in particular by his extensive 1875 trip to America. In America Marshall saw an alternative social expression of the same Anglo-Saxon rootstock from which Britain's industrial might had grown, now growing in a richer and more fertile soil of technology and competitiveness. We can speculate that the importance he attributed to this experience was the result of how readily it fit into his emerging ideas on the ethological link between work and character. American workers, Marshall observed, were possessed of more opportunity and land, and therefore, he thought, were less willing to be directed, more independent and more willing to take charge and lead than their British counterparts. This led American society to be more democratic, more attached to liberty and possessed of enormous actual and potential economic might. For Marshall, America was a powerful object lesson in the social malleability of what he termed the "morality" of workers' behavior under different economic conditions of work.

By the mid-seventies the cultural relativity and social roots of the conditions of the working class had become a key theme for Marshall.[11] All of this created in him a growing urgency to develop an economics with a broader appreciation for the influence of working conditions on character. Thus, for instance, in an 1876 paper titled "Some Features of American Industry," authored shortly after his return, he writes:

> It has been found that economic influences play a larger part in determining the higher life of men and women than was once considered. It has been found that activity and vigour of character cannot be obtained without a generous supply of food; that healthiness of character can scarcely exist in overcrowded cottages; that the time and the money which a generation of workers must sacrifice if the next generation of workers is to be properly brought up can hardly be afforded by those who are in want of the necessaries of life. It is being found that the influences of association and habits of action to which a man is subject during most of his waking hours during at the least six days in the week, are, generally speaking, so incomparably more powerful in the formation of his character than any other influences, that those who have attempted to guide man's destinies, but have neglected the influences which his daily work exerts on him, are like children who have tried to determine the course of a ship, not by controlling her rudder and properly trimming her sails; but by merely blowing on her sails with their breath.
>
> (Marshall in Whitaker, 1975, Volume 2, p. 354.)

The conviction that he could control the rudder and trim the sails of the vessel of economics and use this control to "guide men's destinies" never left Alfred Marshall. A prominent later example of the technical apparatus this led him to construct would be the labor market analysis in the *Principles of Economics*.

Further biographical information that is relevant to tracing this line of influence on Cambridge labor economics, also richly illustrated in Groenewegen's book, is Marshall's immersion in the late Victorian working-class reform movement. There is ample evidence that he and his wife, Mary Paley Marshall, followed with interest the publications, news events and personalities surrounding labor issues. They were on personal (but not always warm) terms with most of the major British social thinkers and reformers of the day. This was notably true, for instance, of Beatrice and Sidney Webb, as well as Charles Booth and his wife. Marshall also made efforts to become acquainted with working-class leaders like Tom Mann and Ben Tillett, the leaders of the dockworkers, whom he may have considered beneath him in class status, and regarding whose tactics he was ambivalent at best (as we will see), but whose ideas he saw as necessary to the wider task of getting the "facts" right about important economic issues. In the same vein, Marshall and his wife spent much of their vacation time dutifully traipsing about factories and working-class sections of England and other European countries. Combining education and travel was, of course, a widespread Victorian trait. But the great seriousness of these travels for the Marshalls, and Alfred Marshall's conviction that they would aid his wider understanding of the world he hoped to capture in his economics is undoubted.[12] Also, his early and thorough knowledge of the history of trade unions and bargaining is evident both in his teaching materials from the 1870s and 1880s, and the extensive discussion of these issues in his first book, the collaboration between the two Marshalls, *Economics of Industry* (Marshall and Marshall 1879, Book III).

All these strands coalesce in Marshall's extensive participation as a member of the Royal Commission on Labour from 1891–94.[13] This commission was called by the Salisbury Conservative government over concern with the growing frequency of strikes by the trade union movement and industrial unrest more generally. Marshall later described his four years of (significant) work on this commission as "the most valuable education of my life" (Groenewegen, 1995a, p. 367).[14] Its appeal to him lay in the opportunity it offered, in that pre-information age, to gather more factual details. The commission was lavishly financed and represented the greatest centralized fact finding effort of the time into the practices of labor markets and institutions, and the life of the "laboring classes." As can be seen from his questioning of witnesses, Marshall also used his time on the commission to test his, by then already well developed, theories on wages, employment and the influence of work on character and parenthood.

We will detail those theories shortly, and examine how they influenced Marshall's views on the methodological usefulness of supply and demand theory in issues relating to labor. Before that, however, it is useful to stand back and place Marshall's views on labor in their social context. Victorian reformers, beginning with the great documenters and collectors of statistics like Rowntree and Booth, were apt, we have seen, to find the causes of poverty in the proximate defects of character – drink, sexual immorality and so on – that they found accompanying poverty-stricken families.[15] From this standpoint the logical aim of reform was to correct such deficiency by moral or religious teaching. The legion of Victorian religious and secular campaigns of moral uplift that sprang from this urge are familiar.[16]

Also prevalent and influential in discussions of the plight of the working poor – particularly in the early Victorian era from 1837 to the 1860s, the generation prior to Marshall's years of intellectual formation – were the Manchester Liberals. Mostly a movement that grew out of opposition to the Corn Laws, promulgated largely in the popular business press such as Bagehot's *Economist*, radical liberalism was dominated by politics more than theory. The most prominent liberal proponents were politicians, such as Richard Cobden and John Bright. Its guiding economic principles were Ricardian economics. On labor issues Manchester Liberals were firm in their support for the 1834 Poor Laws and generally *laissez faire* about the rights of property and capital against those of the state. Significantly, they used economic ideas, such as Malthusian population theory and the "dismal" economics of the wages fund, when convenient. Thus in the early part of the Victorian age, economics became a favorite tool for the repudiation of social reform. In the Manchester Liberal view, only by the advance of capital, unfettered by the state, could the lot of workers ever improve. This infamously harsh viewpoint, a favorite whipping boy of Dickens for example, was *not*, it should be emphasized, the Victorianism upon which Marshall was brought up and which he later embodied.[17]

Marshall was a "late Victorian intellectual" (Groenewegen, 1995a, p. 8; Viner, 1941). The "late" Victorian period, from 1860 to about 1900, refers to a time of still general consensus on the value of free trade in the international sphere, but it emphatically was not a period of dogmatic support for *laissez faire* on domestic issues. It was also a period marked by the extension of the vote to all able-bodied men and hence a growing need by politicians of the two dominant parties – the Tories and the Liberals – to appeal to working voters and their supporters in the educated middle class. In this period, the Liberals represented social views closest to Marshall's, and more so to those of the early Keynes, at least before World War I. Then as now, however, there is no exact analog in popular politics for the views of such creative and unique intellectuals of social thought. Moreover Marshall's reticence and reserve on political matters is famous (and puts him in marked contrast to Keynes). Marshall, with his strong dislike of controversy, was reluctant to openly support any political movement.

In this regard it is important that Marshall's economics hero was John Stuart Mill, the meliorist of the Classical Political Economy tradition, who had recanted the wages fund and who thought that the virtues of competition prized by Adam Smith and the utilitarianism of Bentham could be reconciled with socialist concerns for the poor and even state action. Also, significantly, it was Mill, within the Ricardian tradition, who established the position, later followed in Marshall's *Principles* to a certain degree, that production and distribution theory are not to be treated as exact analogs to one another.

Mill's vision of the progressive society was not meant as just a transitional way station between *laissez faire* capitalism and socialism, but as a realistic alternative to both. This ideal of an organically mixed economy – full of liberty, private production, and widespread competition, but also dedicated to higher values, perhaps even directed by state intervention – always remained Marshall's preferred vision for society. So too did Mill's optimism and faith in the inevitability of social progress remain permanent parts of Marshall's make-up. Marshall left mathematics and the moral sciences and devoted himself to economics with the express purpose of showing that Mill's instincts, suitably translated into modern marginalist garb, were economically sound. It was for this reason that he set himself the task, culminating in the *Principles* and the establishment of the economics degree at Cambridge, to carefully build an "engine of analysis," in Keynes's apt phrase, to enshrine a reasoned "method" that, by wide applicability to changing social problems, he hoped and expected would become a way to the improvement of the problems of the poor. This was his greatest achievement. Ever the evangelist, he also always hoped thereby to convince scientific economists, public statesmen and reformers, and, his favorite target, "ordinary business men," of the soundness of "economic chivalry" – such as voluntarily raising wages. There is little evidence that he had much success in this endeavor.[18]

When these strands are tied, one is struck by the complex and fascinating place it carves out for Marshall in terms of the sketch of the earlier history of labor and unemployment that ended above with the words of the more radical voice of J. A. Hobson. At one level Marshall, in his very person, given the weight of his position at Cambridge and the silent influence he wielded through his students and the positions they attained, and given his success with the *Principles*, exerted a unique "official" voice on many matters of public economic policy, including labor issues. His efforts formed a socially powerful combination for late Victorian Britain. It was constructed of contemporarily potent ingredients of scholarship, professionalism and the consequent appeal to, and appearance of, reason, along with a call to duty on the part of the upper classes toward the lower. It must also have been a pleasing aspect to conservative audiences that Marshall was so much at pains in his commentary on policy questions to emphasize the virtues of the natural, slow and cumulative impact of beneficial social change – also a familiar scientific theme in the *Principles*. Thus the role he often assumed in public appears as a bemused paternal scold, descending from the loftiness of his superior theoretical knowledge to bring calm reason to the heartfelt but ignorant rants of socialists and trade unionists.[19]

An effect, inevitably, was to turn discussions of economic questions into a professional issue that, curiously opposite to his intention of being widely read and influential, could only seriously be discussed by others possessing the insights of his "engine." Previous to this professionalization economic debates had been much shriller and overtly ideological, but more widely debated. Labor questions in particular had often been characterized by, for instance, the evangelical zeal of reformers and trade unionists on one side, and the ominous predictions of chaos and social decline on the side of conservative politicians and dismal economists. Marshall achieved his intended effect of calming and rationalizing such debates. But this very professionalism was also stifling of efforts at social analysis and reform that were not sanctioned by Marshall and/or were more controversial.[20] Partly this was due to the closing of the professional ranks around conventionalism, protected, perhaps unconsciously, by Marshallian qualifications and by the stature of degrees and chairs at important universities, to which professionalism inevitably led. Partly it was due also to Marshall's jealous and protective guard of what he saw as "his" school's reputation, and the extreme caution of his public pronouncements.

This conflict between propriety and a more rude statement of facts, as we might put it, was especially evident in the questions Marshall put to people like Sidney Webb and the trade union leaders testifying before him on the labor commission.[21] Marshall can be seen in his worst light in this evidence. The most charitable interpretation one can place on his performance is an extreme fastidiousness about the necessary complexity of labor market issues. Less charitably, Marshall's questioning often reads like a hostile shredding of the labor witnesses – in marked contrast to his questioning of the business or political leaders appearing before him. It seems that Marshall's public persona, perhaps unwittingly, was in fact often that of defender of the status quo he professed to want to change. Such a view can easily be derived from his public positions and advisory work (see Groenewegen, 1995a, especially Chapters 11 and 16) where his continual public bias against labor's more radical (socialist) political positions is evident. It can also be seen in his habit of enmeshing opponents on the left in an obfuscating web of *ceteris paribus* clauses. This was particularly true of socialist writers of the time such as Henry George, Sidney Webb and Henry Hyndman.[22] Coupled with this palpable bias was an all too fanciful faith in the possibilities of conservative businessmen and politicians reading into those same complex chains of reasons valid grounds for embracing a 'social' outlook on labor questions. Ultimately, Marshallianism, as practiced by Marshall, failed to be much of a force for the changes he "seemed" (his endless qualification aside) to be in favor of. However great the success of his "engine" – and it was considerable – Marshall's parallel efforts at encouraging higher values in business and politics, what he called "economic chivalry," were a delusion on his part.

To end this chapter on the social and intellectual context of Marshall's labor economics, then, we are left with evaluating Marshall as a social *theorist*, which after all is how he should be remembered, not as a controversialist (which he partly was, but for which he was really not suited). At the level of theory, and in the broad sweep of the changing perception of labor problems by Victorian British social thinkers, Marshall's approach represents an interesting place – one that seems to have escaped comment. I am referring to his basic theme of the importance of work and wages on character and family life, and so on future generations of workers and their probabilities of economic and moral success. The early reformers of working-class conditions focused upon the moral defects of workers as the cause of all ills, including, we have seen, unemployment. Later, Hobson's prescient suggestion was that individual character really had little to do with the causes of labor problems, unemployment especially, if the state of trade was demanding to throw someone out of work. Yes the laziest and least productive would go first, but that was not the reason for unemployment. Personal characteristics merely explained the particular incidence of unemployment over the trade cycle. Hobson thus shifted the focus of attention from the individual worker to the system. This is the same overall argument that Keynes was to make 40 years later – although in Keynes's case the argument was importantly modified by his Marshallian pedigree, and it was pitched to an audience much more interested in the answer.

In the end, Marshall represents a curious amalgam of the reformist and scientific trends of his day. Labor, he said, was mostly hindered by poor working conditions, low wages and a consequent lack of a good upbringing and education. But this was the fault of the system. Moreover, this could be seen only with the help of a sound economics, namely his. A sound economics recognizes the social realities and complexities of the labor markets and the subtle ways in which supply and demand interact therein. (As we will see in the next chapter, this means that the supply-demand apparatus might not be nearly as useful for investigations in labor markets as it is in product markets.) Thus Marshall, in his characteristically meek, bland, non-controversial, professional way, intimated that the problems of the poor might be solved through knowledge, good intentions, persuasion to economically chivalrous behavior and, in the extreme, perhaps, even legislation.

6
The Treatment of Labor Markets in Marshallian Economics

I. Marshall's method and treatment of distribution in the *Principles of Economics*

In evaluating Alfred Marshall as an economic theorist and his influence over economics it is crucial to recognize his methodological attitudes and vision for economics. Two strands of his perspective seem most relevant: his attitude toward controversy and his attitude toward truth (Collard, 1990). It is commonplace to regard Marshall as wary of public controversy, almost to the point of extreme timidity.[1]

Yet this was not just a personal trait but also a strategy for gaining professional status for economists. For Marshall, professional economists were to avoid the unseemly appearance of controversy, both theoretical and practical, and were to assume a scientific objectivity on social issues. Part of this self-conscious sense of objectivity lay in the security of the method and theory of the *Principles of Economics*. "The Organon was to be a machine for the discovery of concrete truth." (Collard, 1990, p. 167)

In line with this vision for economics were Marshall's extensive efforts to found the Tripos (Coats, 1967; Groenewegen, 1995a, pp. 531–61), which would supposedly institutionalize the production of such non-controversial "professional" economists. Furthermore, another aspect of Marshall's attitude toward controversy was his attempt to reconcile the old classical theory with the newer neoclassical approach. This is clearly evident in his labor market analysis, where long-run supply and demand becomes "indeterminate" as the old classical themes concerning labor – population, human nature and social institutions – come to the foreground.

In retrospect, it is easy to see now that things were not quite so cut and dried. First with respect to the issue of method, one man's objectivity is often just prejudice to another. It is only fair to note that Marshall injected into his analysis much Victorian moralizing of the type Hobson railed against – particularly with regard to labor markets because of their close connection in Marshall's thought to changeable human nature, and on the influence of parental wages on the most plastic early years of the development of children. But the genius of Marshall was to so intricately weave this moral polemic into his positive analysis that it *seemed* splendidly dispassionate.[2] And as R. C. O. Matthews (1990, pp. 20–3) has stressed in his superb documentation of Marshall's views on labor markets, his fusion of morals and theory was for him a *scientific* necessity when dealing with long-run social forces in which effects today would yield changed preferences and human natures over a long future time.

Picking up on this theme, it is perhaps not unreasonable to skip Marshall's development of the apparatus of supply and demand in the labor market. This strand of Marshallianism is familiar to most economists, and we will encounter it more concisely treated by Dobb in Section III of this chapter. We will instead concentrate on some of the usually forgotten qualifications with which Marshall endlessly complicated his argument. Thus after setting out the mechanical aspects of supply and demand for labor (Marshall, 1962, Book VI, Chapter III), Marshall starts the following chapter (Chapter IV) by stressing the long-term cumulative effects of wages:

> But some peculiarities in this action [of supply and demand on labor] remain to be studied, which are of a more vital character. For they affect not merely the form, but also the substance of the action of the forces of demand and supply; and to some extent they limit and hamper the free action of those forces. We shall find that the influence of many of them is not at all to be measured by their first and most obvious effects: and that those effects which are cumulative are generally far more important in the long run than those which are not, however prominent the latter may appear.
>
> (Marshall, 1962, p. 465)

Chief among the evil effects of adverse labor market outcomes – for Marshall low wages, not unemployment – is the transmission of poverty, lack of opportunity and poor education to children. For Marshall, the main point to stress was that the cumulative nature of social evolution meant that these effects, which "exert a deep and controlling influence over the history of the world," cannot be directly treated by the static method. It is at this juncture, clearly of high importance in Marshall's thinking,[3] that he enters into his advocacy of a policy of encouraging employers to voluntarily pay high wages. For if low wages, though perhaps a natural short-run outcome, can have such long-term cumulative disastrous effects, the opposite is also true:

> On the other hand, high earnings, and a strong character, lead to greater strength and higher earnings, which again lead to still higher earnings, and so on cumulatively.
>
> (Marshall, 1962, p. 468)

As we will see below, Dobb emphasizes this aspect of Marshallianism more than the master himself ever did and draws from it support for positive action such as minimum wage laws and union bargaining. In Marshall's hands these clear-cut policy conclusions would probably have been too "controversial" to consider. Instead we get reserved endorsement of the *goal* of agitation for higher working-class incomes,[4] which is then drained away in the sand of another array of Marshall's endless qualifications.[5]

Also, it should be added in fairness to Marshall that he considered state action as only a last resort, while "policy" had much broader implications. The point is made by Matthews (1990, p. 30) that "policy" to Marshall was preeminently a matter of educating leaders of business and labor in the macroeconomic implications of their actions – that is, they must be enlightened properly, presumably by reading the *Principles*. His hopes for this influence of his writings seem to have come to nothing, but they were sincere. This Victorian faith in progress, and in rationality as advancing civilization, is expressed in Marshall's belief that the social effects of high wages coincided with the private interests of employers and so could be expected to dominate in the long run. It is this context that we come up against a modern New Keynesian notion, as alluded to earlier, in Marshall's explicit and extensive references to "efficiency wages":[6]

> . . . that is, earnings measured, not as time-earnings are with reference to the time spent in earning them; and not as piece-work earnings are with reference to the amount of output resulting from the work by which they are earned; but with reference to the exertion of ability and *efficiency* required of the worker.
>
> (Marshall, 1962, p. 546)

The complication for supply and demand analysis that this implies is a degree of interdependence between the two. High wages call forth better labor and so, in turn, affect the demand price (Marshall, 1962, p. 442). It is in this complex setting that we are to understand Marshall's emphasis on the point that distribution theory does *not* present an exact analog to value theory:

> The keynote of this book [Book VI, "The Distribution of National Income"] is in the fact that free human beings are not brought up to their work on the same principles as a machine, a horse, or a slave. If they were, there would be very little difference between the distribution and the exchange side of value.
>
> (Marshall, 1962, p. 418)

The question we now must answer is: How does his concern with "high wages" and "efficiency" line up with the fact that Alfred Marshall was also a pioneering theorist of marginal productivity theory?

II. Marshall's marginal product of labor, efficiency wages and the national dividend

As Alfred Marshall was a "Late Victorian" in his intellectual views concerning state and society, he was also a "second generation marginalist" in his distribution theory. Usually this is taken as meaning that his incorporation of marginal thinking into the theory of value made the twin blade argument of supply and demand complete. While this is generally true, it does not do his subtly drawn theory full justice. Not only did he incorporate marginal utility and demand with the old classical account of value, and along the way introduce the treatment of time and industry in a way that still is with economics today, he also presented a theory of distribution that was remarkably nuanced, especially when compared to many of his predecessors and contemporaries. His goal, not completely met, was to incorporate the insight of what he saw as contemporary fact within a rigorously drawn account of firm behavior and of national income accounting. It may be that his grasp of his goal was incomplete because he saw so deeply into the limitations that a static analysis presented for a depiction of an inherently dynamic world. But his attempt to reconcile these incompatibilities, to use phraseology of which he was fond, is worthy of honor in itself. For us it is also an important step to visualizing what the problems and promises were for a supply-and-demand-in-the-labor-market theory of unemployment as Keynes inherited it from Marshall.

Marshall's theoretical fastidiousness required that the method by which firms compensated factors of production line up with an airtight aggregate account of total factor distribution. But his hunger for the facts and his focus on "ethology," as we saw in the last chapter, meant this same theory should be compatible with what he saw as one of the leading aspects of modern industrial life – the impact of wages on the character of the worker and his family. Perhaps this is just one instance of what Marshall's biographer Peter Groenewegen (1995a, pp. 783–4) described as Marshall's "aim" in all of his economic work:

> Marshall's ultimate aim in both writing and teaching economics was the hope that the economic knowledge his wider audience gained from his work would assist in the elevation of character by lifting society's standard of life. Mill's prospect of a science of ethology had attracted Marshall as a young graduate because it raises the possibility of a scientific approach to character formation . . .
>
> The demand this objective placed on Marshall's economic writing was twofold. It generated technical requirements for a sound theoretical structure capable of supplying the tools for solving problems of industry, markets, competition, regulation, production, accumulation and progress. In addition, his economics needed to be communicated not only to present

and future academic specialists. It had to be read by the parties more actively involved in the process of social improvement and progress.

One of the "facts" of ethology, as we have begun to see, one that required careful treatment in his distribution theory, concerned a Victorian campaign to improve the character and the work effort of the labor force by raising wages. A particularly important aspect of this was the "high wage economy movement" – a combination of practical businessmen's workplace lore about workers' producing "effort" in proportion to the wages they were paid, and the Victorian reformers zeal to improve working-class character. Its origins lie with the work of Thomas Brassey (1872),[7] a master builder of railroads, bridges and public works in mid-eighteenth-century Britain. Brassey's experience with the work of men in many countries, all of a uniformly unskilled variety, led him to formulate an empirical generalization that Petridis (1996, p. 588) calls Brassey's Law: "This was the claimed tendency for output per wage unit to be the same everywhere." From Brassey's original work, and the advocacy of his MP son, Sir Thomas Brassey, grew a widespread movement campaigning for voluntarily paid higher wages. It was argued that in fact this was in employers' interest as the result would be better work performance. Petridis details how Marshall, among others, very early took on this view as a factual datum and then set about incorporating it into his own version of the marginal productivity theory of distribution.[8]

The problems this presented to such a theory were manifold. Chief among them was the issue of how marginal products could be evaluated if wages themselves interacted with the value of effort from work. For then marginal products were not necessarily independent of wages. Also, this meant that demand for labor and supply of labor was ultimately not independent in such a world. As a result accounting for national output in a competitive setting where every factor was paid its "marginal" product was complicated to say the least. Additionally, Marshall made clear that this precluded simple ethical statements about the "justice" of competitive wages that many of his contemporaries were drawing from the marginal productivity theory. If Brassey was correct, as Marshall believed he was, then paying above what the market would bear over certain ranges could raise labor efficiency, presumably above that at the natural "equilibrium" wage.

As Petridis sees it, Brassey's influence on Marshall began just after Brassey's work was published in 1872, and continued as Marshall's working out of his Organon turned to distribution in the 1880s. Notice how closely this parallels our account of his social views in the previous chapter. Ultimately, however, Petridis views this incorporation as abortive, in that it would have been better treated in Marshall's planned discussion of dynamic issues in a never-finished second volume follow-up to the *Principle's* largely static account.

In this way it also fits nicely with our theme of the degree to which Marshall's economics was ultimately too restrictive to treat the very range of real phenomena that even Marshall, much less Keynes, hankered after. Perhaps recognition of this by Keynes went a long way toward freeing him from those difficult "habits of mind" of which he spoke in the preface to the *General Theory*. Yet Marshall's labor market chapters also point out how much wisdom he hid beneath the calmly constructed edifice of the *Principles*.

Marshall took Brassey's law as an empirical fact. He also saw great promise in the newly emerging concepts of marginal productivity. The clue to the conflict this created was apparent very early in his exploration of distribution in Book V of the *Principles* (p. 423) when he notes:

> But it was only in the last generation that a careful study was begun to be made of the effects that high wages have in increasing the efficiency not only of those who receive them, but also of their children and grandchildren. In this matter the lead has been taken by Walker and other American economists; and the application of the comparative method of study to the industrial problems of different countries of the old and new world is forcing constantly more and more attention to the fact that highly paid labour is generally efficient and therefore not dear labour; a fact which, though it is more full of hope for the future of the human race than any other that is known to us, will be found to exercise a very complicating influence on the theory of distribution.

Thus, Marshall said (1962, p. 456), notice should be taken of a distinction between wages paid for time ("time wages") and those adjusted for effort expended in particular tasks ("task wages" early on, and later, "efficiency wages" or "efficiency earnings").[9] The latter are also identified as wages measured in efficiency units – "that is earnings measured with reference to the exertion of ability or efficiency added."

Having recognized that labor's marginal product depends on the efficiency of work, and that efficiency depends, over ranges, on wages earned, this meant that labor market equilibrium could become indeterminate. Yet full realization of this did not come direct from Marshall's pen. He provided hints of a more complicated situation in labor markets, but also wanted the analytical "engine" of the *Principles* to be logically airtight. Especially was this true when it came to lining up the behavioral theory of the motivations of private labor market agents with an economist's account of measuring the national dividend – what today we would call national income accounting. Though market participants were not impeded either way by this necessity, according to Marshall economists should be: "Problems relating to methods of estimating and reckoning earnings, to which the present chapter is devoted, belong mainly to the province of arithmetic or book-keeping: but much error has arisen from treating them carelessly"(1962, p. 454).

It is fair to say that Marshall's characteristically "reasonable" solution to this problem is what ultimately led him astray. In essence he opted for a non-controversial way out that may have seemed "reasonable," but was perhaps ultimately limiting in a crippling way. He assumed that in static equilibrium all factors of production would earn their marginal product in competitive conditions. Yet this equilibrium itself was dependent on certain assumptions that were incompatible with what Marshall clearly believed were "facts" of labor markets – particularly his deep interest in generational dynamics and the effects of differential wage and "efficiency" for labor. It might be that this is an example on Marshall's part of what Joan Robinson elsewhere (Robinson, 1969, p. vi), describing her own static equilibrium model of imperfect competition, called "a shameless fudge." Petridis (1996, pp. 596–7), again, is acute on this: "So the analysis proceeded on the assumptions that labor was of "normal" or "standard" efficiency working with capital of a given value, generating the result that the marginal net product of labor is equal to its wage." But this did not clear up the ambiguities that he thought it would, and did not aid in understanding Brassey's empirical generalization. Petridis (1996, pp. 596–9), though he does not emphasize Marshall's need for national accounting precision, correctly lays the blame on Marshall's static framework and its restrictive assumptions regarding "equality of efficiency" and "normal conditions," when at the same time he presents arguments of a "modern-efficiency-wage type," with which it is incompatible.

The problem, which would be emblematic of Keynes's own grappling with unemployment in the 1930s, was that Marshall had assumed away the problem he was interested in explaining by his meticulous static construct. If, as he assumed, efficiency earnings tend to equality, and if therefore each factor was working with "normal" capital and normal efficiency, then, yes, net product would be exhausted when each factor was paid its marginal product. But Marshall also wanted to advocate for higher wages – thus, as just one example, his statement that in the case of highly capital-intensive industry, " . . . it would be to the advantage of the employer to raise the time-earnings of the more efficient workers more than in proportion to their efficiency (Marshall, 1962, pp. 457–8)." This and other discussions seem to imply that labor is not naturally paid its maximum – or theoretically optimum – efficiency earnings, or marginal product, under competition. Moreover it was at just such points in his discussion that he often launched into discussions of the cumulative interaction of parents' wages and children's future training and efficiency, advocating the social benefits that would flow from higher wages, ending with careful qualifications on the potential interaction of supply and demand factors and the limits of a too naive marginal productivity theory of distribution. So for instance:

> This doctrine has sometimes been put forward as a theory of wages. But there is no valid ground for any such pretension. The doctrine that the earning of a worker tend to be equal to the product of his work, has by

itself no real meaning; since in order to estimate net product we have to take for granted all the expenses of production of the commodity on which he works, other than his own wages.

(p. 429–30)

or,

We conclude then that an increase in wages, unless earned under unwholesome conditions, almost always increases the strength, physical, mental and even moral of the coming generation; and that, other things being equal, an increase in the earnings that are to be got by labour increases its rate of growth; or, in other words, a rise in its demand price, increases the supply of it.

(p. 442)

In some way we should admire Marshall facing these problems head on – even if he congenitally shied from emphasizing them. The circularity of marginal productivity theory was demonstrated for all in the capital debates of the 1960s and we should not as a profession (though we often do) shy away from the difficulties it presents. Outside of strict static conditions, in which it holds almost as a tautology that "in equilibrium marginal products equal wages," it is difficult to interpret naive statements like Clarks's marginal productivity ethics to the effect that all wages represent just rewards. Nevertheless, like Marshall, many cannot help but endorse his view that: "But though this objection is valid against a claim that it [the claim that wages tend to equal marginal products] contains a theory of wages; it is not valid against a claim that the doctrine throws into clear light the action of one of the causes that govern wages" (Marshall, 1962, p. 430).

In general a careful reader of Marshall's chapters on distribution would even today find an excellent discussion and almost encyclopedic accounting of the factors affecting wages. But they should not come away from this reading feeling very confident that "wages tend toward marginal products" – even if defined in Marshall's preferred efficiency units. Nor would such a reader think this alone tells us much about income distribution. It was almost as if Marshall's method constrained him from his real object. Only by fastidious attention to strict *ceteris paribus* conditions could he make his theory and national accounting framework airtight. But what most interested him – "ethologically" – was defined by the very violation of those *ceteris paribus* conditions. It is a testament to his careful presentation that when Marshall is finished with all of these qualifications the theory seemed so "reasonable." Like in much of Marshallian economics, just as important as the main theoretical structure is what cannot be neatly cut out by the twin blades of supply and demand.

But what of unemployment in all of this? It must be said that in the treatment of this issue, which so engaged other reformers of his time, Marshall had something of a blind spot. His scant comments on it in the *Principles* (Book VI, Chapter XII, pp. 571–3) bring it up only to dismiss it as overblown and surely improving over time (a rather large historical gaffe, considering where unemployment rates were heading as the last edition of the book came out in 1920). To account for this it is perhaps sufficient to note that Marshall's discursive moral-evolutionary dynamics were highly dependent on the author's own peculiar prejudices. This ingredient is suggested by David Collard's assessment of Marshall's influence on Cambridge economics when he argues that Marshall emphasized the need to arrive at "Truth" through the use of his analytic machine – a machine which for all Marshall's qualifications about the long run turned out to be remarkably unsuited to the analysis of unemployment:

> The Organon was to be a machine for the discovery of concrete truth. Keynes remarks (1926, p. 36) that Marshall was not good at the discovery of concrete truth. Beatrice Webb noticed (Koot 1987, p. 180), after staying with Marshall, that he had an extraordinary penchant for making "an astounding observation with no basis in fact."
>
> (Collard, 1990, p. 167)

Webb's comment is telling in the context of Marshall's treatment of unemployment since it would seem that he both denied the view of the Victorian social reformers (like Webb) concerning the growing problem of unemployment and that he based his own views on what could easily be characterized as an "astounding observation with no basis in fact." In the case of unemployment, R. C. O. Matthews (1990, pp. 33–8) has noted that Marshall, somewhat astonishingly, based his analysis of unemployment on his observations of what he considered the "pre-industrial" city of Palermo during his vacation visits to Italy. Matthews summarizes his view as follows:

> It [the observations of Palermo] suggested to him that the history of hiring practices had gone in a circle, with three phases: 1. The worker permanently attached to a feudal patron, but chronically underemployed and also lacking in personal freedom; 2. labour hired and fired on a casual basis; 3. a reversion to a more or less permanent attachment of the worker to one employer, but now because of asset specificity rather than patronage, and with a full whole-time wage being paid, and without loss of personal freedom. The transition from phase 2 to phase 3 had served to reduce the inconstancy of employment.
>
> (Matthews, 1990, p. 34)

This view sheds considerable light on the difficulties a dependence on Marshallianism *as a set of received opinion* would present to a scholar seeking a fuller understanding of short-run changes in unemployment when it was direly needed in the 1920s and 1930s.

However, Marshall's own (scant) treatment of unemployment is less important in itself than in the ambiguous but vastly influential legacy his method left to the profession. In Marshall's hands the Organon suggested that supply and demand organize the discussion, but with due regard to the evolution of social customs and the influence of the economic environment upon character. His analysis was, by modern standards, complex and subtle in the case of the labor market. Starting from a supply and demand framework, he argued that the short-period effects were dominated by long-period concerns which, he hinted, were not amenable to static theorizing. Of these the most important were the issues of human capital specific to individual firms and industries, and the consequent peculiarities of labor as a commodity; and the influence of steady labor attachments on improving the character of the working class. Thus his complex theoretical view of supply and demand analysis, in the case of labor markets at least, becomes merely a skeleton to hang his more evolutionary social and moral outlook upon (see Matthews, 1990, pp. 14–30).

Although one comes away admiring his own use of the Organon, it seems clear, against Matthews, that his emphasis upon the long-period normal supply and demand easily led directly to later confusions and dead-ends concerning employment theory. Although, it perhaps is fair to lay more of this blame upon Pigou than Marshall.

With regard to the labor market, the ultimate irony is that Keynes's own influential views, though clearly opposed to Marshall's conclusions on unemployment, may be more faithful to the master's careful method concerning problems of labor than the chosen successor Pigou. This is because Pigou grew ever more impatient with Marshall's qualifying and fudging, but ever heeded his advice to remain non-controversial. Thus in his hand the *mechanical* aspect of the Organon takes over and unemployment becomes a *simple* matter of a non-clearing labor market.

Keynes, always more attuned to current social "facts" than either Marshall or Pigou, and ever the controversialist, perhaps took more from Marshall's moral philosophy outlook. As Marshall left the characterization of labor supply and demand and its social effects (properly) shrouded in a mysterious brew of institutional and moral analysis, there seems to have been plenty of room for Keynes to elaborate on this part of the Organon. In any event, as we shall see, Keynes never let the Organon blind him to current realities as it eventually did Pigou. And when Keynes felt the need for a new Organon to explain mass unemployment of a kind Marshall never expected, he was able to rise to the occasion as Marshall's more devout successor could not.

III. Dobb: Labor market orthodoxy in interwar Cambridge

To continue our discussion of the Cambridge context of unemployment theory, it is convenient and appropriate to bring our discussion up to the interwar period with the school's official[10] orthodox view as set out in the "Cambridge Economic Handbook" series edited by Keynes from 1914 to 1936. Maurice Dobb's *Wages* came out in that series in 1928 and eventually went through three revisions and over twenty reprintings. Indeed, it survived in print into the 1950s. We will quote below mostly from the original 1928 edition, with some minor references to the second edition written in 1938 as it elaborates upon the arguments of the first. In any case it is clear that this treatment would have been considered fairly standard in Cambridge between the wars.[11]

Coming to Dobb's book today, the modern economist is struck by the author's thoroughness and fairness in his discussion of the "theory of wages" (Chapter IV), and by the wealth of institutional detail relating to historical wage rates, the myriad variety of complex wage payment systems and the social history of bargaining and compacts. One senses the influence of Marshall strongly, but here interestingly blended with Dobb's Marxist historical materialism (which, incidentally, is very much in the background). For our interest, the most important discussion in Dobb's book relates to the analysis of wage institutions in "The Payment of Wages" (Chapter III) and the chapter on the "Theory of Wages" (Chapter IV). In Chapter III Dobb presents a detailed description of several types of wage payment systems, historical and contemporary.[12] Under the heading "The Economy of High Wages,"[13] Dobb offers an argument that would be considered distinctly New Keynesian today, but which is in fact right out of Marshall:

> Recently a great deal has been talked and written concerning "The Economy of High Wages": if the employer pays well, it is said, he will get better work done and so gain more profit. This may come about in two ways. First if the worker and his family live at a higher standard of life, their physical and mental conditions will tend to improve and their working efficiency will tend to increase. Part of this result will tend to be mainly of a psychological character and to be more uncertain and indefinite. Second, the prospect of more wages may act as an inducement to the worker to increase the amount of work that he does, either by working longer hours or by working more intensively.
>
> (Dobb, 1928, pp. 44–5)[14]

Dobb then discusses in detail various alternative methods of contract between workers and employers such as piece rates, premium bonus systems, task bonus systems and Taylorite systems. Having shown how these systems often prove superior from the standpoint of the employer's desire to maximize labor's effort, he asks why is it that we do not see them more universally adopted. His answer (Dobb, 1928, pp. 51–2), citing Ford as an example of a company with a policy of exclusive time wages, is that the nature of certain processes – where the speed of the work is not up to the worker but is a characteristic of the process – may not lend themselves to piece rates. Echoing the "shirker" version of modern efficiency wage theories, Dobb notes that the issue for the employer in these situations is the degree to which supervision is practical. And as in the modern "insider–outsider" view, this will be at least partly a function of workers' cooperation or resistance, he notes.[15] Further, Dobb makes it clear that in the case of skilled work (which to a modern labor-market theorist would imply firm specific human capital) the question often revolves as much around quality of work as around quantity. For all of these reasons, "It is far from true that every case of low output and high costs is curable by an extension of payment by results" (Dobb, 1928, p. 51.).

Turning to Dobb's discussion of wage "theory," we get a nice historical account, stressing, in good Marshallian fashion, continuity with the classicals and an emphasis on flexible, socially relevant theory. The classical theory is seen as "rigid and definitive" in the extreme. Against this:

> . . . only in recent times [read Marshall] have serious doubts developed as to whether the conditions on which wages depend may not be more complicated, and less easily explicable by an easy mechanical formula – whether changes in wages may not react on these so-called "determining" factors as much as these latter influence wages.
>
> (pp. 70–1)

The downfall of the classical theory is traced by Dobb to the chink in the Iron Law of Wages introduced by Ricardo's admission that the subsistence wage was not an absolute physical standard but a matter of social and historic "custom and habit."[16] This influence was eventually used by Marx to disassociate wages from population altogether, except in so far as subsistence created a crude lower limit to wages. Wages thus became *indeterminate* in some degree and subject to struggle between workers and employers (pp. 74–5). But the classical introduction of a demand side argument in the form of a "wages fund" was not enough to save the classical doctrine either. Although it was taken up by Victorian moralists (he quotes Mrs. Marcet) to show trade unions and working-class leaders "the untutored folly of their methods," it eventually backfired when, under the influence of marginalist thinking, it was shown that the wage "fund" was in fact a "flow." It is at this stage also, according to Dobb sometime in the late nineteenth century, that it was realized that advancing wages lead to lower birthrates. This boosts the standing of trade unions and underpins the "high wage economy" arguments.

Dobb sees the marginalist revolution (at least in its sophisticated Marshallian variant) as an advancement over the wage fund arguments, not because it was radically different in kind (he follows Cannan in classifying them both as "supply and demand theories"), but because it was less *deterministic* in its conclusions. This is an interesting and important point as we look forward to the *General Theory*, where one might say Keynes tried to make the same point. But of course Keynes thought he could make the labor market determinate in terms of employment by the consideration of aggregate demand. Thus, quoting Marshall against Clark's crude marginal productivity ethics, Dobb comments "those who were wiser and understood the situation more clearly realized that the new doctrine did not constitute a complete theory of wages" (p. 83).[17] The complete theory, of course, turns out to be a marginalist supply and demand schedule, handled with all the qualifications and reservations Marshall would have added. A long quotation strung together from his discussion is appropriate to convey the accepted version of supply and demand for labor in Cambridge in 1928:

The supply of labour can be used in several different senses. It may be applied to the *number of workers* seeking wage-employment. It may include the *number of hours* which each worker is willing to work . . . It may be further stretched to include the *intensity of work* that is done each hour . . . or even to include the *quality* of work done, depending on the intelligent skill with which it is applied. All of these things are likely to bear some kind of relation to the price of labour . . .

Changes in the wage level will probably react on the quality of the labour supply; and the possibility of this reaction will have to be taken into account as a modifying factor in the theory. But more important than this will probably be the reaction of the wage level on the intensity of work, because earnings provide both an inducement and the physical sustenance to increased energy.

Different amounts of labor will require different prices per unit to call them forth. This will constitute the "supply price" (or "cost price") of different quantities of working energy, and will depend on the physical and psychological resistances which limit an extension of the labor supply.

With regard to the connection between the level of wages and the total population we cannot be more than very uncertain . . . With regard to the supply of labour in other senses, however – the intensity of work, the willingness to work longer hours, the proportion of the population that offers itself for wage-employment – one probably can postulate some connection; and to this extent it will be possible to represent the supply prices of different quantities of labor as a "supply curve," on the assumption of a given aggregate population and a given quality of labour.

The wage level is then seen to be dependent on two variable quantities – the amount of capital advanced to hire labor (or the "Wages Fund") and the supply of labour forthcoming. The former at any one time will depend on the past accumulations of capital, but modified in the course of time by the investor's willingness to add to existing capital by new investments, or on the other hand, by his unwillingness to leave existing accumulations of capital intact ["waiting"] . . .

It will, therefore, be possible to conceive of a "demand curve" for labor as well as a "supply curve," although the shape of this demand curve will differ according to the period of time that one has in mind. Putting the two curves together, we can then have the accompanying picture, with the point of intersection of the two curves as the equilibrium-point where the level of wage will tend to settle down.

(Dobb, 1928, pp. 87–90, emphasis in original)

Already it should be clear that, at least on Dobb's interpretation, the Cambridge tradition of labor market analysis to which Keynes reacted in the twenties and thirties, while clearly a supply and demand theory, was a rather sophisticated one. Following Marshall it made allowances for much institutional detail and was cast in a less rigid fashion than is common even today, wages often exhibiting a degree of indeterminacy. In Dobb's analysis indeterminacy constituted the justification for devoting the second half of his book almost entirely to bargaining and unions. In terms of our introductory discussion of the points made by Keynes in his objections to the "Postulates of the Classical Economics," Dobbs's discussion is most similar to aspects that Keynes classified there as "not theoretically fundamental"[18] – those which bear on the accurate depiction of labor behavior by the labor supply curve. Also, as an aside, it is clear that the version presented by Dobb shows full cognizance of the issues of incentive and monitoring of labor that are the hallmarks of the microeconomics of the New Keynesian economics. Yet it is worth noting that he has next to nothing to say about the issue of "unemployment." As we will see in Chapter 7 on Keynes's own writings, it was this strand of Marshallianism that Keynes internalized, worked within and later exploded. First, we need to continue with the other important Marshallian, A. C. Pigou.

IV. Pigou: Mechanical Marshallianism

But there is another avenue out of Marshall that Keynes implicitly identified when, in the preface to the Handbook series, he identified the founding fathers as "Dr. Marshall and Professor Pigou." It is to this strand of thought, a somewhat more precise and technical Marshallianism we shall see, that we turn to for the explicit reaction of Cambridge economics to the concerns of the Late Victorian social reformers about unemployment.

Marshall himself, as we have seen, actually dealt very little with the problem. Instead, the prime response from Cambridge to the growing popular literature in the early part of the century is by Marshall's chosen successor to the chair at Cambridge and later Keynes's straw (classical) man in the *General Theory*, A. C. Pigou. In 1913 Pigou's *Unemployment* was published in the "Home University Library of Modern Knowledge." Its expressed goal was to encapsulate the latest thinking of the Marshallian neoclassical school as updated in Pigou's own treatise *Wealth and Welfare* (1912), where, according to Pigou and in keeping with Marshall's suggestion that the Organon be the guide to "Truth," "the special problem of unemployment is treated as a subordinate part of a larger and more general problem (Pigou, 1913, p. 253)." So framed it was natural that the question devolved into one of market clearing equilibrium. Following the long-run prejudices of his mentor Marshall, Pigou tellingly introduces his theory as "Unemployment in the Stationary State" (Pigou, 1913, Chapter 5). An extensive quote reveals the core of the approach:

Though, as just stated, the preceding chapter [devoted to criticizing "popular explanations"] has realized no positive results, it has revealed a *method*. For it has made plain the theoretical possibility that wage-rates at any moment and in every part of the industrial field can be so adjusted to the demand for labour of various grades that *no unemployment whatever can exist*. In other words, it has shown that unemployment is *wholly* caused by maladjustment between wage-rates and demand. The road which our investigation must follow is thus indicated. It must assume the form of an inquiry into the influences by which various kinds of maladjustment may be and are brought about.

(Pigou, 1913, p. 51)

Setting a standard that is very similar to the modern labor economics of rigid wages that is once again popular in economic theory, Pigou's investigation led into the imperfections of the labor market that marked it off from the textbook model. These "frictions" from which unemployment would arise even in the fictional stationary state ranged from unions and the inability due to custom to grade each laborer's reward according to his individual productivity to minimum wage laws. Outside of the stationary state, dynamic conditions meant that unemployment was the result of the general phenomenon that wage rates are never "perfectly plastic" (Pigou, 1913, p. 76). Thus Pigou recognized that the change in demand for labour over the trade cycle was an independent cause of unemployment. Yet even here the root cause was the inability of wage rates to adjust. "We are then entitled to the general conclusion that unemployment is likely to be greater, the more rigidly wage-rates are maintained in the face of variations in the demand for labour."[19] Finally, "the mobility of labour" (Chapter 10) completes Pigou's catalogue of the causes of unemployment. It is at this point that Pigou's major policy recommendations are directed and his argument is almost identical to Beveridge's then popular proposals for the Labour Exchanges to increase the efficiency of the market to match employers with employees.

It should be said that reading Pigou's tract of 1913 is a useful antidote to the simplistic view of him and pre-Keynesian economists that has been standard in profession ever since Keynes singled "the Professor" out for crucifixion in his appendix to Chapter 19 of the *General Theory*. In fact, the text offers support for the contention that Keynes's *General Theory*, though constituting a crucial turning point in unemployment theory, is squarely within the Cambridge tradition of his day. First, as Richard Kahn (1976, p. 19) remarked, it is surprising to see Pigou devoting his treatise at the very start to the issue of "involuntary unemployment," a distinction usually presumed to have begun with Keynes.[20] Moreover, it is clear that Pigou had some sort of inkling of the issue of demand-deficient unemployment,[21] if not a coherent theory of it. Besides his remarks on the trade cycle, this is evident in his policy prescription. In addition to the endorsement of Beveridge's labor exchanges, he gives a partial nod to the notion of government counter-cyclical spending policy:

> . . . public authorities are in a position somewhat to lessen the fluctuations that occur in the demand for labour, and hence to diminish unemployment, both by fitting that part of their own demand for goods and services, which is necessarily occasional, into the interstices of the general demand, and also by avoiding unnecessary ups and downs in that part of their demand which is, or can be made, continuous. These practices constitute remedies for unemployment in all circumstances.
>
> (Pigou, 1913, p. 247)

Yet, though Pigou in some respects presents a fairly sophisticated analysis of unemployment, it is clear that his theoretical outlook confines the issue to the operation of the labor market and in particular to the lack of "plasticity" of wages in fthe face of changes in demand. In some ways this is even more evident in his later *Theory of Unemployment* (1933), which so irked Keynes that he felt compelled to devote a whole appendix to its excoriation in the *General Theory*. In fact, a comparison of the two books is rather startling in that the earlier of Pigou's books appears more sophisticated and alive to the issues than the later one. Although written during the depth of the slump, the later book expresses an almost sclerotic retreat into labor-market metaphysics. But since it was written exclusively for a professional audience,[22] as compared to the popular audience for the first book on unemployment, its theoretical underpinning is more transparent. As argued above this is to accord all unemployment to some form of labor market disequilibrium, typically associated with rigid wages. In 1933, Pigou again timidly endorses the temporary injection of public spending in the slump, but makes clear that "wage-policy" is the ultimate "cause" of unemployment. First it is argued that any chronic insufficiency of demand cannot occur:

> . . . the state of demand for labour, as distinguished from changes in that state, is irrelevant to unemployment, because wage-rates adjust themselves in such a manner that different states of demand, when once established, tend to be associated with similar average rates of unemployment.
>
> (Pigou, 1933, p. 252)

And thus, by construction such unemployment as does occur is due to "frictions":

> There will always be at work a strong tendency for wage-rates to be so related to demand that everybody is employed. Hence, in stable conditions every one will actually be employed. The implication is that such unemployment as exists at any time is due wholly to the fact that changes in demand conditions are continually taking place and that frictional resistances prevent the appropriate wage adjustments from being made instantaneously.
>
> (Pigou, 1933, p. 252)

One wonders what Marshall (and Dobb) would have made of this? Lost is all sense of Marshall's complexity and his insight into the role of social institutions and human nature. Also absent is the Marshallian emphasis on Smithian realism in the sense of touching base with real (or even imagined) social facts now and then. It is no surprise that Keynes found this theory so repellent and fascinating at the same time. Remarking to D. H. Robertson:

> Have you read the Prof's book carefully: I find it most disturbing. For if I haven't completely misunderstood, it's simply nonsense from beginning to end . . . For heaven's sake have a good look at the work and tell me if the gist of this is right. Or am *I* talking nonsense? A. C. P. produces as great a sense of Bedlam in my mind as Hayek does. Are the undergraduates to be expected to take it seriously? What a subject!
>
> (CW 12, pp. 310–13)

Thus we have before us the explicit textual treatments of labor markets and unemployment by Cambridge economists other than Keynes, before the *General Theory*. It must be said that it is a mixed bag. Marshall and Dobb emphasized the non-deterministic influence of social institutions at work in labor markets. As a result they were able to account for much of the actual institutional detail of wage practices. The issues raised by modern efficiency wage theories and insider outsider models would have been no surprise to them. They also saw a role for Unions and expressed to a greater or lesser extent favor toward the "social" goal of a "high wage economy," as both practical and desirable. This issue clearly sets them (particularly Dobb) off from the more mechanistic Pigovian analysis. For though Pigou might find the idea of raising wages desirable, his analysis could only see this as leading to unemployment and loss of output.

Interestingly, the modern incorporation of bits of labor market reality into an even more technically oriented discussion by the New Keynesian Economics seems to take Marshall's and Dobb's insights, which they did not themselves see as explanations of unemployment, and make them the explanation of what Pigou would call "lack of plasticity" in the labor market. Perhaps the crucial difference is expressed in Marshall's famous dictum, "natura non facit saltum." He saw the effects of steady employment and higher incomes as effecting a slow evolutionary change on society. It would change over time – he thought – naturally, as society progressed. Dobb (1938, pp. 56–8) in his later editions also endorsed this evolutionary argument, but saw the need for state intervention to secure the needed reforms since, for him, the short-term interest of employers were not clearly coincident with the social effects of higher wages and stable employment. Yet New Keynesian Economics professes to be a short run equilibrium account of involuntary unemployment. In this sense they follow Pigou. Our task now is to look at some of Keynes's own thoughts on labor markets and unemployment, and to trace their evolution up to the *General Theory*. It will be our contention that he was always much closer to Marshall (and Dobb) than to Pigou.

7
Keynes and the Labor Market

I. Keynes as a Marshallian

Given that Keynes was one of those "orthodox members of the Cambridge School" to which he referred in his introduction to the Handbook series, it should come as no surprise that he held views on labor markets and unemployment during his career that reflect the Marshallian tradition laid out above. Keynes's lecture notes prior to World War I, we will see, make it clear that early on he indeed did hold what is best described as a sophisticated and realistic Marshallian view on value and distribution theory. But Keynes's attitude toward the orthodox treatment of unemployment changed significantly as the twenties progressed. It will be our task here to show that Keynes's pre-*General Theory* writings provide evidence that the types of explanations of involuntary unemployment now being proffered as New Keynesian economics would not have been novel to Keynes even before World War I, much less in the thirties. Moreover, his departure from the traditional view of the labor market as self-adjusting in some sense begins in the twenties. Further it will be argued that, though of interest in themselves, these departures remained no more than elaborate qualifications of the classical theory he would eventually reject in the *General Theory*. Thus the source for his own departure from classicism must be sought elsewhere.

To place Keynes within the Marshallian tradition at Cambridge is to recognize both Marshall's enormous but sometimes invisible influence on his pupils and to highlight Keynes's peculiar gifts. It would appear that the characteristics that would mark his career in general, a continuing interest in current social issues, a distaste for 'pure theory,' as such, and a strong attraction to controversy and political involvement, showed very early in Keynes's career as an economist. To substantiate this point we have much evidence. Indirectly, the recent work on Keynes's philosophical apprenticeship with G. E. Moore and his professional work in the philosophy of probability (see O'Donnell, 1989; Davis, 1994) make it clear that he always conceived of his role as that of a moral scientist in the mold of Smith, Sidgwick and Marshall himself. By this is meant to imply his interest in developing habits of thought that would provide practical guides to clear thinking and action about social problems. Thus his *Treatise on Probability* can be read as an attempt at formulating a justification for pursuing the Moorean "good" in the context of human affairs where the outcomes of conduct could not be rigidly specified. This, of course, required a theory that was attuned to particular situations, not a mechanical apparatus. "The object of our analysis is, not to provide a machine, or a method of blind manipulation, which will furnish an infallible answer, but to provide ourselves with an organized and orderly method of thinking out particular problems . . . " (*GT*, p. 297).

In addition, it is evident that Keynes chose topics that were matters of current social import and controversy. At the turn of the century Indian currency reform was one such topic. Later the problems associated with war finance and the restoration of monetary relations between the trading partners of the western world were the dominant economic topics of the day. Of course this is also obviously the case with employment theory as we pass into the twenties and thirties. Keynes's attempts at influencing policy and engaging in sharp polemical controversy are also well-documented aspects of his make up. And as a comparison with the retiring Pigou, as mentioned above, this marks him out from most of his Cambridge contemporaries whose public personas tended toward the Marshallian model.

Yet for all of this Keynes was brought up on Marshall and forever retained traces of the master's influence. These influences included the ever-present attempt to blend historical and institutional analysis with the bare bones of the analytical machine, and a dislike for the purely mechanical aspects of theoretical work.[1] It is perhaps fair to say that besides his taste for controversy (or perhaps due to it), his main difference from Marshall was a more constant attention to, and a more daring theoretical use of, *current* social facts. Keynes exhibited a lifelong interest in the gathering and utilization of economic data. As for examples are his participation in the creation of The Cambridge Economics Research Service and later the Department of Applied Economics at Cambridge and his work on index numbers (see Stone, 1978). Yet as Marshall also displayed a deep interest in the social relevance of his economics, one must be careful in differentiating Keynes and Marshall on this head. Interestingly, we have evidence that this difference with regard to bending both his theory and interests to ever-changing current conditions is what Keynes saw as setting himself off from Marshall; and, what Marshall very early saw as Keynes's major trait as an economist.

In Keynes's memorial biography of Marshall (*CW* 10) he laments the fact that peculiarities of Marshall's personal habits and career led him away from completing the projects he laid out for his life work in his early years. In particular, he notes how Marshall was distracted from producing the further planned volume of the *Principles* which was originally to have included treatments on money and realistic problems of industrial organization, trade and business cycles (see Whitaker, 1990), and that he delayed the eventual monograph treatments of these topics until his grasp of the facts was seriously out of date. He ascribes this to a combination of Marshall's overweening caution in publication and his timidity with regard to criticism. The first trait led him to great lengths to ensure that his historical and institutional analysis was "complete" enough to withstand scrutiny. The second led him into the endless revisions and alterations of the already published volume of the *Principles*. Keynes's biography brilliantly shows forth both the strengths and weaknesses, the good and the bad of Marshall's work and method, and in the process highlights Keynes's different approach to doing economics.

It is for our purposes useful to recall the weakness Keynes saw in Marshall for the contrast it provides with his own work. A series of quotations strung together from Keynes's essay on Marshall (*CW* 10) conveys the main points:

> Marshall, as already pointed out above, arrived very early at the point of view that the bare bones of economic theory are not worth much in themselves and do not carry one far in the direction of useful, practical conclusions. The whole point lies in applying them to the interpretation of current economic life. This requires a profound knowledge of the actual facts of industry and trade. But these, and the relation of individual men to them, are constantly and rapidly changing.
>
> (p. 196)

> In publishing his intellectual exercises without facing the grind of discovering their point of contact with the real world he would be following and giving bad example. On the other hand, the relevant facts were extremely hard to come by – much harder than now. The progress of events in the 'seventies and 'eighties, particularly in America, was extraordinarily rapid, and organized sources of information, of which there are now so many, scarcely existed.
>
> (p. 197)

> [Besides his bad health], he was too meticulous in his search for accuracy, and also for conciseness of expression, to be a ready writer. He was particularly unready in the business of fitting pieces into a big whole and of continually rewriting them in the light of their reaction on and from the other pieces.
>
> (p. 197)

> Given his views as to the impossibility of any sort of finality in economics and as to the rapidity with which events change, given the limitations of his own literary aptitudes and of his leisure for book-making, was it not a fatal decision to abandon his first intention of separate independent monographs in favour of a great treatise? I think that it was . . .
>
> (pp. 197–8)

Economists must leave to Adam Smith alone the glory of the quarto, must pluck the day, fling pamphlets into the wind, write always *sub specie temporis*, and achieve immortality by accident, if at all.

(p. 199)

Moreover, did not Marshall, by keeping his wisdom at home until he could produce it fully clothed, mistake, perhaps, the true nature of his own special gift? . . . The building of his engine was the essential achievement of Marshall's peculiar genius. Yet he hankered greatly after the "concrete truth" which he had disclaimed and for the discovery of which he not specially qualified.

(p. 199)

Economics all over the world might have progressed much faster, and Marshall's authority and influence would have been far greater, if his temperament had been a little different.

(p. 199)

Thus, we may say that Keynes disputed the means by which Marshall achieved his ideal goal of a logical and realistic economics, but not the goal itself. His own method, and in opposition to Marshall's meticulousness with the facts, was to take the salient features of reality that struck his intuition as relevant and important and to weave the theory around these, with the eventual goal of ordering reality and identifying causes. It is well described in an early philosophical paper in which he compares the work of the scientist with that of the artist:

He is presented with a mass of facts, possessing similarities and differences, arranged in no kind of scheme or order. His first need is to perceive very clearly the precise nature of the different details. After concerning himself with this precise and alternative perception, he holds the details clearly before his mind and it will probably be necessary that he should keep them more or less before his mind for a considerable time. Finally he will with a kind of sudden insight see through the obscurity of the argument or of the apparently unrelated data, and the details will quickly fall into a scheme or arrangement, between each part of which there is a real connection.[2]

Moreover, there is reason to believe that Marshall himself saw Keynes's penchant for realism as his major attraction in consideration of his future as an economist. In Keynes's papers exists a set of questions he wrote for Marshall in 1905. Copious remarks are scribbled over them by Marshall, mostly in an attempt to tone down Keynes's strong conclusions. One ends with the following, one must say in light of history, acutely drawn message from the master to the prospective follower:

This is an admirable paper. It is one of the most interesting I have ever seen. It still has traces of the tendency to talk of things in the real world as the may be in a conceivable world. Your propositions are often too unconditional: and if you were to apply them in practice, you would come to grief.

But you are working yourself to take account of realities; and comparatively seldom lash out into "the world behind the looking glass." I repeat what I said before, that I should immensely like to see you become a member of some economics staff, and especially of this. But I know the world is wide.[3]

To follow out this theme of Keynes as a "realistic" Marshallian (as opposed to the scholastic Marshallian Pigou, for example, was to become), and to see more deeply into the Cambridge setting of the development of Keynes's views on labor markets and unemployment, it is useful to divide his career into three phases. The first covers his period as a young don, from 1908, when he began lecturing in Cambridge until 1915 when he went into full-time war service with the Treasury. From this period we get a glimpse of Keynes as a Marshallian on labor markets. But, as we shall see, and the foregoing discussion makes clear, this is a view still evidently quite sophisticated in outlook by modern standards. Second, we look at his writings after the war and running up to 1930. During this period Keynes comes to doubt the efficacy, at least in times of rapid monetary upheaval as he was then witnessing, of the automatic adjustment mechanisms that lay behind the Marshallian analysis of the labor market. Third, of course, is Keynes of the *General Theory of Employment, Interest and Money*. But this will not be directly our concern here, and we have covered its essentials in Chapter 4. In the last section of this chapter, however, we will put forward various views of interpreting its break from the Marshallian positions on unemployment.

II. Keynes as a young don

Keynes's lecture notes from his early years at Cambridge survive among his papers and offer us a very interesting view of the state of Cambridge orthodoxy at that period. They also reveal Keynes to have been quite hardworking (with numerous courses and students) and lively as a lecturer (bringing both his wit and numerous current events and statistics into the argument). It is to his course of lectures on "Principles of Economics," starting in 1911, which we turn to for his then contemporary views on the labor market. Indicative of the state of the profession at that period, as discussed above, and perhaps of Keynes's then current preoccupations, unemployment is not treated anywhere in his lectures as a separate topic. Instead one must glean the source of unemployment from the discussion of the labor market. In keeping with the neoclassical emphasis of normal value and distribution theory this stands as a special case of the theory of long run value:

> As in the case of the theory of normal value, so also in the case of the theory of normal distribution, the more abstract method of treatment must

be mastered not because it describes the facts, but because it supplies an analysis and a classification by reference to which the meaning of the essential facts can be elucidated.[4]

Thus as he had previously done in the lectures in the case of the theory of normal values, Keynes treats the textbook view as merely a skeleton on which to elaborate analysis of the facts. In particular he proceeds by way of listing the conditions necessary for the textbook view to hold (essentially what we would recognize as the first order marginal conditions of a primitive general equilibrium system) and then the possible objections to these conditions met in the real world that might violate the textbook view. Quoting Taussig (1911), Keynes (*KCKP*, UA/6/9) lists the possible conditions required for the theory of normal distribution to hold, and the violation of which will offer clues to the differences between the normal theory and the actual case as follows:

(1) Accurate knowledge on the part of the entrepreneurs of what the marginal efficiency of each factor really is.
(2) Accurate knowledge on the part of each factor as to the employment in which its marginal efficiency is greatest.
(3) Freedom on the part of entrepreneurs and of the owners of the factors to adjust themselves rapidly to changing conditions.
(4) Free competition and complete absence of monopoly amongst the various owners of any factor – i.e. no combination amongst them for the purpose of bargaining with the owners of other factors.
(5) A tendency for the supply of each factor to rise and fall directly with its reward.
(6) A tendency for the demand for each factor to rise and fall inversely with its cost.

Among these Keynes considers the most important divergences between actual and normal distribution to be due to the first three conditions – what he calls "the element of ignorance and the difficulty of rapid adjustment to change." But the rise of unions and large-scale business enterprise calls for recognition of a (then) current tendency toward the fourth condition also being violated. As to the last, he claims there are important cases – "to the possibility of which we must always be alive – where demand and/or supply of a factor is insensitive with respect to changes in its reward." This last violation will come to play an increasing role in his view of labor markets well into the twenties.

Keynes then proceeds to a detailed discussion of particular conditions affecting the return to each individual factor. These end up falling into one or another of the general categories. In the case of wages he (*KCKP*, UA/6/9) follows Marshall and gives the "normal doctrine" as follows:

The net advantage obtained by the exercise of a given degree of efficiency tend to equality in different places and occupations: or more briefly, *efficiency earnings* tend to equality.

As of this period, Marshall's term "efficiency wages" was apparently quite orthodox, especially recalling that this was a lecture to an economics principles course. What was accepted as its meaning is indicated in Keynes's discussion, where he uses it to clarify the misleading use of "time wages" and "piece wages" in defining the equilibrium condition referred to above. In particular it was meant to provide a framework in which the divergences between wages in different firms in the same industry were to be accounted for by reference to the fact that geographical advantages (Keynes mentions "agricultural labor in the north and south" and "coal mines in different districts") and firm-specific capital advantages ("the case of mills with old fashioned machinery") altered labor's productivity. And in a passage that sounds very modern, but in fact is a reference to Marshall, Keynes points out that the efficiency wage doctrine has to be qualified by "the fact that low-waged labor is generally dear if working with expensive machinery." The meaning here is that the value of skilled work is jointly determined by the capital and the laborer's ability to use it.[5]

Thus it may be to the advantage of the employer to raise the time earnings of the more efficient workers more than in proportion to their efficiency.

As in the case of Dobb's book, this complex view of workplace realities allows the theory to accommodate the immense complexity of actual wage practices as attempts to capture the "efficiencies" of labor peculiar to individual firms. Thus, as Keynes's contrast (above) of efficiency wages with the simplistic cases of wages per hour ("time wages") and per unit of output (piece wages) implies, there may be many variations in wage practices in reality:

> In this case [of raising the time earnings of more efficient labor] efficiency partly consists of *speed*. Some elaborate combinations of price and piece rates sometimes in force (sometimes with the object of encouraging speed, sometimes with the object of discouraging it).

Continuing with the elaboration of the orthodox maxim, Keynes next proceeds to a discussion of the term "net advantages." Here, as he admits, he follows Marshall in following Smith. Thus he lists Marshall's accounting of Smith's factors that might provide offsetting advantages and disadvantages to different employments. But again it is Keynes's *qualifications* of the doctrine that are most interesting. Here he covers the ground of information and mobility in a manner that sounds very like modern search theory:

> The normal doctrine assumes mobility between places and between occupations of the same kind. It is obvious that this condition is only partially fulfilled. Principally dependent upon degree of knowledge. Influence of labor exchanges.

He then goes on to J. S. Mill's theme of non-competing groups, also elaborated on by Marshall and Dobb:

> But there is a somewhat different connection in which the question of mobility is important. How far do those who supply labour of specialized

kinds and of different grades or degrees of difficulty form distinct groups? How far is there mobility between different *groups* of labourers?

Again picking up on the basic premise of the modern efficiency wage theories and insider–outsider models, Keynes notes that the answer to this question is "of great importance to the doctrine of wages." If employees have the power to alter their wage without attracting competition, then the normal doctrine is inapplicable. And, bringing it down to social reality, Keynes notes that this theoretical question depends on the actual labor institutions for compact and bargaining:

> Will a change in the wage of one group relatively to the others cause a movement of labourers into or out of it? Upon the answer to this question largely depends the answer to the other question how far one group of labourers may by compact bargaining prey upon the rest of the community and how far the rest of the community can prey upon a particular group of labourers.

His example, a prescient one concerning developments to come in the twenties, is of the "coal miners." It is also worth noting that at this stage and perhaps later Keynes's attitude toward unions displays a distinctly Marshallian ambivalence.[6] He notes, with Marshall, that the implicit combination of capital in large-scale enterprise puts the individual laborer at a large bargaining disadvantage so that "Trade unions are necessary in order to counteract in some degree the initial inferiority of the labourer (*KCKP*, UA/6/9)." Yet he often depicts the victories of unions as "preying" upon the rest of the community and inimical to the maximum national dividend. Later in the twenties, as we shall see, this attitude would be tilted against the unions by political events and his changing approach to the theory of normal distribution.

To conclude with these earliest views, however, it is sufficient to place Keynes within the Marshallian tradition by noting that he ends his view of mobility and its effect upon the equalization of net advantages between employments by noting the influence of heredity and parenting. Since the training and education of children so influence eventual labor supply opportunities, there may be long-term hindrances to mobility that hold up net advantages being equalized. Nevertheless, as of 1914, Keynes considered this only a friction in the efficient operation of labor markets. "Although the original action of the parents counts for much, it is *not* final in its effects."

Thus, in summary, by 1914 Keynes had in hand a very sophisticated Marshallian view of labor markets that recognized the serious complications in the application of the doctrine of normal distribution. Notions very much like the current theories of firm-specific human capital, information deficiencies and search behavior, efficiency wages, and insider–outsider effects were well within his theoretical universe. Yet as the following summation from his lecture makes clear, *these complications were not concerned directly with the notion of unemployment.* That was an issue of the future in 1914:

> We have, therefore, a series of groups of labourers supplying different kinds of services, efficiency earnings in each group tending to equality and partial mobility between these groups. The wage of any group will depend partly upon the supply (adjusted for efficiency earnings) of their labour in relation to the demand, and partly upon their bargaining power.
>
> In these conditions of normal distribution we have the wage so fixed as to employ all, the wages of each being equal to the marginal net product of the last. Actually this state of affairs will be upset, partly by ignorance, partly by some degree of monopoly power on one side or another.
>
> (*KCKP*, UA/6/9)

III. Keynes in the twenties: An emerging social theory of wages

With this background in a sophisticated and subtle Marshallianism, Keynes, fulfilling Marshall's prediction, went out into the wide world hoping to solve current social issues with the aid of Marshall's clear thinking method. Yet as noted, unemployment was not an issue that immediately drew his attention. His first economic works, summarized in *Indian Currency and Finance*, had little to say about unemployment. It was not until after his war experience and the disastrous aftermath, which so repelled him, had enlarged his worldview with a baptism by fire in social and political realities, that Keynes begins to write of the role and behavior of "the labouring classes." In our view this is no coincidence. For the same Victorian vision of society which he saw as destroyed by the war and as responsible for the many social evils that would follow in its wake was the background to the Marshallianism he had earlier internalized.[7]

The argument to be made here is that Keynes's break with traditional views on labor markets, an integral part of his "long struggle of escape from habitual modes of thought and expression," begins in the twenties. Moreover, this struggle involved a move away from the individualist analysis implicit in Marshall's supply and demand framework, but one that maintained the distinctive Marshallian method of integrating positive and normative analysis with reference to current social reality. The result is a "social" analysis of labor markets as a setting for a struggle over distributive shares, increasingly carried out in political terms. The "social justice" argument he uses, and the explicitly social setting, thus marks it off from the current preoccupations of the New Keynesians in that the latter explicitly are attempts to ground labor market behavior in an individualist, labor market analysis. Finally, although this vision underpins his move toward the

General Theory, it is still not the central metaphysical basis of his later discussion of involuntary unemployment. It may, however, provide hints about the useful macro-foundations of labor markets.

Antecedents, and perhaps the whole underlying social vision, to what became a growing preoccupation with the plight of labor show up as early as his *The Economic Consequences of the Peace* (*CW 2*, pp. 1–16). In its general overview of the pivotal historical epoch in which the western nations then found themselves – between the extraordinary growth and stability from 1870, which the war had brought to an end in 1914, and an uncertain, but definitely changed, future – Keynes saw foreboding glimpses of conflict. Much of this he ascribed to the breakdown of the delicate conventions and psychology of the pre-war era. Among these was the implicit acceptance of a large "*inequality* of the distribution of wealth which made possible those vast accumulations of fixed wealth and of capital improvements which distinguished that age from all others" (p. 11):

> . . . this remarkable system depended for its growth on a double bluff or deception. On the one hand the labouring classes accepted from ignorance or powerlessness, or were compelled, persuaded, or cajoled by custom, convention, authority, and the well-established order of society into accepting, a situation in which they could call their own very little of the cake that they and nature and the capitalist classes were co-operating to produce. And on the other hand the capitalist classes were allowed to call the best part of the cake theirs and were theoretically free to consume it, on the tacit underlying condition that they consumed very little of it in practice.
>
> (*CW 2*, 11–12)

Yet the war had disclosed the instability of this bluff and it could no longer be relied upon to give order and continuity to distribution in a manner consistent with the population's notion of justice. "The war has disclosed the possibility of consumption to all and the vanity of abstinence to many. Thus the bluff is discovered; the labouring classes may be no longer willing to forgo so largely, and the capitalist classes, no longer confident of the future, may seek to enjoy more fully their liberties of consumption so long as they last, and thus precipitate the hour of their confiscation" (*CW 2*, p. 13).

This view of the conflict that would rock a society in transition, free of one set of conventions of distribution but not yet in possession of a replacement, was to be forcefully borne out by the dislocations and crises that swept over the British economy for the rest of Keynes's life. At each stage Keynes's commentary, policy advice and analysis reveal his concern with distributive *justice* as a major element in his outlook. But, ever the Marshallian, this was not just a utopian commentary from an ideal ethical standpoint, but an observation of society that became an integral part of his analysis.[8]

Analytically this concern coalesced in the twenties around an argument that, however orthodox economic theory suggested labor markets *should* behave, in fact postwar conditions meant they no longer *could* adjust to wide swings in monetary values (as for instance in the case of the return to gold). Thus throughout the twenties one could say that Keynes, though still basically orthodox in theoretical outlook, was a solid "rigid wage" man as are so many "Keynesians" today. In his case the analysis was framed in terms of a cost-price argument in which swings in the price level called for rapid changes in costs that fell heavily upon labor. The injustice deflationary price instability inflicted on the laboring classes was that it resulted in intensified unemployment. But this positive analysis of deflation was due to the conflict between the sense of fairness of the working class, no longer content to be sacrificed to rentier interests in a historic pre-war exchange rate, and the politicians' and economists' belief that nominal values would automatically self-adjust. Thus the *Tract on Monetary Reform* attacked the assumptions built in to the quantity theory concerning the speed, painlessness and neutrality of the necessary nominal price movements. This, of course, is the context for Keynes's famous quip about death in the long run.

As the twenties wore on and the crises continued, Keynes's views crystallized on unemployment as the major social ill. A common theme in his writings in this period is what he saw as the responsibility for this of stupid and slavish devotion to worn out principles. *Essays in Persuasion*, "the croakings of a Cassandra who could never influence events in time," is a catalogue of accusations of such stupidity by leaders in the twenties. Of particular interest is the line of argument Keynes pursues in his polemic *The Ecomomic Consequences of Mr. Churchill*. Leaving aside the monetary details, Keynes's main claim against the return to gold at the pre-war parity of $4.86 per pound sterling concerned the implicit acceptance it represented of a "deliberate intensification of unemployment." (*CW* 9, p. 218) Here his strong doubts about the orthodox self-adjusting school are clearly in evidence concerning the labor market.

He divides the economy into two sectors. The "external" trading sector would bear the immediate brunt of the new exchange rate on its output and prices. Yet its costs, principally wage costs, would remain tied to the condition of the "sheltered" industries which had no direct connection to foreign competition. The ensuing dislocation concerned the need for the external sector's wages to fall in line with external prices while the prices of laborer's wage goods were fixed in the internal market. To Keynes there was only one possible outcome, unemployment and industrial strife until the "fundamental adjustments" assumed by orthodox theory were forced to come about. Once again the issue concerns the struggle for relative shares that the lack of a social mechanism to change money wages necessitates:

The working classes cannot be expected to understand, better than Cabinet Ministers, what is happening. Those who are attacked first are faced with a depression of their standard of life, because the cost of living will not fall until all the others have been successfully attacked too; and, therefore, they are justified in defending themselves. Nor can the classes which are first subjected to a reduction of money wages be guaranteed that this will be compensated later by a corresponding fall in the cost of living, and will not accrue to the benefit of some other class. Therefore they are bound to resist so long as they can; and it must be war, until those who are economically weakest are beaten to the ground.

(*CW* 9, p. 211)

This is clearly a long way from the qualified acceptance of the normal theory of distribution in Keynes's early lectures. That it was the force of events coupled with a concern for social justice that led him to this position is also made clear in this essay. He mentions the colliers as above all the victims of this misguided policy and notes that if there was a free mobility of labor their sacrifice would not be so great:

If miners were free to transfer themselves to other industries, if a collier out of work or underpaid could offer himself as a baker, a bricklayer, or a railway porter at a lower wage than is now current in these industries, it would be another matter. But notoriously they are not so free. Like other victims of economic transition in past times, the miners are to be offered the choice between starvation and submission, the fruits of their submission to accrue to the benefit of other classes. But in view of the disappearance of an effective mobility of labour and of a competitive wage level between different industries, I am not sure that they are not worse placed in some ways than their grandfathers.

(*CW* 9, pp. 223)

Interestingly, he throws this situation into relief by examining its underlying ethical basis. Not only is it a fact to Keynes that the kind of "automatic" mobility that would ensure fundamental adjustments is gone, but "on grounds of social justice, no case can be made out for reducing the wage of miners (*CW* 9, p. 223)." They are the victims of an ideological struggle that is clouded by the faults of the underlying positive economic doctrine of *laissez-faire*:

The truth is that we stand mid-way between two theories of economic society. The one theory maintains that wages should be fixed by reference to what is "fair" and "reasonable" as between classes. The other theory – the theory of the economic Juggernaut – is that wages should be settled by economic pressure, otherwise called "hard facts," . . . The gold standard, with its dependence on pure chance, its faith in "automatic adjustments," and its general regardlessness of social detail, is an essential emblem and idol of those who sit in the top tier of the machine. I think that they are immensely rash in their regardlessness, in their vague optimism and comfortable belief that nothing really serious ever happens. Nine times out of ten, nothing really serious does happen – merely a little distress to individuals or to groups. But we run a risk of the tenth time (and are stupid into the bargain) if we continue to apply the principles of an Economics which was worked out on the hypotheses of *laissez-faire* and free competition to a society which is rapidly abandoning these hypotheses.

(*CW* 9, pp. 223–4)

Elaborating, for a different era, on Marshall's point that the labor market is much more of a social institution than an automatic mechanism for bringing supply into equality with demand, Keynes notes that "the problem of how to bring about this reduction is as much a political as an economic problem." He therefore proposes a political solution of a treaty agreement between business, labor and the government to effect a uniform reduction of money wages and prices consistent with the new exchange rate, coupled with a surcharge on rentier income, to equalize the burden across all classes. Although in one sense this is just another passing trick of Keynes's immense talent for instant policy proposals, it further illustrates the theme on which we want to end this section. That is that at least from the mid-twenties through to the *General Theory*, Keynes saw the fixing of money wages and their stability as crucial elements of an overall macroeconomic view, and one closely linked, as Chapter 19 of the *General Theory* attests, to price stability. We will touch on this aspect of the *General Theory* in our conclusion to this chapter, below. For now we will bring the argument up to 1936 by considering Keynes's writings on the labor market between 1925 and 1936. But it is already clear that Keynes of the-return-to-gold period was beginning to extricate himself from the traditional emphasis on labor market analysis and concentrate on an integrated view of money and interest as the causal links to employment.

One searches *The Economic Consequences of Mr. Churchill* and Keynes's other writings of the twenties in vain for any hint of an alternative macroeconomic theory. Yet he increasingly emphasizes a view of the efficacy of public works policies to combat unemployment and his attacks on the orthodox view grow ever more shrill. As a matter of characterization of his development one could say that Keynes was clearly shedding his old classical skin in this period, but that the pattern of his new skin was not yet in sight. In terms of labor market analysis this involved more confident uses of his social–political view of money wage setting. Appropriately this shows up most clearly in his political writings of the period, from which a few references indicate the general theme.

In "The End of Laissez-Faire" in 1926 (*CW* 9, p. 287) Keynes declares it is time to "clear the ground from the metaphysical or general principles upon which, from time to time, *laissez-faire* has been founded." There are no "natural" liberties, self-interest does not always lead to greater social interest, and groups of individuals are often superior in achieving social ends than individuals acting together. As an alternative state action should be directed to an agenda the aim of which is to create ways of doing well "those functions which fall outside the sphere of the individual . . . those decisions which are made by no one if the State does not make them" (*CW* 9, p. 291).

In "Am I a Liberal" in 1925 (*CW* 9, p. 305) we see this general position extended to a call for a New Liberalism which would seek a "transition from economic anarchy to a regime which deliberately aims at controlling and directing economic forces in the interest of social justice and social stability." Acceptance of this responsibility is a matter of the facts and of public opinion. "The Trade Unions are strong enough to interfere with the free play of the forces of supply and demand, and Public Opinion, albeit with a grumble and with more than a suspicion that the Trade Unions are growing dangerous, support the trade Unions in their main contention that Coal miners ought not to be the victims of cruel economic forces which *they* never set in motion." (p. 305)

Yet in "Liberalism and Labor" in 1926 (*CW* 9, p. 309) Keynes's early ambivalence against trade unions turns to antagonism. Trade unionists are "once the oppressed, now the tyrants, whose selfish and sectional pretensions need to be bravely opposed." Writing to a socialist author of this period, he is even more explicit: "My opinions on a good many matters are shifting, but I do not yet see clearly where I am being led to. But when it comes to politics I hate Trade Unions."[9] Thus it is not surprising that in "Liberalism and Industry" a proposal for state intervention in the setting of money wage bargains is offered for "the betterment of the economic welfare of the worker."

In 1930 Keynes finally brings forth his *Treatise on Money* after a ten-year gestation. As would be expected it bears at least some marks of the continual transition in his thought over the twenties. We will more completely cover the *Treatise on Money*'s contents in Chapters 10 and 12, where we consider Keynes as a theorist of speculation and of money. Here it is sufficient to note that although the *Treatise* did not contain an adequate treatment of changes in output, its analysis of price fluctuations does ascribe practical significance to the social and political setting for money wage bargaining. Thus "cost inflation" (Keynes, 1930, pp. 166–70) could occur under certain organizations of the wage system. And in a passage that presages the cost-price view of wages that emerges in the *General Theory*, Keynes notes:

> If there are strong social or political forces causing spontaneous changes in the money rates of efficiency wages, the control of the price level may pass beyond the power of the banking system
>
> (Keynes, 1930, p. 351)

This theoretical viewpoint informed Keynes's re-immersion in direct policy issues arising from the worsening slump in the early thirties, and particularly importantly as a member of the Macmillan Committee and the Economic Advisory Council in 1930–31. Peter Clarke (1988) has provided a splendid account of the high policy drama of this period and its intimate relation to Keynes's evolving theoretical views. On theory he wavered, back-tracked and revised as conditions required with a strong sense only of the need to do *something* expansionist, rather than nothing, remarking to Prime Minister Ramsey McDonald:

> When we come to questions of remedies for the local situation distinct from the international, the peculiarity of my position lies, perhaps, in the fact that I am in favor of practically all the remedies which have been suggested in any quarter. Some of them are better than others. But nearly all of them seem to me to lead in the right direction. The unforgivable attitude is, therefore, the negative one – the repelling of each of these remedies in turn.
>
> (*CW* 20, p. 375)

The central unifying theme of his polemics at this point was the need to provide increased aggregate demand (although he did not as yet use that term) through any channel possible. And thus in various places he abandoned old positions to propose protectionist measures, restrictions on overseas lending and reductions in bank rate. Yet he held throughout to the rejection of the usefulness of a "wage policy" of driving down money wages. Thus in the addendum to the Macmillan report, "Proposals Relating to Domestic Policy to Meet the Present Emergency," written by Keynes and signed by him and five other committee members, a purely monetary policy response was rejected in favor of this coupled with expansionist spending.

Labor itself was resolved of responsibility for the slump and then-high real wages in another addendum written under Keynes's influence, "A Reduction of Wages and Salaries." This last also included Keynes's old idea of a National Treaty to equitably set money incomes in times of rapid monetary change. And in debate with Lionel Robbins and Hubert Henderson in the deliberations of the Economic Advisory Council his main opposition was to their practical and theoretical reliance on wage measures. It is in Keynes's personal memorandum circulated to this committee of economists (*CW* 13, p. 180, emphasis added) that we get a clear picture of his final break with the classical notion of the labor market:

> Real wages seem to me to come in as a by-product of the remedies which we adopt to restore equilibrium. They come in at the end of the argument rather than at the beginning. That is to say, we arrive finally at a consideration – as having an important bearing on our choice between the

different alternatives – as to how much each of the several expedients, both those which involve a reduction in money wages and those which do not, are calculated to reduce real wages. But the answer to this will not have much direct bearing on the question how much employment we can expect from each of the several expedients. *Employment is not a function of real wages in the sense that a given degree of employment requires a determinate level of real wages, irrespective of how the employment is brought about.*[10]

Our main conclusion from this evidence is a negative one. By 1930 at least, but actually growing out of a long gestation during the policy debates of the twenties, Keynes rejected the notion that orthodox labor market analysis, even the sophisticated variety that he himself had learned and taught at Cambridge, contained the key to understanding the swings in employment that beset Britain and the world during the Great Depression. He developed in the course of this rejection a loose "social" theory of *wages* in which bargaining over relative money claims by force, fraud, or possibly by compromise might be worked out. Yet this only replaced the distributional and price level arguments of Marshall's doctrine. By 1930, as seen above, he flatly rejected the causal influence of real wages on *employment*. Yet it would have to wait for the *General Theory* for an alternative analysis of employment, now integrated with his theory of interest and money.

IV. Conclusion: The labor market in the *General Theory* in historical context

Our negative conclusion from the evidence of pre-*General Theory* Cambridge labor market analysis is that its contents make it very doubtful that Keynes could have been attempting to found his self-described "theoretical revolution" on labor market arguments, like the New Keynesian economics. Moreover, Keynes's own writings show much evidence of a rejection of what for him would have been orthodox wage theory long before the *General Theory*. Thus arises the old bugaboo, the Talmudic touchstone of Keynes scholarship, that never-ending question all these past decades of macroeconomic debate: Exactly what did Keynes really mean by involuntary unemployment?

In one sense the answer to that is embodied in the rest of this book, in our analysis of the role of financial markets and money in determining aggregate demand. That is where the real action takes place in the *General Theory*. In another sense it is simply enough conveyed by saying that he meant aggregate-demand-constrained unemployment. But we would be amiss if we ended this part of our exploration of the historical sources of the *General Theory* without pausing briefly to note how the discussion of labor market theory and policy that does take place in the *General Theory* fits into the picture of Keynes's developing thought we have just painted.

First, we wish to link up with our earlier discussion, in Chapter 4, of Keynes's attack on the "classical postulates." We can now see that Keynes's particular disputes with the classical postulates of the labor market that we outlined in Chapter 4 were, for him, commonplace, judged by the history of his own writings before 1936. In them we can easily see the outlines of what we have called above his "social justice" view of the labor market. The two most important aspects pointing toward this are his denial that real wages are actually a central factor in determining the level of employment and his objections to the classical labor supply analysis – the second classical postulate.

That laborers cannot bargain over the real wage with any degree of precision when prices are changing unexpectedly and thus may in some circumstances be more interested in relative money wages was, of course, driven home to Keynes by the tumults of the twenties. So was his view that unemployment is not due to obstinacy on the part of labor, holding out for a higher wage. Thus Keynes's rejection of the second classical postulate, while more formally put, is a natural outgrowth of his interwar writings. His vigorous attacks on the idea that drastic deflationary monetary policy, like that enacted in 1925 by Churchill's Exchequer, would merely rescale all prices downward by "fundamental adjustments" is, as we have seen, only the most famous instance of this pattern in his thinking. Moreover, like in the case of the colliers in that episode, who he had correctly predicted would cling to a nominal wage in the face of pressure for reductions, it was clear to Keynes by 1930 at least, that a policy (or perhaps "hope" is a better term) of economy-wide wage reductions would never cure mass unemployment. Yes his opposition to such a policy was a matter of social justice, as he had stressed in arguing that the miners should not bear the brunt of such a failed monetary policy. But more generally, and more importantly, it gave rise to an analytical imperative[11] to recognize the difficulty of such adjustments in a more realistic theory of employment and unemployment. As the *General Theory* sought to demonstrate, this means that an alternative to the classical labor market explanation of unemployment is necessary. To reject wage policies, as Pigou did in the thirties for instance, when your basic theory of the labor market shows them to be the root of the problem is what Keynes was referring to in the preface to the *General Theory* when he spoke of the "practical influence of economic theory" as having been "destroyed" (*GT*, p. vi). This was the principal fault of the "classical" economics to Keynes.

An aside that seems important to note is that this last position, of the *theoretical* importance of Keynes's practical observation of wage adjustment practices, what he saw as their lack of relation to unemployment and the fact that it led him to look more generally at the theory of the economic system for an explanation of unemployment, is not as well recognized as it ought to be. For instance, it is now commonplace to demonstrate Keynes's "unfairness" or "rhetorical petulance" to classical economists, by documenting that most classical economists in England and America had themselves long since abandoned suggesting such a wage policy by 1936.[12] Yes this is obviously true, and is helpful in setting the record straight as to the policy context of the thirties. But his point was not that many economists were recommending wage cuts – many were not – but that those that were not should have fundamental reasons for doing so. The view that casts the history of policy pronouncements in the 1930s as a revelation, or as an indicator of importance for evaluating the progress that Keynes represented for the profession in 1936, requires a strong attachment to a "Keynesian" view of Keynes as the contributor of a novel "sticky wage" theory.

Also, and as he often claimed, Keynes was himself what he would later call a classical economist prior to working out the *General Theory*. We now have before us rather extensive evidence that Keynes also had a long history as a "classical" who rejected a wage policy for the slump. He had personally lived and felt the contradiction between a theory of unemployment that could only offer sticky wages as the cause of unemployment, and what he had increasingly come to see as the contradictory facts of the reality of unemployment. One could say that this contradiction was the most basic motivation for the *General Theory*.

This is so despite the fact, again as we have seen, that Keynes's labor market analysis always dissented from the strict mechanical Marshallianism of the type offered by some of Pigou's work.[13] From very early on, Keynes, following Marshall and in the tradition exemplified by Dobb, emphasized the difficulty of treating the labor market like a commodity market, and saw the outcomes of that market process, as far as wages went, as non-deterministic. (He did not, however, claim that this explained unemployment at any time). As a consequence of this tradition of treating the labor market as a complicated social institution rather than as an auction market, it was perhaps easier for Keynes to elaborate upon his "social justice" view of wages through the policy debates of the interwar years than it was for Pigou. But both of them, prior to the *General Theory*, had no successful alternative explanation for unemployment. Pigou could only fall back on a theoretical lack of wage "plasticity," whatever his changing policy views were. Keynes, in his attack on Churchill's monetary policy in 1925 could only offer vague hand waving about the lack of quickly occurring "fundamental adjustments," and seemed to believe that even without intervention such as he was proposing, that the unemployment of the twenties would correct itself in two years time. *A Treatise on Money* (Keynes 1930, *CW* 5 and 6) similarly failed to offer a convincing account of mass unemployment, as we will discuss in the coming chapters. In the *General Theory*, Keynes finally did offer such an alternative explanation, and it did not fundamentally depend, one way or the other, on the supposed "plasticity of the wages." This is the important point to remember about Keynes's contribution in those tumultuous years.

On a related interpretive point, this evidence convinces me of the opinion, previously put forward by various other writers, that Keynes unfortunately led his readers somewhat astray by opening his book with a discussion of the classical postulates of the labor market and, in particular, doing so in a way that depended upon the full explication his own alternative theoretical construct for a full resolution of his rejection of the classical argument. This resolution finally came, perhaps too late in a complex book for many readers, in Chapter 19 of the *General Theory*, where Keynes fulfills Chapter 2's promise to consider the effects, in his system, of "Changes in Money Wages." This writing strategy was no doubt a rhetorical ploy, designed to offer the classical case as much as he could allow it, while still ultimately showing it to be at fault in its argument for unemployment. Evidence of this degree of concession to the classical case can be seen from our previous development of his labor market work. For one, he chose a rather Pigovian line of expression for the classical postulates, making them much more deterministic and mechanical than in fact Marshall, Dobb or his own previous work would imply. His fixation on Pigou – ostensibly the author of the "classical postulates" – is perhaps understandable, given both Keynes's Cambridge insularity and the towering reputation of Pigou as a theorist. This is confirmed in Chapter 19's appendix by the choice of Pigou's *Theory of Unemployment* for special excoriation.

Also supporting our view of the rhetorical concession made by Keynes in his "classical postulates" strategy is the fact that he had earlier, as we have seen, come to reject *any* influence of real wages on employment. At that point, and influenced by Dobb's view of wages, he depicted them entirely as a residual byproduct of the other outcomes of the system, with no causal influence.[14] This earlier position is a much stronger rejection of classical reasoning than was finally presented in the *General Theory*. For instance, recall his 1931 pronouncement (*CW* 13, p. 180):

> Real wages seem to me to come in as a by-product of the remedies which we adopt to restore equilibrium . . . Employment is not a function of real wages in the sense that given degree of employment requires a determinate level of real wages, irrespective of how the employment is brought about.

Compare this to the following from Chapter 3 of the *General Theory* (*GT*, p. 30, emphasis added):

> The propensity to consume and the rate of new investment determine between them the volume of employment, and the volume of employment is *uniquely related* to a given level of real wages – not the other way around.

This change in emphasis, from a complete rejection of the real wage as anything other than a byproduct of equilibrium, to a situation where real wages are still a byproduct of the level of employment ("not the other way around"), but in which there is now a *unique* relationship between real wages and the level of employment, is due to the adoption of the classical postulates mode of expression. Further, of course, this unique relationship is driven by Keynes's stated adherence to short run diminishing returns as embodied in the first classical postulate, that wages equal the marginal product of labor, throughout the *General Theory* (*GT*, pp. 17–18).

Thus, by *General Theory* reasoning, employment increases were always to be correlated with a fall in real wages. But the resulting employment change is not caused by the wage change. It has been noted before that after the *General Theory* Keynes (1939) seemed reluctant to reject this reliance on the first postulate as well (Brothwell, 1997). But he did recognize that his expression of his argument would be made easier if there accumulated a preponderance of statistical studies, such as Dunlop (1939) and Tarshis (1939) had produced, which failed to find an inverse relationship between employment and real wages. Today, after decades of extensive empirical studies on labor markets, such evidence is best summarized as agnostic on this point (Knieser and Goldsmith, 1987). The sum of evidence suggests that there seems to be no firm relationship over the business cycle between unemployment and real wages. If Keynes had dispensed with Pigou's classical postulates, then an alternative labor market would presumably have become part of the *General Theory's* presentation, and then perhaps the whole confusing "classical postulates" debate could have been avoided.

But that is mostly a sideline to the main argument of both Keynes's book and our own. The main point about the labor market in the *General Theory* was there in plain print for anyone to see who cares to read through to Chapter 19's discussion of changes in money wages. That was that the policy of cutting wages to cure a depression is not only an ineffective route to full employment, but is actually one fraught with further peril. Again, in our historical view we can see this statement of policy as unsurprising. What is new and interesting in Chapter 19 is the now complex machinery of analysis used to present it. It was this engine of analysis, built up in the previous chapters, that finally links together the "general theory" and the "classical postulates" of Chapter 2. Analyzing what might happen if money wages did fall across the board constitutes a definitive comparison of Keynes's theory with the classical one. That Pigou's *Theory of Unemployment* was also slated in Chapter 19 as the representative of the classical view was additionally a link to Chapter 2. This was so both in the attribution to Pigou of the famous postulates, and also because of the fact that Pigou's "long run" standpoint in that book showed the *theoretical* futility of attacking involuntary unemployment from the standpoint of labor market analysis. This is explicit in Keynes's clear explanation of the choice of Pigou's book as a target:

> [Pigou's book] seems to me to get out of *the Classical Theory* all that can be got out of it; with the result that the book becomes a striking demonstration that this theory has *nothing to offer, when it is applied to*

the problem of what determines the volume of actual employment as a whole.

(GT, p. 260, emphasis added)

Finally, what was the alternative analysis of changes in money wages in Chapter 19? It has been analyzed in detail elsewhere (see Cottrell, 1994 for an excellent summary). The major point emphasized by Keynes was that a decline in money wages would not only be difficult and slow, for reasons he had been arguing for decades by this point. More importantly, the final effect would depend on how the wage cut altered the level of aggregate demand. Only if a money wage could be shown to somehow increase either consumption or investment demand could it be expected to increase output and employment (*GT*, p. 259). Accepting this as a theoretical possibility for the case of a wage policy, Keynes applies the Marshallian comparative static method for the rest of the chapter (*GT*, pp. 260–71) to investigate the conditions under which this might be true.

He first rejects any direct positive influence on consumption demand (the majority of consumers would be enduring a wage cut after all). This left the case for a successful wage policy dependent upon what he saw as unlikely scenarios of roundabout repercussions on the marginal efficiency of capital or the rate of interest. Significantly these repercussions all depended on a particularly favorable set of *expectations* being held by entrepreneurs regarding the wage cuts (even in the unlikely event that they could be enacted across the board). For this reason Keynes also advances the proposition,[15] so puzzling within a "sticky-wage" Keynesian view of the world, that it is actually *better* for the stability of the economic system that wages are somewhat sticky in terms of money, rather than fluidly adjusting with every change in the price level. This is because it may give some grounding to investment expectations of what future costs would be.

Having considered the possibilities and put his new model through its comparative static paces, so to speak, Keynes reaches the point we have referred to repeatedly in describing him as a Marshallian in method, of making a judicious choice about the relevant application of his model to the contemporary world. In this case his conclusion is that though theoretically possible, it would be dangerous in practice to expect wage cuts to increase employment – as of course he, among many economists, was arguing in the 1930s. Now, though, Keynes had a theoretical engine – a new Marshallian macroeconomic organon – by which to make the following practical judgment:

> There is therefore, no ground for the belief that a flexible wage policy is capable of maintaining a state of continuous full employment; – any more than for the belief that an open-market monetary policy is capable, unaided, of achieving this result. The economic system cannot be made self-adjusting along these lines.

(GT, p. 267)

Part II A Philosopher and a Speculator

> Another reason for directing attention to speculation is the question as to what place shall be given to the study of it in the theory of economics. Speculation has become an increasingly important factor in the economic world without receiving a corresponding place in economic science.
>
> H. C. Emery (1896)

> Speculation improved his economics and economics improved his speculation.
>
> N. Davenport, in R. Skidelsky (1992)

Part II A Nihilosopher and a
Speculator

8
Looking Backward from the *General Theory*: On the Historical Origins of Keynes's Financial Market Views

I. Introduction to Part II

This part of the book will attempt to set the context for Keynes's understanding of financial markets. The object is to identify the background and setting of what is distinctive about Keynes's views on financial markets in the *General Theory*. It will be assumed that the reader is familiar with the broad outlines of Keynes's basic theme, whereby investment drives output under the influence of financial market behavior.[1] Two specific issues that emerge from his treatment in the *General Theory* will be followed backward into the literature and history of Keynes's place and time. First, where did Keynes get his deep institutional understanding of asset market activity, of the purchase and sale of securities and financial instruments of all kinds? To the extent that this "insiders'" view of the financial markets permeates his "Liquidity Preference" analysis and his views on stock markets in the *General Theory*, this is a pertinent question. In this regard his views on *speculation* and its relationship to the motives of investors is the crucial theme. Second, from whence came Keynes's theoretical treatment of asset market activity presented in the *General Theory* – particularly, the most developed expression of it found in Chapter 17? In this regard we need to delve into the influences on his views of what constituted the subject of Chapter 17, "The Essential Properties of Interest and Money." I will, in a sense, hold out these aspects of the *General Theory* as the touchstone to which our retrospective excursions will be referred back. Again, the aim of this part of the book, however, is not to characterize the text of the *General Theory* but to shed new light on the larger historical context in which it was written. In the last part (Part III) of the book we will present an interpretation of the text of the *General Theory* (not suggested as *the interpretation*, and admittedly just one among a number that can reasonably be formulated) which will explicitly address the usefulness and novelty for interpretation of that work of the background developed here.

Section II of this chapter will highlight some theoretical and factual problems encountered by the Marshallian research program at the beginning of the twentieth century. This is an important preliminary to Chapter 9, where a more detailed and specific account of the monetary work of Marshall is offered, as well as an investigation of an important Victorian analysis of speculation that was to be influential on Keynes's financial views. Section III will show how Keynes's own immediate post-*General Theory* writing established the value for interpreting the *General Theory* of the themes treated in Chapters 9 and 10, in his insistence that it is the monetary side of the *General Theory* that was being most neglected by the book's first reviews. Chapter 10 will then trace the development of these same topics throughout Keynes's career as a monetary analyst up through the *General Theory*.

II. Two problems of later Marshallian economics: "The Representative Firm" and the joint-stock company

As we noted in our discussion of efficiency wage theory in Chapter 6, Marshall's *Principles of Economics* was fraught with tension between the dynamic economy it hoped to capture and the static framework by which it proposed to do so. Indeed, despite the tranquility that Marshall tried to present as the public face of economics, we saw that he was aware of the contradictions that arose between his Organon and the reality he sought to capture. Interestingly, a unified theme can be drawn between two such important difficulties in the Marshallian research program that implicitly point to the later monetary work of John Maynard Keynes. Both of these parallels to the wage question discussed earlier could likewise be interpreted as instances in which "facts" outran Marshall's theory.

The first issue is that which has in recent scholarship (Hart, 1991; Thomas, 1991) been given a formal name as Marshall's "reconciliation problem." This is a modern term to refer to Marshall's well-known early dissatisfaction with Cournot's treatment of increasing returns. Cournot (1838) held the view that if increasing returns for a firm were large and occurred over an extensive range of output compared to that of the industry, they would inevitably lead to monopolization of that industry by the largest firm. Marshall found Cournot's mathematics impeccable. He distrusted, though, their application to the firm-level British scene between 1870 and 1880, even as he believed strongly in the historical power of increasing returns to lower costs and increase standards of living. Thus he had to find a way to "reconcile" his observations of industrial structure with Cournot's analysis and show how increasing returns could be made compatible with competition. Moreover, lest we discount his earlier noted tendency to spend his vacations visiting factory sites as a Victorian eccentricity alone, this was one of those "facts" brought home to him by his travels.

This point, and what he arrived at as its solution in the *Principles*, is highlighted in an interesting letter Marshall wrote to A. W. Flux in 1898:

> My confidence in Cournot as an *economist* was shaken when I found that his mathematics *re* I. R. led inevitably to things which do not exist and have no near relation to reality. One of the chief purposes of my Wanderjahre among factories, etc., was to discover how Cournot's premises were wrong. The chief outcome of my work in this direction, which occupied me a good deal between 1870 and 1890, is in the 'Representative firm' theory . . . As well as the parts that directly relate to the supply price for I. R.
>
> (Pigou, 1925, p. 407)

This letter is cited by Neil Hart (2003, p. 165) in an interesting article where he argues that as far as theory of the interaction of firm and industry is concerned "Marshall was not a Marshallian." Hart explains that Marshall's first attempt at resolving the reconciliation problem was intended as an example of a biological, as opposed to a mechanical, analogy (". . . the young trees of the forest" and so on). It ran in terms that biologically limited any given firm's expansion by the natural life span of its founders. Since they inevitably did not live long enough to convert the advantages of increasing returns to the domination of a whole industry, Marshall surmised, younger firms could spring up to compete with them and utilize the advantages of increasing returns themselves. Thus the life cycle of firms ("trees") was more ephemeral than, and was superseded by, the life of the industry ("the forest"). No one firm could easily come to dominate.

This doctrine eventually set-off a controversy that was played out in the 1920s and 1930s, much of it on the pages of Keynes's *Economic Journal*. Although Clapham (1922) had early on questioned the explanatory power of this doctrine, more serious questioning seems to have begun with the penetrating analysis of Piero Sraffa (1926). Sraffa showed that the conditions under which variable returns are compatible with competition in the Marshallian framework were so restrictive as to be inapplicable to actual industry conditions. Once again we see that the authority of Pigou (1928) was exerted to sterilize Marshallian economics of any inherent contradiction by the construction of the equilibrium firm, a mechanical contrivance that propped up the logical structure but not the empirical relevance of the theory. This impasse led to the "Symposium on the Representative Firm" in the *Economic Journal* in 1930, at a time when the questioning of Marshall's *Principles of Economics* was becoming a central concern of Cambridge economics. Contributions were made by Gerald Shove (1930), Dennis Robertson (1930) and Sraffa (1930).

It is not the point to dwell on the details of the symposium; rather to highlight that it serves as a marker to the tenor of the times at Cambridge, just as Keynes was formulating the *General Theory*. Especially important is that each of these men was a close and respected associate of Keynes. The critique of Marshall's theory of the firm by young Turks like Sraffa and Joan Robinson (see Robinson 1933 for example), in addition to the almost simultaneous deconstruction of Keynes's *Treatise* by the overlapping Cambridge Circus (see Patinkin and Leith, 1978) was both fundamental and wide ranging. No wonder then that activity, like Keynes's later critique of "the classicals," was also so heavily resisted by more "orthodox" Marshallians like Shove, Robertson and Pigou. Perhaps Sraffa's reply to Robertson in the symposium best sums up the critical attitude then prevalent in Cambridge:

> I am trying to find what are the assumptions implicit in Marshall's theory; if Mr. Robertson regards them as extremely unreal, I sympathize with him. We seem to be agreed that the theory cannot be interpreted in a way which makes it logically self-consistent and, at the same time, reconciles it with the facts it sets out to explain. Mr. Robertson's remedy is to discard mathematics, and he suggests that my method is to discard the facts; perhaps I ought to have explained that, in the circumstances, I think it is Marshall's theory that should be discarded.
>
> (Sraffa, 1930b, p. 93)

This leads us to the second, and related, of the two problems mentioned above as then being encountered by Marshallian economics. Again it is one that the wise but wily Marshall, at least implicitly, faced in his own writings. Indeed, one might say that the logic of Sraffa's statement above had been known to Marshall as far back as 1907, at least by 1919, if we take "I think it is Marshall's theory that should be discarded," to mean abandoning sole reliance on the *Principles*.[2] Exact dating depends on when one judges Marshall to have begun on his fabled "second volume" of the *Principles*. This task, which eventually consumed his remaining writing life after 1890, when he was not revising the *Principles*, eventually evolved into the book *Industry and Trade*, published in 1919. One Marshall scholar (Whitaker, 2003, pp. 145–7) dates this to 1907 when the fifth edition of the *Principles* appeared with an interesting new preface that both relabeled the *Principles* as "Volume 1" of a projected two-volume work and described the contents of the *Principles* more modestly than formerly – as the "foundations" of the subject, necessarily to be followed up by a second volume devoted to dynamics, trusts and "recent changes in the character and functions of giant business and of combinations" (Marshall, 1961, p. 46). Based on a remarkable essay of Marshall from 1899 that we cover in this chapter, we would put his interest in the deficiencies of the *Principles* even further back. But precise dating is not important. More important for the theme developed here is taken from a phrase that Marshall introduced in the preface to the fifth edition of the *Principles*: "But *normal* action falls into the background, when

Trusts are striving for the mastery of a large market; when communities of interest are being made and unmade" (Marshall, 1961, p. 47, emphasis added).

We will show that the validity of the assumption adopted in the *Principles* that financial market values were governed by gravitation toward the long-run normal values of a "real" analysis, and that it was therefore acceptable as a *ceteris paribus* condition to assume that gravitation had occurred, was exactly what concerned the later Marshall. Moreover, what form financial market analysis would take once this point was admitted is one way to characterize Keynes' later monetary work.

First, however, we must complete our story of the crisis in later Marshallian economics. Why, as the economy matured, did the "Organon" alone no longer suffice as the sole tool of reasoning that would provide for "cool heads" to go out into the economy and "factually" analyze social problems, as Marshall had originally envisioned? The growing "fact" that had eaten away at the framework of the *Principles*, that years of rearguard action could no longer assimilate (see Whitaker, 2003, pp. 145–7), and which spawned the corrective changes of 1907 and the plan for a new volume, was the rise of the modern joint-stock company, or in more modern parlance the large public corporation. Since Marshall's representative firm depended on the biological analogy of the limited life span of the founders of private firms, without this argument for the reconciliation of "Cournot's problem" the rise to dominance in most industries of the infinitely lived corporation meant a vast reordering of economics as the *Principles* had depicted it.

Among the issues which had been put aside from consideration in the *Principles*, and which this "fact" called for facing head on were the following. The corporation in such conditions, because it would not die with its founders, might be able to fully exploit increasing returns and monopolize an industry. Moreover there was thus the greater incentive for the corporation and potential role for the state to "train" business expertise across generations, and so the supply of such expertise became critical to how well nations would prosper economically. Firms that could get as large as natural production returns allowed might now engage in a kind of strategic competition that was outside the "normal" operations of small-scale firms. Markets and institutions would arise to service the special financial needs of large business, such as the money and capital markets, the produce and stock exchanges and investment banks. Specialized information concerning the interests and operations of these institutions would earn valuable returns. This might also set up many dangers. At the industry level, would the potentially unlimited access to, as Marshall put it, "the money and credit market" allow corporations the means to profitably engage in socially destructive behaviors, limit competition and drive out smaller competitors with smaller financial resources, and form socially harmful "trusts"? In a similar vein,

What were the social welfare implications of the new and more effective tools of marketing and advertising that such large firms had called into existence? Post-Marshallian as these topics may appear, this list was constructed from those treated in Marshall's last constructive publication, *Industry and Trade* (1919).[3]

I also take these topics to be a large part of what later Marshallianism concerned itself with, when considered as a program of research. It would be difficult to precisely date the era of such interests in Cambridge economics, but it was certainly in full swing by the 1920s and 1930s, when Keynes was busy with his reformulation of Marshallian monetary economics and his construction of a short-period macroeconomics. There is ample evidence that many variants of "Marshallian" lines of investigation were included under this large tent. These would include for example Sraffa's (1926, 1930) foundational questioning of the framework of competition in the *Principles*. But it would also include Pigou's (1920) analysis of the incidence and social function of production externalities, as well as his more mechanical attempts to shore up the Marshallian depiction of the competitive firm (Pigou, 1927b) and of supply (Pigou, 1928). It is useful to recall in this context the large credit Joan Robinson gives to both Sraffa and Pigou as well as to Gerald Shove and Richard Kahn,[4] for influencing her thoughts in the influential *The Economics of Imperfect Competition* (1933).[5]

Thus, second, and closely related to the theoretical "static-dynamic" crisis of Marshallian economics noted above, was the factual crisis engendered by the *Principle's* inability to handle an increasingly undeniable feature of modern economies after 1890, the corporate form of organization and governance of business. The argument here is that none of these issues was lost on John Maynard Keynes.

But first we must stop to note that Marshall, though characteristically arguing for as much continuity as possible, himself seems to have noted the growing problems involved for his theory and have tried to address it. Moreover, when he did turn to this problem in writing, in *Industry and Trade* (1919),[6] he showed that these issues required even more attention to the evolutionary aspects of modern economic organization and less static analysis that had been suggested in the *Principles*. Furthermore, this is so despite what his more devout followers were led to in the creation of mechanical analogies like Pigou's "equilibrium firm," and also despite what some of his more severe critics like Sraffa may have thought about the unreality of Marshallianism.[7]

John Whitaker's (2003) excellent article "Marshall and the Joint Stock Company" is the single most compact analysis of this issue in the literature. (Readers interested in the details should consult it.) What we take from his discussion and the related article which follows it by Neil Hart (2003) is that the unstated premise of Marshall's last constructive book was that a "realistic" understanding of industry required something very different from just the largely a priori hypothetical deductions of the *Principles*. Instead, Marshall felt compelled to devote a third of his space (Book I) to a comparative historical account of how the industry of various nations had developed. In the process he proved that his motto from the preface, *"The many in the one, the one in the many"* (Marshall 1919, p. v., italics in original), was not just idle sloganeering. He meant to show that knowledge of cultural antecedents and the process of social evolution in the instances of the industrial development of England, Germany and America were both crucial to understanding their different economic structures and yet contained common messages. In fact, his comments from the first chapter of Book I on this viewpoint read like they could easily have been written by an American Institutionalist. For example:

> But the past lives on for ages after it has been lost from memory: and the most progressive peoples retain much of the substance of earlier habits of associated action in industry and in trade; even when the forms of those habits have been so changed under new conditions, that they are no longer represented by their old names.
>
> (Marshall 1919, p. 6)

This attitude bears fruit in *Industry and Trade*, where Marshall's encyclopedic knowledge of the details of particular industries is married to both his historical knowledge and his implicit search for theoretical structures with which to explain the form and social effect of increasing returns, large units in industry and worldwide trade. Thus he was implicitly showing the value for economic analysis of historical antecedents, of how technology had in the past interacted with social institutions. He also suggested that this reciprocal interaction was likely to evolve new economic problems even as it solved old ones. Whitaker (2003, p. 139) explains that this discussion implied even more than Marshall was willing to admit about the shortcoming of his *Principles*:

> The *Principles* clung to an increasingly implausible life-cycle theory of the representative firm because it played a crucial role in that work's focus on analyzing long-period equilibrium. *Industry and Trade*, displaying a more evolutionary methodology, found no need for it and tacitly abandoned it while maintaining a veneer of consistency.

This is the clue to how Marshall saw the pursuit of the questions noted above, and the way forward for a "realistic" Marshallian economics. In modern industry and trade, competition was a struggle between large firms and small, using and possibly advancing technological change, constantly altering in the process the very grounds upon which competition took place. Long-period equilibrium analysis was particularly unsuited to investigate such dynamic social change. Yet it could not be said that Marshall was willing to admit that these long-period positions might not eventually reassert themselves even on such an evolutionary process. Whitaker detects ambivalence on Marshall's part about what was left of the *Principles* after the admission of the prevalence and growing size of joint-stock companies. His link of this to the issue of long-period analysis is what we wish to stress:

> This [internal economies] opens a significant gap between the *Principles* and *Industry and Trade*, but a much larger one must now be noticed . . . The dominant method of the *Principles* is the analysis of long-period equilibrium situations, considered against a background hypothetically held constant by use of the *ceteris paribus* clause . . . *Industry and Trade* adopts, if quite implicitly, a quite different methodology, reflecting a more evolutionary mode of thought.
>
> (Whitaker, 2003, p. 150)

To put this problem in terms useful for interpreting Keynes's development toward the *General Theory* requires bringing this theme to bear on areas not treated in *Industry and Trade*, although feebly addressed in the last abortive Marshallian effort, *Money, Credit and Commerce* (1922). They are the supply and demand aspects of financial markets and the economic functions and influence of trading opportunities on organized exchanges for produce, credit and equities. As we will see in the next chapter there is more interest displayed in unpublished Marshalliana in this area than there is in *Industry and Trade*. Marshall's biographer Groenewegen gives a full account of the reasons for this. Essentially Marshall ran out of the time and energy necessary to complete this task. But another reason, hinted at by both Groenewegen's account and the work of Whitaker, is that remaking the *Principles* in this direction involved perhaps too large a leap of theoretical imagination for the systematic and cautious Marshall. Keynes was not so inhibited, we will argue.

Thus we have before us a clearer starting point for analyzing Keynes's own personal Marshallian evolution. It was moved, like all Cambridge work in the 1920s and 1930s, by the need to drive the Marshallian method into new fields and to answer new questions. Factually it was concerned with areas of theoretical and practical interest to Keynes: the operation of the money and credit markets and the function and role of speculation. Theoretically it required a structure or an engine of analysis that could accommodate dynamic change – in money, credit, expectations, the state of the news – while still being open to the later Marshall's more evolutionary sensitivities. Moreover it was apparent that this might involve a reorientation of analysis away from Marshall's focus on long-period equilibrium positions. But toward what? That story is a twisting one that concerns the long development of these issues from the early Marshall to Keynes of the *General Theory*. We will trace that development in the coming chapters of this book.

III. Looking backward from the *General Theory*

Before we trace that development it is useful to assume an alternative viewpoint looking from the other end of our telescope on the historical development of the *General Theory*. Just such an important window on the financial analysis of the *General Theory* is offered by Keynes's comments on its immediate reception. To guide our search backwards from the *General Theory* we draw upon two sorts of evidence. First there is the record of Keynes's own statements about his work, much of it emanating from his participation in what the editors of his collected works have aptly dubbed the "Defense and Development" of the *General Theory* (*CW* 13, 14 and 29). Second, there is the wider set of evidence relating to Keynes's theoretical milieu, his contemporaries, predecessors and teachers; his non-economic activities; and his own former writings. In the previous section we concentrated on investigating the deepest background for this wider sort of evidence, which sets up themes we will follow in Chapters 9 and 10. Now we will review Keynes's own comments on the *General Theory*. We shall see that Keynes's own pronouncements on his views offer tantalizing hints, but hints that are difficult to interpret without the aid of the wider historical record.

Keynes regarded the theory of interest as the part of the *General Theory* that was most commonly misunderstood. Almost his entire published corpus of immediate post-*General Theory* (Keynes, 1937a,b,c) writings on the book is dominated by attempts to correct this misunderstanding. Two of these are particularly relevant to our theme.

In the first, contributed to a *Festschrift* for Irving Fisher, Keynes (1937a) provides a nicely schematized version of his position in relation to what he sees as orthodox theory. Here, Keynes asserts an asset holding, general-equilibrium view as a sort of financial market *metatheory* into which a number of particular theories of interest could potentially be fitted.[8]

The metatheory set-up is explicitly a stock equilibrium where wealth owners and arbitragers trade existing assets (including money) until expected rates of return are equalized (that is, Keynes is assuming existence of "second-hand" markets).[9] But there are, nevertheless, flow output effects of this stock equilibrium. If the asset market equilibrium involves a price for some existing capital goods that is higher than replacement costs, new (flow) production of those capital goods will result. As this investment goes forward, rates of return fall as profitable production of each type of investment good reaches the limits of the market, given existing cost and demand conditions. The market for assets to hold is thus assumed to operate in such a manner that, given differences of opinion about expectations of future changes in asset prices, trading occurs between investors until all traders are satisfied. Given their individual preferences and understanding of the state of the news, in equilibrium, each investor's portfolio exhibits *equalized expected rates of return*.

Notice that since money is one of the assets, its spot and future price (implied by bond prices) determines its rate of interest just like all other tradable assets. Money *may*, but need not, by the logic of the equilibrium construct alone, have a predominant influence on all rates of return in this framework. Here, then, is the peculiar two-stage reasoning exhibited both in Chapter 17 of the *General Theory* and in this *Festschrift* article. First there is Keynes's general metatheory by which arbitrage equilibrium is defined. Any theory of interest must be subject to this arbitrageurs' equilibrium. Second, the question is posed as to the level at which this equalized rate of return will settle:

> These propositions are not, I think, inconsistent with the orthodox theory or in any way open to doubt. They establish that relative prices (and under the influence of prices, the scale of output) move until the marginal efficiencies of all kinds of assets are equal when measured in a common unit; and consequently the marginal efficiency of capital is equal to the rate of interest. But they tell us nothing as to the forces which determine what this common level of marginal efficiency will tend to be. It is when we proceed to this further discussion that my argument diverges from the orthodox theory.
>
> (*CW* 14, pp. 102–3)

In private correspondence in 1937 Keynes criticized Hawtrey, whom he accused of mistaking "higgling" – the process of reaching equilibrium – for the more fundamental forces determining equilibrium (*CW* 14, p. 182). The distinction is clear in his conception of the process by which asset market equilibrium is brought about. Keynes is assuming that the informational efficiency and speed of trading that characterizes modern asset markets will result in a higgling process by which returns on assets are equalized in the short period: that is, expected rates of return for all existing assets, measured in a common unit (money), will be equalized. For him, this higgling process is not the place to look for the fundamental forces characterizing the dynamic changes that establish the common level of expected rates of return at which the equilibrium will settle. Those forces are discovered on another plane of reasoning, the one upon which Keynes claims to be staking the novelty of his own position in the *General Theory*.[10]

What is Keynes's theory as to the level of interest rates? Here the peculiarities of money as an asset, the complex psychology of the liquidity premium and even its characteristics of production and substitution in use play a role, as in the argument of Chapter 17. At this point, however, we need only note that all of this is preceded by the general view of asset market processes outlined above. This view is both more general and more commonsensical. In fact, one can find many places where Keynes expresses dismay and dissatisfaction over the failure of his readers to understand what he thus saw as the obvious and non-controversial "essential properties" of all asset market behavior. Consider, for instance, the following:

> To speak of the "liquidity-preference theory" of the rate of interest is, indeed, to dignify it too much. It is like speaking of the "professorship theory" of Ohlin or the 'civil servant theory' of Hawtrey. I am simply stating what it is, the significant theories on the subject being subsequent. And in stating what it is, I follow the books on arithmetic and accept the accuracy of what is taught in preparatory schools.
>
> (1937b, p. 215; see also *CW 7*, p. 222)

For our present purposes, we shall file away this "metatheory" conception of asset market equilibrium and note simply that Keynes considered it both fundamental and obvious. It will be our task in Chapters 9 and 10 to show whence he might have derived such a view and why he would consider it so obvious. Our next task here, however, is to set up the second issue noted above. Given that Keynes considered all asset markets to be subject to the logic of his equi-expectational equilibrium construct, what is the source of his own specific view of this topic – his theory of where assets prices will settle in relation to expected returns on newly produced capital goods? In the *Festschrift* article he emphasizes his views on uncertainty, expectations, confidence and the functions of money in this context (1937a, pp. 105–8). But a more complete discussion of all three issues is gained from Keynes's second post-*General Theory* article, "The General Theory of Employment" in the *Quarterly Journal of Economics* (1937c).

For our purposes three points about that article are important. First, Keynes claims to be interested in trying to re-express "the comparatively simple fundamental ideas which underlie my theory" (1937c, p. 111), and in doing so fills almost all of his space with a discussion of his views on money and financial markets. Second, in pursuing those simple ideas he is very explicit in emphasizing the roles of uncertainty, incalculable expectations and the consequent conventional nature of market psychology that underlies his view of investment behavior. Thus, as has often been remarked, he is here on the terrain of his analysis of long-term expectations in Chapter 12 of the *General Theory*. This is important because it alerts us to the fact that what he sees as unique in his own view is tied up with what he saw as the nature of financial market expectations and speculation. As is well known, these topics dominate the discussion in Chapter 12. Finally, underlying the whole argument is an application of the asset market equilibrium just outlined, where the importance of these characteristics of asset trading in an uncertain world is illustrated (1937c, pp. 116–19).

With this evidence from Keynes's own hand before us, I wish to make the following claims that will serve as the sufficient reason for the direction of the rest of my argument on the roots of Keynes's financial market views in the *General Theory*. Within the context of the problems of later Marshallian economics, as we have detailed it above, Keynes worked to bring Marshallian realism to his theory of how economies can get stuck in unemployment equilibria. In dealing with his monetary framework we must look for the source of two distinct sets of beliefs. First it is necessary to look for the source of what Keynes saw as obvious and necessary; that asset markets settle toward a (stock) equilibrium where market trading drives prices to positions characterized by equalized expected rates of return among assets at the margin, given market opinions. Marshall will figure prominently here.

Second, we must understand his view of what determines the level this equilibrium will seek. This, to Keynes, is what is unique to the *General Theory* view of financial markets and rates of interest. We must therefore seek out the origin of his view of the economic relevance of market psychology, the behavior of traders in the context of uncertainty and how these affect his view of the meaning, function and consequences of asset market speculation. I shall argue that this view emanates less from Keynes's grappling with economic theory than from his practical observations of and participation in actual financial market processes. Part and parcel of his observation, however, from the beginning of his career to the end, was an attempt to classify the rationality of financial market transactors within the terms of his early philosophical work on probability. At this stage, I can support these claims by noting that in pursuing the main question of Chapter 12 in the *General Theory* – the circumstances governing the "prospective yields of capital assets" and so the determining factors governing the influence of the equilibrium rate of interest on new investment – Keynes ends up analyzing the "market psychology" which guides economic actions under uncertain expectations, and he stresses the crucial influence of the degree of "confidence" with which anticipations are held. In this context, Keynes notes the special importance of observation of market processes:

> There is, however, not much to be said about the state of confidence *a priori*. Our conclusions must mainly depend upon the actual observation of markets and business psychology. This is the reason why the ensuing digression is on a different level of abstraction from most of this book.
>
> (*GT*, p. 149)

Parallel to the structure of Keynes's argument, then, our narrative account of the sources of Keynes's views on market psychology will also follow two related paths, detailed in Chapters 9 and 10. At one level we shall pursue a doctrinal history of the economic treatment of asset markets, as he would have known it. Second, we shall offer a history of what Keynes could have known and may have accepted as the "facts of observation" concerning asset markets. Despite what Keynes may have thought, these "facts" and theories are more intertwined than distinct.

9

Stock Equilibrium in Asset Markets and "The Folly of Amateur Speculators": The Marshallian Setting

I. Introduction

In seeking a source for Keynes's theoretical views one is on firm ground in starting from the source of economics as he knew it, Alfred Marshall. In the last chapter we saw how the problems of later Marshallianism coalesced around the dynamics of investment in industries dominated by increasing returns, joint-stock ownership and large units of production. Some monetary and financial topics logically arise from this change in the Marshallian landscape. They include the investigation of methods of trading on organized produce and stock exchanges such as such large dealings in production and capital call forth, the industrial needs these institutions fulfill and the wider social implications of the speculation possibilities such trading may introduce. It also calls for analysis of the activity of "holding" the financial assets traded on such exchanges, especially the now tradable capital assets. As we will see, it was no coincidence that these became exactly the themes of Keynes's own financial market work.

We have also seen in Chapter 7 the extent and nature of Marshall's influence on Keynes with regard to his labor market analysis. Some claims established there relate to his financial market views. First, early in his career, particularly before World War I, Keynes was almost slavish in following Marshall's economics. This is borne out by the surviving lecture notes from the courses he taught in Cambridge at this time. The same can be said of his monetary work. Second, beginning immediately after the war and accelerating over the course of his involvement in England's economic travails in the twenties, Keynes came to abandon what he saw as an illusory faith in economic stability characteristic of Victorian ideals and Marshallian economics. In the case of his financial market views, this first emerges as a response to the breakdown of the gold standard and his attempts to develop an analysis appropriate to a world of floating exchange rates. Third, through all of this Keynes clung tenaciously to a personal Marshallianism that was in equal parts doctrinal and methodological, essentially relying upon the

Marshallian Organon as an organizing framework, but never letting it shackle him or blind him to contemporary reality – as it did blind Pigou for instance.

The documentation for this in the case of his monetary work, however, is more difficult in that Marshall's monetary work is notorious for having exerted its influence by "oral tradition" through unpublished testimony and memoranda (Laidler, 1991). Fortunately, two remarkable documents, never published in Marshall's lifetime and only recently entered into the public domain, can, along with his later published work, help us characterize the full extent to which Marshall's monetary and financial market views provide the analytical bedrock for Keynes's own way of doing financial market analysis, up to and including that in the *General Theory*.

The first is Marshall's essay "Money" (1871, pp. 164–77), written in the early 1870s, and the second is the recently published essay "The Folly of Amateur Speculators Makes the Fortunes of Professionals. The Wiles of Some Professionals," written around 1899. Marshall's essay "Money" relates directly to Keynes's preferred meta-theoretical approach to monetary theory. The second essay, as noted by those who have brought it to light (Dardi and Gallegati, 1992, pp. 581–6), reinforces the point that Keynes' ideas on stock-market speculation, while ultimately radical when considered next to Marshall's, are still firmly within the Marshallian tradition. What Dardi and Gallegati do not pursue, and which we shall, is the light this essay sheds on the full context in which Keynes developed his views on speculation. For there is a fascinating commonality between this later-Marshall essay, Keynes's own work and a once influential, but now largely forgotten, book published in 1896: H. C. Emery's *Speculation on the Stock and Produce Exchanges in the United States*. This book was the text on which all turn-of-the-century academic discussion of speculation was centered. Furthermore, it is to Emery's book, not Marshall's, that Keynes's original attempt to apply his theory of probability to financial market speculation can be traced. Since it was Keynes's attempt to merge his theory of rationality under uncertainty with speculative behavior that marked his views as unique in this field, Emery may be even more important to his thinking in this regard than Marshall.

II. Marshall's 1871 essay "Money"

It was Keynes who first lamented, in his still unequalled short sketch of Marshall's life, the loss of so much of Marshall's thought that was not on value and distribution during his lifetime. A large part of this general lamentation (*CW* 10, Section 4) concerned his reluctance to publish his theory of money.[1] He goes on to document the existence of a "Cambridge oral tradition" in monetary theory that was mainly conveyed through the lectures of Marshall and Pigou, and through the circulation of such unpublished memoranda as Marshall's evidence to the Gold and Silver Commission (eventually published as Marshall, 1926, pp. 19–195). Of particular note in Keynes's biography is his selection of Marshall's 1871 essay "Money" to illustrate this loss. What was it about this essay that so impressed Keynes when Mary Marshall lent it to him to prepare his portrait of Marshall? How did these ideas figure in Keynes's monetary work, which just then was commencing on the *Treatise on Money*? How does this figure into his use of the same Marshallian framework in the asset-market analysis of the *General Theory*? Could this be why he considered that framework so basic and beyond question in the post-*General Theory* writings cited in the last chapter? These are questions which we intend to pursue in this and the next chapter.

To begin with the basis of Keynes's later (meta-theoretical) approach to asset market activity, it is interesting to note that it originates in a surprisingly early attempt by Marshall (1871) to achieve just what Keynes claimed to be doing – for the first time – 60 years later in the *General Theory*. For Marshall begins his essay with the common complaint of monetary theorists that the value of money is never subjected to the same theoretical treatment – "supply and demand" – as is the determination of the exchange value of all other commodities. Thus in the treatment of money

> . . . we do not find a clear statement of that balancing of advantages which in the ultimate analysis must be found to determine the magnitude of every quantity which rests upon the will of man. If we seek for this we shall find that 'the rapidity of circulation' is not the most convenient thing to be made the basis of our investigations.
>
> (1871, p. 166)

Instead of the traditional quantity theory approach ('the rapidity of circulation'), or the old classical reliance on cost of production, Marshall is here proposing, as Whitaker notes in his introduction to the essays, to integrate the two approaches under a supply and demand framework. In the case of money the question to be answered is: "Why does a man keep on hand a large stock of money?" (Marshall, 1871, p. 166). Importantly, he emphasizes that this is not a decision that is made in isolation from one's "total position of wealth" and the various opportunities for employing it – either in productive use or in the prior provision of transaction services ("the ready command over commodities") of otherwise barren money stocks. In Marshall's world – in 1871 – these opportunities were conceived of as the choice between owning a "horse" or a stock of non-interest bearing "coin." But the general view of how the demand for the various opportunities for holding wealth apportions itself among the available stocks of all assets outstanding is – absent the crucial liquidity motive for holding money and the role of expectations of appreciation – exactly that of Keynes in 1936. Asset holders "balance" at the margin the advantages of each and position their wealth portfolio accordingly:

> This then is the balancing of advantages which each individual has to adjust for himself. If he retains but a very small ready command over commodities he is likely to be put occasionally to considerable inconvenience; if he retains a very large one he receives no adequate compensation for the inaction to which so much of his wealth is doomed. He has thus to settle what is the exact amount which on the average it will answer his purpose to keep in this ready form. Each individual settles this and therefore the whole amount retained in this form by the community is determined by this process on the part of each individual member of it balancing opposing advantages.
>
> (Marshall, 1871, 167–8)

We wish to emphasize in Marshall's treatment the outline of a general theoretical framework for asset market analysis, what we called above Keynes's asset market metatheory. In one way it might be described as perhaps the earliest example of Marshall's preoccupation with the economic effects of the passage of time bearing theoretical fruit via the application of his marginalist method. For him asset markets are to be treated as elaborate examples of the market day phenomenon, where the existence of stocks becomes an all-important force in establishing equilibrium prices. Beginning here and carrying all the way through to the complex analysis in Chapter 17 of the *General Theory*, the application of the marginalist method to such a situation involved a conception of an asset market general equilibrium forming out of the balancing at the margin of two sets of differences.

On the one hand, assets themselves have different qualities and social functions – determined by both 'natural' properties (for example, productiveness) and by social practices (for example, general acceptability). On the other hand, individuals have different tastes and preferences over the desired characteristics of their portfolio. In Marshall's simple "world" of convenient money and productive capital goods, preferences varied only over relative degrees of transaction convenience and return. Thus speculation had no role to play. In Keynes's eventual full-blown version of this framework in the *General Theory*,[2] the assets vary by return, carrying cost and liquidity; and individuals' demands for these assets depend on their preferences for return and convenience (now transformed as liquidity preference), and also on their "speculative" expectations of the likely "appreciation" of each asset.[3] Thus in Keynes's world the influence of opinion can become paramount via the activity of the bulls and bears operating on the exchanges.

Nevertheless, in bare essentials Keynes's approach is the same as Marshall's balancing of the advantages of a hoard of coins and a horse. Previously commentators (see Laidler, 1991, 49–64) have noted the extent to which this sets the standard for the later expressions, by Pigou (1917) particularly, of the Cambridge approach to the demand for money and the micro-foundations approach to the quantity theory. That it may also be seen as the basis of Keynes's later asset market analysis is not widely recognized. But the evidence for this view can be traced all through Keynes's work, as I show below. For now it is sufficient to note what Keynes wrote in his memorial essay on Marshall in 1925, in a period in which he was already working on what was to become the *Treatise on Money*, when he singled out this essay for praise and after quoting from it went on to claim:

> We must regret still more Marshall's postponement of the publication of his *Theory of Money* until extreme old age, when time had deprived his ideas of freshness and his exposition of sting and strength. There is no part of Economics where Marshall's originality and priority of thought are more marked than here, or where his superiority of insight and knowledge over his contemporaries was greater. There is hardly any leading feature in the modern theory of Money which was not known to Marshall forty years ago.
>
> (*CW* 5, p. 189)

Even allowing for the hyperbole, this is a strong statement. Even more so when we recall the denigration of Marshall's theory of interest that was to be written by Keynes inside ten years from this date. A problem, then, is exactly what features of Marshall's treatment survived in Keynes's esteem over this ten-year period and which fell from grace? Our argument will be that the metatheory survived, while the full-employment (classical) theory of the "normal" rate of interest did not.

III. Marshall on speculation

For now, however, let us stay with Marshall and offer some evidence of the attitudes toward stock market activity in general and speculation in particular that he might have bequeathed to Keynes. Again there is the issue of unpublished writings to contend with. And again, there is an essay, unpublished in his lifetime, which offers more insight into what was to develop in Keynes's writings on speculation than what Marshall ventured into print.

The published material should be dealt with first. In *Industry and Trade* Marshall (1919, Chapter 5) discusses "Constructive Speculation [and] Organized Produce Markets." His discussion is organized along the lines of explaining the rise of this institution in the "many services to business men and the world at large" which they provide. Chief among these is the shifting of risks to a concentrated locus of knowledgeable and prudent speculators, taking it off the shoulders of more risk-averse end users. This is socially beneficial, despite the opportunity it offers for abuse, as long as the risks it deals in are equally represented on opposite sides of the market. In fact, says Marshall, this is not even truly speculation as it is commonly termed, but is a form of "insurance":

> A produce exchange can best undertake such risks as these, because many minds of first rate ability and many large capitals are occupied there in dealing with just these risks: and because many of the risks are in opposite directions and cancel one another. The broad shoulders of an exchange can carry without effort the intense risk, relatively to his financial strength, which the chance of a rise in price has imposed on one man; and can generally neutralize it by carrying the equal risk, which the chance of a fall in price has imposed on another.
>
> (Marshall, 1919, pp. 258–9)

We will see below that this risk-bearing function of produce exchanges was exactly what Keynes started out believing in his earliest lectures. We will also see that he, as did Marshall, ascribed this socially useful result to the superior knowledge of traders. In fact following from this is Marshall's definition of "manipulative speculation" as the reverse, trading on the basis of purposely false information:

> Manipulative speculation has many forms and many degrees. Its chief method is to create false opinions as to the general conditions of supply and demand.
>
> (Marshall, 1919, p. 262)

Crucial to the ability of manipulators to create such speculation will be the "folly of amateur speculators," marked by the participation in trading of sufficient numbers of dupes, without the knowledge and judgment of insiders:

> For such men do not understand that the affairs of a great speculation require thorough equipment with knowledge that is beyond the reach of the general public: they do not speculate at random; but they act more mischievously and disastrously to themselves than if they did.
>
> (p. 264)

Finally, in what seems like a distinctly Keynesian and modern voice, Marshall notes that the information that these noisy traders operate on is "old news" to experienced insiders:

> But ill-informed speculators generally suppose themselves to be basing their action on the most recent news. Now the latest information

accessible to outsiders has nearly always been acted on by well-informed persons, and has exerted the full influence, belonging to it, before it has reached the public.

(p. 264)

Yet Marshall, while aware of such abuses earlier in the history of economics than is usually supposed, mentions them mostly as aberrations of a socially useful institution:

Thus the power of selling the future command of a thing not yet in possession is liable to abuse. But when used by able and honest men, it is beneficial: as is shown by the havoc, caused by epidemics of unorganized speculation in the value of land, such as are not infrequent in new countries.

(p. 264)

An issue immediately confronting us is one that is continually raised by analysts of speculation (from Victorian times to the *General Theory* at least). One could usefully think of *produce* exchanges as institutions that assist in finding the long-period positions of supply and demand, for they deal in commodities for which there are, more or less, easily ascertained bounds on the necessary information for forming opinions on these matters – such as average acreage planted and annual world demand for wheat stocks. This is not so easy to understand in the case of shares of *stocks*. What is in fact the fundamental basis of such opinions? As we will see it was the transfer of the logic of produce speculation on organized exchanges to the same activity on stock exchanges, where the end users were not producers, but investors and savers, which caused most of the problems in Keynes's developing views of speculation. Eventually we will see he came to doubt that stock market insiders always had accurate information from which to form a confident opinion about "fundamental" long-period values toward which Marshall assumed all constructive speculation was directed.

This leads us to what Marshall published on stock exchanges in his lifetime. Here we are led not to the interesting and competent discussion of *Industry and Trade*, but to the abortive last publication of Marshall's *Money, Credit and Commerce*. It contains a chapter (Marshall, 1923, Book 2, Chapter 4) titled "Stock Exchanges." Overall, as Keynes, in his Marshall sketch, and many other commentators since have noted, the book is not up to Marshall's usual high standards. Unlike *Industry and Trade*, which can be read with profit by economists today, this largely previously written book, pasted together from old drafts, has not worn its years well. Nevertheless, for our story it still contains a few interesting details.

For one, his general description ascribes a function to stock exchanges that sounds very Keynesian in its, admittedly brief, discussion of their psychological value as barometers of the confidence of the investing class:

> Stock exchanges are not merely the chief theatres of large business trans-actions; that are also barometers which indicate the general conditions of the atmosphere of business.
>
> (Marshall, 1923, p. 144)

He borrows freely from the discussion in *Industry and Trade* with respect to the functions and possible evils of speculation, while on the whole rather weakly declaring (as opposed to showing) that stock speculation is on balance beneficial. One allusion, however, to the stock exchange's beneficial exposure of long-period values is interesting to highlight for our later discussion:

> The purchaser of almost any "security" of which considerable quantities are habitually bought and sold on a stock exchange, is generally fortified by the knowledge that expert and well-informed capitalists regard its price as fairly representing its *real value*. Therefore, although stock exchange machinations may occasionally set for a time, an unduly high value, or an unduly low value on a particular "security," yet, in the main, *the judgment of well-informed, capable men protects the general public from grave errors of judgment in their investments*, so long as these are conducted with reasonable caution.
>
> (Marshall, 1923, p. 145, emphasis added)

We will see that this question of the judgment of stock market insiders is one that Keynes, over a long career as both an active participant and an economist, would continuously ponder. His final conclusion in 1936 will be shown in the next chapter as distinctly non-Marshallian on the issue of speculation. Though already touched on, what we can say now about that conclusion bears repeating for its contrast with Marshall and to ward off the notion that it is "all in Marshall" after all. That is to say, we will show that Keynes came to the conclusion that such "real" values are not always there to be determined. Moreover, Keynes eventually achieved the status of a virtual insider through his own dealings, and was always convinced, like Marshall, of the personal morality of most traders. But the mature Keynes would come to depict the judgment of insiders, explicitly when they were playing by the rules of the game, as aimed at an entirely different goal than forecasting fundamental values.

Without abandoning his belief that stock markets really were aiming to discover fundamentals, Marshall ends his chapter by obliquely alluding to part of Keynes's eventual point, the dangers inherent in an exchange where outside speculators in the stock market do not have the insiders' (for Marshall real and true) information:

> It may indeed be said that shrewd, far-seeing speculators sometimes govern their own action, not so much by forecasts of the distant future, as by forecasts of the inaccuracy of the forecasts of that future.
>
> (Marshall, 1923, p. 151)

This quote highlights Marshall's realization that efficient transmission to prices of transparent information about fundamentals was what constitutes the social utility of the institution of stock markets, and that differences between the access of insiders and outsiders to this information could lead to large abuses. For whatever reason, he was not willing to commit his more radical thoughts on this to publication in his lifetime.

Here we turn to Marshall's unpublished 1899 essay. In their excellent introduction to this essay Dardi and Gallegati (1992, pp., 573–81) note that it stands as a sort of halfway house between the traditional view of speculators in English economics[4] and Keynes's later views. In the traditional view speculators had a transient role to play as a class of agents specializing in market arbitrage whose prominent function is to generate and extend "contagious" buying and selling among the less informed mass of amateur agents who form their customers. In so doing, they were liable to cause "some accident which excites expectation of rising prices" to result in "a generally reckless and adventurous feeling" (Mill, p. 1871, p. 542), and this was seen to be a factor in commercial panics and price instability. Dardi and Gallegati emphasize that, prior to this essay, Marshall considered this negative view of speculation appropriate to the analysis of general price instability and the cycle, but was reluctant to admit it as a factor capable of upsetting the tranquil movement from short- to long-period normal values envisioned in the *Principles*.

In the 1899 essay, however, Marshall takes more seriously the possibility that speculation might be more than a passing cyclical factor, and could even upset the establishment of long-period normal positions (and thus, though Marshall himself does not mention it, but which is important for comparison with Keynes, the establishment of the "normal" rate of interest.) As Dardi and Gallegati (1992, p. 572) put it:

> The main interest in these pages lies, in our opinion, in clearly highlighting Marshall's shift of position from a typically nineteenth-century vision of speculation as a picturesque and sometimes objectionable, but essentially marginal phenomenon, to a modern view which places speculation at the very center of the capitalistic engine, as an inseparable component of the working of financial markets.[5]

The basis of the difference in outlook between the old view and the modern view, revolved around the theme of the "informational" context for speculation and its consequent reinforcement or not of the more fundamental forces of "enterprise." For the earlier Marshall, it was not conceivable that speculators could forever forestall the movement of prices toward those consistent with long-period normal values – that is, consistent with equalized rates of return to all sectors of capital. In the unpublished essay, Marshall raises the possibility that it might be in the interest of professional speculators to keep the amateurs misinformed about the true nature of the fundamentals (say the future expected earning capacity of a publicly traded firm.) Thus, and analogously to Keynes's "beauty contest" metaphor, "the first of the valid charges that may be brought against the general economic influence of stock exchange speculation" is "that the shrewdest and most far seeing speculators often govern their action not by their own forecast of the distant future but by their forecasts of the forecasts that will be made by less competent people" (Marshall, 1899a, p. 589).[6] Even worse, attesting to the vast manipulations witnessed in the 1880s and 1890s, when Marshall (1899a, p. 550) comes to consider the "special [role] played in the stock exchange arena by powerful financiers and [the] great operators, who belong to High Finance (la Haute Finance, la Haute Banque, die hohe Bank)," he finds they may also have reason to use duplicity and misinformation. Thus on the whole there is the possibility that the operation of the exchanges, when speculation dominates, may hide the true (fundamental) values more than reinforce them.

Now racy as this may sound, coming from Marshall, there are clear signs that he would have been unwilling to go all the way with Keynes's later views. As Dardi and Gallegati comment, Marshall's whole argument still presupposes that the "fundamentals" are out there to be found. As we will show in the following sections this is one crucial point at which the later Keynes diverges from Marshall's most radical view of speculation. For Keynes the fundamentals eventually lost the attractive value that Marshall's term "normal" was meant to convey.

IV. H. C. Emery: *Speculation on the Stock and Produce Exchanges of the United States*

The analysis put forward by Marshall in 1899 was not entirely original. He apparently relied heavily in his theorizing about the nature and role of speculation upon Emery's *Speculation in the Stock and Produce Exchanges in the United States* (Emery, 1896). In fact in almost all the essentials, Marshall is merely seconding Emery's work. He was referenced extensively, for instance, in the discussion in *Industry and Trade*. Dardi and Gallegati also note that Marshall referred to Emery in his unpublished essay, that his personal copy of Emery's book is highly annotated and that he recorded extensive notes on the book. The reason this is particularly interesting to our theme is that this book appears to have served as the standard reference work for the whole profession, up until the 1920s at least, on just exactly what was going on in the most "speculating" country then known:

> The American people are regarded by foreigners as the greatest of all speculators . . . Speculation proper, as well as the speculative spirit of vast industrial enterprise, has had its most striking development perhaps in the United States. The greatest speculation in produce which the world has ever seen has grown up recently in Chicago, while a speculative market of almost unequaled magnitude is found in the Stock Exchange of New York. While, however, little has been written in the country either to describe the details of exchange methods, or to estimate the function of these exchanges in the economic order.
>
> (Emery, 1896, p. 7)

Emery saw it as his task to fill this gap. In the process he left a document of amazing detail about the then standard practices on the commodity and stock markets. Almost all major writers on the subject of speculation after him seem to refer to this book. In particular, Keynes, who, we will see, relied heavily upon Emery early in his career, used it as the text in his pre-war lectures at Cambridge on "The Stock Exchange"; Irving Fisher, Emery's Yale colleague, thanks Emery for his criticism and quotes him in *The Rate of Interest* in 1907; and Thorstein Veblen seems to have relied upon Emery's description of the exchanges as part of the raw material that went into the crafting of his *Theory of Business Enterprise* (1904, p. 165). Thus it will be very useful to review the highlights of Emery's book to situate Keynes's later use of its contents. The goal of this rehearsal of Emery is to convince the reader that much of what is now thought of as the distinctively Keynesian view of speculation was in fact well known to monetary economists of the early part of this century.[7]

Emery, in opposition to what he saw as a one-sided literature on speculation that tended to emphasize the "evils," with no account given of the positive functions, consciously set out to provide a descriptive account of the exchanges, emphasizing "the fact that speculation in the last half century has developed as a natural economic institution in response to the new conditions of industry and commerce" (Emery, 1896, p. 10). This goal and Emery's great attention to detail and history clearly set his work within the American "institutionalist" tradition. Yet in a comment that offers some insight into the subsequent development of the theory of speculation, Emery notes with reluctance that this approach has forced him to forgo an extensive analysis of the "evils of speculation."[8] Interestingly, his excuse for this lack of balance rests on what he saw as the greater difficulties attaching to that subject:

> The evils of speculation, though more widely appreciated by the public, are by no means so simple of comprehension or so easy of description as

its benefits. An adequate study of this part of the subject would require not only a careful historical study of the deals and manipulations of the speculative market, but a mind trained by wide experience of business life to weigh justly the influences for harm and good.

(Emery, 1896, pp. 11–12)

I suggest that Keynes eventually overcame these difficulties, after his own "wide experience" put him in a position to analyze speculation's influence for harm and for good. But first there was Emery.

Emery offers clear descriptions in Chapters 2 and 3 of the various instruments and practices found on the stock and produce exchanges, and the economic rationale of their organizational rules. He also provides (1896, Chapter 2) a detailed analysis of forward trading, futures contracts, straddles, options and short selling. Further, he shows how the rules of the various exchanges and the development of clearinghouses, evolved to provide a framework of self-policing that would create the fiduciary trust on the part of participants necessary to maintain public confidence in the dealings of the exchanges and so allow them to serve as the central markets they did become. For the student of financial institutions this analysis of what today would be called the "theory of clubs" aspects of the exchanges seems amazingly modern.[9]

More important for our purposes, however, is his historical and theoretical treatment of the economic function of speculation in Chapters 3 and 4. He defines speculation by reference to the development of "trading over time." The oldest examples are found in the purchase of actual goods to hold in anticipation of a rise and later this was extended to prior payment for goods in transit via bills of exchange. Emery notes that the origin of such trades lies in forward trading – a practice that has existed since antiquity, and in organized form since the seventeenth century. In its most general form speculation is just buying or selling through time in hopes of better terms at the end of the period considered. But there is evidence of "futures" dealing of the modern kind only in the last few centuries.

The mark of this form of trading is to be found in a move toward more abstract trading of standardized products or instruments. Real futures occur only with the development of the warrant and grading systems, by which various products – first metals and then various grains – were standardized into grades and the legal rights of ownership were transformed by the issuance of warrants (or receipts) representing generalized claims to a specific quantity of a standardized product, deliverable at a specified future date.[10] He notes that the development of such trading also depended on the centralized concentration of trading and information, epitomized by grain markets in the American Midwest and particularly Chicago in the period 1850–70. There, through the combined influence of the Chicago Board of Trade, the western expansion of the railroads, the development of the grain elevator system and the invention of the telegraph, a new and massive organization of trading activity could take place:

> The development of the system of grading and of elevator receipts is the most important step in the history of the grain trade. It is only with such a machinery that an extension of forward sales in the modern sense is possible, that is of forward sales of goods having no definite existence until the moment of delivery. (p. 38)

Emery makes it clear that, although older forms of "trading over time" – such as the trade in receipts of actual specific lots of grain prior to the establishment of generalized "futures" – also offered opportunities for holding for a speculative gain, the modern exchanges greatly altered the scope of speculation. No longer was it tied to actual quantities of goods traded and it became just as easy to speculate for a fall as for a rise in price (pp. 38–46). Here we see the development of two crucial distinctions that would later mark both Keynes's and Marshall's analysis of speculation. They are:

(1) that the exchanges are first and foremost a method of locking in terms over time by both producers and end users – a form of price hedging – in which regard, their primary economic function was to be defined in terms of "risk-bearing";

(2) that such primary activity also creates secondary opportunities for "speculative" time dealing by a separate class of *speculators*. "All time-dealings arise from a desire to provide in the present for the events of the future. Speculative time-dealings arise when an anticipated difference in the present and future prices of a commodity in question leaves room for a possible profit" (p. 33).

As we have seen in the case of Marshall, already, and as is well known from Chapter 12 of the *General Theory*, future criticisms of speculation by economists after Emery would turn on the judgment of the role these "insiders" play in fulfilling the primary function of the exchanges.

Emery takes as his paradigm case of speculative trading the grain future. This is important because it will be seen that the theory of the economic function of speculation that Emery puts forward – that we are arguing to be so influential in economic circles in the beginning of the twentieth century – is also based on an analogy to the commodities exchanges. Yet even in Emery's discussion, and later increasingly also in Keynes's discussion, this theory makes only an uneasy transition to the "stock" exchange. The reason for this is already in sight: it is very difficult to establish exactly what in the stock market setting constitutes the counterpart to the hedging of intertemporal risk by primary producers and users of commodities that form the *raison d'etre* of the produce exchanges.

Emery (pp. 74–94) does a remarkable job of making the mechanical anal-ogy to "futures" for the stock exchange by detailing the extensive practice of "borrowing and lending" stocks and margin sales which accompanies stock speculation.[11] This practice, combined with the fact that "stocks and bonds possess in themselves that quality of representiveness which is secured for commodities only by means of classified grades and a warrant system," means that in "the conduct of business on the stock exchanges, the same general principle is found as prevails on the produce exchanges, with some marked differences in the actual methods employed" (p. 74). Yet, hav-ing laid out a fine description of these methods, he is, nevertheless, forced to admit a difference:

> There is not the same economic reason for future dealings in stocks as in produce, for while any kind of produce is something the supply of which is itself a future thing, and so often cannot be contracted for except for future delivery, a particular stock on the other hand is, in the main, fixed in amount. The stock to be delivered is all in existence at the time of sale, and there seems to be no reason, except for speculation, for postponing its delivery.

> (p. 77)

To get on to Emery's *theory* proper as presented in Chapter 4 "The Economic Function of Speculation," it is worth repeating that it is grounded in an attempt to show speculation as a "normal" business practice, exem-plified by the activity on the produce exchanges. His previous historical analysis of the development of these exchanges is crucial here, because he essentially argues that the modern speculators – those who secondarily trade in "futures" as opposed to the end users and producers – represent a mod-ern extension of the division of labor among factors of production. In this case the element of risk bearing that had previously been part of the return to the occupations of farmers, grain merchants and grain users, for instance, could now be seen as the specialized function of the grain exchange specu-lators.[12] The speculators, engaged in both buying and selling futures that are never intended to result in the actual delivery of grain, make their profit (or loss) by forecasting future price movements and by taking positions.

The social impact of this development is the creation of *worldwide* markets which channel all information affecting the supply and demand everywhere into the formation of a single world price for staple commodities. Two quo-tations drawn from Emery's discussion will serve to illustrate his view and to set the context for Keynes own attempt (*GT*, pp. 150–3) to define the his-torical epoch of speculative capitalism in the *General Theory*:

> With this change [to worldwide markets after 1850] the market for all the great staples became a world market, and the total demand and total

supply began to determine a single price for all places. The chances of local fluctuations in price became greatly lessened, for the local scarcity or abundance might be offset by opposite conditions elsewhere. At the same time the fluctuations possible because of these distant conditions became of much more importance. Formerly the merchant, from a thorough knowledge of his own market, was well-prepared to assume its speculative risks. Now he was called on to face a wider *Konjunktur*, and to assume the risk of changing values dependent on world-wide conditions . . . With the advance in knowledge, the trading element and the speculative element in their business had come to be more sharply distinguished, and the more important the speculative element became, the greater was the burden on those who pursued their business for its trading profit.

(Emery, 1896, pp. 107–8)

What was now needed by the trader was a distinct body of men prepared to relieve him of the speculative element of his business, that is of the risks of distant and future changes, just as he had formerly relieved the producer of his distinctly trading risks. A new body was wanted to cope with the *Konjunktur*. And as the need grew, the speculative class became differentiated from the trading body as the latter had been differentiated from the producing body . . . Now they became a third class, distinct from both producers and exchangers. Whereas formerly each man bore his own risks, the new class has arisen to relieve him of these risks; instead of all traders speculating a little, a special class speculates much.

(pp. 108–9)

Now we have before us Emery's basic theory, which will already bear testament to the early date at which economists engaged in discussion of such notions as the role of market insiders and the positive function of risk-bearing by organized exchange speculation.[13] How did Emery extend this reasoning to the stock exchange? He notes that the history of this exchange in the United States owes much to the "enormous increase in private securities which came with the building of the railroads" (pp. 112). Thus, though not directly the result of the commercial revolution in world trade responsible for the produce exchanges, the stock exchange was derivative from this revolution. Again, scale was a factor as the size of the public and private investments required for large-scale railroad and telegraph building created risks beyond the means of even the largest individual investors. "The small investor, like the merchant, could hardly take such chances; and, like the merchant, he found a class ready to assume all the risk of buying or selling his security, and a market that fixed prices by which he could intelligently invest."

But instead of focusing on the opportunities to hedge risk as the primary social function of speculation in the case of the stock exchange, Emery picks up on what had been a subsidiary theme in his discussion of the produce exchanges in their putative powers of "direction." For the produce exchanges, he had emphasized the influence that speculative prices exerted on consumption. "Speculation, then, tends to equalize consumption over a long period by causing economy in anticipation of a shortage, and free use in anticipation of bountiful crops" (p. 145). In the case of stock market speculation this "directive" influence becomes the now commonplace[14] one of simultaneously providing the liquidity necessary to make large-scale investment palatable to individual investors and, through channeling information into prices fixed on the exchange, ensuring the best distribution of resources among these investments (pp. 148–50).

Interestingly, at this point, Emery conducts a running argument against much of the then existing literature, most of it German, in an attempt to establish something very much like the market efficiency view so well known from recent finance literature. For the most part this concerns various refutations of attacks on the social beneficence of stock-exchange-directed investment. More interesting than his arguments, which are not very convincing, are the topics he is thus committed to examine. These include trading under the influence of market insiders ("manipulators") as opposed to trading on "the best information" that is yielded by "expert investigation" (pp. 151); the question of whether stocks prices fluctuate because of speculative activity or they are speculated in because of fluctuating value (p. 152–3); the accuracy of the market's opinion concerning the economic impact of political changes in the news (pp. 154–5); and the influence of and extent of the opinions of the non-speculative classes (the "artisan," the "professional man of small income" and "banks, trust companies, insurance companies and the like") on stock exchange prices.

Thus once again we are reminded that there is nothing new under the sun. Many of the issues that concerned Keynes, and which still concern some modern writers (Shiller, 1991) about exchange market speculation, were well-known to Emery in 1896. To conclude, notice the distinctive aspects of Emery's view that will later show up in Keynes's writings, albeit altered and transformed. First, there is a positive function for the exchanges that grew out of the circumstances of the development of the industrial and commercial world over the latter half of the nineteenth century, particularly in America. But the primary function of each type of exchange – either for risk bearing and/or for directing resources – also created secondary opportunities for the accumulation of wealth for certain classes of economic actors that was unintended, though inseparable from the primary function. Thus speculators are part of the machinery of the modern economy. In fact, a guiding theme in Emery is a self-conscious attempt to attack as misguided the then prevalent opprobrium attached to the role of speculators. Emery stressed that speculators were merely the messengers of a new, more risky commercial environment. Killing them off by legislative decree would not alter the message that by the turn of the century western economies had come to depend upon these exchanges both to engage in large-scale investment and to transact commodity exchange on a world scale. A question remained, in the course of answering which both Keynes and Veblen (1904) would eventually take their distinctive tacks on Emery. Could the casino-like aspect of this system – admittedly ancillary from a social evolutionary standpoint – ever come to doom the productive process on which it feeds?

V. The historical record and Keynes's developing views on speculation

It is now time to tie up some of the threads of this argument by bringing the evidence on Marshall's work and on Emery's views on speculation to bear on an evaluation of Keynes's own analysis of financial markets. I shall emphasize that one must recognize the change and development of Keynes's ideas in this and other contexts. In the case of his evolving views on speculation I argue that, until the 1920s, his views of the economic function of speculation were quite orthodox and based largely on Marshall and Emery. He for the most part defends speculation as economically beneficial, though even at this early stage he introduced some interesting theoretical nuances which emanate from his views on probability. In fact, one might say that what is today usually seen as the "Keynesian" theory of stock markets and long-term expectations based on uncertainty and convention, grew from a seed planted when the young Keynes, fresh from his struggle with the logic of probability in relation to conduct, came upon Emery in his early lectures at Cambridge.

This development, I will argue, is visible in Keynes's changing views of the informational context in which speculative decisions are made. Thus, beginning in the twenties, and increasingly over the course of the thirties, he came to appreciate that, in certain contexts, speculation might be capable of independently exercising an adverse effect on economic activity. Much of this change of view concerned his evaluation of world economic events in these turbulent decades. But his personal experiences as an investor played a role as well. By the time of the *General Theory*, his critique of the deleterious effects of the "casino" aspects of modern capitalism had hardened into a stance virtually indistinguishable from Veblen's view in 1904. In all of this analysis, however, he remained firmly wedded to the framework set down by Emery and investigated by the later Marshall. That is to say, the question of the economic impact of speculation always turned on the question of whether or not it was mere reaction to and possible exaggeration of underlying "real" economic forces, as the traditional benign view supposed. Also constant throughout this development is a staunch unwillingness, more adamant than Emery's own attitude, to blame the speculating class itself for the troubles of speculation. For Keynes, blame should lie with the organization of a system in which the instability of events and the consequent precariousness of confidence could give rise to the predominance of speculation over enterprise. Not surprisingly, this also came down to an issue closely related to Keynes's early work on probability and its relation to practical reasoning.

Recognizing the links to probability and to Keynes's practical experience forces us to touch base with many points of the now complex interdisciplinary Keynes literature. The work of Skidelsky (1983, 1992, 2000); O'Donnell (1989); Moggridge (1992) and Davis (1994a) will be important sources. Starting with Skidelsky (1983) many writers have suggested that Keynes's philosophical views are at the base of his economics. Without entering into the disputatious secondary literature this claim has spawned, it is worth noting that we do see a continual influence from this side in Keynes's evolving views on speculation. I do not here suggest that there is a simple one-to-one mapping of Keynes's philosophical views into a theory of speculation. Such a mapping would depend crucially on the knowledge context one assigns to speculative activity, and the theoretical "whole" in which the effect of speculation is judged to be operative. My argument will be that it was precisely on these issues that Keynes changed his mind over the course of his career.

In the matter of Keynes's own speculative activity, Donald Moggridge, in his role as editor of Keynes's *Collected Writings*, has done the Keynes scholar an invaluable service in recording the essential facts and documents concerning Keynes as an investor. These materials plus Moggridge's own editorial comments (*CW* 7) are essential reading for anyone wishing to understand this little investigated side of the many-sided Keynes.

The main facts – that he traded on his own account and with capital provided by friends and relatives; that this often took the form of highly leveraged speculative positions; and that he also engaged in giving investment advice both to his college, King's, and to insurance companies – are well-known. Less well-known, and more important for our story, are the detailed ups and downs of Keynes's own investments and the mostly internal supporting documents Keynes wrote for insurance companies and bursar meetings, which Moggridge collected together. What these materials indicate is that Keynes showed as much verve, but not always as much success, at investing as he did at doing economics; and, that, also similar to his economics, he changed his investment "philosophy" over his career. Both Moggridge (1992, p. 586) and Skidelsky (1992, pp. 24–30, 41–6, 340–3, 557–8) attribute to his personal financial experiences a large degree of influence over Keynes's more theoretical interests in speculation[15]. Moggridge in fact describes Chapter 12 of the *General Theory* as "largely autobiographical." I happily give limited support to this view, although it is more complicated and less clear-cut than either of the two biographers had space to investigate. Most importantly, Keynes's theoretical views on speculation must be placed in the wider intellectual context we are here investigating. Keynes's discussion in Chapter 12, for instance, owes at least as much to Emery and *Probability* as it does to his investment experience. Finally there is the issue of chronology. What classification of time best captures the evolution of Keynes's views on speculation? It is customary for economists to tell this story as one of successive sheddings – or in less sophisticated versions one tremendous wrenching molt – of Keynes's many-layered classical skin, eventually emerging as the full-blown "Keynesian" suggested by each particular author's interpretation of the *General Theory*. In the case of his evolving views on speculation, this analogy, while not entirely inappropriate, is difficult to maintain. Some of the patterning of his previous skins remained intact, while some elements were merely rearranged into a larger, more complex pattern. Thus, as Skidelsky has surely convinced us by now, Keynes's history contains at least as much continuity as change. The challenge is to reconstruct an evolution that played itself out against the backdrop of Keynes's many lives. What follows is an attempt at such a reconstruction.

10
The Evolution of Keynes's Views on Asset Markets and Speculation

I. The young don as philosopher of speculation, 1909–14

For the earliest evidence on Keynes and speculation we turn to the lectures he gave in Cambridge before World War I. Complete notes in his hand for many of these courses are in the Keynes papers at King's College. Two of these are particularly relevant to our concerns. First there is a series of lecture notes dated 1910 entitled "Modern Business Methods II."[1] Second, there is a set of notes for lectures Keynes gave over the years 1909 to 1914, titled "The Stock Exchange and the Money Market."[2] There is some overlap between the treatment in these two courses, but the general impression is that when it came to discussing the organization of the exchanges and speculation, Keynes relied heavily on Emery's discussion in both, sometimes lifting whole passages from his book (with attribution) and for much of the rest paraphrasing him. In one sense Emery is taken as a source of the "facts" about the machinery of the exchanges. For example, consider the following characteristically cocksure remark by Keynes:

> These lectures will be extremely elementary, and only occasionally will any questions of intellectual difficulty arise. The greater part of them will be concerned with simple statements of fact, and to quite an appreciable extent with the explanation of the meaning of terms. A good deal of the apparent difficulty of stock exchange questions arises out of the unaccustomed terminology in which they are expressed. When once the meaning of the words is clearly understood, nothing more is required than a common share of general intelligence.
>
> (KCKP UA/6/3/6)

Keynes also advises that the student will learn much more by "contracting the habit, which every economist, however theoretical his tastes should have, of reading regularly one of the financial weeklies." That this was not just idle advice is attested to by the superb illustrations from current

126

financial events with which Keynes interleaves the lectures. But in a telling remark, considering the future course Keynes's career would take after 1914, the young don also notes that the stock market is "essentially a practical subject, which cannot properly be taught by book or lecture. *Further, I have myself no practical experience of the questions involved*" (KCKP UA/6/3/6, italics added). No practical experience yet, that is.

Rather than repeat Keynes's version of Emery, it will be helpful to show the context in which the discussion of speculation was situated, and then discuss his sole departure from Emery's book. The context is best conveyed by the section headings of the courses as Keynes outlined them in the following notes:

Company Finance and the Stock Exchange[3]

1. Types of shares
2. The flotation of a company
3. Management of a company
4. The Balance Sheet
5. The Stock Exchange
6. Speculation – definition, economic function, methods – bears, bulls, options, the account, carry over, contango
7. The Different Classes of Securities – Aggregate value, consols and their history, trustee stock, fluctuations of capital value
8. The current rate of interest – determining factors – risk, ease of sale, likelihood of future increases, "lock up"
9. Foreign Investment – geographical distribution

Modern Business Methods II[4]

1. The Organization of the Exchanges
2. Dealing in Futures
3. Speculation in Stocks and Bonds
4. The Economic Function of Speculation
5. The Effect of Speculation on Price
6. The Regulative Influence of Speculation
7. The Assumption of Risk by the Speculative Market
8. The Evils of Speculation
9. Questions to be answered[5]

A familiarity with and borrowing from Emery's book is apparent in almost all (Sections 1–8) of the "Modern Business Methods" course. Furthermore, in the first course on the "Stock Exchange," part of the same material appears under Sections 5 and 6. Perhaps the most interesting of these is the discussion of the "Economic Function of Speculation." The extent of its dependence on Emery can clearly be seen in the following summary by Keynes:

> Thus the function of an organized speculation is limited to certain classes of goods. Its object is to relieve trade of the risks of the fluctuating values by providing a class always ready to take or deliver a property at the market price; and, in so doing, to direct commodities to their more advantageous uses, and the investment of capital into the most profitable channels.
>
> (KCKP UA/3/265)

Keynes disagrees with Emery, however, in his evaluation of the proper *definition* of speculation, a subject that arises in Emery's attempt to differentiate it from gambling. Two interesting threads of intellectual history intersect at this point. One is the common turn-of-the-century suspicion of speculators as mere gamblers.[6] The other is the now well-known fact that early in his career, Keynes was as much, if not more, involved in the philosophy of probability as he was in economics. Emery (1896, pp. 98–101) had set out to defend organized exchange speculation from this "gambling" charge. It is at this point in his lecture on Emery that Keynes steps in, having in 1910 completed his fellowship dissertation on probability, in which he explicitly deals with both the nature of chance and gambling, the relation of notions of probability to the conduct of everyday life, and the very issue of the morality of gambling.[7]

In order to analyze Keynes's very interesting discussion of the distinction between gambling and speculation, it is useful to briefly recall the account in the *Treatise on Probability* of "practical reason and ethics" (see *CW* 8, Chapter 26 and O'Donnell 1989, Chapter 6). What marks off Keynes's analysis of speculation as different from those by contemporaries is its strong grounding in his own particular theory of probability. In applying his theory of probabilities as rational degrees of belief relative to the knowledge in the possession of the individual, Keynes wanted to show that conduct could be moral and rational if based on a probabilistic estimate of the good consequence which would follow from action. But he insisted that such conduct must give due regard to the "weight" attached to the evidence one possessed in formulating these probable consequences, and the relative "moral risk" of the probable outcomes. The issues of probability in relation to knowledge and the confidence with which we hold that probability (summed up by his term "weight") are perhaps sufficiently well-known to Keynes scholars by now to pass over without comment. But the attendant concept of "moral risk" is worth examining in the present context for the light it sheds on Keynes's evolving views on speculation.

Moral risk is essentially a device for breaking out of a strict reliance on mathematical probabilities in assessing the morality of actions. It is a way of distinguishing between courses of action which might have equal probable goodness (that is, the actions are equal in expected value: the projected goodness multiplied by its probability), but have unequal probabilities of occurring. Keynes (*CW* 8, p. 347) asks:

> Is it certain that a larger good, which is extremely improbable, is precisely equivalent ethically to a smaller good which is proportionately more probable? We may doubt whether the moral value of speculative and cautious action respectively can be weighed against one another in a simple arithmetical way, just as we have already doubted whether a good whose probability can only be determined on a slight basis of evidence can be compared by means merely of the magnitude of this probability with another good whose likelihood is based on completer knowledge.

As O'Donnell's (1989, pp. 122–33) excellent discussion of this issue makes clear, there is a connection between this concept and Keynes's views on the evils of gambling. As O'Donnell puts it, Keynes "suggested that in some situations there was a greater rationality in playing safe (the more probable smaller good), than in living dangerously and risking much for the larger but more uncertain gain" (O'Donnell, 1989, p. 123). In the case of gambling – "at poker, for instance, or on the Stock Exchange" – Keynes (*CW* 8, pp. 352–3) applies this framework in combination with a strong belief in the declining marginal utility of money to argue that the gambling is only immoral when the players vary widely in initial wealth. For though, on average, a fair gamble will result in zero return for long-term players, wealthier players will be able to outlast the poorer and so easily beat a succession of them as each lacks the resources to play as long as the wealthy players. Thus:

> The true moral is this, that poor men should not gamble and that millionaires should do nothing else. But millionaires gain nothing by gambling with one another, and until the poor man departs from the path of prudence the millionaire does not find his opportunity.
>
> (*CW* 8, p. 353)

He adds in a footnote a sentiment that is repeated both in his official testimony on gambling laws (*CW* 28, pp. 395–7) and in the *General Theory* (*GT*, pp. 159–61) discussion of the stock market:

> From the social point of view, however, this moral against gambling may be drawn – that those who start with the largest fortunes are most likely to win, and that a given increment to the wealth of these benefits them, on the assumption of a diminishing marginal utility of money, less than it injures those from whom it is taken.
>
> (*CW* 8, p. 353n)

Our reason for rehearsing these elements of Keynes's philosophical work becomes clear when we read his first attempts, in the lecture notes, to define the essential nature of speculation:

The Nature of Speculation

(1) Where the risk is incalculable
    e.g. some political insurance at Lloyds
(2) Where the risk is more or less calculable
    (a) the risks not averaged
        e.g. roulette at Monte Carlo
    (b) the risks averaged + commission
        life insurance
        fire insurance
(3) Where the speculator's knowledge or judgement is superior to that
    of the market
    1 and 2a – Gambling
    2b – Insurance
    3 – Speculation – Not identical with "taking risks"
    Perhaps bookmaking partakes of all these.

The essential characteristic of speculation is, it seems to me, the possession of superior knowledge. We do not mean by the risk of an investment its actual future yield – we mean the degree of probability of the yield we expect. *The probability depends upon the degree of knowledge.* In a sense, therefore, it is subjective. What would be gambling for one man, would be sound speculation for another.

. . . If we regard speculation as a reasoned attempt to gauge the future from present known data, it may be said to form the basis of all intelligent investment. *But it is better, I think, to regard the speculator as a person who endeavors to make a profit by means of a power of forecasting the future superior to the ordinary.*

(KCKP UA/6/3/93,95, italics added)

Notice that Keynes's analysis of the relation of speculation to gambling runs, just like his theory of probability, in terms of *judgments* relative to the knowledge in one's possession. Also note that he is already attaching importance to the distinction between financial risks which are calculable and those which are incalculable (what he would later call "uncertain" risks). Since the pure chance attached to speculative positions on the part of the small casual investor means he should attribute little *weight* to his judgments, his activity *is* simply gambling. By 1910 Keynes is arguing that the position of market insiders, having due regard to the constant flow of information Emery stressed is centralized on the exchanges, and to their superior ability (as Marshall argued), defines professional speculation as rational action. Now the question arises: How does speculation on the exchanges fit with the ethical view which Keynes expressed with regard to gambling in the *Treatise on Probability*? For much like the millionaire's immoral advantage over the poor gambler, the market insider would have clear advantages over the more ignorant investors on the exchanges. That is they might, if two things were true according to Keynes's own theory of probability. First, it would have to be possible to secure the knowledge that made for the insiders' superior judgment (that is, such knowledge could in principle *exist*). This follows directly from his definition of probability as a logical relation between a proposition (the price of U.S. Steel will rise) and the evidence related to it ("fundamentals" or market psychology). Second, it would require the exchanges to be organized in such a way that it is relatively easy for the insiders to prey on the outsiders. Notice that both of these topics were considered by Marshall in his essay on the folly of amateur speculators and by Emery in his defense of the stock exchange. What is remarkable about Keynes as of 1910, especially considering what he would say in the *General Theory* 25 years later, is that with regard to the first question, at that stage he clearly believed in what we would now call calculable fundamental values: "I shall regard the possession of superior knowledge as the vital distinction, and the only vital distinction between the speculator and the gambler" (KCKP UA/6/3/98). Given this conviction it is not surprising that, at this juncture, he did not even raise the possibility of speculation derailing the beneficial risk-bearing and directive influences of the exchanges on economic activity. This is reflected in the fact that despite his disagreement with Emery over the proper *definition* of speculation, he immediately follows this discussion by repeating Emery's view of the "Economic Functions of Speculation." It is contained too in the praise he clearly expresses for professional speculators. At one point in the lectures he equates the morals of professional speculators to those of bookmakers, quoting approvingly the following passage from the *Economist* (September 25, 1909):

> Take professional bookmakers or betting men, for example; they work as hard at their business as human beings can do, and their earnestness is remarkable. Thoughtful men of few words, they are as grave as judges, as reflective as metaphysicians, and as serious as bishops; whatever their faults may be, they cannot be accused of frivolity or of not working for their living.
>
> (KCKP, UA/6/3/94)

This is a far cry from the words of the excoriator of casino capitalism who would later compare the activities of professional speculators with "a game of Snap, of Old Maid, of Musical Chairs" and whose perhaps most widely remembered passage would be the famous "beauty contest" metaphor for stock market speculation. Or is it? I want to argue that one can rationally reconstruct the development of the Keynes of uncertainty, gloom and the "dark forces of time and ignorance which envelop our future," the Keynes who appears in Chapter 12 of the *General Theory*, from the cocksure, inexperienced young philosopher lecturing about speculation he had never engaged in or witnessed at close hand, while still maintaining the framework of rationality and probability he had laid out in what Skidelsky (1983, p. 119) calls "the most important book in his life." Keynes's theory of probability was grounded in relevant knowledge. His own knowledge of speculation and his opinion of the amount of knowledge embodied in speculative activity, however, is something that changed dramatically over his career.

Consider the issue of speculation from his overall philosophical standpoint. In 1910 Keynes judged the risks undertaken by speculators to be subject to more or less calculable probability estimation by those who had the knowledge and skill to forecast prices.[8] Following Emery, he judged the "goodness" of their activity to consist in the beneficial functions of risk-bearing and directive influence. Moreover, he also agreed with Emery that this probable goodness of the speculators' activity led "on the whole" to the favorable functioning of the economic system – indeed it was an organic outgrowth of the form of commerce grown up in capitalism since the 1850s, a social organization about which Keynes had no doubts in 1910. Given that he also followed Emery in reporting the possibility of abuses by insiders – what Emery (1896, Chapter 5) called "the evils of speculation" – Keynes's estimate of the weight of evidence in favor of the above positive judgments must have been high. Or conversely, in 1910 Keynes evidently attached little weight to the proposition that the moral risk of speculative activity could lead to abuses that would outweigh its positive benefits.

From this perspective, Keynes's own theory of practical reason and probability in relation to conduct serves as a guide by which to chart the changes in his attitude toward speculation over the quarter century between his first optimistic writings on speculation and his eventual critique of it in the *General Theory*. We can expect that his confidence in the "goodness" of speculation on the whole might be upset either by a reevaluation of the basis in knowledge according to which speculators speculate; and/or an upward revision of his judgment of the moral risk attached to allowing speculation free rein. Keynes's later writings show evidence that he changed his mind on both of these issues.

II. The philosopher starts speculating, 1919–23

The 1920s mark a major period of change in Keynes's way of thinking and living. Robert Skidelsky (1992, p. 173) dates this change quite precisely in Volume 2 of his wonderful biography of Keynes when he comments:

> The years 1924 and 1925 were more obviously watershed years than 1923. He broke decisively with *laissez-faire*; by attacking the return to the gold standard, he burnt his boats with the Treasury and the Bank of England; and he married Lydia Lopokova. Events and the processes of his own thought radicalized him, so that he emerged the self-conscious champion of a new economic and political order.

In this section, we will try to chart one current of this sea change in Keynes's outlook by canvassing his radicalization with regard to the issue of speculation. Our story depends on the seemingly odd fact that Keynes became an intellectual radical at the same time that he was amassing a financial fortune through his own speculative activity. I thus want to weave the story his writings reveal with some evidence of his own experience as an investor. Adopting Skidelsky's dating, we divide up our analysis of the twenties into two sections, each corresponding to a basic change in Keynes's thinking and a change in his investment activity. The first period, extends from Keynes's return from the Paris peace talks to the publication of his *Tract on Monetary Reform* in 1923. It was during this period – in August of 1919 to be precise – that Keynes first began speculating on a large scale, on the foreign exchange market (Moggridge, 1992, p. 348). It was also in this period that he began to write professionally about speculation.

The foreign currency market is an exchange we have not seen discussed by any of the writers up to this point for the obvious reason that currency speculation was impossible under the pre-war fixed exchange rate system. Keynes, first with his partner Oswald T. ("Foxy") Falk, a colleague from the Treasury during the war, and then on his own, used his early understanding of the machinery of the forward market, what he thought of as his superior insight into the likely course of monetary policy and the exchanges, and the resources of friends and relatives, to take highly leveraged[9] speculative positions in the various European currencies, the dollar and the rupee. Early in 1920 he was short on marks, lire and francs and long on dollars. According to Skidelsky (1992, p. 41) this strategy was founded on the belief that "as British prices rose faster than American ones, sterling would go down against the dollar; whereas with the inflation rate in France, Germany and Italy higher than in Britain, sterling could be expected to appreciate against their currencies." But in late May, things went wrong. Francs, lire, and marks appreciated against sterling, exacerbating the effects of an already depreciating dollar. As Skidelsky (1993, p. 43) describes the situation: ". . . finally on 27 May Keynes was forced to liquidate his positions. He lost all his group's capital, and owed his broker nearly £5000. His debt – including his "moral debts" to his family and friends – came to just under £20,000."

After this date, Keynes rather quickly erased these debts by borrowing heavily and jumping back into the market and for the rest of the twenties he steadily accumulated wealth, not without setbacks, by further speculations in currency, commodities and stocks (*CW* 4, pp. 8–9). The main point is that Keynes's record in the twenties seems to place him closer to the "gamblers" than the "speculators" as he defined these in his 1910 notes. "The first thing that strikes one . . . is that he was not uniformly successful as an investor. In the 1920s, for example, in five of the seven years between 1922 and 1929 Keynes did *worse* than the *Bankers' Magazine* index"(Moggridge in *CW* 4, p. 9). It is important for our story that these early setbacks were reflected in a changing attitude toward speculation in his economic writings. He starts out the twenties mostly praising and defending currency speculation. But later, beginning in 1923, he began to doubt his own earlier characterization of speculators as necessarily superior forecasters or holders of privileged information. But this did not mean that Keynes came to see speculation in this period as an independent economic force, much less a social problem in need of remedy.

Keynes's confident attitude of the early twenties is reflected in his descriptions of both the currency exchanges, including the all-important forward market, and of the commodity exchanges. Keynes was one of the first monetary economists to write about the mechanism of forward exchange markets. In particular his analysis of the determinants of the forward-spot premium in the *Tract* are an instance of the Marshallian stock equilibrium approach to asset markets – here extended to "hot" short-term money chasing the highest return internationally in a fluctuating exchange world.[10] But while describing the "machinery" of the foreign exchanges, he was also defending speculation from the charges then being leveled against it by government officials and the press. In fact much of what he wrote was for the press[11] and it is to that literature that we now turn.

For the *Nation and Athenaeum* in 1923 Keynes wrote an article titled "The Foreign Exchanges and the Seasons" that is reflective of much of his writing at this time. Keynes opposes the usefulness of the purchasing power parity doctrine in explaining short-run exchange rate movements (*CW* 19, pp. 87–8). He suggests rather that the exchange rate is much more sensitive to "seasonal" trade demands imposed by worldwide commodity production and distribution and to the influence of "speculation." Because of the strong influence of speculative expectations "a country's exchange is more sensitive than its price level to what the world thinks is going to happen but has not happened yet." But the expectations of speculators are not independent of what actually happens. As Keynes now knew from painful experience, they cannot afford to run contrary to events for long:

> Speculators can only cause the exchange to rise or fall at an earlier date than it would have done otherwise. For they have to reverse their

transaction in due course, buying back or selling out as the case may be; so that, whether the thing which they anticipated has happened or not, their influence washes out sooner or later. Generally sooner rather than later, because the mass of speculators take short views and lose heart very quickly if there is any delay in what they had anticipated. . . Most people vastly exaggerate the effect of speculation on the course of the exchanges. . . It is only really important on the very rare occasions on which it precipitates a panic – that is to say, imitative action on a large scale by numbers of people who are not speculators at all, but just terror stricken.

(CW 19, pp. 87–8)

This sentiment also shows up in what was Keynes's most extensive foray into journalism, editing and partly writing the *Manchester Guardian Commercial*'s special "Reconstruction Supplements" in 1922. Much of the currency exchange discussion from these supplements eventually ended up in *A Tract on Monetary Reform*. I will treat extensively the monetary theory analysis of *A Tract on Monetary Reform* in Chapter 12 in a consideration of Keynes as a monetary theorist. Here we wish to trace only his ideas on speculation *per se*.

In the preface to the 1923 French edition of the *Tract*, we get a very clear and colorful view of Keynes defending currency speculation as he excoriates the French Minister of Finance's opinion concerning the "mysterious and malignant influences of speculation":

This is not far removed intellectually, from an African witch doctor's ascription of cattle disease to the "evil eye" of a bystander or bad weather to the unsatisfied appetites of an idol. In the first place, the volume of speculation, properly so called, is always extremely small in proportion to the volume of normal business. In the second place the successful speculator makes his profit by anticipating, not by modifying, existing economic tendencies. In the third place, most speculation, especially "bear" speculation, is for very short periods of time, so that the closing of the transaction soon exerts an influence equal and opposite to its initial effect.

(CW 4, pp. xvi–ii)

In the body of the *Tract*, as in Emery's treatment, speculative markets are viewed as a productive aspect of the modern commercial system. But now Keynes's eye is on the influence of rapid changes in money values on the overall activity level in this commercial system. "Whether one likes it or not, the technique of production under a regime of money contract forces the business world always to carry a big speculative position; and if it is reluctant to carry that position, the productive process must be slackened" (*CW* 4, p. 33). In the case of changes in the value of money, even Emery's specialized risk-bearing class cannot remove all of this risk. Thus the speculator, as Keynes emphasized in the preface just quoted, is not the cause of, though he also cannot prevent, the main social evil confronted in the *Tract*, volatility in the price level.

Another angle on speculation is found in the sole theoretical chapter, Chapter 3, "The Theory of Money and of Foreign Exchanges," where Keynes analyzes the role of forward markets in currency. His general theme is very Emery-like again, emphasizing the risk-bearing factor.[12] It is at this point that his equilibrium asset holding model, the stock equilibrium approach he had learned from Marshall, reappears. Speculators drive the premium or discount between the spot and forward rate to the point where "opinion" is balanced as to the "preferences of the money and exchange market for holding funds in one international center rather than another" (*CW* 4, p. 103).

It may happen that there is so much speculative activity on one side or the other of the market that the existing resources prepared to move money from one center to another are exhausted. This may temporarily drive the difference between spot and forward rates to a level "which represents an altogether abnormal profit to anyone who is in a position to buy these currencies forward and sell them spot." Only when enough new money is drawn into the exchanges will the normal relationship between spot and forward resume. Keynes contends, however, that these episodes reveal the sagacity of the market opinion in predicting future changes:

> . . . when the differences between forward and spot rates have become temporarily abnormal, thus indicating an exceptional pressure of speculative activity, the speculators have often turned out to be right.

He then repeats a claim made by Emery, who had gone to the trouble of using data on commodity prices to illustrate the stabilizing effect of speculation on prices. "When the type of professional speculation which makes use of the forward market is exceptionally active and united in its opinion, it has proved roughly correct, and has, therefore, been a useful factor in moderating the extreme fluctuations which would have occurred otherwise" (*CW* 4, p. 109). Thus in the *Tract* Keynes supports Emery's positive view of the "economic function of speculation," extending it to the foreign exchanges:

> Where risk is unavoidably present, it is much better that it should be carried by those who are qualified or are desirous to bear it, than by traders, who have neither the qualifications nor the desire to do so, and whose minds it distracts from their own business. The wide fluctuations in the leading exchanges over the past three years . . . have been due, not to the presence of speculation, but to the absence of a sufficient volume of it relative to trade.

> (*CW* 4, p. 113)

What then is new in Keynes's account in the early twenties? Two issues do begin to surface that presage his later views on speculation. First he begins to differentiate his analysis among the various speculative exchanges. Second he begins to rethink the philosophical basis of speculative expectations. Yet it is important to distinguish among the various exchanges when evaluating Keynes's developing views on speculation. In the remainder of the chapter I will argue that from mid-twenties onward Keynes focused on such doubts and criticisms as he held toward speculation almost entirely on stock market speculation. Moreover, this critique of stock market speculation, while it may have had some basis perhaps in his own experiences as a speculator, was also bound up with his changing views about the knowledge context appropriate to each market.

The beginning of his rethinking of this matter emerges in another of the *Manchester Guardian* articles, one that did not make it into the *Tract*. This article was published in 1923 under the title "Some Aspects of Commodity Markets." Here Keynes provides a lucid and concise discussion of the functioning of commodity markets and their rationale. Moreover, it is at this date that he first conducts a serious empirical analysis to complement his interests[13] in commodity markets. Annually, from 1923 to 1930, Keynes compiled his own data series from disparate industry and government sources into his memoranda on "Stocks of Staple Commodities" written for the London and Cambridge Economic Service (*CW* 12, pp. 267–647). Reading these memoranda is an important reminder of the depth of Keynes's knowledge of the details of the markets he was both engaged in and writing about.

It is no surprise to find that the theoretical treatment in the *Guardian* article is essentially that of Emery. The role of the exchange is to bear the risk of price fluctuations in standardized traded commodities (*CW* 12, pp. 259–62). But there arises here an interesting change from his 1910 discussion. Whereas in 1910 speculation was defined by "access to superior knowledge and forecasting ability," now Keynes appears to doubt this view – at least so far as commodity markets are concerned. He describes thus the standard view he now objects to:

> In most writing on this subject great stress is laid on the service performed by the professional speculator in bringing about a harmony between short-period and long-period demand and supply, through his action in stimulating or retarding *in good time* the one or the other.
>
> (*CW* 12, p. 260)

To this he objects:

> This may be the case, but it presumes that the speculator is better informed on the average than the producers and the consumers themselves, which

speaking generally, is a rather dubious proposition. The most important function of the speculator in the great organized "futures" markets is, I think, somewhat different. He is not so much a prophet (though it may be a belief in his own gifts of prophesy that tempts him into the business), as a *risk bearer*. If he happens to be a prophet also, he will become extremely, indeed preposterously, rich. But without any such pretensions, indeed without paying the slightest attention to the prospects of the commodity he deals in or giving a thought to it, he may, one decade with another earn substantial remuneration *merely* by running risks and allowing the results of one season to average with those of others; just as an insurance company[14] makes profits without pretending to know more about an individual's prospects of life or the chances of his house taking fire than he knows himself.

(*CW* 12, p. 261)

Notice the almost complete reversal here of his discussion of the distinction between gambling and speculation in the 1910 lecture notes. There gambling and speculation were different from each other and from insurance. In gambling the risks were either unknown or individual risks could not be "averaged" across instances (that is, they constituted uninsurable risk). Fire and life insurance, then, was a case of ascertainable average risk plus commission over the expected value. Speculation, though, Keynes had defined in 1910 as betting on price changes by reference to superior knowledge and ability. Now, in 1923, the speculator is no longer a prophet but just a functionary, depending on the law of averages and the fact that producers and sellers of commodities are willing to pay a risk premium for the security of sure future prices. Perhaps the shock of actually turning out to have been wrong with regard to some of his own market prophesies convinced Keynes that the activity was not one which would yield to superior intellectual ability. In any event, in the case of commodity markets specifically, this view never changed in Keynes's later writings, though he continued to be actively involved in these markets for the rest of his life – both as a trader and a reformer (see *CW* 12, Chapter 3; 21, pp. 456–70; 27, Chapter 3).

To summarize this section then, after the experience of the war had increased his confidence in his own financial judgment, and, crucially, introduced him to the world of City finance, Keynes became more deeply involved in speculation: as an investment advisor, financial journalist and policy analyst, and as a speculator on a large scale. His writings of this period, from 1919 to 1923, consist essentially in extending Emery to the analysis of foreign currency exchanges, and defending speculation from contemporary criticisms. He was still in all respects save one, less like the Keynes of the *General Theory* than was Marshall in his essay of 1899. The difference was Keynes's unique combination of practical experience of financial markets and his ability to weave insights from this experience into a philosophical analysis of the rationality of speculation. This gift would finally allow him to outpace his master by the end of the twenties, when he seriously turned his efforts toward economic theory.

III. Speculation and the credit cycle, 1923–30

Following our interest in Keynes's dual interests in the theory and practice of speculation into the period after 1923, but before the *General Theory*, immediately involves us in the issues of the credit cycle and the stock market. First, Keynes's own investment activity over the period 1923–30 was marked by what he called the "credit cycle" investment theory (see Skidelsky, 1992, pp. 24–7). It implied an active strategy later described by Keynes as "holding . . . shares in slumps and disposing of them in booms" (*CW* 12, p. 106). This policy is predicated upon an ability to predict the turning points of the slumps and the booms. In view of our premise that Keynes's investment activity, his policy concerns and his work in economics were often intertwined, it is not coincidental that this same period saw Keynes seriously grappling with the economic theory of the financial markets. His goal was to find an economic theory of the credit cycle which would illuminate the events of these turbulent years. The result, and our second reason for marking this period as distinct, was *A Treatise on Money* (*CW* 5 and 6). The *Treatise* can be seen, as Robert Skidelsky (1992, pp. 314–19) has argued, as Keynes's "summing up of the 1920s." This is particularly apt when we come to realize that the *Treatise*, like the Roaring Twenties, which ended in bust, was a deeply conflicted and contradictory experience.

To describe the role of speculation in Keynes's *Treatise on Money* is a complicated task, involving as it does the panoply of theoretical and applied arguments he put forward there to analyze the "credit cycle" and its relationship to monetary factors. The task is made even more difficult by the fact that the book seems to grow and transform itself as it goes along. Starting out firmly rooted in the quantity theory and the natural rate tradition, the *Treatise* ends up pointing in crucial ways toward the *General Theory*. I will situate the theoretical model of the credit-cycle and its contributions to Cambridge monetary theory in Chapter 12. Here I wish to make the case that the *Treatise* in many ways represents Keynes's most mature treatment of speculation, and in the all-important analysis of the actual operation of stock market speculation (as opposed to its macroeconomic implications) it loses little in comparison with Chapter 12 of the *General Theory*. Furthermore, it is from the *Treatise*, with its detailed treatment of the institutions of modern financial markets, that we get final confirmation of a theme we have been developing since our discussion of Emery concerning the differentiation among the various exchanges. For in the *Treatise*, Keynes separately analyzes the potential moral risks attached to the activities of commodity, currency and stock speculators.

The *Treatise* analysis is designed both to highlight the degree to which "monetary" phenomena exacerbate and amplify the credit cycle, conceived as a movement away from a theoretically "real" or "fundamental" equilibrium, and also to suggest policies by which the cycle could be controlled. An important aspect of this argument concerns the lack of a social mechanism for automatically (and in a short span of time) restoring the equality between saving and investment (linked in the *Treatise* to the benchmark full-employment, natural rate equilibrium). In fact, Keynes claims that cyclical changes in the production of capital goods are not only not offset by counterbalancing changes in the value of these goods, but that the reactions of prices and the financial system during the cycle actually exacerbate and prolong the disequilibrium.[15] With this in mind, it is not surprising that the treatment of speculation in the *Treatise* stresses the role speculation might or might not play in restoring the fundamental equilibrium once it has been upset by some real disturbance. We shall look at each exchange's role in this regard.

The *Treatise*: Speculation on the foreign and commodity exchanges

The role of the foreign exchanges is the easiest to approach. In the *Treatise* Keynes virtually repeats the analysis he put forward in the *Tract* as to the machinery of the forward market.[16] Now, however, the practical question is how any one country can achieve autonomy in managing its bank rate when the exchanges tend to enforce equalization of rates of return across countries. Again, as in the *Tract* discussion, Keynes suggests that the central banks themselves enter the forward exchanges to offset any temporary disturbances from abroad that might interfere with domestic policy. Furthermore, to give some latitude to the domestic monetary authorities, Keynes suggests maintaining as wide a gap in the "gold points" as is possible. This policy would downplay the sensitivity of the exchanges to expectations of return by introducing a degree of "doubt" to the speculators in short term "hot" money. Thus it seems fair to conclude that as of 1930 Keynes's earlier positive view of currency market speculation was still retained.

As for the commodity exchanges, there is also a large degree of overlap with the discussions of the early twenties. But now we begin to see the outlines of a "moral risk" argument along the lines of the *Treatise on Probability* analysis quoted above. The issue is clearly laid out as a matter of the goodness of the "organic whole." That is to say, whatever social function we know speculation to have in its own market must be set off against the probable effect this "micro" function will have on the total situation. A similarly structured argument is to be found in both the *Treatise* and the *General Theory* with regard to stock market speculation. It is only in the stock market case that Keynes judges speculation to have failed the test. Thus by 1930, while in many cases his views on speculation *per se* remained the same, it is the organic wholes themselves which are being reconstructed.

Commodity markets form an integral, if small, part of the analytical framework of the *Treatise*. They represent the financial institutions that perform the social function of carrying stocks of "liquid capital" over the course of the cycle. In analyzing the real side of the cycle, and the crucial determinants of the rate of investment, an important issue to Keynes is the possibility that commodity markets might provide a counterbalance to fluctuating production of these goods by accumulating buffering stocks carried over between boom and bust. This had played a large role in Hawtrey's (1919) analysis of the cycle (see Keynes's discussion in *CW 7*, pp. 116–31, especially pp. 117–18), and in the *Treatise* (p. 119).

Keynes claims that after studying the statistics – the same data we noted above that he had personally compiled for the London and Cambridge Economic Service on commodity stocks – he had come to believe that "the true surplus stocks of liquid capital, which at any time are existing, are too small to have any decisive influence on the replenishment of working capital" (*CW 7*, p. 119). The question then is to describe why the commodity exchanges, to which Emery and Hawtrey had ascribed a smoothing effect on consumption, and to which they and Keynes ascribed a "risk-bearing" function, could not hold sufficient carryover stocks during the bust to provide the means of easily re-igniting the succeeding boom.

In an interesting twist on the Emery argument, Keynes argues that because a volume of carryover large enough to provide the needed buffer represents such heavy "carrying costs,"[17] speculators would only be able to bear it if the price were brought down to such ruinous levels as to halt any further production. Notice that this does not indict commodity market speculation as such, it just dethrones it (in company with many financial markets in the *Treatise*) from a position as a social homeostatic device. Keynes's use of the risk-bearing argument to model the larger issue of the trade cycle demonstrates his ability to creatively combine both his deep knowledge of the empirical magnitudes and institutional facts of a situation with a slight tweak or rearrangement of existing theoretical tools, and in so doing to throw a dramatic new light on a practical economic issue. Thus here, he turns in on itself Emery's influential doctrine of the positive risk bearing function of commodity market speculation. It is just because the market can so accurately evaluate its own risk that it cannot perform an automatic equilibrating function for the economy as a whole:

The conclusion of this section may be summarized by saying that our present economic system abhors a stock of liquid goods. If such a stock comes into existence, strong forces are immediately brought into play to dissipate it. The efforts to get rid of surplus stocks aggravate the slump, and the success of these efforts retards the recovery.

(*CW* 6, p. 131)

One further important issue in this context concerns the form of analytical framework chosen. Keynes elaborates this analysis of the commodity markets in the *Treatise* by working out a formula for relating price fluctuations to carrying costs (pp. 125–7) and a "theory of the forward market" (pp. 127–9)." In all of this the modern reader is again reminded, just as in the case of the *Tract* discussion of the foreign exchanges, of the degree to which Keynes, in practically all of his financial market analysis, relied on the Marshallian stock equilibrium framework. Moreover, the fact that this theory seemed to him so plastic – a "metatheory" as we described it earlier – is reinforced by this material: he presented his foreign exchange market analysis proper, his and Hawtrey's arguments concerning stocks of liquid working capital, and his analysis of the bulls and bears on the stock exchange (to which we now turn), all in the same framework. And, looking forward, readers familiar with the *General Theory* analysis of the "Essential Properties of Interest and Money" will immediately notice that this framework, and the attention paid to the "costs of carrying" stocks of liquid goods, are both incorporated almost fully into that more abstract argument.

The *Treatise*: Speculation on the stock exchange

We are now left with the stock exchange, the final stage upon which Keynes's drama of speculation, enterprise and thrift is played out in the *Treatise* (and, later, to more applause, in the *General Theory*). It is worth emphasizing that in both the *Treatise* and the *General Theory* stock market speculation occupies center stage. In fact, a problem we encounter in describing the historical evolution of Keynes's ideas between the *Treatise* and the *General Theory* is that in almost every matter of *detail* (as distinct from the theoretical frameworks in which these details are embedded), save one, the treatments of stock market speculation are *identical* in both books. The historian is thus presented a twofold task: First, it seems important to highlight both the fact of, and the source of, Keynes's evident turn against stock market speculation around 1930. This is important as a historical corrective to the commonly held conception that Keynes invented the analysis in Chapter 12 of the *General Theory* out of whole cloth. In documenting the context of this aspect of the *Treatise* we are actually providing neglected background to the later work. But there is a second task to be confronted, namely the identification of what is novel in Keynes's use and description of stock market speculation in the *General Theory*. To address this question we will draw a final parallel between Keynes's early theory of practical reason and his later economics. In particular I will show that the issue revolves around the status accorded to the "knowledge" utilized by traders speculating on the stock market. To put it in more Marshallian terms, the difference between the *Treatise* and the *General Theory* reflects the altered status accorded to long-period normal values in each.

In the *Treatise*, organized stock market speculation plays a major role in the origin and dynamics of crises, or movements away from savings-investment equilibrium (see Horwich 1964, pp. 416–26 and Leijonhufvud, 1981). Keynes clearly recognized by this time[18] that the day-to-day value ascribed to equities by the price fixed on the exchanges may bear little relation to the fundamental income earning potential of a corporation (*CW* 6, pp. 322–4). Instead he describes these values as a matter of public sentiment concerning the form in which to hold wealth – either securities or "idle balances." Since both are fixed in total quantity over the short run by the volume of existing bank deposits and the outstanding "old shares" traded on the stock exchange, the rate of interest and stock prices adjust to allocate these existing stocks in such a way as to satisfy the portfolio preferences of the marginal bulls and bears (*CW* 5, pp. 127–31). "Thus the actual level of security prices is . . . the resultant of the degree of bullishness of opinion and the behavior of the banking system" (*CW* 5, pp. 224).

The theoretical role of this view of stock market speculation in the *Treatise* is embedded in a complex version of the quantity theory, whereby changes in stock market activity interact with the rate of interest and the price level via changes in "industrial and financial circulation" (Keynes's breakdown of the stock of money) over the cycle.[19] But although speculators may alter the interest rate (or conversely alter security prices) temporarily, and so cause saving and investment to diverge, they cannot do so indefinitely. Each stage of the cycle has a built-in corrective in the *Treatise*:

> . . . as soon as the price of securities has risen high enough, relatively to the short-term rate of interest, to occasion a difference of opinion as to the prospects, a "bear" position will develop, and some people will begin to increase their savings deposits . . . Thus in proportion *as the prevailing opinion comes to seem unreasonable to more cautious people*, the "other view" will tend to develop, with the result of an increase in the bear position.
>
> (*CW* 5, p. 229, emphasis added)

Note the fact that in the *Treatise* there is thus a "reasonable" basis for the opinions of speculators. This is because in the *Treatise*, as opposed to the *General Theory*, there is always a long-period fundamental value for securities:

> In the long-run the value of securities is entirely derivative from the value of consumption goods. It depends on the expectation as to the value of the amount of liquid consumption goods which the securities will,

directly or indirectly, yield, modified by reference to the risk and uncertainty of this expectation.

(CW 5, p. 230)

It is for this reason that Keynes is largely unconcerned in the *Treatise* with the level of security prices *per se*. Speculation on the exchanges is only of concern in so far as it causes swings in the amount of money needed to satisfy the financial circulation; such swings may leave an insufficient amount of money to satisfy the industrial circulation. This of course is the mechanism in the *Treatise* by which speculation might "stimulate new investment to outrun savings, or contrariwise" (*CW* V, p. 230). From this view follows his fairly mild (by comparison with the *General Theory*) policy evaluation:

> I should say, therefore, that a currency authority has no *direct* concern with the level of value of existing securities, as determined by opinion . . . The main criterion for interference with a "bull" or "bear" financial market should be, that is to say, the probable reactions of this financial situation on the prospective equilibrium between saving and *new* investment.
>
> (CW 5, p. 230)

In the *Treatise*, then, speculation on the stock exchange might possibly influence economic activity. If the speculators, because of their reliance on non-fundamental short-run psychological motives, line up on the "wrong-side" of the two views during a transition to a new higher or lower "real" rate of interest, they can exacerbate the "credit cycle." As of 1930 Keynes had not yet extended this market externality to the long period. He does, however, seem to have felt some degree of tension in his position, with respect to the underlying philosophical presuppositions regarding the rationality of such speculative activity. Toward the end of the *Treatise* we find him explicitly addressing this issue:

> How far the motives which I have been attributing above to the market are strictly rational, I leave it to others to judge.[20] They are best regarded, I think, as an example of how sensitive – over-sensitive if you like – to the near future, about which we may think that we know a little, even the best informed must be, because, *in truth, we know almost nothing about the more remote future*.
>
> (CW 6, p. 322, emphasis added)

The puzzle is how we are to reconcile this statement with the argument above that speculators' activities will inevitably and quickly draw prices toward long-run fundamental values. For if "in truth, we know almost nothing about the more remote future," how can we ever know the "long-run . . . value of securities . . . [which is] entirely derivative from the value of consumption goods"? One answer to this question is yielded by a close comparison of the *Treatise* with the *General Theory* on the subject of stock prices. For many of the elements of what has come to be referred to as the Keynesian theory of stock prices – a view which is conventionally attributed to the analysis of "long-term expectations" in Chapter 12 of the *General Theory* – received almost identical treatment in the *Treatise*. Thus one way to bridge this crucial period of transition in Keynes's thought is to identify what the two books have in common. This will help us to isolate what *is* new in the *General Theory* with respect to speculation.

The following is a comparison of quotations from the *Treatise* and the *General Theory* in respect of stock market valuations:

T: The value of a company's shares, and even its bonds, will be found to be sensitive to a degree, which a rational observer from outside might consider quite absurd, to short period fluctuations in its known or anticipated profits. (*CW* 6, p. 322)	*GT*: Day-to-day fluctuations in the profits of existing investments, which are obviously of an ephemeral and non-significant character, tend to have an altogether excessive, and even an absurd, influence on the market. (*GT*, pp. 153–4)
T: . . . it must be well known to anyone who follows the prices of ordinary shares that their market valuation shows a strong bias toward the assumption that whatever conditions and results have been characteristic of the present and the recent past, and even more those which are expected to be characteristic of the near future, will be lasting and permanent. (*CW* 6, p. 323)	*GT*: In practice we have tacitly agreed, as a rule, to fall back on what is, in truth, a convention. The essence of this convention – though it does not, of course, work out quite so simply – lies in assuming that the existing state of affairs will continue indefinitely, except in so far as we have specific reasons to expect a change. (*GT*, p. 152)
T: But if this is true of the best informed the vast majority of those who are concerned with the buying and selling of securities know almost nothing whatever about what they are doing. They do not possess even the rudiments of what is required for a valid judgement, and they are the prey of hopes and fears easily aroused by transient	*GT*: As a result of the gradual increase in the proportion of the equity in the community's aggregate capital investment which is owned by persons who do not manage and have no special knowledge of the circumstances, either actual or prospective, of the business in question, the element of real knowledge in the valuation of investments by

events and as easily dispelled. (*CW* 6, p. 323)

T: For the value of a security is determined, not by the terms on which one could expect to purchase the whole block of the outstanding interest, but by the small fringe which is the subject of actual dealing Now this fringe is largely dealt in by professional financiers – speculators you may call them – who have no intention of holding the securities long enough for the influence of distant events to have its effect; their object is to re-sell to the mob after a few weeks or at most a few months. . . thus so long as the crowd can be relied upon to act in a certain way, even if it might be misguided, it will be the advantage of the professional to act in the same way – a short period ahead. (*CW* 6, pp. 323–4)

T: Apart, moreover, from calculations of greater or lesser ignorance, most people are too timid and too greedy, too impatient and too nervous about their investments, the fluctuations in the paper value of which can so easily obliterate the results of so much honest effort, to take long views or to place even as much reliance as they reasonably might on the dubieties of the long period; the apparent certainties of the short period, however deceptive we may suspect them to be, are much more attractive. (*CW* 6, p. 324)

those who own them or contemplate purchasing them has seriously declined. (*GT*, p. 153)

GT: It might have been supposed that competition between expert professionals, possessing judgement and knowledge beyond that of the average private investor, would correct the vagaries of the ignorant individuals left to himself. If happens, however, that the energies and skill of the professional investor and speculator are mainly occupied otherwise . . . They are concerned, not with what an investment is really worth to a man who buys it "for keeps," but with what the market will value it at, under the influence of mass psychology, three months or a year hence. Moreover, this behaviour is not the outcome of a wrong-headed propensity. It is an inevitable result of an investment market organized along the lines described. (*GT*, pp. 154–5)

GT: Moreover, life is not long enough; human nature desires quick results, there is a peculiar zest in making money quickly, and remoter gains are discounted by the average man at a very high rate. The game of professional investment is intolerably boring and overexacting to anyone who is entirely exempt from the gambling instinct; whilst he who has it must pay to this propensity the appropriate toll. (*GT*, p. 157)

Taking this evident similarity of the analysis of how stock prices are determined as given, Keynes clearly had developed most aspects of his mature treatment of speculation and financial market processes by the end of the *Treatise*. But, as he wrote to his mother in 1930, it was an analysis that did not hang together well: "Artistically it is a failure – I have changed my mind too much during the course of it for it to be a proper unity" (*CW* 13, p. 176). On the one hand he had painted a picture of a financially dependent system in flux, where cyclical movements away from fundamental "real" equilibria were more than just passing inconveniences. Speculation on the exchanges – particularly the stock exchange – could exacerbate these cyclical movements. Nevertheless, there remained at the core of the natural rate analysis powerful attractive tendencies pulling the economy back toward long period equilibrium. In the second volume of the *Treatise*, dealing with applied and historical analysis, however, what had been asides about speculation on the stock exchange in the more theoretical passages of the first volume grew into a philosophical disquisition on the fundamentally uncertain knowledge context of investors' and speculators' activities.

Thus, by the end of the book, there coexisted in an uneasy juxtaposition a classical Marshallian view alongside a Marshallian–Keynesian view. The Marshallian–Keynesian view was a unique blend of Emery's workmanlike role for speculators and Marshall's optimizing investors equalizing expected returns in a sophisticated stock equilibrium setting. But the larger classical framework in which this was set, the most sophisticated and complex financial market analysis of Keynes's career, conflicted with what he saw, on a different plane of reasoning, as the peculiar rationality of modern financial market practices. In the *Treatise*, then, we might say that Keynes, more firmly in grasp of the actual reality of financial markets than Marshall, and less timid about the possible evils of speculation than Emery, provided a theoretical rationale for Marshall's concerns about the Folly of Amateur Speculators in 1899. What was left for the *General Theory* to add?

IV. Conclusion: "Faithful" investing and speculative economics, 1931–36

What was the larger theoretical role for speculation in the *General Theory*? It will be left to Part III to provide much of this answer. But given the stress I have placed on the similarity of Keynes's analysis of asset markets in the *Treatise* with that in the *General Theory* I should end by noting some of the differences encountered in the latter work. In keeping with the story to this point I shall note both a change in Keynes's personal investment activity and a change in his view of the knowledge context of speculation. More important than these, though, is the "general theory" itself. Now he had a theoretical framework, an economic system, which combined with his philosophical speculations about asset markets to form a proper theoretical – and artistic – unity.

Keynes's own investment experience in the turbulent markets of the late twenties and early thirties is instructive more for his turn in philosophy than any spectacular personal crisis. Unlike Irving Fisher for instance, Keynes did not lose everything in the Crash of '29. In fact, he had very little *to* lose, his portfolio of U.S. securities being very slim at the time.[21] But he did lose substantially during the late twenties, on some speculative commodity transactions which, being carried on borrowed money, forced him to liquidate some of his shares in the City during a bear market. This, plus the declining value of what he had left (mostly shares in the Austin Motor Company) meant that his net worth went from £44,000 in 1927 to £7,815 in 1929. Events of precisely this sort were reflected in the *Treatise*. Perhaps the crash in 1929 also caused him to reevaluate his investment strategy. In any case, by 1930, he had come to regret the whole project of attempting to time the market according to the credit cycle theory and had begun a policy he variously referred to as "duty" and "faithfulness." To use his *General Theory* terminology, in his own stock market investments, Keynes turned from "speculation" to "enterprise". Clearly, he meant this as more than just a slogan, though, and began a new policy of investing to hold based on long-term prospects. Moggridge (*CW* 12, pp. 9, 16–17), for instance, offers evidence of the extreme concentration this led to in his portfolio. Often half of his holdings were constituted by three or four issues.[22]

There is much evidence on the reasons for this change in strategy in his internal investment writings of the period. To investing partners, his life insurance colleagues and his fellow bursars at Cambridge, he repeatedly urged this as both the most responsible and the most profitable policy. In a 1938 memorandum for the Estates Committee of King's College, titled "Post Mortem on Investment Policy" he recounts the experience of the last 20 years since he had "first persuaded the College to invest in ordinary shares" (*CW* 12, p. 106). Regretting his earlier mistaken belief in the "credit cycle policy," he explains:

> As the result of these experiences I am clear that the idea of wholesale shifts is for various reasons impracticable and indeed undesirable. Most of those who attempt it sell too late and buy too late, and do both too often, incurring heavy expenses and developing too unsettled and speculative a state of mind, which if it is widespread, has besides the grave social disadvantage of aggravating the scale of the fluctuations."
>
> (*CW* 12, 106)

He then goes on to report the three principles upon which he now thinks successful investment depends. It is worth quoting these whole as they so accurately describe the policy he in fact followed from at least 1930:[23]

(1) a careful selection of a few investments (or a few types of investment) having regard to their cheapness in relation to their probable actual and potential *intrinsic* value over a period of years ahead and in relation to alternative investments at the time;

(2) a steadfast holding of these in fairly large units through thick and thin, perhaps for several years, until either they have fulfilled their promise or it is evident that they were purchased on a mistake;

(3) a *balanced* investment position, i.e. a variety of risks in spite of individual holdings being large, and if possible opposed risks (e.g. a holding of gold shares amongst other equities, since they are likely to move in opposite directions when there are general fluctuations).

The corresponding ideas in the *General Theory* are immediately apparent. What *was* different about the discussion of the stock market in Chapter 12 of the *General Theory*, compared to the analysis in the *Treatise*, was a clear change in policy stance toward speculation. In the *General Theory* Keynes no longer saw the central bank as capable of offsetting the influence of speculation in all instances and went so far as to propose increased transactions costs to make frequent speculative purchases more difficult. "The introduction of a substantial government transfer tax on all transactions might prove the most serviceable reform available, with a view to mitigating the predominance of speculation over enterprise in the United States" (*CW* 12, 160).

But why did Keynes come to suspect the influence of stock market speculation in the *General Theory*? The answer concerns the possible dramatic effect he suspected speculation could have on real investment in new capital goods, both through the yield that such investments would be expected to earn in times of high liquidity premiums and through the collapse of the prospective yields to new projects, due primarily to a collapse of investor confidence. Since investment drove output and employment in the *General Theory* any inhibition of investment was necessarily a social evil. But the link between stock market speculation, confidence and the level of investment was not one which Keynes made very clear. It required an inclusive and generous reading of the *General Theory* to keep the necessary parts of the argument together. And one hole in the argument is never actually filled: How exactly do stock prices for particular firms influence those firms' demand for new investment? Nevertheless, let us reconstruct the argument as it stands.

First, this macro argument for the importance of stock market prices and confidence in determining investment had to come to grips with the strong *attractive* and *equilibrating* tendencies Keynes had ascribed to fundamentals in the *Treatise*. In the *General Theory* this purpose was served by his analysis of the Marginal Efficiency of Capital. Like the economic function of stock markets, this too had its outwardly rationalistic appearance in the form of the simple Fisherian discounting formula that reduced the complexity of the investment decision to a single value to be compared with the current rate of interest. Yet it is emphasized time and again in the *General Theory* that the prospective yield that goes into this formula is *not* an easily ascertainable quantity. It is, in fact, in investigating the basis of prospective yield that Keynes is led to his philosophical disquisition on stock prices, confidence and long-term expectations just reviewed. In sum, in his "psychologizing" of the basis of the prospective yield in Chapter 12 (and in those post-*General Theory* essays we started with above) Keynes stressed that these expectations are based precariously on little current knowledge, that they are not readily checked by experience and that the marginal efficiency of capital is therefore subject to wide swings connected to changes in the confidence with which estimates of it are held. In the *General Theory*, there is no natural rate, no long-term value to which this psychological value is returned, as there was in the *Treatise*. Thus in the *General Theory* (*GT*, pp. 48–9) Keynes defines the "long-period" level of employment as the level of employment that would result from the continuation of a state of expectations for a period long enough so that all current investment is based on one unchanging set of expectations. It is not that he expects a state of long-term expectations ever to actually last for such a period, but he is replacing the similarly fictional concept of the Marshallian long period with one based upon a given psychological state among investors.

His application of this theory to the evaluation of the potential adverse social impact of speculation, however, revealed a deeper complexity to the role of speculation than is at first apparent. As mentioned, this new theory plus the post '29 experience of the U.S., gave Keynes reason to reevaluate his estimate of the offsetting moral risk involved in interfering with the normal functioning of the modern stock-exchange equipped investment process. As always, his critique emphasized the fault of the system, not the speculators, who were after all just operating by the rules of the game. But the rules were themselves the result of organic social evolution, as Emery had emphasized, and it is clear in the *General Theory* that they are not easily manipulated. Thus the final complexity of Keynes's view rests with the intricate and delicate relationship he sensed exists between the normal functioning of speculative markets and the tone this functioning gives to investor confidence and expectations. This is why he could not provide a functional form for the influence of speculation. For example, after further considering the stock market as an organic social whole, he is forced to backtrack, and notes that it may not be possible to constrain speculation without undermining the liquidity it is the markets' social function to provide. Thus his advice to impose transactions costs on exchange trades ran up against a dilemma:

... the liquidity of investment markets often facilitates, though it sometimes impedes, the course of new investment. For the fact that each individual investor flatters himself that his commitment is "liquid" (though this cannot be true for all investors collectively) calms his nerves and makes him much more willing to run a risk. If individual purchases of investments were rendered illiquid, this might seriously impede new investment, so long as *alternative ways* in which to hold his savings are available to the individual. This is the dilemma.

(*CW* 7, pp. 160)

It was a supreme fault of such a system that it so craved liquidity that it left itself open to extremes of instability. This is why Keynes was so pessimistic about the prospects of a purely financial policy toward slump in the *General Theory* (*CW* 7, pp. 164).

Keynes's remarks upon the importance he attached to his psychological analysis of financial market processes after the *General Theory* should thus be taken seriously. Market psychology was integral to the *General Theory*, just as it was alien to the *Treatise*. The description of stock market trading is very similar in the two books. Yet the recognition in the *General Theory* of speculation's potential social impact, and the acknowledgment that its philosophical basis in knowledge is more tenuous, makes that work unique. It should now be apparent, however, that the development of this aspect of Keynes's thought had a long history prior to the *General Theory*.

Part III "Shifting Equilibria" in a Monetary Economy

In my opinion the main reason why the problem of crises is unsolved, or at any rate why this theory is so unsatisfactory, is to be found in the lack of what might be termed a monetary theory of production.

The distinction which is normally made between a barter economy and a monetary economy depends upon the employment of money as a convenient means of effecting exchanges – as an instrument of great convenience, but transitory and neutral in its effect . . .

That, however, is not the distinction which I have in mind when I say we lack a monetary theory of production. An economy, which uses money but uses it merely as a link between transactions in real things and real assets and does not allow it to enter into motives or decisions, might be called – for want of a better name – a real exchange economy. The theory which I desiderate would deal, in contradistinction to this, with an economy in which money plays a part of its own and affects motives and decisions and is, in short, one of the operative factors in the situation, so that the course of events cannot be predicted, either in the long period or in the short, without knowledge of the behavior of money between the first and last. And this is what we ought to mean when we speak of a monetary economy.

J. M. Keynes (1933)

11
The Development of Cambridge Monetary Thought 1870–1935

> . . . it is bound to remain to me a source of some bewilder-
> ment that at some time in the period following 1930 the
> idea that monetary analysis (whether conducted in terms
> of V or K or S and I) is concerned with the behaviour of
> output as well as of prices should have apparently struck
> Keynes, or at any rate the able little group who were then
> advising him, with the forces of a new discovery.
>
> Robertson (1926 [1949])

I. Introduction

It would be extremely misleading to suggest that no economists before
Keynes had considered the issues surrounding the demand for money; its
relation to speculation; the interest rate and employment; and the savings
and investment nexus that are now considered part and parcel of his, and
all, macroeconomics. In fact not only was economics in general rife with
such discussions in the first three decades of the twentieth century (Haberler,
1937; Saulnier, 1938; Laidler, 1991, 1999), but contributions from Cambridge
economists were an important part of this debate, (Robertson, 1940; Eshag,
1963; Shackle, 1967, Patinkin, 1976, 1982; Presley, 1979; Leijonhufvud,
1981; Bridel, 1987). Moreover both of these literatures have been well
documented.[1]

The general agreement across the different studies of this period is that the
issues of interest to monetary economists from Marshall onward, but
increasingly in the interwar years, formed the material out of which the
General Theory issued. A partial list of topics treated there would include: the
proper conceptualization of monetary economics as a part of value theory,
the role of the quantity theory of money, the integration of monetary and
real economics, the evaluation of monetary policy, the documentation and
theory of the trade cycle, forced savings, the determination in monetary
economies of savings and investment behavior, and the always closely

connected treatment of the demand and supply of "free capital" (Marshall's term), or of "loanable funds"[2] (the term used by many later economists). This is a long list, and it still neglects international topics. In what follows I will take the existence of this documentation as given. All historians should now agree that the potted history according to which Keynes invented out of whole cloth in 1936 a theory of interest, employment and money which had no precursors among his "classical predecessors" was, as Laidler has perhaps most forcefully argued, a myth.

Of course that has been one of our points of departure throughout the book thus far. This does not mean, however, that all is settled. In fact, room is thereby opened up for a variety of historical narratives. One such perspective is a brief and seemingly non-judgmental account of Cambridge monetary thought, *From Marshall to Keynes* (Eshag, 1963). In another, Presley (1979) provides us with a useful account of the economics of Dennis Holme Robertson and his close interaction with Keynes. Another asks the question of what happened to this literature in the context of the creation of postwar macroeconomics (Laidler's 1999 story of the creation of IS/LM analysis). Yet another is driven by Don Patinkin's search – on his own account unsuccessful – for predecessors to his own "real-balance" interpretation of Keynesian macroeconomics (Patinkin, 1976, 1982). Finally, Bridel (1987) uses this literature to argue that the central, but insufficiently argued, insight of Keynes in 1936 was the principle of effective demand (that output adjusts to imbalances between savings and investment). By this "Neo Ricardian" argument, Keynes's avowedly short-period liquidity preference theory of interest – what Keynes thought actually determined interest instead of savings and investment – should be thrown out because effective demand can only properly be grounded in Sraffa's (1960) long-period classical setting.

All of these perspectives contain as elements of their broader themes investigations into the wealth of literature on monetary economics and the business cycle from the first three decades of the twentieth century. We will find this literature useful for our own purpose: to trace the development of those ideas which specifically moved Keynes toward his position of 1936. It is useful at this point to restate from Chapter 1 our view of what that position was. What was new or revolutionary in Keynes's argument of 1936 was his claim that modern competitive systems, naturally and without policy intervention, need not – note I do not say could not or will not – equilibrate at full employment.

Part I treated the development of views on the operation of labor markets from Marshall to the *General Theory*, with an emphasis on English (and especially, Cambridge) economics. We argued that it is crucial to understand the details of how Keynes's entire conception of economics was conceived in Marshallian terms in his formative stages as an economist. In the context of labor markets, however, we saw there were at least two routes taken out of

Marshall's work, those of Dobb and Pigou. Interestingly, as an aside, only through Pigou – not Dobb and Keynes – were we able to find antecedents to modern "New Keynesian" economists' emphasis on microfounded sticky wage explanations of unemployment. We traced the development of Keynes's personal view of the labor market in this context. We saw him outgrow a juvenile dependence on Marshall's *Principles of Economics* and suggested the influence of Dobb's more explicitly "indeterminate" characterization of Marshallian labor market analysis in the 1920s. We then traced Keynes's own development of a specific application of this way of looking at labor markets, as unemployment rose and persisted into the thirties: described there as Keynes's "social justice view." As opposed to both the then current work of Pigou on unemployment, and the modern economic tradition that views unemployment as explained by sticky wages, we argued that Keynes wrote the *General Theory* as an alternative monetary explanation that would fill the void he felt was left by the inability of a rigid-wage argument to explain the mass unemployment then occurring.

Part II then returned to the Victorian age and followed the evolution of Keynes's understanding of money, asset markets and speculation, again culminating in the *General Theory*. We saw that Keynes began his academic career almost slavishly dependent on Marshall. But even then, and growing with his personal investment experience, he brought the subtle reasoning of his philosophy of probability – and its emphasis on the rational basis of action (or not) in knowledge – to bear on the analysis of speculation. Additionally, we saw his ever-present dependence on Marshall's stock theory of the demand for money throughout this development.

Finally we have now reached Part III, which will examine Keynes's most developed commentary on the essential properties of interest and money, and its antecedents in interwar business cycle theory. We will be more concerned in this part of the book with the text of the *General Theory*. In the process we also will offer an alternative framework for capturing a complete picture of the theoretical development that ended in the *General Theory*: a general analysis of how employment and output interact with money, interest and speculation. By "alternative," I mean an alternative to the more conventional method of expressing Keynes's message in the *General Theory* that was adopted by the mainstream of the economics profession in the postwar era: the IS/LM model.

Thus in Part III we are using the record of the history of business cycle theory referred to above, but very selectively as is required by our purpose. Two books from that literature that most relate to our argument should be mentioned at the outset. One is the account by Shackle (1967) of Keynes's development of the *General Theory* from the *Treatise on Money*. His emphasis on the monetary character of Keynes's view of underemployment equilibria is particularly close to our own. We will support its stress upon the liquidity preference theory of interest in what follows. We will reject, though,

Shackle's reliance on the Swedish *ex ante-ex post* method. The other is Leijonhufvud's "Wicksell Connection" (1981), an extremely useful characterization of a common framework for savings-investment analysis that he suggests dominated discussion of macroeconomic coordination problems in the 1920s and 1930s. We will have much more to say about these topics in future chapters. We will argue, however, that Leijonjufvud's negative account of how the *General Theory* fits into this framework needs correction. First we begin in the rest of this chapter to establish some further elements of contact between Keynes and the general monetary and business cycle literature of the early decades of the twentieth century.

II. Early twentieth century monetary and business cycle theory

Different authors stressing different aspects of this record may irritate readers looking for "the" story of this period. That circumstance is the nature of complex historical narrative, though, not even considering the influence of contemporary tastes in macroeconomics. What I think can be agreed upon by all of the scholars noted above, or so I will assume in this section, is the following. Marshall left a legacy of many unanswered or underdeveloped, but still pregnant, monetary and business cycle questions. His pupils and immediate successors, the "Cambridge" economists of the era from 1910 to 1936 (most prominently Pigou, Robertson, Lavington, Hawtrey and the earlier Keynes), took these hints as the starting point for their own contributions to monetary theory. In so doing they vastly extended Marshall's insights. In particular the theory of asset demand in the context of balancing preferences at the margin of asset portfolios – already highlighted above – seemed to have been known to each of these economists, and was developed by them in different ways. Likewise, they were each interested in the question of business cycles, or what they termed "the credit cycle."

Starting from Marshall's elaboration of Mill, each saw this as asking how the monetary system caused the economy to deviate from the long period positions that had been the subject of Marshall's *Principles* (though the early Robertson is an outlier here). Moreover, starting from where Marshall left this question, Robertson, Hawtrey and Keynes developed explanations of the cycle which involved the potential for savings to diverge from investment. In the course of this investigation they independently recognized the possibility of the occurrence of "forced" savings, or the potential of the monetary system to redistribute income from consumers to producers. This could encourage "overproduction" of capital goods during a boom, which, if it proved to be unsustainable, could lead to an "overinvestment" crisis and the downward phase of the business cycle.

Also broadly agreed upon is the existence of a Wicksellian influence on Cambridge in the form of the fashioning of cycle theory around divergences between the "market" and "real" rates of interest. This distinction plays a role in, at least, the *method* of the argument over the "credit-cycle" among Cambridge economists. For instance, Wicksell authored an English language paper in the *Economic Journal* of 1907 (before Keynes's assumption of the editorship of that publication in 1911) titled "The Influence of the Rate of Interest on Prices." Additionally a Wicksellian style of reasoning was self-consciously adopted by Keynes in his *Treatise on Money*. Robertson also took this stance in his *Economic Journal* article of 1934, "Industrial Fluctuation and the Natural Rate of Interest." Thus there are ample grounds for supporting a Wicksellian influence on Cambridge in this period.

Yet there are also reasons to doubt Cambridge's full familiarity with, much less endorsement of, Wicksell. One is the late date (1936) at which Richard Kahn translated Wicksell's *Interest and Prices*. The other is the well-argued point of both Bridel (1987, Chapter 3) and Laidler (1991, Chapter 3, 1999, Chapter 4) that Marshall's theories of investment, of interest and of the cycle aleady relied upon something like Wicksell's cumulative process. Nevertheless, if we follow Leijonhufvud (1981) in thinking of the "Wicksell Connection" as an analytic category rather that as a strict historical dependence on Wicksell's writings – one whereby crises are centered around the analysis of the savings–investment nexus, and the potential failure to smoothly equilibrate after a change in the profitability of new investment – then this scenario no doubt captures much of what went on in Cambridge, as well as in Austria, Sweden and the United States, before the *General Theory*. Again this seems now to be generally accepted.

Shifting to more contentious – but I think broadly agreed upon – ground, consider the question of the influence from the rest of the world on Cambridge and so on Keynes. Explained either as a consequence of the then limited availability of translated foreign literature, or as a consequence of the ingrained insularity of the Cambridge school, their conduct of this debate often ignored certain Scandinavian, Austrian and American developments. One consequence that has been treated extensively below is the clash of Cambridge and the Austrians. Thus the arrival of Austrian theory in Britain, in the person of Hayek in the 1930s, though it broke no new ground in the doctrine of forced savings (which was already well known to Pigou, Keynes, Robertson and Hawtrey), did legitimately seem strangely couched to a Cambridge audience. For one, it relied on what seemed an esoteric Bohm-Bawerkian capital theory – a theory that was eventually shown to English-speaking audience to contain great faults[3] – and on a very formal assumption of full employment, compared with the more realistic Cambridge account. It also was partly Walrasian in origin and micro-founded, both in ways that would naturally be seen as alien by Marshall and his followers. This might explain some of the mutual mistrust and misunderstandings of Hayek and the Cambridge school in the 1930s, analyzed in the coming chapters. But, we will argue that the important substantive elements of disagreement between the parties lay deeper than such misunderstandings. It should also be mentioned in this context that institutional rivalry between Cambridge and the London School of Economics, as well as strong ideological differences over the slump and depression between these two influential poles of British social thought, should not be forgotten (see Caldwell, 2003 and Hoover, 2003).

Then there is the role of Swedish economists and their alternative conception of the natural rate, identified in the literature as the Stockholm School. Laidler (1999, Chapter 3) is very good on laying out their contributions and their particular interpretation of Wicksell. He properly stresses that their method, more than any particular theory, is the important element of the School's legacy for macroeconomics. Two particular methodological strains of their work are the emphasis on carefully analyzing the stages of the dynamic process of disequilibrium between savings and investment that ensue in many otherwise divergent accounts of the cycle, and the related, but seemingly alternative, treatment of quantities based on *ex ante* expectations versus the *ex post* settlement by which markets or the economic system may reconcile these expectations. The first methodological precept is what lead to Hicks's "temporary equilibrium" approach in *Value and Capital* (1939), and so is beyond our consideration. But the *ex ante-ex post* method was urged upon Keynes by Bertil Ohlin during the writing of the *General Theory* and figured prominently enough in the immediate postpublication criticism of that book (which we will treat below) that Keynes felt compelled to respond (Keynes, 1937). Moreover, Shackle (1967) makes much of the view that only through this method can the monetary interpretation of the *General Theory* be properly presented. This point was opposed in Chapter 2 both by reference to Keynes's own view and on analytic grounds.[4]

III. Specific Marshallian monetary antecedents

As we have done with the first two parts of the book, we should briefly review the Marshallian thought on the subject of this part of the book, to set the stage for what follows. Eshag (1963), Bridel (1987) and Laidler (1991 and 1999) have covered this ground well, so we are afforded the luxury of relying on the record they present to suggest our interpretation.[5] As above, there is again the issue of Marshall's seeming reticence to present his views on money and the business cycle to a full public viewing until age had reduced his ability to do so. And again, his earlier work from the 1870s and 1880s – often unpublished but circulated to colleagues in Cambridge – is actually the best source of his views. His eventual publication of *Money, Credit and Commerce* (1923) was, as has already been referred to, a belated and abortive repetition of these fragments.

Earlier, we have treated his paper on the demand for money from the 1870s and his various treatments of speculative markets. To complete the picture we need to briefly explore his analyses of the interaction of this demand with the supply of money, his theory of the determination of the interest rate and his views on the business cycle.

It was originally Marshall's plan that he would extensively treat business cycles in a separate treatise along the lines of the coverage of 'normal value' in the *Principles*. In fact he refers to this issue implicitly at the end of that book, in his famous last chapter on "Progress in Relation to Standards of Life" (Marshall, 1962, p. 601) where he says:

> And now we must conclude this part of our study. We have reached very few practical conclusions; because it is generally necessary to look at the whole of the economic, to say nothing of the moral and other aspects of a practical problem before attempting to deal with it at all: and in real life nearly every economic issue depends, more or less directly, on some complex actions and reactions of credit, of foreign trade, and of the modern developments of combination and monopoly. But the ground which we have traversed in Book V ["General Relations of Demand Supply and Value," containing his crucial short to long period analyses] and VI ["The Distribution of the National Income," containing his discussion of wages, rent, quasi-rent, interest and profit] is, in some respects, the most difficult of the whole province of economics; and it commands, and gives access to, the remainder.

This should alert us to the fact that, as early as 1890, Marshall considered his famous 'engine of analysis' and his coverage of normal prices and distribution to be no more than a starting point for the solution of "practical problems." One might also note that he did eventually treat in separate places "foreign trade" (Marshall, 1879) and "the modern development of combination and monopoly" (1919). Unfortunately his coverage of "the complex actions and reactions of credit" never adequately received its hoped for book-length treatment. Thus Marshall students have spent a century poring over his unpublished writings, his testimony before various official commissions, and his fragmentary writing on these topics, for such insight as they could gain. We will reserve to the end an interpretation of how much his eventual treatment of these issues leaves of his original theoretical structure in the *Principles*. First we should review his fragmented, but often incisive, monetary theory.

The most difficult element of Marshall's thought is his theory of interest. Significantly, it was ultimately to be the least satisfactory to Keynes. In the *Principles* Marshall defined what was essentially a "real" theory whereby the demand and supply of capital determined the rate of interest, via the marginal productivity of capital in production ("the principle of substitution"), and a marginal utility of theory of savings (the psychic pain of "waiting"). Yet this simple argument was just the beginning of a long chain of reasoning.

Marshall – ever the realistic and cautious interpreter of theoretical arguments – considered this insufficient to explain the actual determination of the rate of interest.

First there was the complication – later to appear prominently in the *General Theory* – of the existence of old stocks of existing capital goods and new flows of investment activity. The old "appliances" would be revalued if expectations of profitability or the rate of interest were to change. The market for "free capital" was defined by the supply of real savings ("waiting," or abstaining from consumption) and the demand for capital determined by the expected profit on new investment opportunities. To some extent returns on the existing stock of appliances relative to the cost of producing new ones set rates of return for various old investments ("quasi-rents" in the language of the *Principles*) that served as signals to direct new free capital to the highest rate of return.

There followed discussion of the relative shape of the respective supply and demand curves, and of the stability analysis various such assumptions would make. As Bridel (1987, pp. 15–24) has well illustrated, Marshall put much of his confidence in this regard into the inverse relation of demand and the interest rate, realizing that savings might be more complicated in interest sensitivity. Linking this part of Marshall to Keynes's discussion in the appendix to Chapter 14 of the *General Theory* (*GT*, p. 189), would tend to convince one of the validity of Keynes' quip that "'Interest' has really no business to turn up at all in Marshall's *Principles of Economics* – it belongs to another branch of the subject." But what is surprising is that Keynes clearly knew there was much more to Marshall's monetary theory than the *Principles*.

For one thing, Marshall had a clear account in other places (see Bridel, Chapter 3) of the relation of this real theory to its expression via monetary phenomena. In fact it was really to follow out his many hints in this direction that a whole generation of Cambridge theorists, including Keynes, devoted much of their professional lives. So for instance his stock theory of the demand for money was put to work by Marshall to investigate the dynamic properties of monetary changes and price-level movements. This leads naturally into an account of his cycle theory as well.

The role of the supply of gold under the gold standard and the influence of an influx of its quantity to a country was first discussed by Marshall in his evidence to the Gold and Silver Commission of 1888–89, some of which was reprinted in *Money, Credit and Commerce* (1923). The focus of his discussion is the banking system, where the initial influx is concentrated, which is thereby led to lower the rate interest on loans and increase credit. The complexity and versatility of his "cash-balance" approach to the demand for money (and other assets) comes in at this point. Money may be demanded, as we have seen above, for its convenience services in conducting *transactions*, but there is also the possibility – first shared in 1886 with the Royal Commission on the

Depression of Trade and Industry – of a second *precautionary* motive to demand cash to hold, or what he called the "law of hoarding":

> . . . viz, that the demand for a metal for the purposes of hoarding is increased by a continued rise in its value and diminished by a continued fall, because those people who hoard believe that what has been rising in value for some time is likely to go on rising and vice versa.
>
> (Marshall, 1926 [1949], p. 6)

Speculators thus borrow this increased money supply to buy goods that they expect to rise in price, and their activity then raises prices. As this raises the demand for currency for transaction purposes, there is a cumulative process of expanding money and prices which is satisfied and brought back into equilibrium with the increased supply of money as the price level is bid up. After the transition, prices are higher, and interest returns to its old level. His story may not be much, but it importantly hinted at the role of the banks in causing savings and investment to differ, as well as giving a homely Marshallian quality to the strict mechanical arguments of the quantity theory.[6]

Many commentators see the later development of Marshall's ideas as leading in two directions. One is the sort of money demand analysis of Lavington and Pigou (and ultimately Patinkin), which built on the real-balance changes, and related spillover effects, that would be set off as prices, desired money demands, and quantities of assets changed. These writers improved the clarity of Marshall's vision and eventually, with Keynes and Patinkin as the logical endpoints, worked out the stock-flow issues at the heart of such adjustment problems. Patinkin went so far as to consider such disequilibrium dynamics the essence of Keynesian economics.

The other strand of development of Marshall concerns the nascent cycle theory he employed. Actual interest rates are, he was clear, determined on the loan market. The discount rate for short loans is largely governed by the supply and demand of bank credit. The long-term rate was more a matter of average profitability in industry. Ultimately the anchor of the long rate, and to a lesser extent the discount rate, was the real return to investment, which derived from the real supply and demand for capital. But in the short run many mistakes could take place. "Error" was the catchword here, and error could arise from mistaken movements in the real rate, mistaken expectations of price rises augmented by speculation, unexpected discovery of new monetary metal, or mistaken expectations by bankers. Thus the ability of the monetary sector to distort the real demand and supply of "free capital," and the potential error of private actors gave rise to cycles (Bridel, 1987, pp. 36–47; Laidler, 1999, pp. 81–86).

A spectacular event, like a war, or a bumper harvest, leads to a rise in business confidence and in bank lending. Speculators, as above, begin the cycle as they act in a cumulative way to bid up prices, overestimating their prospects. Marshall relied on Mill (1871) for the emphasis on "error," but contributed an original element in describing how unanticipated price changes might interact with inflexible wages and changes in money interest rates to cause disequilibria in labor and goods markets, and so account for changes in employment and output. Credit is eventually curtailed (for unexplained reasons) as expectations dim, forcing a crisis. Credit contracts and prices tumble in the downward phase. A period of caution and business doldrums ensues, until the next upturn. Thus for Marshall – and even Keynes, at least through the *Tract* (*CW*, 4) – price stability is a necessary and sufficient remedy for crises. But even here, Marshall saw the practical problems in achieving price stability, and instead called for indexation of loans and wages.[7]

It would be a mistake to read too much into Marshall, especially viewed retrospectively from Keynes of 1936. Most of his discussion of these topics is short and not given the systematic development of the *Principles*. It is important, however, for the hints it left to his students and successors, as Bridel (1987) and Laidler (1991, 1999) both make clear. It is also somewhat remarkable – in relation to the "it's all in Marshall" vein of thinking – to see how Marshall, in a few short paragraphs, threw out material that seems so pregnant from the standpoint of later developments. Thus for instance his much-repeated line: "But though men have the power to purchase they may not choose to use it" (Marshall and Marshall, 1879; pp. 154–5; and repeated in Marshall, 1962, pp. 591–2). Also, from the same sources follows a description of the cycle that seems eerily suggestive of the *General Theory*:

> For when confidence has been shaken by failures, capital cannot be got to start new companies or extend old ones. Projects for new railways meet with no favour, ships lie idle, and there are no orders for new ships. There is scarcely any demand for the work of navies, and not much for the work of the building and the engine-making trades. In short there is but little occupation in any of the trades which make fixed capital. Those whose skill and capital is specialized in these trades are earning little, and therefore buying little of the produce of other trades. Other trades, finding a poor market for their goods, produce less; they earn less, and therefore they buy less: the diminution of the demand for their wares makes them demand less of other trades. Thus commercial disorganization spreads: the disorganization of one trade throws others out of gear, and they react on it and increase its disorganization.
>
> The chief cause of the evil is a want of confidence. The greater part of it could be removed almost in an instant if confidence could return, touch all industries with her magic wand and make them continue their production and their demand for the wares of others.

IV. Marshallian monetary and cycle theory as a precursor to the *General Theory*

As we saw in Part II in relation to our discussion of Marshall's views on speculation, here also there is good evidence that Marshall's depiction of the downward phase of the cycle was not the same as Keynes's 1936 intent to define unemployment equilibria. Bridel (1987, pp. 36–51) is insightful on this. He makes it clear that Marshall always held that the forces that would determine long-run normal values were separable from, and impervious to, the passing influence of monetary and cyclic factors. First there is the depiction of the long and the short money rates themselves, in particular their subordination to the real rate available on new capital. Second, there is what Bridel (1987, p. 46) calls the main weakness of Marshall's monetary views, his failure to demonstrate, or refer to empirical evidence is support of his important point that the market rates of interest will be driven to oscillate around the 'equilibrium' rate of interest which is defined by the real demand for capital and its associated marginal productivity.

This is one crucial point on which we will see Keynes of 1936 diverge from the Marshallian tradition. The traditional Cambridge (and general neoclassical) analysis is premised on the question of how the monetary system can distort the real system, which in itself always tends toward equilibrium. Keynes would eventually put forth the view that a monetary system might – for real, essential, reasons – 'naturally' equilibrate at less than full employment.

Thus, although we have emphasized continuities between Marshall, the school of thought he founded, and the various positions held by Keynes before 1936, there is still a crucial distinction to be made between all of these and the *General Theory*. This distinction is important and should be stressed, for Keynes's outlook by 1936 was different than Marshall's in crucial ways that should not be obscured by more superficial commonalities. Yes, Keynes was not completely fair to his predecessors. Most of them realized that output could change and that unemployment could arise over the cycle. Perhaps most surprisingly, Keynes seems to have chosen to cite hardly any of Marshall's monetary theory. But we also have to agree with Bridel (1987, pp. 47–8), when he speaks of the fundamental difference that did eventually set Keynes's vision of a modern economic system apart from Marshall's:

> Undoubtedly there always existed a clear-cut dichotomy in Marshall's mind between the 'general laws of value and distribution' and the causes of the trade (or credit) cycle. The 'mutual relations of the disorganization of credit, production and consumption' (Marshall, 1962, p. 592, n.1) have nothing in common at all with the basic marginalist theorems. Trade cycle forms a separate subject of "supreme importance' (1962, p. 592, n. 1), but the 'main study needed [to bring remedy to it] is that of

the organization of production and credit' and not an integration of these 'complex social and economic forces of the world in which we live' into the determination of 'normal values.'

(1879, p. 148) [18]

Second, it is important to focus on the time lag in argument here between the 1870s and the period after World War I. That Marshall's view in his *Principles* had become somewhat anachronistic by the twentieth century is a theme we visited in Part I. Furthermore, Marshall's long-standing failure to publish his specifically monetary work robbed the Cambridge school of an up-to-date and coherent treatment of monetary ideas until quite late. (And when Marshall's work did finally appear, it took the form of an imperfect recycling of his ideas from the nineteenth century.) This task was left for his students to pursue after World War I. Thus Laidler (1991, Chapter 3; 1999, pp. 81–3), among others, has shown in this regard how Marshall reaches back to John Stuart Mill (1871), in his first (later shunned) book with his wife, Mary Paley Marshall (Marshall and Marshall, 1879) and in a paper on "Remedies for Fluctuations of General Prices" from 1887. Laidler (1999, Chapters 4–6) then shows the development of Marshall's ideas by his students in the post-1912 through 1936 period. This undeveloped bit of Marshall was also recycled by the master, most notably in the last chapter of the *Principles* (1962, pp. 590–2). We would also add to this list the enduring importance of Marshall's unpublished 1871 essay "Money." In a sense, then, the very lack of an account of those "complex actions and reactions of credit," of which Marshall spoke at the end of the *Principles*, became the stimulus for Cambridge monetary theory in the 1920s.

This recalls our earlier discussion of Marshall's theory of the "representative firm" and increasing returns. Like his view of the firm and the "Cournot problem" in the *Principles*, Marshall's monetary analysis was already anachronistic by the turn of the century, and certainly by the period after World War I. This seems to have been little noticed, but is nevertheless an important aspect of the development of Cambridge economics. Marshall's monetary views never received the projected update that he considered necessary – an update of the sort that was at least partly accomplished with his "realistic" treatment of new forms of business organization in *Industry and Trade* (1919). Yet, as we noted earlier, *Industry and Trade* represents a view that is in serious conflict with the analytical treatment of the *Principles*. Therefore it is relevant to ask: How much of the structure of the *Principles* would have been left standing after a similarly thorough treatment of money and credit? Furthermore, the same features of economic development that render *Industry and Trade* problematic for the *Principles*, arguably also complicated Marshall's work on a monetary book. As we saw in Part I his concern with the "Cournot problem" centered on the rise of publicly traded joint stock companies. In his essay "The Folly of Amateur

Speculators" (unpublished in his lifetime) we saw this issue transferred to the concurrent rise in opportunities to invest and speculate on the stock exchange. Proceeding beyond his published monetary and cycle work, he was worried about the possibility that the stock exchange might misdirect capital and stall the establishment of long-period positions. Part of this evolving vision was contained in his treatment of industrial organization in *Industry and Trade* (1919).[9] There he saw the further development of large corporations influencing management, industry structure and competition. That book also traced the evolution of the division of labor to the new markets for handling "risk," as insurance and commodity markets became outlets for specialization in this aspect of business, relieving firms of the risk of future changes in output and supply prices. But, though he clearly saw the function of hedging and insurance, he did not produce a well-developed treatment of stock trading. *Money, Credit and Commerce* (1923) did little to correct this.

That Marshall did intend to develop his analysis along these lines is confirmed by his biographer Peter Groenewegen (1995a, pp. 313–21) in his analysis of Marshall's lectures at Cambridge. Groenewegen shows that the content of his monetary lectures in the period 1884–90 centered on conventional nineteenth-century topics: Mill's theory of business cycles, gold and bimetallism and Bagehot's theory of banking. They then moved steadily during the 1890s toward what we would today describe as "corporate finance." Thus in comparing student notes from 1892 taken by A. L. Bowley to those taken by Walter Layton in 1904, there is much greater attention paid to "the role of share price fluctuations in business fluctuations" (Groenewegen, 1995a, p. 319). There then follows a report of Layton's hypothesis about the development of Marshall's lectures that fits well with our theme:

> This was that they reflected his massive research into commerce and industry for the book he was then preparing and which in these years involved substantial study of the stock exchange, share prices and even accounting practice, as shown by his notes on these subjects preserved in the Marshall Library.[10]

In this light, the previous section of our book (Part II) can be viewed as a narrative of how Keynes came to produce such a treatment of stock trading and speculation out of the fragments left by Marshall, Emery and his own developing experiences with investment and probability. Thus one way to interpret Keynes's concerns from the end of World War 1 onward, when he really first seriously turned to economic theory, was that he was following out Marshall's concern with the "mutual relations of the disorganization of credit, production and consumption" (Marshall, 1962, p. 592, n. 1). On this interpretation, in 1936 Keynes then took his already developed view of stock trading (as published in the *Treatise*) and reworked the ground of Marshall's fragmentary treatment of how this interacts with money, interest and employment to offer new insight into the macroeconomic implications of the rise to dominance of the public corporation. But unlike Marshall, and his other pupils, we shall see, Keynes eventually concluded that the possibility existed that the organization of speculative trading activity in a monetary economy was capable of altering, and not just producing temporary divergence from, the full-employment long-period positions of the *Principles*.

V. Marshall's pupils

But the story is even more complex, because as time wore on Marshall became less important to Keynes than did his own generation – Marshall's pupils. As stated earlier, much good work has been done on the content of Cambridge monetary economics after Marshall and before the *General Theory*.[11] There is no need to repeat it here. Thus, in this section we will review that literature for issues that illuminate the discussion of the "essential properties of interest and money" in the *General Theory* and how they interact with investment and employment. We postpone until the next chapter the contributions of Keynes to Cambridge economics.

Two branches of this Marshallian legacy are identified in the literature: the extension of Marshall's stock approach to the demand for money, and the development of Cambridge cycle theory. In terms of closeness to Marshall's own vision concerning both of these topics, one should single out the work of Frederick Lavington and Arthur Cecil Pigou. The dependence on Marshall's framework is somewhat less with our next figure, Ralph G. Hawtrey, who nonetheless also used the Marshallian demand for money analysis in his story of the cycle. The other Cambridge cycle theorist of note, besides Keynes himself, was D. H. Robertson. As all analysts agree, Robertson's theory started out as a real analysis of the cycle in his first book, *A Study of Industrial Fluctuation* (1915 [1948]). He eventually wedded this theory, after his growing involvement with Keynes in the 1920s and his developing awareness of Marshall's monetary work, into a joint study of real and monetary effects in *Banking Policy and the Price Level* (1926 [1949]). A more readable and less terminologically extravagant restatement of this cycle theory is found in the third edition of the Cambridge Economic Handbook *Money* (1928a).

The stock demand for money

Pigou (1912, pp. 423–38, 1917) and Lavington[12] (1921, Chapter 6) both offered more precise, updated and extended presentations of Marshall's basic stock demand for money and other assets. The details of this crucial development of the asset demand for money in the face of alternative assets is well discussed in many places (Eschag, 1963, Chapter 1; Laidler, 1991, pp. 60–58,

1999, pp. 87–9; Patinkin, 1982, pp. 165–88; Bridel, 1987, pp. 52–7, 96–100). Both Pigou and Lavington pushed Marshall's basic framework to new contexts. Significantly these contexts concern the changes wrought on the economy by the rise of public corporations and the increasing specialization of financial markets that we discussed above. One lies with extension of the demand for money to include – using later terminology familiar to post-*General Theory* economists – not only the transaction motive, but also the precautionary motive and a primitive form of the speculative motive. In terms of the assets to be chosen from, the set they treat expands to include not only money and real investments (as in Marshall's 1871 essay), but also financial assets and shares of equity traded on the stock exchange. As a representative sample consider the following from Lavington (1921, p. 30):

> The general principle is familiar enough. As a person extends the application of resources in any particular use, the yield from each successive unit of resources so applied satisfies a less and less urgent need. Accordingly he presses their employment in each use up to that point where in his judgment the marginal yield is equal all round; for if this yield differed as between any two uses it would pay him to transfer resources from one to the other. Resources devoted to consumption supply an income of immediate satisfaction; those held as a stock of currency yield a return of convenience and security; those devoted to investment in the narrower sense of the term yield a return in the form of interest. In so far therefore as his judgment gives effect to his self-interest, the quantity of resources which he holds in the form of money will be such that the unit of resources that is just and only just worth while holding in this form yields him a return of convenience and security equal to the yield of satisfaction derived from the marginal unity spent on consumables, and equal also to the net rate of interest.

This is strongly reminiscent of Keynes's later "liquidity preference theory," lending credence to the proposition that Keynes's claim to originality on this head were exaggerated.[13] More importantly, this is further evidence of the enduring influence of Marshall's essay *Money* on the later development of the Cambridge school and its ability to alter its form with changing theoretical needs. Nevertheless, without going to the hair-splitting lengths of Patinkin (1982, Chapter 6), the case can also be made that there is less than all of Keynes's liquidity preference in this analysis, and that should be emphasized.

First, it should be realized (as can be easily seen from a reading of the originals) that these are very brief analyses by both Lavington and Pigou. Also they are never integrated into their own cycle work, much less into a complete theory of interest, output and employment. We also agree with Patinkin – and we will present the case more fully in Chapter 14 – that

Keynes's use of this asset framework turns on the issue of properly recognizing the impact of stocks and flows on the demand for assets. Such is clearly not true of Lavington in the quote above. He seems to confuse the *flows* of income spent on consumption goods and saved, with the *stocks* of assets and the relative attractions of each as a way to hold those savings. We will see that Keynes was much more precise about this.

Pigou's and Lavington's analyses were Marshallian in that they were meant to answer the question of how the quantity of money would determine the price level. As Laidler has well put it, emphasizing the negative aspects of this literature risks forgetting that they were not written from the standpoint of post-1940 economics:

> Now we must be careful not to make too much of the above criticism of Cambridge monetary theory [concerning its confusion over stocks and flows]. Seen through the eyes of anyone brought up on the monetary economics of the Keynesian and Monetarist 'revolution' its lack of precisions about these issues is no doubt a glaring fault. But the Cambridge economists were, like Fisher, interested in analyzing the determinants of "The Value of money," to invoke the title of Pigou's 1917 paper. For *this* purpose (and not, for example, for constructing some theory of real income determination the need for which had not yet arisen) their supply and demand approach was surely adequate.
>
> (Laidler, 1991, p. 64)

The Cycle

The central interest of Cambridge economists by the interwar years was to formulate a theory of the cycle. Two early attempts at this were also devoted to systemizing Marshall's thoughts. Pigou (1912) and Lavington (1922) thus recapitulate the Marshallian emphasis on "errors" in expectations. Perhaps the coherence that was lacking in Marshall's account was best supplied by Lavington, who, in addition to restating Marshall, states his dependence on Pigou and Robertson and on W. C. Mitchell (p. 7). Thus to some extent we can look to this as the orthodox, backward-looking, Marshallian position in Cambridge as of 1922.[14] This sets these works in opposition, we will see, to the exciting new work that was then being done by others.

Lavington's book as a whole is readable and concise, if now presented with what might strike the modern reader as a bit of Victorian stiffness. For our purposes, a reading of it establishes the degree to which Marshall's (and so Mill's) influence extended, in an almost unchanged manner, into the post-World War I era, the book's explicitly stated context. In this regard, Lavington's cycle book provides an interesting contrast in outlook to Keynes's thinking at the time. Both Keynes's *The Economic Consequences of the Peace* (*CW*, 2) and *A Tract on Monetary Reform* (*CW* 4), are permeated by a strong sense of the need to remake the broken social mechanism of pre-war Europe. Lavington is clear in recognizing ". . . the exceptional difficulties arising from the war," yet he considers these social problems to be better seen as a continuation of factors that also afflicted the previous century (Lavington, 1922, p. 11–12). He then restates Marshall's (and others) widely accepted *description* of the course of a typical cycle. Thus there is a major emphasis on business psychology and the resulting mistakes made in anticipation of the returns to be got from the investment in capital goods. Lavington also offers, as was mentioned earlier in the context of Pigou's *Unemployment*, a detailed account of the role of entrepreneur expectations and the role of the banks in cycles. In fact, Lavington's account of this theory may be better than Marshall's. His narrative well represents the different theoretical plane upon which cycles were discussed in the Victorian literature which Keynes was brought up on – that is different from the obviously more serious and highly theoretical discussion, of which Marshall was a master, devoted to the establishment of long-period equilibria.

Even so, one might be surprised to see Lavington's use of the term of "effective demand" and its course over the cycle (Lavington, 1922, p. 25),[15] his frank concern with the unemployment caused by the downswing (pp. 100–4), and his emphasis on the "uncertainty" faced by investors forecasting the future (Chapter 4). In the end, however, it is also clear that these are considered by Lavington to be passing influences on an otherwise well-operating system. In fact, at one point, he partly apologizes for his use of "speculative" reasoning in ascribing cycles to something as inconsequential as the system's sensitivity to errors in business confidence (p. 61). The view which Lavington champions contains some of the raw *elements* of Keynes's later attempt to formulate an equilibrium theory of unemployment, but in the end it amounts only to a tidy retelling of Marshall's viewpoint. This reluctance to formulate a more theoretical account of the cycle is evidence that in 1922, at least one part of Cambridge cycle theory relied more on the *precedent* of Marshall's and Pigou's wisdom than on any theoretical *demonstration*:

> This reasoning is definitely speculative; its use can be justified only by the great obscurity of the many influences working within the business cycle. It has, however, this in its favour, that it leads to the conclusion which is apparently accepted by such economist as Dr. Marshall and Professor Pigou: the conclusion namely that the active principle animating business cycles is to be found in changes in the general level of business confidence.
>
> (Lavington, 1922, p. 61)

It is not plausible to nominate Lavington and Pigou as the groundbreaking Cambridge cycle theorists of the interwar years. This title must go to Robertson, Hawtrey and Keynes. Their great quest, even starting before the war, *was* to offer a formal theory of the credit cycle. In the process of doing so their first-rate creativity, more than Lavington's and Pigou's reverence, prepared the way for Keynes's treatment in 1936.

To treat Hawtrey first is appropriate both because his first book was published before the war, in 1913, and because his "monetary" theory of the trade cycle is a closely linked development of Marshall's outlook. Although his standing as a civil servant at Treasury could suggest a status as an outlier to the Cambridge tradition, the historians of this school (see especially Bridel's excellent treatment, 1987, pp. 57–78) make it clear that he built firmly on a foundation of Marshallian analysis, and also that his work became the generally accepted interwar source for the cycle at Cambridge.[16]

We do not have the space or the need to treat his (and later Robertson's) extensive writings as they deserve, and as they have been treated by others whose books I urge interested readers to consult.[17] For our purposes the elements most crucial to Hawtrey's theory of the cycle are the following. He clearly set out an analysis of how savings and investment could diverge based on the actions of the banks, and of how changes in the interest rate would react to this disequilibrium situation. Hence he took a crucial step, as Bridel clearly shows, toward establishing a Cambridge version of the loanable-funds theory of the rate of interest, to which Keynes was to later contrast his 1936 theory of interest. Second he explicitly centered his analysis on the flows of income and spending – using the term, and very nearly the concept, that Keynes would later call "effective demand," as early as 1913.

A crucial variable in Hawtrey's story of how banks could alter savings to be different than investment involved a belief – shared with Marshall and many Marshallians of this period, probably including the Keynes of the 1920s – that actual investment was determined by a prior accumulation of savings – what Bridel (1987, pp. 82–3 and 94–6) terms a "lump-sum-of-savings." In Hawtrey's analysis, which is centered on retail stocks of unsold goods, bank lending to dealers in these stocks cause this *real* savings to rise over the upswing of the cycle, as it lowers the market rate of interest (Marshall's "discount rate") below the rate of profit expected on these stocks and so increases investment in them. The upswing, once started, cumulatively sets off more savings and lending and increased inventories for as long as the boom lasts. The upswing also, however, contains the seeds of its own destruction for Hawtrey, in that the boom also causes a drain of reserves ("currency"). Here comes in his use of Marshall's stock demand for money. Increased activity among consumers and retailers sets consumers to trying to keep nominal balances increasing with rising *output* and prices. Eventually this increased "cash drain" (as we would call it today) violates a critical level of reserve ratios (endogenous to the banks, not strictly enforced by central bank policy). Lending stops expanding. Then begins a reversed downward phase.

Keynes, we will see, was later to comment in correspondence with Hawtrey that this account suffered from two basic flaws. The first was that

Hawtrey seemed to Keynes to systematically confuse the higgling of the market with the establishment of more fundamental equilibria. But that was only a flaw relative to the wish to account for the economy getting stuck in *equilibria* with unemployment. Hawtrey himself saw his cycle analysis, as Marshall did, as a purely disequilibrium phenomenon. It was a process in which natural forces would eventually re-establish the long-period position of the economy. Thus cycles did just that, cycling around full-employment long-period equilibria. But Hawtrey also thought, stepping back from his theory, that the world of modern money and credit made long-period positions themselves inherently unstable. Except when credit is stagnant, "one of the most important of the economic conditions which the quantity theory takes to be 'given' will be an acceleration or retardation of the in the creation of credit. In practice it seldom, perhaps never, happens that the state of equilibrium is actually reached" (Hawtrey, 1919, p. 46). At all other times, for Hawtrey, the point was to show what was happening to consumers' "income" and "outlay," and to savings and investment in relation to this cyclical expansion and contraction of credit. An obvious question arises. If the long period never arrives, how powerful are the forces supposed to establish it? Keynes would later construe this situation as one of short-period equilibrium. Hawtrey could not see his way clear to this result.

A second "fault," when considered from the standpoint of the *General Theory* surely, but also a fault of a theory of the cycle, was that Hawtrey focused his analysis on one particular type of investment, retail inventory; and one particular cause, monetary changes. Keynes was later to criticize the focus on inventories in the *Treatise*. This point marks his growing realization – obvious to readers of the *General Theory*, but also obvious to Marshall and Lavington and Robertson for instance – that the most important part of changing aggregate demand is changes in fixed capital equipment. Keynes should be seen as in debt to Hawtrey's income approach and his focus of "aggregate demand," as well as the seed of doubt he sowed in Keynes mind about the attractive quality of long-period equilibria. The twist was that Keynes eventually saw the behavior and consequences of consumers and investors in *real* terms, not just monetary ones, and found the adjustment of consumers and the establishment of equilibria to depend on income.

Neglect of fixed capital was not a fault of Dennis Holme Robertson's extensive writing on the cycle. He too first published before the war – in fact, as he states in the very witty preface to the reprint of the book *A Study of Industrial Fluctuation* (1915 [1948], p. vii), after only *four* years of study of economics. Robertson was then not yet the staunch defender of Marshall and the Cambridge tradition in monetary theory that he was later to become. At least that is true as far as the cycle was concerned (he would probably say its ingredients were there in Marshall all there all along, once one realized it). His early vision of the cycle (Presley, 1979, pp. 9–59, provides a good account) was fueled more by the work of Aftalion (1909) and

Labordere (1908),[18] especially because he saw these two authors as the best on the "real" causes of the business fluctuation. Hence, and in contradistinction to Hawtrey's, Robertson's first book is intoxicated with invention and real capital production, with capital goods' inherent indivisibility and the possibility that, once started, a capital project depends on a real accumulation of consumables to fuel the work on it until it can be completed and come online. If, either alone or in combination, this stock of consumables were to run out before this was possible, if the investment goods themselves so rose in cost because of diminishing returns, or if the expected return to using investment goods were to fall, a crisis would ensue.

Thus it is possible to explain the cycle as a phenomenon of "overinvestment." Although this term should be understood here in Robertsonian language as a point of the upswing "beyond which any further investment would involve a sacrifice of present enjoyment disproportionate to the enjoyment which will be afforded by the new consumable goods which it is proposed to create" (Robertson, (1915) [1948], p. 240). This language and viewpoint is important, as it illustrates Leijonjufvud's (1981) major point that Robertson, and all major business cycle theorists of this period were interested in what he calls "intertemporal coordination problems." In the Austrian capital-theoretic language encountered later in the thirties, this would be termed a change in the "period of production."

Much attention is also paid by Robertson in this book to the real – and to a lesser degree the psychological – effects of unexpected fluctuations in harvests (1915 [1948], Part 1, Chapters 4–7). This quasi-Jevonian element of his theory rests with a "real" twist on the nineteenth-century emphasis on "harvests" as a precipitating factor of the cycle. Now they do not just set off spontaneous excitement among investors, bankers and speculators, but impact real demand as well. Examples of these are on railways and ships designed to carry crops to market and so on investment in new rolling stock and ships, on construction and on the production of stocks of consumption goods. Conversely, the role of "error," of banks, credit and money is, by Marshallian standards of the day, conspicuously downplayed.[19]

Yet Robertson is today admired, and justly so, as a monetary economist, the author of the very successful Cambridge Economic Handbook *Money* (successive editions printed from 1922–48). The explanation for this is straightforward. His first book was just the beginning of his economic studies, rushed into print before he went off to the war. It was only after the war, in collaboration with Keynes,[20] that he became the outstanding monetary analyst we now think of. Yet Robertson never repudiated his first book's outlook and his belief that the cycle was at root, as its primary cause, a function of technological invention and its real effects concerning capital investment. In this way we can say that his later works, like *Banking Policy and the Price Level* (1926 [1949]) were attempts to integrate his "real" theory with the more conventional ones of a monetary and "error" variety – "the two which appear at the present time to be commanding an ever-increasing measure of assent" (Robertson, 1926 [1949], p. 1). Another way to put this is that after further reading and consideration he tried to bring his "real" theory more into the mainstream of the Cambridge discussion of the business cycle. Indeed the very nature of this mainstream was indicated by the then popular title we earlier saw Keynes using for Cambridge economics' enigma of the twenties: the credit cycle. The result of this effort was a short book – *Banking Policy and the Price Level* (Robertson, 1926 [1949] – which introduced so many bizarre and never-again used terms that even so committed a monetary antiquarian as David Laidler (1999, p. 93) calls it "impenetrable."

But it is a book which is nevertheless important to the development of interwar business cycle theory, as Laidler goes on to say, because it introduced to English language readers the concept of "forced savings" (Robertson, 1926 [1949], Chapters 5 and 6). This concept, around which much controversy would later ensue between Hayek and Keynes, depended on the banking systems ability (à la Hawtrey) to alter the savings that consumers would voluntarily make by extending excess credit to producers in the process of making loans. Unfortunately termed "induced lacking" (after Robertson's abortive attempt to introduce "lacking" as a term for savings),[21] this phenomenon was indicative of the pre-*General Theory* concern in Cambridge with the cyclical possibility of inequality between savings and investment, and the possible – significantly not necessary – "evil" it represented.

We will analyze this more completely in Chapter 12, and its Austrian version in detail in Chapter 13. Suffice it to say here that Robertson was highlighting a method by which an increase of bank loans to producers beyond "voluntary" savings, could "rob" consumers as it bid these goods out of their reach. Using the standard Marshallian stock demand for money, Robertson postulated this to occur because consumers' desired *nominal* money stocks would be found to be worth less in *real* terms as they found that producers had bid up prices (but presumably not those famously sticky wages). Nominal incomes of consumers would not go so far in terms of goods as a consequence, and there would be redistribution to producers. Compared with the emphasis in the coming Austrian version, however, Robertson's version was not a uniformly pessimistic one about there always being an "evil" effect of monetary expansion, as Laidler (1999, pp. 96–8) shows. In fact, he argued that if the consumer decided individually to spontaneously increase their money balances ("abortive lacking" or "hoarding"), say because of increased uncertainty about the future, this could be self-defeating in the depressing effect it would have on investment.[22] It would then possibly be beneficial for the bankers to "induce" a bit of forced savings by an offsetting increase in bank loan expansion which would maintain investment. One sees echoes here of the type of thinking that later went into discussion of the "paradox of thrift."

VI. Keynes and Marshallian monetary economics

For our purposes note the following about the "monetary" version of Robertson's *real* theory of the cycle, keeping in mind the notion first testified to by Robertson himself, that his and Keynes's work of this period was essentially a joint product.[23] First, it is a theory based on the notion that *voluntary* savings change either because peoples' incomes do, or because consumers spontaneously change attitudes toward their asset balances. It is not too great a leap from this, at least in retrospect, to a theory of flow consumption (or savings) as a function of flow income, and a complementary stock theory of asset demand determining the rate of interest. As it would turn out, in this short-period theoretical context, the crucial lack is an equilibration mechanism for income. This was explicit in Hawtrey's disequilibrium analysis of bank credit and implicit in Robertson's sequence analysis via the loanable funds market. For the Cambridge cycle theorists of the interwar period, the point was to trace out the steps by which increased bank lending induced savings and investment to differ, and how this process brought along a chain of real activity (the building of Marshall's "appliances") and of changes in real-balances.[24] Yet a boom so created, according to this theory, contains the ingredients of its inevitable demise. As expectations are ultimately grounded by the real productivity of capital and the underlying unchanging 'normal' profit rate, they will ultimately revert to long-run values. How this would happen is the essence of each twist on the "crisis." Hawtrey saw the eventual shortage of reserves as the critical factor. Robertson was particularly focused on the indivisibility of large capital projects. Even Robertson's doctrine that forced savings might occur during the boom – a phenomenon that Keynes, having once held, would later depart from in the *Treatise* (see Bridel, 1987, pp. 109–11 and pp. 124–26) – is just a temporary disturbance to this unchanged long-period position.

Common to all these theories was the presumption that the system would eventually be pulled back to its equilibrium values of savings, consumption, income and interest. Hence the point made repeatedly by Keynes in the *General Theory* – and much denied by his Cambridge contemporaries – that such theories assumed these values would coincide with full employment. Obviously – and Keynes was inaccurate if not dishonest to imply otherwise – many economists, at Cambridge and elsewhere, saw for many years before 1936 that unwilling unemployment was possible, and indeed in the twenties and thirties actually occurring, and that income did change over the business cycle. But, just as obviously, they maintained that the cycle played out against the unchanging background of Marshall's long period. Sticky wages might impede the adjustment process, and/or bank lending, and/or "error" in expectations, or perhaps the cycle was ultimately due to the very nature of technological and capital intensive growth itself.

In other words, Cambridge cycle theorists were not big believers in the seamless ability of the system to coordinate the intertemporal allocation of resources. This intertemporal coordination problem, though, was judged by them to be a temporary phenomenon, not to be confused with Marshall's more fundamental forces. By 1936 Keynes came to question this judgment. Hence, we conclude that, though the Cambridge setting offered as sophisticated a cycle theory as there was anywhere in the interwar period, and though it did contain many of the ingredients and discussions that we can now see became the material out of which the *General Theory* would be written, and that though it may be true that Keynes was in fact not very generous in attribution to his predecessors and contemporaries, crucial further steps were yet to be taken.

12
Keynes's Development as a Cambridge Monetary Theorist

I. Introduction

Needless to say, Keynes was an integral member of the intellectual circle working in the Cambridge tradition of monetary and business cycle theory that we have just surveyed. His life work spanned the arc that we just traversed, from Marshall to the *General Theory*. As we approach the *General Theory* end of this arc, as we have seen in all other sections of the book, events, and his own evolving views of them, rather than those of his contemporaries', increasingly acted upon his mind. Having now isolated the importance of an overarching theory of money and the economic system to his attempt to explain unemployment, it will be our task in this chapter to treat Keynes as a Cambridge monetary theorist, which until the *General Theory* primarily meant Keynes as a monetary cycle theorist. Once again we will see the immense importance of Marshall, an influence that only slowly decayed and never disappeared.

After World War I, Keynes ranked himself with the younger generation that we have noted above as "Marshall's Pupils." In that light he was distinguished by several factors. First, even in an early flirtation with "forced savings," he displayed a continuing interest in monetary factors, both for their own sake and in relation to the cycle. Second, he was unique among his contemporaries in his own personal experience as an investor, and his incorporation of that experience into his economics. Last he was marked, compared to them, by the ever-fluid changes of his outlook in the face of what he saw as changing circumstances and by the related attempts to apply his theoretical formulations to events. So for instance, while Ralph Hawtrey seems never to have changed his mind, and Dennis Robertson mostly could be said to have grown into more monetary knowledge, all to be fitted under his original 1915 framework, Keynes modified his positions often as events unfolded.

Thus the larger view of Keynes as a theorist that emerges is that, though for most of his life he worked from within the "citadel" of Marshallian monetary economics and the later elaborations of it by his Cambridge colleagues, he became the "Marshallian" that most rebelled against Marshall's teachings. The radical nature of this final break will be chronicled in Chapters 14 and 15. Here we want to trace the elements of his work in the period of his career prior to the *General Theory* and particularly to note any elements that, in retrospect, served as precursors of the views on interest and money in the *General Theory* that we are calling attention to. In one way his radical turn was fueled by the equally radical nature of the economic crisis of the thirties. His reaction to that crisis could be rated as an overreaction, exacerbated by his controversial nature, as Dennis Robertson certainly thought it was. If that reaction eventuated in a better understanding of the economic system, as many of us believe it did, his controversial presentation of that theory can be rated as scientifically beneficial.

II. The historical context for Keynes as a monetary economist

In the preceding chapters we have covered in some detail Keynes's concerns as regards labor and speculation over his whole career. We were also bold enough to suggest that Keynes really gave little sign of serious interest in economic theory before 1923,[1] when he finished his semi-journalistic *Tract on Monetary Reform*. Perhaps this interest was sparked by his lack of a proper economic model by which to critique Britain's policy of returning to the gold standard at the pre-war parity exchange rate. Maybe it was also due to presenting his hoped for formal treatment of the quantity theory in relation to the credit cycle, *A Treatise on Money* (1930). Yet already in the *Tract*, we will see, and continuing in the *Treatise on Money*, Keynes was formulating a distinctive view of what characterizes a modern monetary economy. Looking at Keynes's intellectual odyssey from the standpoint of the eventual formulation of the *General Theory*, we can say that his experiences before 1930 were, though not written down as formal economic theory, nevertheless important in a number of ways to his later theoretical work in economics.

For one his apprenticeship with Marshall gave him a firm grasp of the foundations of a sophisticated version of orthodox economics. Moreover his early devotion to the theory of probability as a guide to reasoned conduct meant he was fully aware of the influence of rationality, and its limits, in human behavior. This was especially true of behavior under uncertainty. As we have seen, Keynes's journalistic activity and involvement in public affairs led him to a predilection for politically relevant economic models. Writing as easily and successfully for journalistic audiences as he did, satisfied his innate, and Bloomsbury-sharpened, relish of controversy. It may also have dulled his habits of academic attribution beyond conventional recognition. Additionally, his moneymaking activities gave him a practitioner's perspective on financial market behavior, which intertwined with his more theoretical and philosophical views.

To this we must not forget to add that during the years of World War I he also had ample experience, not always happy, of the administration of public affairs. The insight he drew from this is important for a number of reasons. It meant that he thought he understood the political pressures, theoretical prejudices and workaday habits of civil servants. It also seemed to convince him of the value of a degree of academic detachment. Thus we know from his biographers that after the Peace Treaty he resisted all calls to again serve "inside the beast" until World War II. Until then, the role of outside commentator – sometimes Cassandra, sometimes shaper of opinion, always a creator of instant policy solutions, whether taken seriously or not – was his preferred role.

Finally we should note that in his many policy discussions Keynes was at one with his Cambridge colleagues in his activism and his critical stance toward an unbridled *laissez-faire* approach to the economy. Keynes always believed that modern capitalism required intervention, management and active guidance in order to perform optimally. The set of activities that he saw as the responsibility of the state only grew as the twenties wore on. Many modern readers of Keynes, especially economists, consider this his major fault, evidence of blindness on his part to the social virtue and economic utility of wide-ranging freedom for individual choice. But Keynes, and as we have seen to some extent Marshall, looked upon the different interventions that they both argued for, be they moral suasion of private actors or the extension of state responsibility for output as a whole, as ways of *enlarging* of the field for individual choice. Lessening the scourge of involuntary idleness – the primary defect of capitalism as Keynes saw it by 1936 – was the greatest arena for this enlargement.

These points have all been more or less supported by the foregoing discussion. One point of this chapter's particular angle on Keynes's "many lives" is to show that when he did start to take economic theory seriously, as he did in *A Treatise on Money*, he may have started from Marshall and the Cambridge school, but did not thereby neglect all of the foregoing. Primarily, then, we need to show how Keynes grew in the twenties and thirties in terms of what at the end of Chapter 10 we called his "model." All of the references we cited at the beginning of the Chapter 11 are excellent further sources of the details on this. We will often rely on the results of this extensive scholarship and on selections from Keynes's texts. Our purpose is not to be encyclopedic. That is, one way of understanding Keynes's theoretical position in 1936 is by envisioning him as taking some elements of basic Marshallian monetary theory, elaborating upon Hawtrey's disequilibrium expenditure and change-of-income approach to cycles, all of his contemporaries' interests in the savings and investment nexus, and freeing this viewpoint from the dominating role of Marshall's long-period and its associated "natural" rate of interest. A key element in this process, as we will see in the next two chapters, is a doctrine of the essential properties of interest and money. One way to express the result is the standard multiplier model.

Another angle, the one we pursue here, is through those essential qualities of a monetary economy.

III. Pre-war lectures: "The Theory of Money"

Prior discussions have emphasized Keynes's pre-World War I dependence on Marshall for material from which to lecture Cambridge undergraduates. Monetary theory is no exception. Keynes's *Collected Works* (*CW* 12) contain sufficient evidence of these lectures, which when combined with histories of the period already cited, make only a brief outline of the lectures' contents necessary. Essentially we can class Keynes as an early and committed expositor of the Cambridge version of the Neo-classical quantity theory of money. By that I mean to emphasize that he wholly took on board Marshall's monetary views. We may even suspect, that, like many an overburdened and inexperienced young lecturer, the young Keynes gave these ideas little of his own thought, which was conspicuously reserved for *Probability* during this period of his intellectual development.

That said, as mentioned in our two previous investigations of this period, Keynes left evidence of being an able and interesting lecturer on money, even if he was investing little of his own brain power in the subject. As an example (*CW* 12, pp. 759–64), Keynes goes into some length on empirical estimates that had then been made of the velocity of money, discusses Irving Fisher's experiments with Yale students along these lines, invites the students to calculate their individual velocities of money and provides a personal estimate of his own (Keynes's estimate of his personal velocity in those pre-World War I years was 34).

Overall, however, the lectures convey a complacency regarding monetary theory that would have been very much at odds with the writer of the *General Theory* 25 years later. Again this suggests the extent of the fundamental change in outlook he underwent in that time span. At this early stage of Keynes's career there were two paramount aspects of the Cambridge economists' complacency about the theory of money. One, external to the theory proper but important, was that Britain's own monetary institutions – the stable pound sterling, its then 200-year tradition of banking institutions and its successful history with the then spreading international gold standard – were the envy of the world. This we know was to dramatically change, in ways that profoundly affected Keynes, under the pressure of World War I and its aftermath. Second, and just as important for our narrative of Keynes's intellectual growth, is the fact that Keynes and his Cambridge colleagues confidently believed that they were working in a place and in an economics tradition in which the majority of the issues then facing monetary economics – issues of both practical and theoretical importance for monetary economics and its ruling paradigm, the quantity theory of money – had been already largely settled by Alfred Marshall. What were these basic questions?

These can be quickly paraphrased[2] from Keynes's lectures. At the outset of "Elementary Lectures on Money" (*CW* 12, pp. 690–1) are laid out the main topics to be covered. In the first course of eight weeks these included: the elements of a good currency, nominal and real prices, the determination of the general price level, index numbers, causative factors in differences in purchasing power of currencies across countries and across time, and the relationship of price changes and interest rates. The second course of lectures covers roughly what we would today call "the monetary transmission mechanism," including how changes in the quantity of gold change prices, winners and losers from inflation, bimetallism, Gresham's law, foreign currency systems, the Anglo-Saxon versus the Germanic banking systems and the regulation of paper currency. After this, Keynes's notes are incomplete and those that remain create some confusion about his exact treatment of more advanced topics, coincident with our above survey of the overlapping material on speculation and corporate finance, but at minimum[3] there are notes for part of a more advanced treatment of money of which the editors of the *Collected Works* (*CW* 12, pp. 723–83) have printed the theoretical sections. Under the "causes determining the value of money" an algebraic treatment of the interaction of the supply and demand for the stock of gold and a demonstration (marked "derived from Marshall's lectures") of Marshall's famous rectangular hyperbola graphical representation of the demand for money (pp. 733–4) is presented. This is followed by a long discussion of the factors affecting the supply of gold. Many empirical estimates of gold stocks[4] are given in this context. Further, Keynes shows a clear knowledge of Marshall's analysis of "hoarding" (pp. 754–6) and the use of money as an asset. In addition to a clear explanation of each of these topics individually, Keynes uses them to demonstrate his opinion that the quantity theory, true as far as it goes, is only a starting point for monetary analysis.

Despite his debt to Marshall, it is easy to imagine that Keynes's lectures offered a superior treatment of the Marshallian monetary oeuvre – superior even perhaps to Marshall's own eventual account in *Money, Credit and Commerce* (1923). Of particular interest for us, his comments give evidence that, even if he had not yet seen the Marshall essay "Money" from 1871 at this early point,[5] he was already well aware of the stock-equilibrium nature of the money market. Consider, for instance:

> The relations between value and cost of production seems relatively unimportant in the case of the precious metals, because the rate of consumption being slow, the value at any moment appears to be determined rather by the volume of the stock. But the amount added to the stocks in any year is more or less regulated, more now that formerly, by the cost of production and the value at the moment. There is therefore, an *equation* between present value and present cost of production. Moreover in the long run the total volume is determined by the costs of production in the preceding years. Hence there is a sense in which it is true to say that the volume and,

therefore, the value of money is governed in the long run by cost of production. But inasmuch as at any moment the existing conditions of supply have a small effect on the value, it is misleading to say that the value at any time is determined by cost of production *at that time*. It is true, of course, that we must nearly always add the qualification 'in the long run;' but when the long run is a *very* long run, so long that the ultimate event cannot even be *foreseen*, the doctrine loses most of its importance.

(*CW* 12, pp. 751–2, italics in original)

There is also an almost verbatim account of the Mill-Marshall theory of the effect of a sudden influx of gold and of the cycle that we outlined in the last chapter. Thus as we saw with the theory of wages and of speculation, Keynes before World War 1 was a confirmed believer in, and enunciator of, Marshall's analysis. He also, as expressed in his now famous review of Fisher (Keynes, 1911), seems already fully aware of the relative rarity of Marshall's monetary thought outside of Cambridge. What did a favored Marshall student know about the effects of money on the economy in 1911?

The proof of the Quantity Theory has given us general grounds for supposing that an increased volume of currency tends to raise prices, but it supplies no indication of the actual steps by means of which this effect is produced . . . To fill in this part of the argument is, therefore, essential for its completion. The only economist who, so far as I know, has made any attempt to do so is Professor Marshall. His theory of it, moreover, has only been published insofar as it appears in evidence before the G. and S. Commission of 1888 and the Indian Currency Committee of 1898. It is not, therefore so widely known as it should be, and you will find scarcely any allusion to it in works on the theory of money. It is a great misfortune that Prof. Marshall has never published his theory in a full and complete form. What I shall have to say is entirely derived from him, either from his printed evidence, to which I refer you, or in conversation.

(*CW* 12, pp. 776–7)

IV. Debates with Dennis Robertson and "forced savings"

Though it is generally agreed that Keynes did not develop his monetary analysis into anything essentially original before the war,[6] one document (that remained unpublished in his lifetime) is something of an anomaly in this respect. An anomaly both because it was written before the war, as a paper to be delivered to the "Political Economy Club" meeting of December of 1913, and because it marks the beginning of a flirtation with a type of nascent forced-savings/over-investment theory.

Also important is that this paper marks the beginning of an intellectual collaboration between Keynes and Robertson that was to be important after the war, and that for a time propelled forward both men's ideas on business cycles. Looking forward to the next chapter, this also establishes that

Hayek's Wicksellian forced savings analysis of 1931 would not have seemed very novel to Keynes and Cambridge, at least in its basic message that bankers lending more to producers than was voluntarily saved by households could lead to a crisis. The topic of his paper (*CW* 13, pp. 2–14): "How Far are Bankers Responsible for the Alternations of Crisis and Depression?" The initiation of this stage of Keynes's thought seems to have been sparked by his reading of the initial form – as a Trinity College Fellowship Dissertation – of Robertson's "real" theory of the cycle, that we presented in the last chapter. Recall from that discussion that Robertson's goal was to produce an account of the cycle that was due to changes in investment demand sparked by new investment opportunities, particularly those associated with new technological invention. We noted that Robertson, in the eventually published version of this work (Robertson, 1915 [1948]), lamented that previous writers had so exclusively relied on the monetary system to explain crisis, as did Mill and Marshall. His alternative explanation was offered as a "real" theory. In that aspect it was a variant on "overinvestment" theories: it suggested that, in the normal course of economic progress, invention sparked discontinuous jumps in new investment which tended to outpace the community's willingness to save. Notice this already assumes that the investors and savers are different sets of economic actors, with different motives which the economic system may or may not always reconcile. This combined with an appreciation of the large scale and 'lumpiness' of capital projects, created the possibility for Robertson that the crisis in the cycle occurs when capital projects, still at the stage of construction, are abandoned.

The monetary details of this process were not touched on by Robertson in his 1915 book. This is the stage at which Keynes enters the debate, inaugurating a discussion that would lead to close collaboration between the two after the war. Accordingly, many writers have commented on how closely intertwined were the work of these two men after World War I (Presley, 1979; Bridel, 1987, Chapter 6). For instance, there is good reason to believe that Robertson's *Banking Policy and the Price Level* (1926) and parts of his Cambridge handbook *Money* (1922), especially the crucial third edition of *Money* (1928) which contains a less elaborate version of his (their?) forced saving argument, owe a good deal to Keynes. For a time this led to Keynes and Robertson working so closely that Robertson was to report (1926, p. 5):

> I have had so many discussions with Mr. J. M. Keynes on the subject-matter of Chapters V and VI [which contained the crucial definitions of savings and of forced savings], and have re-written them so drastically at his suggestion, that I think neither of us now knows how much of the ideas therein contained is his and how much is mine.

What was the nature of these discussions? Absent much surviving correspondence, the details are lost to history. But one way to rationally reconstruct the relation between the theories is to say that Robertson (1915 [1948]) provided a characterization of a "real" theory of the cycle and Keynes's role was to seek the monetary mechanism at work in Robertson's story. It is just as plausible, however, especially based on the evidence of Keynes's early lectures – that Marshall, Hawtrey and Irving Fisher had already set Keynes thinking along these monetary/real[7] lines.[8] In any event it is the economics that is of interest to us now, and the evidence from the period 1915–30 of the writings and correspondence of Robertson and Keynes reveals for us the basic economic theory relevant to this stage of Keynes's thought. Let us investigate the issues at stake in this collaboration.

The kernel of the problem is well seen from Keynes's 1913 (*CW* 13, p. 2) paper, where we see Keynes referring to "the most ordinary theory of the way in which banking considerations come in [to the explanation of the cycle], chiefly associated with the name of Professor Irving Fisher." Precipitated by some event, a cumulative run up in prices is started that raises expectations of a continuing boom by both the demanders of business loans ("producers") and the (myopic) bankers who supply them. This continues so long as the expected profitability of the new activity endures. Eventually when these same bankers find "to their horror" (p. 3) – perhaps because of a shortage of gold reserves – that they can no longer sustain the reserve ratios associated with sound banking, they curtail lending and "the papers announce the next morning that the trade boom is at an end" (p. 3).[9]

Keynes says he finds this theory – which could as well be attributed to Marshall as to Fisher – to be "clever, rather than satisfactory. It does not seem to be laying bare fundamental things" (*CW* 13, p. 3). In order to go beyond it he suggests we begin by shifting to another theory, that of "overinvestment," in order "to give the clue to some useful ideas." There follows a bare outline of what appears to be Robertson's theory, though the "overinvestment" theory goes without an author in this paper.[10] Keynes's main point is that these two views can be brought together by an explanation of bankers' role in overinvestment. The bankers are essential to this process because savers do not directly lend to the producers of capital goods. Rather they do so through banks – a standard part of the debate that would later in the thirties eventuate in the "barter-monetary" economy distinction. Banks enable new projects by providing short-term financing for new capital projects, hoping the projects, once they are producing revenues, will be re-financed on a long-term basis by the debenture markets. In this crucial interval the banks hold the key, because they have available what Keynes will later call "idle balances," here called that part of savings which households keep in "suspense" (p. 4), and which in aggregate give "the machinery of banking" the reserves to lend from:

Thus in any given year there are two sources from which goods (or, if you like, for it is the same thing, funds) are available for capital works – that part of the existing resources which is deliberately set aside by individuals for investment, and that fraction of the resources, which individuals hold in suspense and leave with their bankers, which bankers advance directly or indirectly for capital purposes.[11]

Hence in any year the value of material goods actually utilized by capital works may run ahead of or fall behind the value deliberately saved, according as the advances of bankers are made, to a greater or lesser extent, for purposes of capital expenditure. I should say that there is a tendency to over-investment (as distinguished from over-savings) when the proportion of the funds in the hands of bankers which is fixed in permanent capital works is increasing

(*CW* 13, p. 5).[12]

If we now jump forward to Robertson's (1926) Chapter 6 where his (and Keynes's?) forced savings doctrine is first presented, we will see the full development of this theme. In one sense what is presented there is a story about how banks can fuel investment during the boom in excess of the voluntary savings of a society considered as a closed system. As Robertson (1926, p. 71) puts it in his idiosyncratic jargon: "From our present point of view, the fundamental feature of the upward swing of a trade cycle is a large and discontinuous increase in the demand for Short Lacking [savings of real goods destined for short term "circulating capital" uses], occurring as the essential preliminary to an expansion of output." This increased demand for the stock of consumables needed to fund production of capital is a problem for the following reason:

. . . there seems no doubt the supply of Short Lacking is not sufficiently elastic to cope with such pronounced and discontinuous increases in demand, and that the responsibility for meeting them rests almost entirely upon the banking-system.

(Robertson, 1926, p. 72)

Here arises the same contradiction that Hayek was to later worry about, leading to his Wicksell-inspired monetary rule to set the money rate equal to the real rate:

Under such conditions it seems unreasonable to expect the banking system *both* to ensure that appropriate additions are made to the quantity of circulating capital *and* to preserve the absolute stability of the price level.

(Robertson, 1926, p. 72)

In reality Robertson feels the boom will be accomplished by the banks letting the price-level rise (just as Keynes had said of the "usual story" of the cycle in 1913). This increases the supply and demand for "short lacking" and the boom and the price level proceed apace.

Now enters the "machinery of banking (explicitly footnoted by Robertson as being suggested by Keynes at one point in the argument, p. 76). As the expansion develops, banks cumulatively raise "money rates of interest" (p. 76), sell "Government securities" (p. 77) and, ultimately, have to resort to "direct limitation of new loans" (p. 77), in an effort to simultaneously discourage and accommodate the new loan demand. This also is where, compared to Hayek's later theory, Robertson's more sanguine view of "over-investment" comes in. Thus he doubts the benefit of maintaining as a goal of monetary policy that lending always be consistent with voluntary savings. Even if that could be accomplished, says Robertson, such a course may choke off "socially beneficial" expansions of investment and output (pp. 78–80). It is also mentioned at this stage by Robertson that the controls of the banking system are asymmetric, and that it is more important to try to prevent excessive deflation on the down side of the cycle, than to prevent moderate inflation in the upturn. There is *no* control available to induce producers to take loans in the downturn and "there may be *no* rate of money interest in excess of zero" which will stimulate increased activity (p. 81).[13] Thus it is not surprising, as we saw in the last chapter, that Robertson recommended "some degree" of forced savings as beneficial, "the necessary price we have to pay for what we call progress (Robertson, 1928, p. 145)."

What is even more important for our story is that this firmly establishes a Cambridge version of a forced-savings doctrine, held by Robertson and at least for a time entertained by Keynes, long before Hayek's arrival on the scene in 1931. This makes it clear that Cambridge was not just talking past Hayek, misunderstanding his capital-theoretic foundations, as some have claimed (Caldwell, 1995). Instead Cambridge monetary theorists were well prepared for what Hayek was suggesting, as they had already faced this issue in the decade prior to 1931. Keynes, at least, had in fact moved beyond this stage by then. But we will save that argument for the next chapter.

Let us end this section by noting two things. First, Keynes's own flirtation with Robertsonian cycle theory was short lived. Second, that his stated reasons for doubting that theory points us toward another aspect of Keynes's interwar monetary thought represented both in his *Tract on Monetary Reform* (1923) and *Treatise on Money* (1930), namely, the consequences of rapid inflations or deflations on the distribution and level of income, and the consequent benefit of stabilizing the price-level. Given our above account of the close working relationship between Keynes and Robertson, it is interesting to note Robertson's own view, looking back from 1948 (Robertson, 1915 [1948]), p. xi). After noting Keynes's role in the development of his own theory, Robertson recalls:

While Keynes must at the time have understood and acquiesced in my step-by-step method, it is evident that it never, so to speak, got under his skin; for in his two successive treatments of the savings-investment theme in his two big books he discarded it completely.

Yet while it is obviously true that Keynes abandoned Robertson's method, it is instructive to note how he phrased his objection. He objected to two things. The first is the fact that Robertson's theory did not provide a role for the rate of interest. He also objected to Robertson's conclusion that central banks need not aim at price stability. That this was the case is not surprising, because throughout the twenties Keynes was deeply interested in the goal of stable money and in the Bank of England's "bank-rate" or interest rate policy. The first stage of this interest is evident in his summation of the monetary condition of the post-War Europe in *A Tract On Monetary Reform* (*CW* 4).

V. The *Tract*: Portrait of a monetary society in crisis

A central piece of our story concerns Keynes's involvement with financial policy and what might be termed "financial journalism" in the 1920s. Although much of this was written for a wider audience than professional economists alone, it stands the test of time and the subsequent development of monetary economics quite favorably. *A Tract on Monetary Reform* of 1923 (*CW* 4) well represents this aspect of Keynes's interests. It reproduces some earlier material he had written for the "Reconstruction Supplements" to the *Manchester Guardian Commercial* and generally stands as Keynes's comment, as a monetary analyst, on the post-World War I monetary problems of the former combatants. In the *Tract* Keynes revealed himself as a firm opponent of price-level instability and a proponent of the Cambridge version of the quantity theory, now applied after the war to a fluctuating exchange regime. Besides its trenchant account of the social consequence of inflation, the *Tract* is notable for the application of Cambridge monetary theory to two issues then headlining the news: the extent to which governments can and should use the monetary printing press for public finance and the, then new, supply-and-demand-determined system of fluctuating exchange rates.

The dependence of Keynes's *Tract* on Marshall and Pigou's theory of money is well known. Also notable, and much less commented upon, is that his theoretical interests there parallel his critique of the "forced savings" analysis discussed above – particularly in the concern with distributive and productive effects of changes in the value of money. Thus as far as the mechanics of monetary analysis go, Keynes was squarely within the orthodox Cambridge tradition of his day. In fact, his tastes in monetary theory as of 1923, as far as they are expressed in this popular book, were not even as innovative as the Robertson framework. Keynes of the *Tract* appears quite satisfied to investigate his subject with more traditional (and for his journalistic audience more intelligible) monetary tools. We do see, however, that Keynes in the *Tract* was beginning to speculate on the special qualities of an economic system that had outgrown in crucial ways Marshall's simplifying assumptions and his "real" economics.

The *Tract* argued that governments' unconstrained creation of money – reflecting the contemporaneous German hyperinflation – was the result of weak central government inflicting a tax on individuals' holdings of money – the holdings that Marshall had seen as flowing from the utility of the socially given convenience of money. Governments levy such a tax repeatedly, by continuously increasing this rate of money creation beyond that "foreseen" by the public. Yet this effect was not, Keynes argued, fully explained by the orthodox analysis in terms of a simple change in the "velocity of money." This is because, after the abuse of the value of money is realized, holders of money will come to expect it and will reduce their balances by even more than the extra note issue would imply. Ultimately, if the inflation is rapid and ruinous enough, this may create the conditions of the policy's own demise, as consumers' already minimized holdings of the debased currency are made worthless, and ultimately abandoned. But lagging expectations and the persistence in the public mind of the illusion of the stability of the monetary standard for fixing terms of contracts, (necessary and useful in normal times), meant that there was considerable room for weak governments to levy steep inflation taxes.

The conventional interpretation of the *Tract*[14] emphasizes Keynes's orthodoxy. This is supported by Keynes's use of the quantity theory of money: he even presents the theory as an equation in chapter 3 (*CW* 4, pp. 61–70), referenced to Marshall, Pigou and Fisher.[15] What is "modern" of Keynes in this respect may be his early use of a crude empirical method. So throughout the book there are numerous "tests" of his conclusions by resort to simple tables of time-series figures, his preferred use of statistics. All of this is well-known.

We wish to emphasize another side of the book. The interest of *A Tract of Monetary Reform* to our theme, not so well documented but of particular import in looking at the development of his later writings, is its presentation of a nascent view of the structure of post-war economies, of the new problems such a structure presents, and of the economics appropriate to it.[16]

To start to make this contrast it is useful to hark back to Marshall's *Principles*. There we find a society made up of small competitive family firms ("undertakers"), which possess both organizational skill and enough of a long-term outlook to engage in the savings and investment (motivated by the returns to waiting and the productivity of investment) necessary to capitalist production. Workers in these firms are skilled or unskilled earners of a wage, which varies somewhat indeterminately yet within limits set by the productivity gains that can be got out of higher wages, according to their efficiency. They produce goods destined for their own and other's consumption, aided by the skills and habits which their parents were able to provide them with, and in cooperation with the productive capital ("appliances") provided by the undertakers. There is also vague recognition of a class of money dealers who both receive savings and finance new investment, but this is clearly not the main interest of the book.

Marshall felt that his portrayal of the capitalist economy in the *Principles* was basically faithful to its important structures.[17] He nonetheless recognized that it left out various factors that became of increasing significance as the nineteenth century progressed. Despite his awareness of his omissions, he still believed that the *Principles* gave him an adequate basis for investigating his preferred theoretical object. This object was the market transaction and the relative price structure that would eventuate in his hypothetical long period, when the forces of competition could fully play out. The dynamic story that underpins the static equilibrium system he so constructs concerns how firms and industries might adjust under such a regime of unchanging competition. But Marshall was also a fastidious and orderly thinker. Thus his distribution theory was carefully crafted to define wages, profits, interest and rent in such a way that they would consistently add up to the total national dividend. One aspect of his overall vision was to depict a coincidence of interests between the classes of society in maximizing this dividend. He also hoped to provide an "engine of analysis" that would be useful for further economic studies. We have seen, however, that in addition this strategy set up unresolved tensions between his construction of a static equilibrium framework and his goal of including the major forces at work in the economic system of his day.

If we go even deeper, Marshall's most fundamental interest is often said to be the interplay, via "utility," between a society's wants and its activities. Ultimately, though, that reveals only his metaphysical taste in theorizing, and so refers to the forces to which he felt comfortable appealing: utility and productivity.[18] In any event, Marshall's hankering for realism meant he was not content to dwell long on abstract concepts. Hence the *Principles* is resplendent with the institutions, firms and characters of the British Victorian marketplace. The skilled craftsmen, the chivalric businessman, the frugal saver, all make up the cast in this drama, and are intended to show the relevance of his system. Indeed, it was Marshall's hope – never realized – that these characters would even themselves come to understand his economics. Of course, as discussed above, Marshall and Marshallianism had therefore to deal with the theoretical "threats" and the realistic "challenges" that were thereby created for this framework. The difficulty of treating large scale increasing-returns to production and the related rise of the infinitely lived public corporation within the theoretical context of this system was the most important of these challenges.

Further, recall that Marshallianism's particular weakness, the task Marshall most glaringly left undone in his own revisions of the *Principles*, was shown above to be the failure to update his monetary analysis in light of these challenges. The last chapter established that the next generation of Cambridge monetary economists after Marshall more or less explicitly realized and started their own work from an awareness of this weakness of Marshallianism. As we will subsequently claim that one aspect of the essence of the *General Theory* is its analysis of what is essential and different about a monetary economy (say from Marshall's or Smith's "real" economies), it is of interest to chronicle Keynes's developing alternative conception of a modern monetary economy. A bare outline of this vision is presented in the *Tract* (*CW* 4, pp. xiv):

> We leave saving to the private investor, and we encourage him to place his savings mainly in titles to money. We leave the responsibility for setting production in motion to the businessman, who is mainly influenced by the profits which he expects to accrue to himself in terms of money. Those who are not in favour of drastic changes in the existing organization of society believe that these arrangements, being in accord with human nature, have great advantages.

Hence arises the subject of the *Tract*:

> But they cannot work properly if the money, which they assume as a stable measuring-rod, is undependable. Unemployment, the precarious life of the worker, the disappointment of expectation, the sudden loss of savings, the excessive windfalls to individuals, the speculator, the profiteer – all proceed, in large measure, from the instability of the standard of value.

What analytical framework is appropriate to investigation of the distributive and productive effects of changes in the value of money?

> For the purpose of this enquiry a triple classification of society is convenient – into the investing class, the business class and the earning class. These classes overlap, and the same individual may earn, deal, and invest; but in the present organization of society such a division corresponds to a social cleavage and an actual divergence of interest.
>
> (p. 4)

This same basic conception of economic society underlies the *General Theory*. As will also be true in the *General Theory*, the driver of this system is the investor. How did we reach this point historically and institutionally, asks Keynes in the *Tract*? In the nineteenth century, the countries of the west developed a system of "contracts for the *investment of money*" and the fixity in money of these terms is the prime characteristic of our whole "*investment system*." This system further evolved, as the nineteenth century turned into the twentieth, into "many arrangements . . . for separating the management of property from its ownership" (p. 4,). These arrangements are typified by bonds, annuities and shares of common stock. All are contracts to receive more or less fixed sums of money at a future date. One important aspect of this development was that it created an atmosphere in harmony with the expansion of business and of population, and thus formed part of the ideological and spiritual supports of the growth of the system. It was also important that this system effectively mobilized large-scale production in a way that Marshall's family firms could not. Thus we can contrast Marshall's old style *real* system with Keynes's *monetary* economy, in that the latter system is fully congruent with the existence of large-scale production and public corporations:

> By this system the active business class could call to the aid of their enterprises not only their own wealth but the savings of the whole community: and the professional and propertied classes, could find an employment for their resources and (it was believed) small risk.
>
> (*CW* 4, pp. 5–6)

This arrangement worked remarkably well so long as monetary values were stable, which they generally were in the west for the hundred years before World War I. Keynes illustrates all of these cultural phases with an extended analysis of the British Consol, which during Victorian times provided the preferred vehicle for holding wealth and the symbol of the investing class:

> Thus there grew up during the nineteenth century a large, powerful, and greatly respected class of persons, well-to-do individually and very wealthy in the aggregate, who owned neither buildings, nor land, nor businesses, nor precious metals, but titles to an annual income in legal-tender money. In particular, that peculiar creation and pride of the nineteenth century, that savings of the middle class, had been mainly thus embarked.
>
> (p. 12)

This was one part of the investor class – the rentiers – who had a particular stake in the post-war negotiations over the value of long-term money contracts. In some of the cases these investments –along with the distribution of income and the cultural assumptions they supported were wiped out by inflation (for example, Germany). An irony of this process is that it was sometimes aided by these same investors' mistaken belief in the eternal fixity[19] of money values (for example, Germany). In others the presumed inviolable nature of these contracts (in commodity terms) became, Keynes says, an obstacle to progress (for example, France in the *Tract* and ultimately, Keynes would come to think by 1925, Britain). Essentially it meant encumbering those societies, already facing large war debts, with a crippling tax structure designed to serve the interests of the investor class. Expediency and social justice warranted reducing this tax burden by partly robbing capital value from the investors via an adjustment of the money terms payable for his bond holdings. Not to do so risked a ruinous inflation, social unrest, and the interruption of capital accumulation. Moreover, the end result would be the same, or worse, for investors anyway, he argued. Reasoned deliberate policy, managed currency reform and explicit capital duties were thus the way to proceed. Then normal business could resume again.

But what of the other two classes? "The business class," who actually organize production and deal in stocks of commodities, do so for the simple reason that they expect to be able to sell their output or inventory for more money than it took to produce or buy the stocks. Thus the expectation of rising prices generally stimulates business activity and that of falling prices retards it. In situations of rapid change, "when prices are rising month by month," such a businessman will enjoy windfall gains "upon which he had not calculated" (p. 17). Both because of lagging expectations, and the resulting fact that the nominal rate of interest never rises enough to keep the real-rate stable, no skill is required for speculation in an extreme inflation. "Anyone who can borrow money and is not exceptionally unlucky must make a profit, which he may have done little to deserve" (pp. 17–18). Thus begins Keynes's life-long conviction that the businessman is best depicted in terms of "expectations" and of "prospective prices." We saw above that this is explicit in terms of the general statement of "expectations as determining output" in the *General Theory*. It is also explicitly present in the structure of *A Treatise on Money*. In Chapter 17 of the *General Theory* we will see it formalized in the discussion of the own rates of interest analysis, which in simplified terms could be seen as asking: given real productivity, carrying costs, and price expectations, under what circumstances can employment of productive capital be assumed to yield a greater sum in terms of money than the holding of money balances?

Returning to the *Tract*, what makes an extreme instability of money values on the upward side so insidious for society – high- or hyper-inflation – is that producers can be virtually guaranteed the ability to make money without attention to the skills of enterprise. Businessmen in such situations thus cease to value productivity and thrift and lose interest in all long-term term commitments. "The welfare of his enterprise in the relatively distant future weighs less with him than before, and thoughts are excited of a quick fortune and clearing out (p. 23)." To make matters worse, this fall of the businessman's social utility and personal honor, as Marshall would have put it, is paralleled in society by a fall in the esteem in which the normal activity of business is held:

> To convert the business man into the profiteer is to strike a blow at capitalism, because it destroys the psychological equilibrium which permits the perpetuance of unequal rewards. The economic doctrine of normal profits, vaguely apprehended by everyone, is a necessary condition for the justification of capitalism.
>
> (*CW* 4, p. 24)

Finally, if depreciation of money discourages investment and discredits enterprise, what of that third great division in this economic portrait of society: the earning classes. Interestingly, and in accordance with our survey of his contemporary views on labor in Part I, Keynes in 1923 thought that the working classes had "improved their *relative* position in the years following the war, as against all other classes except the 'profiteers'" (p. 27, italics in original). Moreover – and even further evidence, if such were needed of the pre-*General Theory* orthodoxy of the rigid money wage argument – earners' incomes increased because social and bargaining conditions during the war and in its aftermath were such as to reverse what Keynes describes as "a commonplace of economic text-books," namely "that wages tend to lag behind prices" (p. 25). The result was that real wages rose in Britain and the United States. In keeping with his earlier-noted disapproval of labor unions, they are here seen as the major cause. Also there is the psychological motive of worker blackmail of employers in the context of the widespread resentment of them as war "privateers." Curiously, Keynes fails to even mention the vast labor shortage that sending a whole generation of young men to fight and often die in the trenches must have caused, not to mention the simultaneous total mobilization of the society for war production. In any event, as of 1923 Keynes's concern for the plight of labor lay in the future.

The conclusion of this line of Keynes's thought contains elements that are both conventional and suggestive of developments to come. First are the distribution effects:

> We conclude that inflation redistributes wealth in a manner very injurious to the investor, very beneficial to the business man, and probably, in modern industrial conditions, beneficial on the whole to the earner. Its most striking consequence is its *injustice* to those who in good faith have committed their savings to titles in money rather than things.
>
> (*CW* 4, p. 29, italics in original)

A further macroeconomic consequence of inflation – one that Keynes will come to play down in the context of further unemployment in the thirties – is that savers who are dependent on an "atmosphere of confidence" are thereby discouraged and thus investment (under the lump-of-savings theory of investment he had yet to throw off) would be hurt.

But when we turn to deflation things are even worse. In this case, the "investors" do well in money terms, but at the cost of disrupting the production process and so hurting both businessmen and wage earners by the occurrence of unemployment. Here is a situation that sounds more like the *General Theory* – one of insufficient aggregate demand, but now exclusively translated through price expectations (*CW* 4, p. 34, italics in original):

> Now it follows from this, not merely that the *actual occurrence* of price changes profits some classes and injures others . . . but that a *general fear* of falling prices may inhibit the productive process all together. For if prices are expected to fall, not enough risk takers can be found who are willing to

carry a speculative "bull" position, and this means that entrepreneurs will be reluctant to embark on lengthy productive processes involving a money outlay long in advance of money recoupment – whence unemployment. The fact of falling prices injures entrepreneurs; consequently the fear of falling prices causes them to protect themselves by curtailing their operations; yet it is upon the aggregate of their individual estimation of the risk, and their willingness to run the risk, that the activity of production and of employment mainly depends.

We can use this quote to focus on a theme explored in Part II, where we saw at this stage Keynes's wavering, but still intact, positive view of speculation as informed risk taking. Recall that he had at this stage begun to conduct his own speculation on commodity and currency exchanges. He then thought of the activity of speculation, perhaps somewhat hubristically, as a further division of labor by expertise, in this case creating specialists at bearing risk. Yet even the better-informed foresight of expert traders does not go so far that it can deal with wide swings in the value of money. Thus with the negative "externality" of uncertainty about future monetary values and the concern that this could lead to falling price expectations in mind, we see that in the *Tract* Keynes is already contemplating (negatively) the employment effects of such situations. He presents it there as a major problem of the post-World I world, and one which economic theory is ill prepared to deal with.

How to fix this problem? At this stage Keynes judged a restoration of stable or slightly rising price expectations, via a managed currency, to be the way to restore confidence in the future and so restore investment. Price stability was not just a goal for its own sake, but a means to the end of restoring confidence in the future and thereby restoring prosperity.

VI: "A Piece of Financial Machinery"

On a different plane, the *Tract* introduced a complex and technical chapter on "The Theory of Money and of the Foreign Exchanges" (*CW* 4, pp. 61–115). As indicated by that title – and by the juxtaposition in this chapter of sections devoted to "The quantity theory of money," "The theory of purchasing power parity," "The seasonal fluctuation," and "The forward market in exchanges" – Keynes thought the topic of how a monetary economy normally dealt with fluctuating prices to be important in itself. But the forward market linked up with the overall theme of the *Tract* in that Keynes thought of it as a way for both international trading firms and central banks to lock in future prices, and thus contribute to restitution of a stable value of money and therefore to prosperity. On the one hand, a stable managed currency with the aim of a stable price level (subject to choosing the proper index) would, by itself, increase confidence among traders and producers.

But further, and despite the stabilization of this index, seasonal swings in commodity prices for both production and consumption could be minimized, said Keynes, by off-loading the particular risks of a commodity to knowledgeable commodity speculation specialists. This is in line with our discussion in Part II, where we showed the enduring positive view that Keynes held of the social utility of commodity speculation and traders. Thus commodity futures traders played a very beneficial role through the hedging of future costs and revenues and the smoothing of seasonal price fluctuations. But only after the war, under a regime of floating exchange rates, did it become evident that traders on an international market also faced the risk that the currency exchange rates could themselves change.

Keynes was fully aware, in the *Tract*, of the economic truism (as it is known today) that one can either fix internal prices and let the exchange rate of a currency fluctuate, or vice versa. Although it must be said that Keynes did not see this as an either/or dichotomy, but one of degree. If they came into conflict, Keynes was in favor of changing the exchange rate and stabilizing internal prices. This was because of the crucial social role of money contracts and the system of production and distribution they supported. Keynes was also aware that the late nineteenth-century gold standard was able to keep *both* relatively stable, but he considered this as due to an unrepeatable coincidence of special circumstances. For one, gold discoveries and new processes for extracting it from ore were made at fortuitous times to keep pace with a growing world output.[20] For another, banking systems grew in both credit-granting facilities and in techniques of economizing on gold. Thus he judged that the gold standard had become a partly managed system even before the war.

In any case the war and its aftermath had upset the relationship between internal prices and exchange rates to such an extent that to bring the whole system into line again would require some degree of "normalization" before any thought was to be given to fixing exchanges. Keynes preferred a managed system in which stability of the price level would be the first goal of monetary policy, and exchange rate stability a secondary – he thought not wholly incompatible – goal. And if this normalization was to mean something other than the pre-war exchange rate of £1 = $4.86, so be it. One might say that when the "Return to Gold" did come a few years later, Keynes was proven practically correct on the distributional and productive disaster it would cause. That event also eventually signaled to Keynes that standard economic theory as he knew it was not of much assistance in accurately analyzing and predicting the consequences of such a decreased aggregate demand – or in his language of the twenties a "forced deflation" of wages and internal prices – for employment and output.

Here we are concerned to highlight a more technical aspect of the *Tract*. It is an analysis that will aid our eventual understanding of Keynes's presentation of the essential properties of interest and money in the *General*

Theory. In the *Tract*, though, it arises in a very different context than its more abstract use in the *General Theory.* We refer to Keynes's analysis of the forward market in currency, which provides the kernel of the idea of own-rates of interest as used both by Sraffa in his 1931 critique of Hayek and by Keynes in 1936.

We can set up the *Tract* discussion of this issue by reiterating Keynes's view that businesses had not learned to deal with the new era of floating exchange rates. He also observed that the conventional account of the relation of internal price fluctuation to exchange rate fluctuation – the purchasing power parity theory, best enunciated in his time by Gustav Cassell (1922) – was clearly not sufficient to explain short-term fluctuations in exchange rates. The twenties had shown that exchange rates had fluctuated more than was justified by short-run changes in prices. There thus arose in this period "a piece of financial machinery" – the forward market in currencies – of which, Keynes claimed in the *Tract*, there was not sufficient knowledge among traders relative to its importance. He thus took it upon himself to provide an explanation (*CW* 4, pp. 94–115).

We noted in Part II that Keynes's early account of forward exchanges coincided with his own personal experience of speculation. Further, Skidelsky (1992, p. 159) tells us that both the inflation tax discussion and this "forward market" section of the *Tract* were so based: "Both techniques were illuminated by his own experiences, the first as Treasury official in the war, the second as a post-war currency speculator." Thus we encounter again Keynes's characteristic mix of concrete financial experience and high level monetary theory thinking.

Keynes starts his analysis by observing that the practical use of forward markets by manufacturers and merchants dealing in foreign markets is to match spot transactions, where cash is exchanged today, with forward transactions to guarantee a fixed exchange rate upon delivery of the goods so contracted for. End users can thereby ensure that they are "protected from the consequences of any fluctuation in the exchanges in the meantime (p. 95)." He then offers extensive data on different currencies at different periods since the war to show that the prices set on these forward exchanges fluctuate, in amount and sign, switching from future currency being "at a discount or at a premium on spot" (p. 100). Commissions are set competitively, though, and are consequently often "small in relation to the risks that are avoided" (p. 100). That so few traders know or use the currency forward market, is due, – Keynes thinks – to superstitious avoidance of markets that are thought to be speculative. Additionally, such facilities are lacking in some countries, and even where it is available hedging against currency risk is not a complete protection if a commodity's value is poorly represented by the exchange rate alone, without accounting for the accompanying changes in internal prices.

Nevertheless "what it is that determines the amount and the sign (whether plus or minus) of the divergence between the spot and forward rates" (p. 102) is the real object to be explained. As we will see in the following chapters, this is a part of the *Tract* (pp. 102–15) of particular interest. Here Keynes steps back from the day-to-day aspects of his own experience, to outline a theory of this intertemporal price.

He begins with an example: the predominant influences on holding money at short-term at that time were the rates obtainable on London sterling deposits versus the rates on New York dollar deposits. If dollars in terms of pounds one month forward are at a discount of half a cent, traders can ensure themselves this half cent turn by selling the dollars spot for pounds and buying them back one month forward. Thus for merely being the owner of pounds in London during the month, as opposed to depositing them in dollars in New York, one can lock in this rate of return:

> That he should require and can obtain half a cent, which, earned in one month, is equal to 1½ percent per annum, to induce him to do the transaction, shows, and is, under conditions of competition, a measure of the market's preference for holding funds during the month in question in New York rather than in London.

Thus the market makers – sometimes called traders or arbitragers – are not themselves betting on the exchange rate's rising or falling. They are covered, and not holding a speculative position. The predominating influence over this preference in practice, Keynes claims, is differences in the current short-term interest rates offered by banks in the various financial centers:

> "That is to say, forward quotations for the purchase of the currency of the dearer money market tend to be cheaper that the spot quotations by a percentage per month equal to the excess of the interest which can be earned in a month in the dearer market over what can be earned in the cheaper." (pp. 103–4)

A few points important to our later understanding, and Keynes's later use of a more general framework of such rates, are worth noting. The first is that equilibrium on this market is a complex matter, defined by the expectations of the end users but enforced by the process of arbitrage. The end users' needs and opinions cause changing numbers of buyers and sellers to line up on different sides regarding falling or rising exchange rates. Who might these "end users" be? They will be the true customers of the exchange – traders who encounter seasonal differences between supply and demand – and speculators. (Keynes thus says – as did Marshall of commodity market participants – that the most risky speculators operate on a "spot" cash basis, uncovered by a forward contract.) Whoever they are and whatever position they take, market participants will fall into one or the other camps of Marshall's old "Bulls and Bears."

Alternatively, the arbitrageurs and marketmakers – those who make these opportunities possible – take covered positions based on the current opinion of the market, for which they secure only a small competitive "turn" on their trades. This means the extent of trading is ultimately limited by the cumulative financial resources that have been committed to future trading by these market makers.[21]

Such trade, at its most abstract, is of the nature of Marshall's stock equilibrium – which we have repeatedly emphasized throughout this book. There are two levels to the equilibrium of such markets. At one level, arbitrage activity between markets (as in the example including the spot exchange market, the forward exchange market and two bank-deposit markets) continually ensures that all interest rates and exchange rates will satisfy a condition of equality of profit opportunity for traders – often today called covered interest arbitrage. Thus the return on a deposit in London is equal to that on a deposit in New York at current exchange rates. But the forward premium or discount is a barometer of how strongly preference is felt for holding money in either place; and this is a matter of expectation about how prices will change from the spot rate. Therefore, at another level, it will be the needs and expectations of the end users that fix the terms at which future delivery or receipt of a currency can be had at any time. Given expectations and the needs of trade, these users enter the market on the side of supply or demand, and so move the "price" (the discount or premium) until it justifies this distribution of opinion. Outside of the action of arbitrage, speculators or traders would have a motive for buying or selling forward contracts as long as the current price does not reflect their degree of confidence in their expectations. Thus what moves the forward difference from the spot exchange is something that alters this opinion. What could such a "change in the news" be for the exchange market?

In the *Tract*, the predominant influence on established markets is "the interest rates obtainable on 'short' money" (p. 103), as stated previously. A second factor that dominates this, sometimes, is:

the various uncertainties of financial and political risk, which the war has left behind . . . the possibility of financial trouble or political disturbance, and the quite appreciable probability of a moratorium in the event of any difficulties arising, or of the sudden introduction of exchange regulations which would interfere with the movement of balances out of the country and even sometimes the contingency of a drastic demonetization.

(p. 105)

A third factor is the possibility of a dramatic change in expectation of what the future exchange rate will be. The result will depend on "whether it is the sellers or the buyers of forward dollars who predominate" (p. 106). If this change occurs in the presence of a difference in rates of interest between the two currencies, and in opposition to the distribution of funds suggested by the interest differential alone, then the price (discount or premium) will have to induce the arbitragers who are making the 1 1/2 per cent per annum (to use Keynes's example again) on the interest rate difference, to move funds. It is also necessary that they have the necessary funds available. The traders will then execute orders to buy or sell currency forward until a price is established that both compensates bulls and bears according to their changed expectations and ensures enough of a difference to "yield the arbitragers sufficient profit for their trouble" (p. 106).

Now we are talking about a movement in the exchange due to a definite speculative change. It may be so drastic a change as to lead to further, fourth, factor which occurs when there is speculation that is "exceptionally active and is all one way." In this case the rise of a bullish or bearish sentiment about a currency may exhaust the resources of the market and its makers. Then the discount or premium of the forward over the spot exchange rate may reach abnormal levels and may represent an "altogether abnormal profit to anyone who is in a position to buy these currencies forward and sell them spot" (p. 107). Only when new capital is thus drawn into the market by this high prospective return – or, Keynes does not add but we may presume must be true, the spot exchange rate is dramatically changed – can this price difference disappear.

Finally, notice that Keynes truly thinks of the professionals – the market makers – as playing a passive role here. Essentially they are a "piece of financial machinery," enforcing the necessary equilibrium of equal profit opportunities, by arbitraging across various transactions and markets in search of any remaining certain profit. "Normal" operation of the forward market – like the stability of a system built on money contracts – depends on the durability of a set of psychological expectations. Currency professionals are not villains on this view, but rather expert operators on relative risks who make the valuable opportunities of their trade available to the wider economy.

What of speculators? Also in keeping with our Part II treatment of Keynes's opinion of speculators, they are seen here as accurate predictors of currency movements:

> It is interesting to notice that when the differences between forward and spot rates have become temporarily abnormal, thus indicating an exceptional pressure of speculative activity, the speculators have often turned out to be right.
>
> (*CW* 4, p. 108)

It is interesting to speculate – as Keynes does not here – on the grounds upon which such speculation could ultimately be judged to be a "social bad." For one, speculative trading might be bad if – harking back to Marshall's "Folly of Amateur Speculators" – it led investment away from the long-run values of the real-rate of interest (for instance in the two countries whose money is at stake) and so led to a misallocation of capital. In a way a form of this view does fit with Keynes's conception of a monetary economy in crisis in the *Tract*. Unstable money values – and wide swings on currency markets as the exchange system tries to deal with these changing prices – leave room for unproductive activity to be – at least temporarily – profitable.

Thus in the short-term speculative activity may draw in otherwise productive businessmen, who are motivated by ways to earn more money in proceeds than their outlays. Given that Keynes considers that the "normal" operation of forward markets has a useful social function, the possibility of socially harmful speculation would turn on the *scale* of the activity. To use a later analogy from the *General Theory*, "speculators may do no harm as bubbles on a steady stream of enterprise. But the position is serious when enterprise becomes the bubble on a whirlpool of speculation" (*GT*, p. 159). It is when speculation draws in money resources from otherwise productive investment that it is to be judged socially harmful. Even worse, if this activity is seen as the dominant way to make money then employment and accumulation of real capital will suffer. In the *Tract* this latter negative externality is not brought clearly into focus, and no model of the possible spillovers into employment and output is offered. If we can only stabilize the price level – Keynes of the *Tract* is saying – such speculation will not be profitable and expectations and enterprise based on a stable price level will ensure the return to normalcy – for investors, businessman and earners.

VII. From the *Tract* to the *Treatise*

When the return to gold did come in 1925, Keynes rated it as a "policy of the feather brained order (*CW* 9, p. 246)." As is now well known, particularly since Donald Moggridge's (1972) full reconstruction of this episode of interwar policy, this was because Keynes did not think British internal prices had yet achieved consistency with the pre-war exchange rate of $4.86. By Keynes's calculations this would have required a further 10% reduction in British internal prices. The only way to achieve this – not told to the public, but known he said at the Treasury, at Threadneedle Street in the halls of the Bank of England and by the Professors who recommended this policy – was by forcing prices to fall in line with the new, overvalued exchange. Such forced normalization of prices is what in 1925 Keynes ironically called the necessary "automatic adjustments." But driving down the internal price level was not a painless or easy task:

> The Bank of England is *compelled* to curtail credit by all the rules of the gold standard game. It is acting conscientiously and "soundly" in doing so. But this does not alter the fact that to keep a tight hold on credit – and no one will deny that the bank is doing that – necessarily involves

intensifying unemployment in the present circumstances of this country. What we need to restore prosperity to-day is an easy credit policy. We want to encourage business men to enter on new enterprises, not, as we are doing, to discourage them. Deflation does not reduce wages "automatically." It reduces them by causing unemployment. The proper object of dear money is to check an incipient boom. Woe to those whose faith leads them to use it to aggravate a depression.

(*CW* 9, p. 259)

This is all quoted from his resulting 1925 comment, "The Economic Consequences of Mr. Churchill" (*CW* 9). That essay forms a fascinating record of the application of the *Tract* analysis to Britain's then controversial decision – now well-recognized as a debacle – to return to the gold standard at $4.86. Besides its clear use of the *Tract*'s monetary analysis of distribution – and its role as the beginning of Keynes's realization of the social injustice of balancing monetary changes on the back of labor (discussed above in chapter 7) – what is principally interesting in light of the later development of the *General Theory* is what it reveals about the state of Keynes's macroeconomic views in 1925.

Though "The Economic Consequence of Mr. Churchill" shows Keynes's growing disdain for orthodox economics, and though the *Tract*-style analysis is deployed as an effective journalistic critique of the decision to return to gold at an overvalued exchange rate, Keynes had no alternative economic "model" with which to back up his "intuition" that the forced deflation would be a long and painful experience, causing Britain much unemployment and lost output. Thus the movement of the exchange toward $4.86 is described as a "movement away from equilibrium" (*CW* 9, p. 245). Export industry must immediately adjust output prices to the new international reality, but they cannot easily adjust internal costs. This will only come with a general deflation. "But I think that Mr. Churchill's experts also misunderstood and underrated the technical difficulty of bringing about a general reduction of internal money values" (p. 250).

What Keynes claims should have been said – but could not be said for political reasons – is that to do so will involve forcing down wages. "To begin with there will be a great depression in the export industries." But this is only the start of a campaign to bring down all wages. "Now wages will not fall in the sheltered industries merely because there in unemployment in the unsheltered industries, therefore you will have to see to it that there is unemployment in the sheltered industries also. The way to do so will be by credit restriction." Keynes's casual treatment of how much unemployment will be caused is the most notable aspect of this analysis when considered in light of the *General Theory*. The clincher is that Keynes clearly describes such deflation-caused unemployment as a temporary disequilibrium phenomenon. How long will the authorities have to hide the real intent of their policy? In the guise of a critical but honest advisor, Keynes in 1925 would tell the government:

> We ought to warn you, though perhaps this is going a little outside our proper sphere, that it will not be safe politically to admit that you are intensifying unemployment deliberately to reduce wages. Thus you will have to ascribe what is happening to every conceivable cause except the true one. We estimate that about two years may elapse before it will be safe for you to utter in public one single word of truth. By that time you will either be out of office or the adjustment, somehow or other, will have been carried through.
>
> (*CW* 9, p. 253)

VIII. *A Treatise on Money*

We have already analyzed the treatment of speculation in Keynes's attempt – in *A Treatise on Money* (*CW* 5 and 6) – to provide an alternative model of the cycle as an inevitable, but self-correcting, deviation from long-period equilibrium in a monetary economy. In fact, in Chapter 10, we found that on the level of the liquidity preference analysis of financial markets, there is really very little difference between the *Treatise* and the *General Theory*. In this final section of the present chapter I wish to comment briefly on the mechanics of the *Treatise* "model" of the cycle, and on how that book envisioned the operation of a monetary economy.

The ambitions of the *Treatise*

The first thing to say about the *Treatise on Money* is that it represents Keynes's attempt to marry Wicksell's natural rate/money rate concept with the Marshallian version of the quantity theory, and thereby to construct a theory of the credit cycle. Keynes's discussion of the quantity theory tradition and of the history of discussions of the transmission effect from monetary changes to the 'real' economy is titled "The 'Modus Operandi' of Bank Rate" (*CW* 5, Chapter 13). He details there the theories of Marshall and his pupils, the Wicksellian tradition, and older discussions of the way in which money influences real activity. He declares that the state of this aspect of economics is notably undeveloped and unsatisfactory. His complaint about Marshall centers on the latter's committee testimony that we discussed above. "The emphasis here is on 'speculation,' which lends a false color" (p. 172). Much better is Hawtrey, getting closer to the influence of money on real activity and seeing financial machinery as something more than functionless speculation. Hawtrey, though, concentrates too much on the effect of new money on "investment by dealers and middlemen in liquid goods." In fact, Keynes shows that this notion was earlier refuted by Thomas

Tooke as far back as 1838 (p. 174). The best theory on offer, says Keynes, "though there are obscurities to overcome,"[22] is Wicksell:

> Wicksell conceives of the existence of a 'natural rate of interest,' which he defines as being the rate which is 'neutral' in its effects on the prices of goods, tending neither to raise nor to lower them, and adds that this must be the same rate as would obtain if in a non-monetary economy all lending was in the form of actual materials. It follows that if the actual rate of interest is lower than this prices will have a rising tendency, and conversely. It follows further, that so long as the money rate of interest is kept below the natural rate of interest, prices will continue to rise – and without limit.
>
> (*CW* 5, p. 176)

But this is about as far as the influence of Wicksell on Keynes goes. Wicksell does not make many other appearances in the *Treatise*. One gets the impression that Keynes's use of Wicksell is to invoke the voice of authority for what he already was going to say. This is implicit in that Keynes does not even mention Wicksell's capital theory discussions. He really had very little patience for such discussions – considering them useless and abstract. And as we will see in the next chapter, when confronted with the Austrian capital-theoretic version of Wicksell, in the shape of Hayek's theory of the cycle, he declared it to be totally nonsensical. What was attractive in Wicksell was his agreement with Keynes's already-held view that the influence of money was to be sought in its influence on long-term investment:

> At any rate, whether on or not I have exaggerated the depth to which Wicksell's thought penetrated, he was the first writer to make it clear that the influence of the rate of interest on the price level operates by its effect on the rate of investment, and that *investment* in this context means *investment* and not speculation.
>
> (*CW* 5, p. 177, italics in original)

More important than its use of themes from Wicksell, another ambition of the *Treatise* is its self-conscious attempt to offer an updated treatment of monetary theory – and to provide an alternative to what Keynes saw as the outdated quantity theory. This element is clearly stated in the "Author's Preface" (*CW* 5, p. xvii):

> In Books III and IV of this treatise I propose a novel means of approach to the fundamental problems of monetary theory. My object has been to find a method which is useful in describing, not merely the characteristics of static equilibrium, but also those of disequilibrium, and to discover the dynamical laws governing the passage of a monetary system from one position to another.

In comparison with the *General Theory*, therefore, much attention is justly focused in the secondary literature on the *Treatise* on whether Keynes has output and employment adjusting there,[23] and on the role in this regard of his celebrated "fundamental equations." This is a valid point of comparison between the two books in that it offers the starkest contrast to the *General Theory*, but it risks neglecting the things that carry over between them. In Keynes's view (*GT*, pp. vi–vii), the carryover is substantial – especially as regards the *Treatise's* analysis of financial markets and the determinants of the rate of interest.

The *Treatise* was, in fact, a complicated mix of monetary theory, institutional analysis and policy applications (historical and current). In order to investigate the credit cycle, and to provide a new theoretical foundation for studying modern monetary economies, Keynes felt it necessary to introduce many "salient features" (p. xvii) of modern money and banking and of monetary policy. Moreover the second volume, "The Applied Theory of Money,"[24] is given over to attempts to apply the framework of the first volume, "The Pure Theory of Money," to episodes of monetary history and policy. Given this enormous ambition and his many other activities in the twenties – along with the fact that his opinions concerning monetary theory were changing rapidly as the decade and the writing of this book wore on – perhaps it is not surprising that Keynes found it difficult to bring the project to a successful conclusion. Thus another thing to say in general is that the *Treatise* was an "artistic failure" – but especially its theoretical model of the cycle. Many of Keynes's contemporaries noted this, and, indeed, we have seen that he did so himself.

At the most abstract, and in the retrospective shadow cast by the *General Theory*, this failure of his "model" was due to Keynes's inability in that work to break away from the notion of a unique, full-employment, long period equilibrium construct. Nevertheless it was a grand failure of a book – sabotaged as much by its enormous ambitions as by this theoretical struggle. For many reasons, then, its now forgotten contents are worth picking over. Its failed model allows us to compare the vision of the *Treatise* with Keynes's later view of an economy prone to less-than-full-employment equilibria, and by contrast to highlight Keynes's theoretical advances in the *General Theory*. Moreover, the former book's institutional detail is of enduring relevance, and recognition of its rich detail allows one to construct a more continuous evolution from the *Treatise* to the *General Theory*. Finally, the occasional flashes of Keynes's brilliance that are buried in the *Treatise* still make for enjoyable and informative reading in their own right.

The "Fundamental Equations for the Value of Money"

Before going further, it is worth discussing briefly Keynes's theoretical methods in the *Treatise*. Chiefly we want to convince the reader that his much-abused "fundamental equations" were part of a conscious effort on his part to replace the oversimplified "real" economics of Marshall and the quantity theory with recognition of the vast consequences of introducing money and the financial system into economic theory. Keynes may have failed to provide a completely coherent framework for analyzing such a system, but his *quaestia*, as he put it, is still interesting.

What did the "fundamental equations" consist of? They are identities which specify the conditions of equilibrium of the level of two, he thought importantly separated, sub-price indices of the general price level. The first one focuses on the household sector. It identifies the factor incomes (often identified as "efficiency earnings") and expenditure and savings levels which will stabilize the price of consumption goods. The second is related to the investment good sector and the behavior of business "entrepreneurs." The price level of investment goods is in equilibrium when the cost of production of investment goods is equal to the profits from investment. Hence the definition of profits as net of "windfalls" – that is, net of abnormal profits. When the level of profits is different from this, then the current price at which investment goods are selling will earn entrepreneurs windfall gains (or losses). The two sectors are related to one another in the *Treatise* ". . . by the fact that the division of the output between investment and goods for consumption is not necessarily the same as the division of the income between savings and expenditures on consumption" (*CW* 5, p. 123).

Keynes's failure to provide a proper theoretical framework in theory for analyzing the credit cycle stems in part from how many complicated details of a monetary system were stuffed into the two *portmanteau* "fundamental equations" – what we earlier saw Marshall in the *Principles* call the "actions and reactions of credit" on the economy. Perhaps it was subconscious at the stage of the *Treatise*, but in this way Keynes seemed to indicate, as Hawtrey had earlier done, that the conditions of long-period equilibria were so stringent, so distant from the actual conditions and the active forces for change at work in a real monetary economy, as to be of little use in analyzing them. Yet if Hawtrey saw this as a reason to be humble as to the goals of monetary theory, the haughtier Keynes considered it as an achievable challenge. Thus the "fundamental equations for the value of money" (*CW* 5, Chapter 10) were at one level supposed to supersede, for a monetary economy, what the similar identities of the equation of exchange achieved for an earlier stage of economics.[25] Notwithstanding that they were more appropriate to modern conditions – and that reference to them would show that oversimplified quantity-theory chains of reasoning from cause to effect in terms of the volume of money, the price level and the velocity of money were thus inadequate – Keynes accepted that they were still just the starting point of monetary analysis:[26]

. . . all these equations are purely formal; they are mere identities; truisms which tell us nothing in themselves. In this respect they resemble all other versions of the quantity theory of money. Their only point is to analyse and arrange our material in what will turn out to be a useful way

for tracing cause and effect, when we have vitalized them by the introduction of extraneous facts from the actual world.

(CW 5, p. 125)

What were these "extraneous facts" that would "vitalize" the *Treatise's*
identities and make them appropriate to a monetary economy? To begin,
all of the background assumptions that we saw above as emphasized by
Keynes in the *Tract* have first to be assumed. Among these was the distribution of income in such a monetary economy between the investing, business and earning classes. Additionally, it was important that many new
opportunities for saving and investment behavior were available in a
sophisticated financial economy. Also important was the conventional
behaviors of these classes and the influence of changes in the value of
money on their expectations, as well as on the expectations of the laboring
classes. To these Keynes added recognition, as both Hawtrey and Robertson
had before him, that the decisions to save and to invest are made by different sets of people for different reasons. What stood between these actors
in the modern economy was the whole machinery of banking and credit.
Further, said Keynes, and following from a true stock-flow recognition of
Marshall's, Lavington's and Pigou's, real-balances version of the demand for
money, the decisions to save out of income also involve a second decision
as to the form of asset in which to hold savings. As we have seen in Part II,
this creates a role in the analysis of savings and investment for the whole
complex of "liquidity preference theory" considerations: the expectations
and asset holding behavior of investors, of the banks, of market professionals and of entrepreneurs.

Also of importance is Keynes's elaborate and valuable presentation of the
uses of money in a modern monetary system in the *Treatise* (*CW* 5, Chapters 2,
3 and 15). This analysis was also to be assumed in the *General Theory*, but is
most often lost on modern readers. The original details are worth consult-
ing, but the most important aspect of the scheme to remember is its identification of two somewhat independent routes by which money circulates
through the economic system. The "industrial circulation" is that part of
both "income" and "business" deposits by which the factors of production
are paid, and by which money is spent on annual output. Its velocity k_1,
bears a fairly stable relation, given payment and banking customs, to economic activity. This is not so of the "financial circulation," which is the flow
of payments through the financial markets and through banks coincident
with the credit-creation process – in short, the flow of money spent for those
activities of financial markets that we have analyzed in Part II.

In the *Treatise*, Keynes relates the use of this part of "business" deposits to
his elaborate analysis of liquidity preference among "bulls and bears." He
notes that the operation of these markets, by comparing expected returns on
financial and real productive investments, governs the rate of new capital

production. Since thereby investments in real capital involve the pace of activity on financial markets – the scale of investment depended on the expansion or destruction of deposits by the banking system – and since it is by abstaining from real investment and holding money that a "bear" position is satisfied, the financial circulation is much less stable than the income circulation. Thus the financial circulation velocity k_2, does not bear a stable relationship to economic activity.

The total amount of the financial circulation depends, therefore, partly on the *activity* of transaction but mainly on the magnitude of the 'bear' positions – both of these things being likely to be phenomena of rapidly *changing* prices rather than of an absolutely high or low level.

(*CW* 5, p. 225)

All of this combined to emphasize that, in a monetary system, long-period equilibrium was a very complicated affair. This is in addition to the complications we detailed in the last chapter that were already inherent in Marshall's non-monetary vision of a long-period equilibrium enforced by 'real' competition alone. One might suppose that the very complexity of the monetary forces considered in the *Treatise* would have suggested to Keynes that a monetary economy might be one in which financial activity was capable of stalling Marshall's competitive process. But this insight lay in the future. And this despite the fact that the model of the *Treatise* contains even more reason to expect inherent instability of prices than the complexity of the equilibrium conditions of the fundamental equations alone would suggest. For it is actually a book about cycles – or how easily such conditions will not be met. Therefore much of its discussion is devoted to detailing how deviations from this equilibrium were inevitable, and how they cumulatively set off other secondary accentuating factors in a complex and unpredictable mix. An extensive quotation is worthwhile to make the nature of the complex *Treatise* vision of long-period equilibrium clear:

This means, indeed, that in equilibrium – i.e. when the factors of production are fully employed, when the public is neither bullish nor bearish of securities and is maintaining in the form of savings deposits neither more nor less than the 'normal' proportion of its total wealth, and when the volume of savings is equal both to the cost and to the value of new investments – there is a unique relationship between the quantity of money and the price levels of consumption goods and of output as a whole, of such a character that if the quantity of money were to double the price levels would double also.

But this simple and direct quantitative relationship is a phenomenon only of equilibrium as defined above. If the volume of saving becomes unequal to the cost of new investment, or if the public disposition toward securities takes a turn, even for good reason, in the bullish or in the bearish direction, then the fundamental price levels can depart from their equilibrium values without any change having occurred in the quantity of money or in the velocities of circulation. It is even conceivable that the cash deposits may remain the same, the savings deposits remain the same, the velocities of circulation may remain the same, the volume of monetary transactions may remain the same, and the volume of output may remain the same, and yet the fundamental price levels may change.

Such an exact balance is, of course, only a theoretical possibility. In the actual world a change in anything is likely to be accompanied by some change in everything else. But even so the degrees of change in the quantity of money, the velocities of circulation, and the volume of output will not be related in any definite or predictable ratio to the degrees of change in the fundamental price levels. Indeed this is notoriously the case at the acute phases of a credit cycle.

(CW 5, pp. 132)

One is struck by what seems an excessive amount of action that is here shoehorned into just two identities! Yet Keynes was conscious of a long tradition in economics of such heroic reductionism. For example, this is still twice the number of equations on which the simple one-sector quantity theory depends. Even allowing for a doubling of the amount of insight that may be gained from treating the economy as two sectors rather than as only one, and accounting for the many permutations and re-arrangements of these equations that Keynes in the first book of the *Treatise* often substituted for insight, the model there is simplistic. But one interesting aspect to be gleaned from comparing Keynes's views between 1930 and 1936 is that they suggest an evolution toward a belief in *more* inherent stability for the modern economic system – at least in so far as prices are concerned. This is despite the fact that throughout he maintained a belief in the efficacy – if not, ultimately, the sufficiency as regards prosperity – of a stable price level policy for stabilizing inherently unstable investment expectations.

On one level Keynes's eventual view of a more stable system of prices in the *General Theory* is due to the well-known insight he later gained from the self-limiting multiplier process for changes in employment and output. At another, as we saw in Part I, he had come to see that the stability of output prices depended on an inherently stable level of factor earnings not because wages were rigid in some artificial sense, but because the marginal efficiency of wages was indeterminate within some limits. But on yet another wider view of price stability this insight was due to Keynes's acceptance that a monetary economy – an economy, as he says in the preface to the *General Theory* (*GT*, p. vii), "in which changing views about the future are capable of influencing the quantity of employment and not merely its direction" – prices could be stable *because* output adjusts.

The "widow's cruse fallacy"

Such an insight is reinforced by consideration of the famous "widow's cruse" conundrum of the *Treatise*, which is found discussed alongside that of the fundamental equations in Chapter 10 of the *Treatise* (*CW* 5, pp. 125–6). The first fundamental equation defines equilibrium for households as being satisfied when the net income of factors of production (net of "windfall" profits or losses) is equal to the expenditures and savings of these factors. If this condition is met, the price level of commodities will be stable. The second fundamental equation defines equilibrium of the price of investment goods as being satisfied when the proceeds of investment are equal to the cost of production of investment goods (only normal profits are being earned). Thus in equilibrium windfall profits will be zero.

As argued by Keynes in the quote above (on pages 334-35), there are many things which can upset this equilibrium. Disequilibrium, where $I \neq S$, can arise from changes in the disposition of factor incomes between savings and investment, from changes in the expectations of financial market participants and from changes in the expectations of businessmen concerning their degree of bullishness or bearishness toward the future profitability of investment in real capital. But, surprisingly, the spending or saving of the seemingly inevitable "windfalls" which would emerge for businessmen ("entrepreneurs") in the process of the cycle is not among the disequilibrating factors cited by Keynes. That is to say, what happens if the entrepreneurs "chose to spend a portion of their (windfall) profits on consumption" (p. 125)?

> . . . the effect is to *increase* the profit on the sale of liquid consumption goods by an amount exactly equal to the amount of profits which have been thus expended. This follows from our definitions, because such expenditure constitutes a diminution of saving, and therefore an increase in the differences between I' [the cost of production of new investment] and S. Thus, however much of their profits entrepreneurs spend on consumption, the increment of wealth belonging to entrepreneurs remains the same as before. Thus profits, as a source of capital increment for entrepreneurs, are a widow's cruse which remain undepleted however much of them may be devoted to riotous living. When, on the other hand, entrepreneurs are making losses, and seek to recoup those losses by curtailing their normal expenditure on consumption, i.e., by saving more, the cruse becomes a Danaid jar which can never be filled up; for the effect of this reduced expenditure is to inflict on the producers of consumption goods a loss of an equal amount. Thus the diminution of their wealth, as a class, is as great, in spite of their savings, as it was before.
>
> (*CW* 5, p. 125)

This "widow's cruse" argument was later dubbed by a "fallacy" by the Cambridge Circus – the name given to the group of young economists who met in Cambridge after the *Treatise* was published to argue over its tenets (*CW* 13, pp. 337–43). It offers a convenient window into the failings of the *Treatise* model when considered in light of the *General Theory*. In its raw form it appears to be a fantastic assertion – that changes in the proportions of "windfall" profits that are consumed on the part of entrepreneurs lead to an unstoppable process whereby, either investment due to the rising price of consumption goods bought by entrepreneurs is sent spiraling upward in a (class-wise) self-funded way, or profits are sent spiraling downward in a vain attempt by entrepreneurs to tighten their collective belt. It appealed to Keynes because it formally makes his much-stressed point in the *Treatise* that it is investment ("enterprise") and not saving ("thrift") that makes for prosperity.[27] Yet to understand how even so powerful a mind as Keynes's could be confused by his own model into believing this proposition it is helpful to consider how such a proposition would be treated in the *General Theory*.

Notice that his suggestion here is reminiscent of the later Keynesian "paradox of thrift." Though no specific statement of this paradox is offered in the *General Theory* – and though it has become a bête noir of rigid anti-Keynesian rhetoric – it is actually a plausible deduction from the idea stressed by Keynes in both the *Treatise* and the *General Theory* that increased savings could be socially bad, *under conditions short of full employment*. What turned the "fallacy" into a valid "paradox" between the *Treatise* and the *General Theory*?

One plausible explanation of the seemingly bizarre "widow's cruse" assertion – especially for one otherwise so attached to "realistic," policy applicable, models as we have seen was Keynes – is that no disequilibrium adjustment of expenditures and output is defined in the formal analysis of the *Treatise*. Instead only prices are allowed to fluctuate when the fundamental equations are out of equilibrium. It is true that Keynes of the *Treatise* often described how an economy that had gotten into the process of disequilibrium – either naturally, or in the face of a policy-induced change – would suffer numerous consequences in terms of expenditures and employment. But the *equilibrium* level of each equation still evidently exerts an ultimately attractive force. Thus, as Keynes says in the quotation above, the equilibrium level of prices is only consistent with full employment. In the *Treatise* (as in Marshall's works), it was implied that this state of affairs would naturally be re-established.

The plausibility of this line of thinking on Keynes's part is borne out by the preface to the *General Theory* (*GT*, pp. vi–vii). There we find Keynes describing the difference between the two books as "probably clearer to myself than it will be to others" and "in my own mind is a natural evolution in a line of thought which I have been pursuing for several years." What was Keynes's view of the difference between the two books?

When I began to write my *Treatise on Money* I was still moving along the traditional lines of regarding the influence of money as something so to speak separate from the general theory of supply and demand. When I finished it, I had made some progress towards pushing monetary theory back to becoming a theory of output as a whole. But my lack of emancipation from preconceived ideas showed itself in what now seems to me to be the outstanding fault of the theoretical parts of that work . . . that I failed to deal thoroughly with the effects of *changes* in the level of output. My so called "fundamental equations" were an instantaneous picture taken on the assumption of a given output. They attempted to show how, assuming a given output, forces could develop which involved a profit-disequilibrium, and thus required a change in the level of output. But the dynamic development, as distinct from the instantaneous picture, was left incomplete and extremely confused.

As Skidelsky succinctly puts it (1992, p. 448), "A theory which assumed fixed output could not explain what caused output to vary." What was missing from the *Treatise* was the notion that the "dynamic development" of the system could be something other than a Marshallian-style leap between full employment positions which were themselves defined outside the monetary realm, even if, following Wicksell, Keynes recognized that these positions might contain different "natural" rates of interest. In other words, Keynes was groping toward a new position – perhaps spurred on by following out the consideration in the *Treatise* of expenditures 'a la Hawtrey,[28] perhaps spurred on by the Circus's objections to the "widow's cruse fallacy," or perhaps led-on by the multiplier analysis of Richard Kahn (1931) and Jens Warming (1932). Dating does not matter so much. What does matter is that Keynes was led to the truly radical theoretical notion that Marshall's full employment long-period positions might *not* have the attractive force that would ensure their eventual establishment – or re-establishment after a shock – once monetary factors were admitted into the analysis. In the *General Theory*, Keynes was to posit that macroeconomic stability might, curiously, be *more* enduring than the *Treatise* had suggested – just because of the prevalence of monetary factors. The price to be paid for this short-period stability, however, is the possibility of involuntary unemployment.

13
Sraffa and Hayek on "Own-Rates of Interest"[1]

> . . . when the definitive history of economic analysis during the nineteen-thirties comes to be written, a leading character in the drama (and it was quite a drama) will be Professor Hayek.
>
> J. R. Hicks (1967)[2]

> Nor should we be surprised that Sraffa, with his taste for the concrete and his characteristic irony, has at the same time put us on our guard against a certain loose manner of conducting politics and tackling economic questions.
>
> G. Napolitano (1978)

I. Introduction

In the last chapter we touched on the relationship between Keynes's *Treatise on Money* and the Wicksellian tradition of monetary theory. Keynes was first of all attracted to Wicksell's clear statement that the transmission mechanism from money to the 'real' economy was via the influence of the money rate of interest on *investment*, and not on *speculation*. Second, Keynes took on board Wicksell's distinction between the *money* rate of interest, set in financial markets with the participation of the central bank, and the *natural* rate of interest, determined by the profit rate on new uses of capital. If these rates are the same then money is *neutral* with respect to the price level. If they depart from each other, prices will rise or fall as the money rate is below or above the natural rate.

As we also stated in the foregoing chapter, there is reason to believe that Keynes did not fully endorse – or maybe even understand, as of the *Treatise* – the whole of Wicksell. Keynes pled that his poor knowledge of the German language, and the late stage in the development of his thought at which he became aware of Wicksell's work, meant that Wicksell actually had little influence on the composition of the *Treatise* (*CW* 5, p.178). These reasons accord well with our analysis to this point of the Cambridge monetary theory tradition and Keynes's role in it. Marshall, Hawtrey and Robertson were the main authors on business cycle theory to which Keynes was responding in the *Treatise*. Yet the full import of the Wicksellian tradition for the development of the *General Theory* really comes after the *Treatise* – although Keynes's reaction and use of that tradition is inseparable from the analysis of the *Treatise*. A hint of what was to come is evident in Keynes's brief discussion of Wicksell in the *Treatise*. Keynes casually comments in passing, correctly it turns out, that Wicksell's view of the neutrality of money meant that his "natural" rate of interest must be the "same rate as would obtain if in a non-monetary economy all lending was in the form of actual materials" (*CW* 5, p. 177). Nothing further is made of this notion in the *Treatise*, but we will see in what follows that it would loom large in importance as the transition to the *General Theory* proceeded.

To set out the context for this aspect of the transition in Keynes's thought, in this chapter we explore the meaning and significance of the pre-*General Theory* use of the conceptual tool of "own-rates" of interest. We are thus drawn to a short but dense critique in 1932 by Piero Sraffa of F. A. von Hayek's *Prices and Production*, (1931) Hayek's reply and Sraffa's rejoinder (Sraffa, 1932a,b; Hayek, 1932). This exploration will prepare us for the next chapter that deals with the use Keynes made of this concept to illustrate the essential properties of interest and money in Chapter 17 of the *General Theory*. Significantly for our story, included in Sraffa's review is his use of the own rates of interest tool in a critique of the more general Wicksellian framework.

Two important issues are raised by Sraffa, which were also of importance for Keynes at this point. One is the just mentioned "method of neutral money" proposed by Wicksell and his followers as a way to highlight the effects of money on the economic system by the comparison of "real" (or barter) and "monetary" systems. Second, Sraffa analyzes a particular use of this method by Hayek, the forced savings account of business cycles in *Prices and Production* (1931). As we have seen, this idea had been familiar for some time to the monetary economists of the Cambridge School. Sraffa's critique thus reinforces Keynes's rejection of Robertson's version of "forced savings" as an important aspect of economic crises. Sraffa's evaluation of the "method of neutral money" is more ambiguous, arguing that the method may be recommended if followed consistently, as he thought Hayek had not. But Keynes's development of this idea was to be entirely different than Sraffa's original use. We will see that he takes the concept of "own-rates" of interest from Sraffa's and Hayek's long period setting, and uses it to identify what is essential to the properties of a monetary economy in short-period equilibrium – one for which long-period forces may often be irrelevant. In this way the Sraffa-Hayek exchange links with a theme we have been building throughout Parts II and III: how Keynes suggested we theoretically represent a monetary economy.

This debate also plays a role in the larger historical context of interwar business cycle theory, particularly in England. Partly this is due to the role of *Prices and Production* as the central text, and the high water mark, of the career of one of Keynes's central rivals in the attempt to explain the Depression, F. A. von Hayek. Much has been written about this rivalry, some of it centered on discussion of the desirability, or not, of "going back to Hayek" to reformulate a way forward for economics (Lachmann, 1986). Alternatively, it has been suggested that this debate is important as an argument for "going back to Sraffa" (and avoiding the detour of Keynes) for a reformulation of economics (Kurz, 2000). We have nothing to add to either of those questions. Except, that is to say, as it is considered relevant that we conclude that Sraffa's review was on sound ground, of lasting significance and was influential on Keynes.

Outside economics proper, there were doubtless other issues of a personal or political nature involved in the debate between Sraffa and Hayek.[3] One is the degree to which Hayek and his work was used to launch a conservative challenge to the preeminence of Keynes and Cambridge on the British scene of the 1930s. Modern scholars committed to subjectivism in method, to Hayek's political ideals, to "Austrian" economics, or even to Sraffian economics, often point to the supposed ulterior motives of Sraffa's critique of Hayek, and to Sraffa's later supposed role in launching an "anti-subjectivist" movement, as elements of some sort of conspiracy to bring down Hayek. Our reading of the political landscape of the 1930s is simpler. It seems more probable that Hayek's diagnosis of the "crisis" of the Great Depression, and his suggestion for how to use monetary theory to analyze it, was abandoned both by the economics profession and, more widely, on the intellectual and political scene of the 1930s, owing to its inherent shortcomings. First, there is the fact that Hayek's proposed theory was ultimately judged by most contemporary economists to be incapable of showing what it hoped to show: that "crises" were the inevitable result of changing the quantity-times-the-velocity of money in a system. Second, the associated policy pessimism – Hayek believed that crises should be left to sort themselves out – was simply unacceptable politically and professionally in the context of the 1930s.

Readers with different views, however, can nevertheless take our story as an analysis of a relatively little-examined aspect of this period – an aspect reflecting only the development of economics itself. In what follows we will focus exclusively on the role of the exchange between Sraffa and Hayek in the development of Keynes's *General Theory*. We will here simply concentrate on what was written by Hayek and Sraffa at the time, and later by Keynes, on the topics introduced above.

II. Setting the stage

Prices and Production (1931, 1935)[4] consists of a series of four lectures Hayek presented at the London School of Economics in 1930. They were intended to outline the "Austrian" approach to the explanation of business cycles originating in the work of Mises and extended by his student Hayek. Presented to an English audience largely unfamiliar with Austrian work, Hayek's lectures must have seemed excitingly novel. Moreover, the fact that they purported to delve into the causes of the great question of the day, industrial depression, added to the purely theoretical interest. As should not be surprising, the fascination with Hayek was a combination of a putatively higher level of abstraction[10] than monetary theory had then attained (today we would ascribe this to a better "technique"), and a novel combination of disparate parts of the existing literature. Lionel Robbins, who was largely responsible for bringing Hayek to England, gave voice to the feeling that here was something new and significant in his glowing foreword to the book:

> I hope that the publication of Dr. Hayek's Lectures, which stand in the mid-stream of this [the Austrian business cycle theorists] great tradition, will do something to persuade English readers that here is a school of thought which can only be neglected at the cost of losing contact with what may prove to be one of the most fruitful scientific developments of our age.
>
> (Hayek, 1931, p. x)

Hayek's approach was an eclectic[5] blend of the Austrian capital theory of Bohm-Bawerk, the short-run quantity theory effects of the early British monetary theorists and the relative-price and interest rate theories of Wicksell. Thus it is easy to see how Hayek and Keynes were both vying for the same theoretical space in economics. But instead of Keynes's championing of price-level stability, Hayek proposed that a legitimate monetary theory would turn only upon relative price effects (Hayek, 1935, pp. 22–8). For this reason he attacked the idea of a general price level as theoretically unsound[6] and declared that the corresponding notion of a general value of money was superfluous (pp. 25–6):

> And, indeed, I am of the opinion that, in the near future, monetary theory will not only reject the explanation in terms of a direct relation between money and the price level, but will even throw overboard the concept of a general price level and substitute for it investigations into the causes of the changes of relative prices and their effects on production.
>
> (Hayek, 1935, pp. 25–6)

Correspondingly, Hayek's explanation of business cycles centered on the effect of monetary policy on the relative prices of capital and consumption goods. Here is the centrality of Mises's forced saving theory and the Wicksellian natural-rate doctrine to his argument. In Hayek's scheme, the natural rate was the rate which equalized "the supply and demand for real capital" and if the bank rate (or actual rate) differed from this, the result was a divergence of "voluntary" saving and investment. It was the interest rate as an intertemporal price ratio between current (consumption) production and future (capitalistic) production that signaled the investors to invest more than was "natural," and thus led to the creation of "forced savings." Crises and cycles, then, resulted from what Hayek considered the *inevitable* destruction of capital that followed such a misdirection of production by bank-influenced prices. This basic argument is much like Robertson's, but its dependence on Bohm-Bawerk's capital theory gave it a different, as Kaldor tells us, more technically exotic, feel – for a time.[7]

Following Wicksell, Hayek focused on the natural rate ("equilibrium rate") as the rate which would equalize investment and voluntary saving as they would occur in a "nonmonetary" barter economy. The influence of money in this scheme came purely through its role as the medium of exchange. This is what will turn out to be the most important difference from Keynes. Since saving and investment actually took the form of money transactions, the banking system (including the central bank) had the ability, said Hayek, to induce actual savings and investment to diverge from their "natural" proportions. This occurred when the money rate was set above or below the natural rate. In what Hayek saw as the normal course of the boom the too low money rate misdirects production toward a more capital-intensive mix (in Austrian parlance a "lengthening of the period of production").

Where Hayek saw himself as differing with Wicksell was over the role which the "natural rate" could serve as a guide to policy in an expanding economy. As a then contemporary writer on 1930 interest rate theory put it, there were

> . . . four tests which Wicksell gave for his "natural" rate: viz., (i) stabiliza-tion of the general price-level; (ii) equalization of current savings and investment; (iii) the identity of the "natural" rate with the non-monetary barter rate; and (iv) its identity, again, with the prospective yield on future real capital.
>
> (Adarkar, 1935, pp. 30–1)

Of these four results of an actual rate being set equal to the natural rate (for Hayek by a "neutral" money policy of maintaining the money supply con-stant), Hayek found a contradiction between (i) and the rest. In other words, he argued that while setting the natural rate equal to the money rate would give expression to the voluntary decisions captured in (ii) through (iv) it could not at the same time keep the price level constant in an expanding economy:

> Nevertheless, it is perfectly clear that, in order that the supply and demand for real capital should be equalized, the banks must not lend more or less than has been deposited with them as savings . . . And this means naturally that . . . they must never allow the effective amount of

money in circulation to change. At the same time, it is no less clear that, in order that the price level may remain unchanged, the amount of money in circulation must change as the volume of production increases or decreases. The banks could either keep the demand for real capital within the limits set by the supply of savings, or keep the price level steady; but they cannot perform both functions at once.

(Hayek, 1935, p. 27)

Thus, Hayek stakes out his position. He views the goal of a "neutral" monetary policy (that is, one that allows for the full expression of voluntary decisions over saving and investment) as a proper one. Giving full vent to individual decisions requires setting the money-rate equal to the natural rate. And since this policy is incompatible with attention to the general price level (as already Robertson had suggested and Keynes had rejected), Hayek believes we must abandon any such fuzzy aggregative concepts as the price level and focus our attention on the relative price effects of a monetary policy:

But it seems obvious as soon as one once begins to think about it that almost any change in the amount of money, whether it does influence the price level or not, must always influence relative prices. And as there can be no doubt that it is relative prices which determine the amount and direction of production, almost any change in the amount of money must necessarily also influence production.

(Hayek, 1935, p. 28)

III. "Assuming away the object"

This is the argument that so fascinated economists in the thirties. Like many theoretical developments it contains in equal parts, methodological prescription and positive analysis. Hayek insisted that a valid monetary theory must proceed from the "method of neutral money." This involves comparing a hypothetical barter price system in equilibrium with the disturbances to that system that result from changes in monetary policy.

Sraffa clearly saw this dual nature of Hayek's thesis, as his critical review analyzes both Hayek's chosen framework and his use of that framework. Thus both an *internal* and an *external* critique of Hayek's argument is presented by Sraffa.[8]

In Sraffa's view, however, it is not possible to consider these elements in isolation. The basic flaw of the theory originates with the method. The subtlety of the review is the manner in which Sraffa weaves the internal contradictions of the theory into the basis of the external critique. It is useful to begin with this external criticism.

The external critique in Sraffa's review addresses the important issue of the place of money in a theoretical representation of the economy. His complaint is that while Hayek professes to be analyzing the influence of money on relative prices he is in fact concerned with a wholly different question:

> But the reader soon realizes that Dr. Hayek completely forgets to deal with the task he has set himself, and that he is only concerned with the wholly different problem of proving that only one particular banking policy (that which maintains constant under all circumstances the quantity of money multiplied by its velocity of circulation) succeeds in giving full affect to the "voluntary decisions of individuals," especially in regard to saving, whilst under any other policy these decisions are "distorted" by the "artificial" interference of banks.
>
> (Sraffa, 1932a, p. 45)

By Sraffa's account the reason that Hayek strays from the path he sets out for himself can be traced to the theoretical method he employs; the technique of "neutral money."

> The starting point and the object of Dr. Hayek's inquiry is what he calls "neutral money"; that is to say, a kind of money which leaves production and the relative prices of goods, including the rate of interest, "undisturbed," exactly as they would be if there were no money at all.
>
> (Sraffa, 1932a, p. 42)

The flaw of this method, as Sraffa sees it, lies in using the manipulation of a framework which is exactly as if "there were no money at all" as the object of his inquiry into *monetary* theory and policy. Sraffa notes that the neutral economy might be useful if it were to be employed by way of comparison with various real monetary economies. Then it would be possible to compare the disturbances to the monetary economies with those to the non-monetary "neutral" economy. "This would bring out which are the essential characteristics common to every kind of money, as well as their differences, and thus supply the elements for the merits of alternative policies" (p. 43).

Instead of this, however, Hayek conducts his investigations completely within the context of the neutral economy, which by his own admission conceives money only as a medium of exchange. By doing so, Sraffa claims that Hayek denies those very characteristics that define a monetary economy:

> The differences between a monetary and a non-monetary economy can only be found in those characteristics which are set out at the beginning of every textbook on money. That is to say, that money is not only the medium of exchange, but also a store of value and the standard in terms of which debts, and all other legal obligations, habits, opinions,

conventions, in short all kinds of relations between men, are more or less rigidly fixed.

(p. 43)

Since Hayek's starting point of a hypothetical "neutral" barter economy considers only money which is "used purely and simply as a medium of exchange," his inquiry cannot admit the "most obvious" effects that a monetary policy will have in a real money economy where

> when the price of one or more commodities changes, these relations [described above] change in terms of such commodities; while if they had been fixed in commodities, in some specified way, they would have changed differently or not at all.
>
> (Sraffa, 1932a, pp. 43–44)

In sum, Hayek's method of neutral money "amounts to assuming away the very object of the inquiry."

Having said this, Sraffa as a reviewer is faced with a dilemma. For if the whole method of the work under review undermines the investigation from the start, what more is the reviewer to say about author's use of this method? Sraffa bases his discussion of Hayek's use of the "method" of neutral money on his critique of that method. If Hayek's method of analyzing the influence of monetary disturbances on savings, accumulation and relative prices emasculates the role of money from the start, then some other factor besides the monetary disturbance must explain his results. As Kaldor reminds us Hayek seemed to be proposing that the influence of monetary policy on these matters was, in fact, the whole of the explanation of the great enigma of the thirties: industrial depressions. But if this conclusion is based on the use of a system that is "as if there were no money at all," an alternative explanation is needed. This explanation is the task of the internal critique of Sraffa's review:

> Dr. Hayek invariably finds, when he comes to compare the effects of alternative policies in regulating this emasculated money, that there is an all important difference in the result, and that it is "neutral" only if it is kept constant in quantity, whilst if the quantity is changed, the most disastrous effects follow. The reader is forced to conclude that these alleged differences can only arise, either from an error of reasoning, or from the unwitting introduction in working out the effects of one of the two systems compared, of some irrelevant non-monetary consideration, which produces the difference, attributed to the properties of the system itself. The task of the critic, therefore, is the somewhat monotonous one of discovering, for each step of Dr. Hayek's parallel analysis, which is the error or irrelevancy which causes the difference.
>
> (Sraffa, 1932a, pp. 44–5)

IV. "Incantations and a little poison"

In terms of Hayek's "internal" argument sketched above, Sraffa addresses himself to two cardinal points: forced savings and the natural rate of interest. Both of these involve Hayek's basic conception of the influence of changes in the quantity of money on the economic system.

In the first case Sraffa is interested in clarifying the distinction, so crucial to Hayek's theory of monetary induced cycles, between "voluntary" savings and "forced" savings. Sraffa recognizes that Hayek's use of this analytical distinction rests on the alleged *permanence* of the capital accumulated in the voluntary case as opposed to the "inevitable" destruction of that accumulated in the forced saving case. In Hayek's argument, monetary expansion may increase saving and accumulation for a time, but when the quantity of money ceases to expand any such involuntarily financed capital will be dissipated as consumers revert to their former proportions of intertemporal money expenditure. This "spoilage" of capital is what Hayek describes as an economic crisis. What is crucial to this argument is some mechanism for ensuring that the initial (those prior to the monetary expansion) proportions of money income saved and consumed will always be re-established when the expansion comes to an end:

> . . . the use of a larger proportion of the original means of production for the manufacture of intermediate products can only be brought about by a retrenchment of consumption. But now this sacrifice is not made by those who will reap the benefit from the new investments. It is made by consumers in general who, because of the increased competition from the entrepreneurs who have received the additional money, are forced to forego part of what they used to consume. It comes about not because they want to consume less, but because they get less goods for their money income. There can be no doubt that, if their money receipts should rise again, they would immediately attempt to expand consumption to the usual proportion . . . then at once the money stream will be redistributed between consumptive and productive uses according to the wishes of the individual concerned, and the artificial distribution, due to the injection of the new money, will, partly at any rate, be reversed. If we assume that the old proportions are adhered to, then the structure of production too will have to return to the old proportion.
>
> (Hayek, 1931, pp. 52–3)

There are numerous questionable aspects of this argument that Sraffa notes in passing.[9] Many of these were addressed in Hayek's later developments of his theory in the thirties and forties. Though these technical aspects are interesting, and in fact offer further opportunities to contrast the outlooks of Sraffa and Hayek, they are not the central elements of the argument at hand.

For the sake of an internal critique Sraffa provisionally accepts the groundwork established by Hayek and asks a very simple question. What is to ensure that accumulations of capital that result from the forced savings will ultimately be consumed? As Sraffa sees it, there is no reason to differentiate between accumulations that result from forced or voluntary savings. For Sraffa, once income has been redistributed by the inflation and saved in the form of capital assets, there is nothing to distinguish those assets from "voluntarily" accumulated assets.

> As a moment's reflection will show, "there can be no doubt" that nothing of the sort will happen. One class has, for a time, robbed another class of part of their incomes; and has saved the plunder. When the robbery comes to an end, it is clear that the victims cannot possibly consume the capital which is now well out of their reach. If they are wage-earners, who have all the time consumed every penny of their income, they have no wherewithal to expand consumption. And if they are capitalists who have not shared in the plunder, they may indeed be induced to consume now a part of their capital by the fall in the rate of interest; but not more so than if the rate had been lowered by the "voluntary savings" of other people.
>
> (Sraffa, 1932a, p. 48).[10]

For the purposes of Hayek's argument that inflation induced accumulation produces the seeds of the ensuing crisis the crucial element is the "inevitable destruction" of the "forced" accumulation. Sraffa, as noted above is not persuaded it must be dissipated just because of its source, and he claims that "Dr. Hayek fails to prove the contrary" (p. 47). In his reply to Sraffa, Hayek admits the centrality of this argument to his thesis ("My theory stands or falls on this point"), and thus it is worthwhile to consider his further defense of it.

Sraffa, in effect, has cut to the heart of the "great mystery" (Hicks, 1967, p. 205.) of *Prices and Production* that so fascinated economists of the period. Hayek's story, when viewed as one of a stable long-period position that is returned to after a cyclic deviation, is a standard account of interwar cycle theory. What was unique about it is the grounding in forced lengthening and inevitable reversion of the period of production that constitutes the action in Hayek's case for monetary induced cycles. The trouble for commentators, then and since, has been to account for the mechanism of Hayek's "concertina effect." Given that changes in the quantity of money seem neutralized from the start by Hayek's chosen methodological framework, Sraffa is required to conduct a "parallel analysis" of the operation of the system. In the case of forced savings the problem is to explain why the "involuntary" nature of the accumulation requires that it be dissipated when the monetary expansion comes to an end. The set piece of Hayek's analysis is his conception of a critical "proportion" between consumer and producer goods that constitutes the Bohm-Bawerkian view of the quantity of capital as the average period of production. It is noteworthy that he defines this proportion in terms of "the money stream" or "total expenditure" directed to the two categories. Thus the influence of monetary expansion on the "structure of production" comes through altering the proportions between these critical money streams. Under conditions of forced savings this change in proportions is brought about by additional credits granted to producers by the banks. When this lending slackens the question is what causes the accumulated capital to be destroyed?

If the crisis is a "reversion" to the previous "proportions" the only way that it can come about is by a redirection of part of the spending stream from producers (who were "robbing" consumers of part of their natural proportion during the inflation) back to consumers. Hayek asserts that this comes through a rise in money receipts of consumers once the expenditure of the producer's credits work back through the system. This is where Sraffa *internally* evaluates the argument and connects it to the external critique already presented.

His argument is as follows. If the essential element of the story is the change in proportions of the spending stream, it cannot be monetary expansions themselves that account for the crisis. This reasoning is driven home in the exchange by both Sraffa's and Hayek's comments on another case of monetary expansion alternative to the forced savings case. As a point of explication, Sraffa notes in passing that by Hayek's reasoning "if the banks increased the circulation but apportioned the additional money between consumers' and producers' credits so as not to disturb the initial "proportions," nothing would happen" (Sraffa, 1932a, p. 48). In his reply, Hayek confirms this view and attributes it to the German edition of *Prices and Production* where he had stated that a monetary expansion could only avoid misdirecting production "if it were possible to inject the additional quantities of money, . . . into the economic system in such a way that no change in the proportion between the demand for consumers' goods and the demand for producers' goods would be brought about" (Hayek, 1932, pp. 244–5).

The key point for Sraffa is that that something other than monetary effects are in fact responsible for Hayek's conclusions. If a monetary expansion that balances increased credit to producers and consumers in the "natural proportion" does not induce crises, then a monetary expansion is not the *sine qua non* of the cycle. Sraffa's parallel analysis concludes that, instead, it is the "supposed power of the banks" to misdirect these credits that does all the work in Hayek's theory:

> What has happened is simply that, since money has been thoroughly "neutralised" from the start, whether its quantity rises, falls, or is kept steady, makes not the slightest difference; at the same time an extraneous element, in the shape of the supposed power of the banks to settle the

way in which money is spent, has crept into the argument and has done all the work. As Voltaire says, you can kill a flock of sheep by incantations, plus a little poison.

(Sraffa 1932a, p. 49)

V. "Essential confusion"

Having concluded that the consequences Hayek claims for forced savings cannot be explained within the context of his theory (at least without "a little poison"), Sraffa is led to consider his second cardinal point, the distinction between real and money rates of interest. The connection between this distinction and the forced savings issue is that, in Hayek's argument, forced savings result from the monetary policy of lowering the money rate below the natural rate. As Sraffa notes, Hayek's use of this disinction is "mainly given by way of criticism and development of the theory of Wicksell." Quoting from *Prices and Production*, Sraffa identifies the main theme of Hayek's theory of the relation of money to the rate of interest:

> In a money economy, the actual or money rate of interest may differ from the equilibrium or natural rate, because the demand for and the supply of capital do not meet in their natural form but in the form of money, the quantity of which available for capital purposes may be arbitrarily changed by the banks.
>
> (Hayek, 1931, pp. 20–1: quoted in Sraffa, 1932a, p. 49)

In keeping with his emphasis on the "method of neutral money," Hayek sets up the natural rate as a benchmark by which to measure the neutrality of monetary policy. A policy is neutral if it sets the money rate equal to the natural rate. His contention is that such a neutral monetary policy, while it would leave the natural system undisturbed ("as if there were no money at all"), could not simultaneously stabilize an aggregate price level if the economy were expanding. Thus, the appropriate guide to policy becomes the maintenance of a stable quantity of money and not the maintenance of a stable price level.

Sraffa's critique of this part of Hayek's argument is that it represents a confused conception of the relationship between money and prices (or conversely between a barter and a monetary economy):

> An essential confusion, which appears clearly from this statement, is the belief that the divergence of rates is a characteristic of a money economy: and the confusion is implied in the very terminology adopted, which identifies the "actual" with the "money" rate, and the "equilibrium" with the "natural" rate. If money did not exist, and loans were made in terms

of all sorts of commodities, there would be a single rate which satisfies the conditions of equilibrium, but there might be at any one moment as many "natural" rates of interest as there are commodities, though they would not be equilibrium rates. The "arbitrary" action of the banks is by no means a necessary condition for the divergence; if loans were made in wheat and farmers (or for that matter the weather) "arbitrarily changed" the quantity of wheat produced, the actual rate of interest on loans in terms of wheat would diverge from the rate on other commodities and there would be no single equilibrium rate.

(Sraffa, 1932a, p. 45)

In order to further illustrate the "essential confusion" involved here, Sraffa again "internalizes" the argument. Taking at face value Hayek's argument that the natural rate" is indeed the rate that would obtain in a barter state, Sraffa asks a not so obvious question. What would loans and interest rates look like if money did not exist, and how would they be different from rates of interest in a money economy? His answer: if we really were in a barter state, the only meaning that loans, savings, or investment could have would be defined in physical terms, money being nonexistent by definition. Thus, "natural" rates of interest would be rates defined in "real" or physical terms. The ratio between the amount of a physical commodity today to the amount it trades for at some future date would be the physical analog to rates of interest.

And, in fact, Sraffa points out that his barter-like rates are not so hard to imagine as we might think. "In order to realize this, we need not stretch our imagination and think of an organized loan market among savages bartering deer for beavers. Loans are currently made in the present world in terms of every commodity for which there is a forward market."[11]

Armed with this concrete conception of what a rate of interest means in barter terms, Sraffa goes on to conduct a "parallel analysis" of Hayek's scheme. In such a barter world, equilibrium means that "the spot and forward price coincide . . . and all the "natural" or commodity rates are equal to one another, and to the money rate." But, if the supply and demand get out of long-period equilibrium for any reason, the spot and forward prices diverge, and the "natural" rate of interest on that commodity diverges from the "natural" rates on other commodities. In other words, "natural" rates are not necessarily "equilibrium" rates if by equilibrium it is meant prices equal cost of production and by "natural" we mean barter-like (money-less) intertemporal loans. Consequently, Hayek's attempt to equate the equilibrium rate with the putative natural rate represents an "essential confusion."

This is most easily grasped in terms of Hayek's own preferred situation of an expanding economy. If, following Hayek's language, this means an increase in output of the producer goods industries, the only way to attract the new resources to this production is for the expected rate of return in the production of these goods to increase. Recall that Hayek explicitly wanted to address himself to an investigation of the effect of monetary influences on relative prices. He also claimed to have rejected a reliance on "vague" concepts of averages, such as the price level. He was thus led to found his argument for a neutral monetary policy on the cyclical influence of money on relative investment flows in an accumulating economy. His policy prescription was to eliminate "forced savings" by holding the quantity of money (multiplied by velocity) constant. The theoretical rationale here was that the quantity of money must not change if the money rate is to reflect the natural rate.

Now Sraffa has shown that, if one really wants to define natural rates in barter-like terms, it is a necessary relative price effect that these rates will naturally diverge in an economy with accumulation going forward. The basis of Sraffa's argument is that any new accumulation is directed to different employments by divergences of market prices from the "natural" price, a standard price theory argument. "It will be noticed that, under free competition, this divergence of rates is as essential to the effecting of the transition [to a more capitalistic economy] as is the divergence of prices from costs of production; it is, in fact, another aspect of the same thing" (Sraffa, 1932a, p. 51).

The consequence of Sraffa's internal argument is that a theoretical investigation that utilizes the concept of a natural rate of interest to reflect a barter state of saving and investment, must deal with the fact that in an accumulating economy "there may be as many "natural" rates of interest as there are commodities." Parallel argument results in a contradiction for Hayek's system:

> But in times of expansion of production, due to additions to savings, there is no such thing as an equilibrium (or unique natural) rate of interest, so that the money rate can neither be equal to, nor lower than it: the "natural" rate of interest on producers' goods, the demand for which has relatively increased, is higher than the "natural" rate on consumers' goods, the demand for which has relatively fallen.
>
> (Sraffa, 1932a, p. 51)

In effect, Sraffa has caught Hayek in an internal contradiction of his own making, escape from which requires abandonment of some part of his framework. Hayek must abandon a unique natural rate as an argument for a constant money policy, abandon the whole Wicksellian conception, or fall back on one of the flawed aggregates he began by disavowing to deliver him from this quandary. This becomes particularly clear when, in reply to Sraffa, Hayek adverts to the possibility (or necessity) of a multitude of natural rates. Sraffa's rejoinder seems to seal the case:

> Dr. Hayek now acknowledges the multiplicity of the "natural" rates, but he has nothing more to say on this specific point than that they "all would be equilibrium rates." The only meaning (if it be a meaning) I can

attach to this is that his maxim of policy now requires that the money rate should be equal to all these divergent rates.

(Sraffa, 1932b, p.251)

In summary, Sraffa's internal case against Hayek's use of the money-natural rate framework rests on the proposition that a literally defined "real" (natural, barter) rate of interest does not exhibit the characteristics that Hayek requires of it. That is, in Hayek's chosen context of an accumulating economy (outside the stationary, or "balanced growth" long-period state), there is no unique barter rate to identify the money rate with, as required for neutrality. Divergence of rates and disequilibrium is not restricted to monetary economies, but also characterizes such real economies as Hayek's argument contrasts money systems with.

VI. Curtain call: The method of neutral money once again

By conducting a parallel analysis from within Hayek's framework, Sraffa exposes the gaps in the Hayek's argument. Monetary expansion cannot be claimed as the source of forced savings reversals and a *deus ex machina* has to be brought in the form of "the supposed powers of the banks." No unique natural rate can be identified in an expanding economy. Thus utilizing the natural rate as the theoretical maxim of monetary policy becomes problematic even in a conceptual sense. Furthermore, the literal meaning of barter rates contradicts Hayek's presumption that the natural system is inherently stable, exhibiting the unique natural rate, while monetary influences are inherently destabilizing in their potential for disturbing the natural equilibrium. Instead, Sraffa shows the virtual necessity of divergent, disequilibrium rates in an accumulating barter system.

Yet this entire critique was conducted within the purview of Hayek's own theoretical framework. And, as noted above, Sraffa considers it a methodological dead end from the outset. ("But from the beginning it is clear that a methodical criticism could not leave a brick standing in the logical structure built up by Dr. Hayek.") It is, therefore, not surprising that the internal critique would eventually bring back into full view the inherent contradictions of conducting monetary theory from the standpoint of a theoretical system which proceeds as if there were no money at all.

If interest rates defined in barter terms necessarily exhibit divergences in a growing economy, the natural rate loses any meaning as a policy guide. Playing on Hayek's own theme of immanent criticism of Wicksell, however, Sraffa claims that his point about barter rates does not necessarily indict Wicksell:

This, however, though it meets, I think, Dr. Hayek's criticism, is not in itself a criticism of Wicksell. For there is a "natural" rate of interest which, if adopted as bank-rate, will stabilize a price-level (i.e. the price of a composite commodity): it is an average of the "natural" rates of the commodities entering into the price-level, weighted in the same way as they are in the price-level itself. What can be objected to Wicksell is that such a price-level is not unique, and for any composite arbitrarily selected there is a corresponding rate that will equalize the purchasing power, in terms of that composite commodity, of the money saved and of the additional money borrowed for investment.

(Sraffa, 1932a, p. 51)

For Sraffa, this offers a solution to the dilemma of the "method of neutral money." For any aggregate "natural rate" selected, it would be possible to identify a monetary policy that would be "neutral" in the sense that saving and investment would be the same in money terms as they are in "natural terms." In other words, a money rate set equal to the composite natural rate would result in savings and investment retaining equal value in the sense that the money value of that savings and its value in terms of the selected composite commodity would remain relatively stable (that is, the "purchasing power" of money saved and invested would be stable in terms of that composite commodity). Of course this would also mean that monetary policy only could be neutral in the sense of corresponding to a "particular" non-monetary economy, out of an infinite possible number. Thus Wicksell has an escape hatch from Sraffa's internal critique. But, as Sraffa notes in his reply, this "way of escape is not open to Dr. Hayek, for he had emphatically repudiated the use of averages." (Sraffa, 1932b, p. 251).

It is at this point that the immanent critique of the natural rate doctrine transcends the framework of neutral money. Having shown a logically consistent version of the aims of the method of neutral money, Sraffa steps back to consider the result:

Each of these monetary policies will give the same results in regard to saving and borrowing as a particular non-monetary economy – that is to say, an economy in which the selected composite commodity is used as the standard of deferred payments. It appears, therefore, that these non-monetary economies retain the essential feature of money, the singleness of the standard; and we are not much the wiser when we have been shown that a monetary policy is "neutral" in the sense of being equivalent to a non-monetary economy which differs from it almost only by name.

(Sraffa, 1932a, p.51)

Thus the escape route of aggregated real rates can define a neutrality of a restricted type. Money can be neutral in the sense of stabilizing the purchasing power of a composite commodity, which serves as the numeraire standard of an analog "barter" system (like Hayek's "natural" system). Likewise, a monetary policy can be devised under which saving and investment, in terms of either money or the composite commodity, is equivalent. But this, again, brings up the original question of what a non-monetary economy would look like. Sraffa's view, revealed above, is that the essential feature of money is the fact that it is the single standard for all transactions. Consequently, a true non-monetary economy is one "in which different transactions are fixed in terms of different standards." For this kind of economy, neutrality of the "average-real-rate" variety will not do, since "there are no monetary policies which can exactly reproduce their results" (Sraffa, 1932a, p.51).

By a rather circuitous route this point redefines the conclusion of the external critique presented at the beginning of the review. Sraffa had started by saying that if the method of neutral money is to be useful to monetary investigations it seems reasonable that the comparison it utilizes be made between a monetary economy and a non-monetary economy:

> This method of approach might have something to recommend it, provided it were constantly kept in mind that a state of things in which money is "neutral" is identical with a state in which there is no money at all: as Dr Hayek once says, if we "eliminate all monetary influences on production . . . we may treat money as non-existent."
>
> (Sraffa, 1932a, p. 42)

Thus the parallel analysis into "neutral money" and various kinds of real money would resolve itself into a comparison between the conditions of a specified non-monetary economy and those of various monetary systems.

VII. The goals of monetary theory

On the evidence of Sraffa's critique of Hayek and the Wicksellian framework, we conclude that Sraffa and Keynes held out very different goals for monetary theory. What Sraffa saw as a legitimate use of the method of neutral money involved conducting two simultaneous analyses: one into an economy that is characterized as monetary, and one into a non-monetary economy. Manipulating the same parameter, we ask: what will be the results in each case? Any difference between the two is due to the factors chosen to represent money.[12]

Keynes was an altogether different economist than Sraffa. Keynes's goals, and his penchant for applicable and simple theoretical structure, would not have been satisfied by Sraffa's fastidious following out of logical conundrums. Keynes wanted economic theory to provide a framework in which the persistence and volume of unemployment that was characteristic of the thirties could be explained in a fashion consistent with what he already knew of the details of the monetary economy. In fact, recent research by

Sraffa scholars reinforces this conclusion, showing that Sraffa himself was not happy with the use of the own-rates-of-interest argument by Keynes in the *General Theory* (Panico, 2001).

That should not necessarily surprise us – at least once it is realized that Sraffa's goal, like Hayek's, was to analyze the relationship between monetary effects and distribution *within a long-period setting*. Keynes on the other hand, we will see in detail in the next two chapters, had reached the conclusion that persistent unemployment could not be properly conceived as merely a "deviation" from an assumed long-period position. Indeed, it is fair to say he came to reject the attractive force of Marshall's long period positions themselves. Thus for both immediate practical reasons, and his own developing theoretical interests, Keynes came to believe that unemployment in a monetary economy could best be characterized as being in *short-period equilibrium*. But his short-period (and long-period) equilibrium is not the same as Marshall's. It is, as we showed in Chapter 2, critically dependent on the expectations of entrepreneurs and asset holders. In order to make this point clear, it is appropriate to repeat a part of the quotation that heads Part III. It comes from a short essay that Keynes penned while he was at work on the *General Theory*, and in which he specifically announces his changing opinion of the notion of equilibrium:

> The theory which I desiderate would deal, . . . with an economy in which money plays a part of its own and affects motives and decisions and is, in short, one of the operative factors in the situation, so that the course of events cannot be predicted, either in the long period or in the short, without knowledge of the behavior of money between the first and last. And this is what we ought to mean when we speak of a monetary economy.
>
> (*CW* 13, pp. 408–9)

Seventy years on from that decision on Keynes's part, and with much further development of economic theory behind us now, we may gain some insight from putting that methodological choice in perspective. To begin it is clear that Keynes's method is not completely the same as that which developed at the most abstract level of economics after World War II – that of so-called General Equilibrium Theory. Starting from Walras, rather than from Marshall as Keynes had, general equilibrium developed as a system of disaggregated market exchange. This view was presented in a series of mathematical proofs that demonstrated that a set of prices exists which will simultaneously satisfy a system of exchange in which for each good there is a separate, but interrelated, market. Although the place of money in that theory can best be described as "controversial," the correspondences between it and traditional notions of equilibrium and rates of interest are clear. On the question of equilibrium, this literature developed a whole new concept, alternative to the traditional modes of both long and short period analysis, which goes by the name of "intertemporal equilibrium." Its central proposition is that trading, via a fictitious auctioneer, reconciles at once all prices in all markets for all time periods. Interestingly, the roots of this idea are sometimes traced to Vienna and the Austrian school – in fact even to Hayek himself.[13] The generally recognized culmination of this line of thought is Arrow and Debreu (1954) and Debreu (1959), and its most influential text is Arrow and Hahn (1971).

With regard to rates of interest, the intertemporal general equilibrium model is characterized by a multiplicity of them. Hence this framework also reveals "own-rates of interest" – for goods traded across time – where time is treated as an analog of space. These rates are computed as the ratio, implied by equilibrium prices for the same good at different dates. Since all the prices are relative and since all trades famously "happen at once," any two dates imply commodity quantities which are equivalent in that they will trade for each other – prices such that a unit of good x at time t is exchanged for b units of good x at time $t + 1$, for example. Such commodity rates of interest are derived from the equilibrium "price vector," – for all commodities for which there are at least two trading dates specified. Thus all goods are treated equally and can therefore potentially exhibit own rates of interest. But these rates actually play no active role in the equilibrium. That is to say, they contain no information that is not contained in the equilibrium prices already, and thus are just second-hand ancillary computations from those prices. At the risk of repetition, it is well to be clear on this. From the intertemporal general equilibrium point of view, there is nothing to be gained by analyzing interest rates. Agents are not motivated in this model by their existence, and no aspect of equilibrium turns on them. Note also, it is therefore the case that this theory offers no mechanism – some devotees go so far as to claim that it would be a senseless and uninteresting question to ask – by which rates of interest would equalize. Finally, since the producers who "supply" the goods, just like the factors that go into "producing" these goods (the production process is not extensively specified), are all supposed to operate by maximizing profit at the predetermined market prices, no notion of differential rates of return, or profit, or its equalization, is likewise entertained in this framework.[14]

One might legitimately ask: Does a theory that cannot accommodate the existence of money belong in a history of Keynes's economics at all? Walrasian general equilibrium is very distant from Keynes's economic concerns. But we are here stepping back from our main narrative to categorize his equilibrium within a taxonomy of notions of equilibrium more familiar to most economists. In that sense – and given the enormous impact of the general equilibrium framework on modern economic theory – it is incumbent on us to briefly mention this very abstract view of equilibrium.

With little notice, therefore, General Equilibrium of the Arrow–Debreu intertemporal variety declares off-limits one of the bedrock issues of economics. Ever since Adam Smith (1776) economists have attempted to show how the capitalist system, through investment, competition and the process of buying and selling on markets,[15] would (or would not under certain conditions) lead "naturally" to a state where all producers of goods earned a uniform rate of profit. In 1890 Marshall took this as the given object of his *Principles of Economics*. Down to this day, most teachers of economics still preach this notion to undergraduates being initiated into the study of the field. Indeed, in *A Tract on Monetary Reform*, Keynes held that the associated meaning of long-period "normal" profit was part of the common perception of justice that underlies the economic system:

> The economic doctrine of normal profit, vaguely apprehended by everyone, is a necessary condition for the justification of capitalism. The businessman is only tolerable so long as his gains can be held to bear some relation to what, roughly and in some sense, his activities have contributed to society.

If the equality of rates of return is to be jettisoned from the apparatus of economic theory – no matter with what degree of logical consistency, and with whatever mathematical elegance – are economists thereby saying that this tendency no longer has any force in the economic system?

This question should give pause about the use of general equilibrium theory to an economics profession that is often blinded by admiration of mathematical technique. Thus from this standpoint, it seems clear that general equilibrium theory – if it is not to be considered only as a mistaken detour or a sophisticated parlor game – has only a restricted place in economic theory. It forms a comment upon the intricacies of exchange – and the stringent requirements necessary to display this intricacy in Bourbakian terms. But "intertemporal equilibrium," taken as a comment on real monetary economies, only masks, the bigger, more important, question of how real economies move through time. If the social process of economic competition exhibits any semblance of order, one that economics can rightfully theorize about, it must tend toward a pattern of order by which expected rates of return converge – whether to a mean or a stable distribution of rates.[16] Otherwise economic activity would appear as little more than a state of flux. At a minimum, this is how Keynes viewed the economic process and economic theory.

It was just such difficult intertemporal coordination issues that were of interest to the interwar monetary and cycle economists. They were convinced that money, banking, financial markets, equity markets, forward and future markets, warehousing and dealing in commodities, were all institutions or practices which had evolved by the economic system as ways of dealing with time – time to trade on expected future income, time over which to hold assets for some future use, time to organize and capitalize large scale production for which one person alone lacked the financial wherewithal and so on. We have, in fact, already chronicled a good part of this analysis in Parts II and III of this book.

These interwar economists also contended, and tried to show in their economics, that these institutions had rules of operation that had consequences for the real economy. Sometimes they were ambivalent over whether the operation of these individual markets or institutions could be reconciled with the greater good of the economy as a whole. Thus Pigou saw investment "error" and "speculation" in commodities as inevitable, and as potentially harmful, activities. Many writers expressed doubt that the banking system could adequately express the voluntary wishes of savers in its role as the provider of credit to business. Sometimes, as in Robertson's forced savings, they thought this inability of the banking system was nevertheless beneficial to stability and prosperity. Alternatively, sometimes they saw intertemporal coordination practices as operating fully in tandem with economic prosperity of the economy as a whole – as for instance was always the case in Keynes's view of commodity speculation as the bearer of the tradable risks of enterprise.

Keynes was thus just one of a long string of economists – in truth stretching back to the nineteenth century – who wanted to integrate monetary theory and real analysis. Marshall, Fisher and Wicksell said much the same thing. Most of those before Keynes, though, operated on the assumption that intertemporal and monetary effects would play out against an uninterrupted operation of the fundamental forces acting on accumulation and costs of production, namely productivity and thrift. The first force, in the form of new technology, made rising standards of living potentially possible. The second force, they thought, ensured that society actually did invest in that technology. Hence, also, the traditional emphasis on thrift as a personal and social virtue. Only by giving free rein to these forces, it was thought, would economic growth and the material well-being of society progress. Especially was this so if the cyclic change of the system always revolved around, and reverted to, a dynamic position of equilibrium that itself was growing and not affected by monetary factors. Keynes was not denying the contribution to economic progress of these factors – particularly that of productive investment in new technology (although he was sometimes over-pessimistic and wrong about the continuation of opportunities for new technology). But he was saying that the savings did not automatically translate into investment when people had other means and motives to hold their savings. Moreover, it was a fault of the system, in Keynes's view, that there is less saving available to invest in capital when the economy is underperforming with regard to unemployment and output.[17]

David Laidler (1999) has shown that after World War II consensus opinion – conveniently dubbed the IS/LM model – formed around bits of Keynes's *General Theory*, combined with many elements of interwar business cycle theory and expressed in a language congenial to the Walrasian system we just discussed. This post-*General Theory* consensus in macroeconomics was married to an acceptable microeconomics of relative prices in the so-called Neoclassical Synthesis.

Here we are interested in the concept of equilibrium that developed in this period. In that regard, post-war Macroeconomics reverted to the pre-*General Theory* notion of business cycles as deviations from an economy's otherwise full-employment path through time – deviations that would of necessity return to this long-period equilibrium as just described. This is certainly a logically defensible position – as a story to pitch to undergraduates. More advanced wisdom, however, requires that we recognize that this conception ultimately falls back on describing macroeconomics by a theoretical construct whereby the system will always 'naturally' return to full employment. Thus, why deviations occur at all must be due to an assumed imperfection in some functioning of the economy compared to how it would operate in the (textbook) "perfect" case. We have seen numerous examples of this in the foregoing: a faulty monetary-banking sector, "error" with regard to investment (which could potentially be corrected), or a rigidity in a nominal price compared to the presumed ideal of a fully plastic system. Each alone – or together in any combination – could prevent the rapid equilibration through time that was assumed would ensure continuous full employment. Thus an appeal to Wicksell, Marshall, Pigou, Robertson, Hawtrey and the Swedes for the roots of the post-*General Theory* macroeconomic consensus, as we find in Laidler, makes a large measure of sense. But there is more to the *General Theory* than this.

Another aspect of the post-war tradition in macroeconomics is that the "short" of short period came to indicate a time interval – one that can be objectively measured by the historical record of macroeconomics. Perfectly legitimate empirical estimates thus form the basis of this measure. One example is the length (in quarters) that the National Bureau of Economic Research has used since the 1930s to "date" economic cycles. By this instrumental measurement of economic time, long-periods are a succession of such short-period economic cycles. The equilibrium position of the economy is thus implicitly conceptualized as a moving average of actual output – say over ten years. Short-period deviations are then defined as the actually occurring gross domestic product (GDP) as it varies from this moving mean. All modern economists have become familiar with charts displaying macroeconomic history in this way.

"Potential" GDP and "actual" GDP are shown as varying through time. Potential GDP is displayed as the moving ten-year average. Superimposed over this is the actual GDP at each quarter. Such records can be very useful and are a staple of popular macroeconomics. They nevertheless have had to contend with the deeper question – often reflected in undergraduates' puzzlement over those years in which the chart indicates "greater than full" employment – of what "equilibrium" means here. One problematic aspect hidden by this display of data is the casual presumption that long-period states can be identified by the moving averages that form potential GDP. But potential GDP, so defined, is not actually a measure of operating capacity at all – nor is it, strictly speaking, an analytical category at all. It only summarizes, in a smoothed fashion, the empirical record of actual GDP itself. Long period positions are therefore an analytical category for which this estimate of "potential" GDP cannot proxy.

I will argue in the next two chapters that Keynes can be understood as offering an alternative macroeconomic definition of equilibrium in the *General Theory*. It does not seem useful to quibble with his definition, or any other, per se – as if there is only one appropriate equilibrium concept. Such "fundamentalism" of the economic variety, much like the religious kind, rarely leads to useful conversations. But economists should be fully aware of the meaning of the concepts of equilibrium that they are employing. If for no other reason, we should be aware because the usefulness of various notions of equilibria varies with the task at hand. No one notion is likely to be the "best" or the "only" appropriate to a range of questions – or is likely to shed the same kind of understanding on any particular question. What should be asked in this context is: What was Keynes's question, and how does his notion of equilibrium help to answer it?

Keynes's question in the *General Theory*, as we have noted, was how to characterize a monetary economy that could possibly exhibit lasting periods – he called them equilibrium positions – of both full-employment and less-than-full-employment. We saw in Chapter 2 that this led him to a particular analytical view of what would constitute long period positions and "expectations as determining output." It should now be clear that this was the outcome of many years of study and of his witness to an economy seemingly stuck in crisis. At one level, the equilibrium that Keynes is arguing for in the *General Theory* can be characterized as the level of employment and output (relative to existing equipment) that results from the expectations of entrepreneurs as to expected profits, along with the expectations of asset holders toward the choices they are offered in which to hold wealth, all combined in an equilibrium of aggregate demand for output as a whole with culturally given habits of household consumption (and saving). Parts of this analysis have come down to us as conventional treatments of the consumption function, aggregate demand and asset market equilibrium. This story as regards Keynes's progress toward the *General Theory* has been told before.

Another way to interpret the *General Theory* is emphasized in what follows. Not because it is in conflict with the expectations-based multiplier theory, but because it appears to have been neglected in the literature on Keynes and macroeconomics. This interpretation emphasizes that employment depends directly on the monetary character of the economy – as

Keynes interpreted the essential properties of interest and money. By this account, the level of employment that entrepreneurs will undertake to offer is the amount that balances the expected rates of return, valued in a single standard, from employing capital to produce goods, from holding real assets and from holding financial assets. It is possible that the rate of production that entrepreneurs are satisfied to undertake, given their expectations, will be less than that required for the full employment of the system. The next chapter chronicles Keynes's attempt to show this.

14

Keynes: "The Essential Properties of Interest and Money"

The idea that it is comparatively easy to adapt the hypothetical conclusions of a real wage economics to the real world of monetary economics is a mistake. It is extraordinarily difficult to make the adaptation, and perhaps impossible without the aid of a developed theory of monetary economics.)

J. M. Keynes (1933)

I. Introduction

In 1947, Keynes's biographer, pre-publication critic and collaborator R. F. Harrod summed up the *General Theory* as follows:

> The theory of interest is, I think, the central point in his scheme. He departs from old orthodoxy in holding that the failure of the system to move to a position of full activity is not primarily due to friction, rigidity, immobility or to phenomena essentially connected with the trade cycle. If a certain level of interest is established which is inconsistent with full activity, no flexibility or mobility in the other parts of the system will get the system to move to full activity. *But this wrong rate of interest, as we may call it, is not itself a rigidity or inflexibility. It is natural, durable, and in a certain sense, in the free system inevitable.* That is why he lays what may seem an undue emphasis on the doctrine that interest is essentially the reward not for saving but for parting with liquidity. Given the complex forces affecting liquidity preference, such and such is the rate of interest that will naturally and necessarily and, so long as underlying forces remain unchanged, permanently obtain. Yet that rate of interest may be inconsistent with the full activity of the system.
>
> (Harrod, 1947, pp. 69–70, emphasis added)

Such an extensive quotation is justified by two remarkable qualities of the statement. First, Harrod's statement, when fully digested, can be seen to embody a viewpoint at odds with almost all major conceptions of the meaning of Keynes's theory of employment. As a moment's reflection over the quotation will reveal to the modern economist, this "central point in his scheme" is not compatible with any standard "Keynesian" exposition of underemployment equilibria. In the "Keynesian" case, the *definition* of unemployment is its correspondence with some sort of "rigidity" in an otherwise smoothly operating general equilibrium system. Among some old Keynesians, the rigidity was explained as the interest rate becoming stuck in the "liquidity trap" by pessimism so severe that no amount of inducement could satisfy the public's craving for liquid balances. When this case was recognized as both theoretically and empirically implausible (see Keynes's own view in *GT*, p. 207), attention shifted to inflexibility in the labor market. By the logic of the neoclassical synthesis, deviations from full employment had to be due to some non-clearing rigidity in the labor market. It was the final recognition of this point that led to both the breakdown of the Keynesian consensus and the most modern "Keynesian" theory: New Keynesian Economics. This literature, like the one Keynes grew up with, is dedicated to formulating microfoundation explanations for "rationally" explaining why the labor market might not clear.[1]

Notwithstanding these analyses, Harrod tells us Keynes concluded that "no flexibility or mobility in the other parts of the system will get the system to move to full activity." What might Harrod be driving at with his assertion that Keynes's central point is a "wrong rate of interest," that this rate "is not itself a rigidity or inflexibility," but is "natural, durable and in a certain sense . . . inevitable"? That question is answered by recourse to the second remarkable quality of Harrod's statement, which is that in a concise, shorthand way he expresses the central concerns of Keynes's own post-*General Theory* restatements of his revolutionary new theory. In these papers (*CW* 14, pp. 101–8, 109–23, 201–15, 215–23), Keynes addresses himself almost entirely to monetary concerns, trying to elaborate his theory of employment via his theory of the interest rate.[2] A variety of different approaches and points are raised in these papers, including Keynes's views on uncertainty, expectations and the role of money and interest in his theoretical explanation of unemployment equilibria. Taken as a whole, Keynes's post-*General Theory* defense of his position reveals his feeling that his monetary theory of the interest rate clearly distinguishes him from his predecessors and contemporaries, and was generally being misunderstood by his interpreters. The implication of both Harrod's statement and Keynes's own post-*General Theory* emphasis on monetary matters in defending his theory is that *a complete understanding of Keynes's theoretical attempt to explain unemployment is fundamentally related to his views on money and interest.*

It is the purpose of this chapter to try to elucidate that part of Keynes's monetary theory that is implicit in Harrod's statement and explicit in Keynes's 1937 defense by analyzing a neglected aspect of Keynes's monetary views: "the own-rates theory of interest" put forth in Chapter 17 of the *General Theory*. In so doing I hope to be able to show that Keynes's monetary analysis in the *General Theory* constitutes a break from the received theoretical tradition that we have viewed from various angles in the previous three chapters.

Colin Rogers (1989) shows the extent to which the Wicksellian tradition that we saw critiqued by Sraffa in the last chapter can be used analytically as a foil against which to contrast Keynes's more "monetary" theory of the rate of interest. Rogers is following out a theme from Leijonhufvud's (1981) earlier careful reconstruction of the "Wicksell Connection" among the various theories of the interwar cycle theorists. Leijonhufvud uses this analytical device to give modern focus to the historical tradition of savings and investment analysis which we have just surveyed. One of Leijonhufvud's main points is that the monetary theory of Keynes's *General Theory* constitutes its greatest departure from the Wicksellian tradition. We might quibble with the historical accuracy of giving Wicksell sole ownership over this tradition (thus ignoring Marshall's important role), but it is a well-taken analytical point. For Leijonhufvud, however, this break with the natural/market-rate analysis is seen as a strictly retrograde move on Keynes's part. In the concluding chapter, Chapter 15, we will critique Leijonhufvud on this point on his own chosen analytical grounds, resurrecting the analysis of Chapter 17 of the *General Theory* to support the argument for the theoretical advance Keynes made on the Wicksellian tradition.[3]

In the present chapter I will document the largely theoretical stance of that analysis by conducting a detailed textual exegesis. The emphasis will be on the radical nature of Keynes's monetary views in the *General Theory* and the break they represent in relation to the Wicksellian and the Marshallian traditions. The goal will be to show that it is possible to interpret the incomplete, often misunderstood, but always tantalizing Chapter 17 of that work as an alternative framework in which to understand the importance that Keynes attached to the influence of expectations, conventional psychology and liquidity in the determination of asset values and therefore to the rate of interest. The method, like in the rest of this book, will be historical, attempting to link up the argument of Keynes's with ideas contained in works historically relevant to his – either that of students, colleagues or contemporary theoretical adversaries. This will then conclude the long historical journey of this work and shed light on the meaning of Harrod's view that the interest rate was the key to Keynes's system. We also hope to show that the framework of analysis discernable in Chapter 17 offers fresh insight into the possibilities of a monetary analysis alternative to the traditional ones.

The Post Keynesian school (Davidson, 1972; Shackle; 1972, 1974; Kregel, 1973) explicitly ground their interpretation of Keynes in the monetary points that Keynes raised in 1937. Consequently, our work here shows that a substantial agreement with the Post Keynesian view of the importance of Keynes's monetary innovations can be given analytical focus by the "own-rates" approach. This focus, it is hoped, offers an alternative to that school's sometimes nihilistic attitude toward equilibrium theory.

II. From Sraffa to Keynes: The state of monetary theory, 1935

As a bridge over the uncharted, and perhaps forever unknown, question of what personal role was played by Sraffa in the eventual form of Chapter 17 of the *General Theory*, we can utilize the thoughts of a Cambridge student of the early thirties, a disciple of Keynes, Adam Smith prizeman and eventually Professor of Economics at the Banaras Hindu University, Mr. Bhalchandra Pundlik Adarkar. Adarkar's *The Theory of Monetary Policy* (1935) provides an interesting contemporary survey of the major monetary theories of the thirties and constructive work on the usefulness of this body of theory for practical monetary management.

Besides the fact that Adarkar provides a concise discussion of the complete range of interest rate theory at the time, he forms an important intellectual link in our study by virtue of his knowledge of Keynes's monetary theory in the transition period from the *Treatise on Money* to the *General Theory*. Keynes's influence is clearly stated in Adarkar's preface:

> It will not be difficult for the reader, however, to discern the intellectual genealogy of this effort and he will at once perceive how deeply indebted I am to J. M. Keynes, that leader of modern monetary thought, in much that I have to say in the following pages.
>
> (Adarkar, 1935, p. viii)

From this, we can feel confident that Adarkar's view will reflect Keynes's views on monetary matters, from this crucial period during the composition of the *General Theory*. For our purposes, two chapters are especially interesting: Chapter 7 on "Mr. Sraffa's Commodity Rate" and Chapter 11 titled "Is Barter Theory Relevant?"

In the latter of these two, Adarkar sets out to investigate "the question as to what extent the theory of a non-monetary economy is likely to be useful in the understanding of monetary phenomena." He notes that the concept has been much used by modern writers on monetary problems, but that "the attitude of most writers in this matter has been altogether dubious, if not misleading." "Cassell, Wicksell and Hayek" are explicitly mentioned as cases where "hypothetical considerations of a non-monetary character have been introduced in monetary theory in connection with our problem [the idea of a natural rate]." His approach to the question is to consider a number of different conceptions of barter since these "hypotheses . . . are not *in pari materia* but relate to distinct concepts of the non-monetary economy" (Adarkar, 1935, p. 86). Adarkar distinguishes between two conceptions of a barter economy. The first is a Robinson Crusoe economy used by Bohm-Bawerk and Rosher to illustrate capital accumulation. This economy is not really a barter economy so much as it is without exchange, and here the acts of investment and saving actually occur in physical terms. More interesting for our purposes is what Adarkar calls "an advanced social economy, in which there is exchange but no *medium* of exchange, in which goods are exchanged against goods" (p. 87). Hayek's ideal barter state is identified with this moneyless economy where "only those investments can be carried out which are justified by the available real savings . . . [which] avoids the disparity between savings and investments, resulting from our adherence to money" (Adarkar, 1935, p. 89). But the assumption that such a moneyless state would be more stable than a monetary system, Hayek's thesis, is questioned by Adarkar. He points out that "relative valuations of goods, services and other forms of wealth are liable to fluctuate therein as much as they do in a money economy." In fact, he thinks that such a non-monetary economy would be *less* stable since all of the factors making for disruption "*viz.*, psychology, natural and physical phenomena, discoveries and so forth are present," but the monetary factor, "the only one that implies some sort of control," is "absent" (p. 88). As we will see, this closely reflects Keynes's own ideas about a barter state.

Because of this instability, and because focusing on barter phenomena encourages us "to forget that what we are primarily concerned with is money itself and its mysterious interactions on the processes of production, distribution and consumption," Adarkar finds such non-monetary systems of little use in either monetary theory or policy. Interestingly for our thesis, he connects this rejection with an abandonment of the whole natural-rate doctrine utilizing Sraffa's review of Hayek. He says that even if we accept the automaticity of savings and investment in the barter state, "it does not help us to ascertain the *ideal* rate of interest that should be adopted under the *money* system." Relying on Sraffa's example, he points out that even in the barter state, the natural rate is not unique but varies with the number of commodities considered. "Moreover, even if we succeed in constructing such an average 'barter' rate, we have no reason to suppose that rate, *because it secured the savings-investment equalization, under barter, it would do so here also*; . . . It is for this reason, among others, that we have to reject the very ingenious concept of the 'natural rate'" (p. 90).

Is barter theory relevant? To a disciple of Keynes in 1935:

> There is no need, however, to suppose that a return to barter would mean the elimination of all the economic problems arising from changes in relative valuations. True, money sometimes distorts the vision and puts false appearances on the realities of economic life and thus necessitates our probing deeper, viewing kaleidoscopically what is happening in the realm of realities. But this is not the same thing as to visualize the modern money economy as a mere disfigured replica of its cruder ancestor.
> (Adarkar, 1935, p. 91)

In Chapter 17 of the *General Theory*, Keynes lifts Sraffa's barter rates (redubbed by Keynes as own-rates) out of that "disfigured replica of its crude ancestor" and sets them down in a modern money economy. In Chapter 13, we established the corrosive effect that Sraffa's commodity-rates approach represents to the whole Wicksellian natural-rate, loanable funds framework. We now need to pick up the development of its more constructive uses in illustrating Keynes's liquidity preference theory. Once again, Adarkar proves a useful bridge in that in the same book in which he disparaged the usefulness of the natural-rate doctrine he also reviewed "Mr. Sraffa's Commodity Rate" (1935, pp. 41–4). Working without the benefit of the *General Theory* and missing entirely the ironic critique implied by Sraffa's use of own-rates, Adarkar finds little use for the concept in his own concern with monetary policy. He seems to have thought that Sraffa was in fact proposing that his average commodity rates be adopted as a policy guide. Nevertheless, the very naiveté of his criticisms, coming as they do from a student of the Keynes of the *Treatise*, provides a useful transition to Keynes's own use of the concept.

Adarkar's chapter is mainly focused on the possible use of Sraffa's average commodity rate as a standard by which the banking authorities might set the money rate. To this task, he finds it inadequate due to its instability. What is particularly interesting, however, is that Adarkar critiques the bare concept of the commodity rates from the standpoint of the rich institutional detail about monetary markets of Keynes's *Treatise on Money*. Again, he foreshadows many of the issues that will appear in Keynes's own use of this concept.

Adarkar points out that Sraffa's commodity rates bear a strong resemblance to Fisher's attempt to reckon "real" rates of interest "for each separate commodity by correcting the money rate for a change in its new spot price" (Adarkar, 1935, p. 42). But the difference between them, he notes, is that Fisher wanted to consider the difference between two spot prices separated in time while Sraffa's rate is completely calculated on current market evaluations as reflected in simultaneously existing spot and future prices. Thus, Fisher's real rate "is a *de facto* affair, on which monetary policy could only hold a *post mortem;*" but Sraffa's rate "is a living fact on which we could rely for active guidance in that if disequilibrium arises, the forward prices indicate it" (p. 42).

It is this forward-looking aspect of commodity rates that peculiarly adapts them to Keynes's preferred mode of monetary theory: uncertainty about the future. And, of course, what Sraffa implied in his review was that precisely those functions of money which relate to uncertain intertemporal situations were the ones Hayek and the natural-rate theorists were ignoring at the peril of irrelevance to a "real monetary economy." Adarkar details the implications that such psychological aspects of money hold for commodity rates.

First, he mentions that in a risky market the equilibrium position of spot and future prices will not exactly coincide due to the "cost of hedging." "As

Keynes has shown (*CW* 6, pp. 127–31), in equilibrium the spot price exceeds the forward price, the 'backwardation' amounting to as much as 10 percent in the case of seasonal crops" (p. 43). In the *General Theory*, this normal backwardation is subsumed under one element of his conception of own rates, the liquidity premium. Adarkar further notes that a true reckoning of such rates must take into account "costs of warehousing, insurance [and] deterioration" of the stocks held over; "the *speculative* element" in spot and forward dealings; and the "current ideas and expectations of businessmen as to the probable course of future production" (p. 44). Each of these influences, we will see, also has a counterpart in Keynes's own-rates framework. While for Adarkar these influences made it "questionable whether we could depend upon such data to discover the norms and equilibria of industry," in Keynes's hands these concerns will constitute a "monetary theory of production" based on both real and monetary influences. It may be that one implication of this theory is that there are no long-enduring "norms and equilibria" by which we can regulate the economy through monetary policy, as was the goal of the natural-rate theorists. But in terms of explicating Keynes's central concern with interest and money in defining unemployment equilibriums theoretically, Adarkar foreshadows Keynes's own argument, to which we now turn.

III. Keynes: The theory of interest and the theory of employment

Chapter 17 comes in 222 pages into a complicated *theoretical* attempt to define unemployment equilibria as a potential resting point of a capitalist economy. As many of his pre-publication correspondents and post-publication critics have commented, its discussion runs on a more general plane of reasoning than the more closely argued model that precedes it.[4] Yet, it obviously must be understood as a part of that greater work. For this reason, it is prudent to preface our detailed investigation of Chapter 17 with a brief look at Keynes's argument up to that point. Keynes's theory of the equilibrium positions of the economic system was "general" in its insistence on the possibility of a range of outputs and employments being consistent with the normal functioning of the system. Keynes's conclusion was that a less-than-full employment equilibrium was the normal case within this possible range. In arriving at this conclusion he felt that the fundamental analytical breakthrough in his own thinking had been the realization of "the psychological law that when income increases, the gap between income and consumption will increase" (*CW* 14, p. 85). It was from this simple idea that he derived his fundamental building blocks of the multiplier and the theory of effective demand. Keynes thought that the neglect of aggregate effective demand, or "demand for output as a whole," had made the classical theory inapplicable except in the special case of full employment. His analysis of their argument in Chapter 2 attributes this neglect to a reliance on the second classical postulate and Say's Law. For Keynes, the way to exhibit such a range of equilibria was to throw out the second postulate and to supply the missing equation for effective demand. Because savings is not necessarily directed to productive use, the level of aggregate demand fluctuates. The result is uncertainty over future levels of activity. To Keynes, this meant his aggregate demand theory would have to deal with saving and investment activity in an uncertain environment. This motivates the fascinating discussions of expectations in the *General Theory*.

Keynes situated the main effect of uncertainty in the investment activity of business. Having cut the strict productivity moorings from beneath the classical theory of interest, it was necessary for Keynes to provide an alternative formulation. Thus, the last element in his system was the liquidity preference theory of interest. This filled the gap in a manner consistent with his analysis of the psychological uncertainty of investment behavior.

In brief, given short-period conditions, output and employment depend upon aggregate effective demand, which is wagged up and down by fluctuating investment behavior (the consumption function being stable). A complex of productivity, monetary and expectational conditions, all packed into the portmanteaux of the liquidity preference function and the marginal-efficiency-of-capital schedules, determines investment behavior and thus output and employment. According to Keynes, when it is realized that output and employment are not givens, but are uniquely correlated with the level of effective demand, the *practically* obvious existence of involuntary unemployment can be *theoretically* explained. It is only in the context of this argument that his definitions of involuntary unemployment and full employment can be understood.

Keynes left it to Chapter 17 to fully draw out his theory of interest and money for reasons clearly set out in the first paragraph of that chapter:

> It seems, then, that the *rate of interest* on money plays a peculiar part in setting a limit to the level of employment, since it sets a standard to which the marginal efficiency of a capital-asset must attain if it is to be newly produced. That this should be so, is, at first sight, most perplexing. It is natural to enquire wherein the peculiarity of money lies as distinct from other assets, whether it is only money which has a rate of interest, and what would happen in a non-monetary economy. *Until we have answered these questions, the full significance of our theory will not be clear.*
>
> (*GT*, p. 202; emphasis added)

IV. The essential properties of interest: Own-rates in a monetary economy

In synthesizing a general theory of interest and money that is compatible with his general theory of employment, Keynes draws on Sraffa's commodity rates as an exploratory tool, now following out the implications of this notion for what Sraffa termed "real monetary economies." Methodologically, this involves Sraffa's admonition to Hayek about starting from concrete situations as well as Adarkar's references to the failings of commodity rates to capture the full institutional detail of a monetary economy. Chapter 17 will provide a way to understand Harrod's comments about Keynes's central concern with a "wrong rate of interest" that is "not itself a rigidity or inflexibility," but is "natural, durable, and in a certain sense, in the free system inevitable" (1947, p. 70). To use Keynes's own words, "Until we have answered these questions the full significance of our theory will not be clear."

Keynes immediately gets down to concrete cases introducing commodity-rates as a natural definition of interest on both money and other types of assets:

> The money rate of interest – we may remind the reader – is nothing more than the percentage excess of a sum of money contracted for forward delivery, e.g. a year hence, over what we may call the "spot" or cash price of the sum thus contracted for forward delivery. It would seem, therefore, that for every kind of capital-asset there must be an analogue of the rate of interest on money. For there is a definite quantity of (e.g.) wheat to be delivered a year hence which has the same exchange value today as 100 quarters of wheat for "spot" delivery. If the former quantity is 105 quarters, we may say that the wheat-rate of interest is 5 percent. per annum; and if it is 95 quarters, that it is *minus* 5 percent. per annum. Thus for every durable commodity we have a rate of interest in terms of itself . . ."
>
> (*GT*, p. 222)

Footnoting Sraffa, Keynes works through an example, similar to Sraffa's cotton spinner, of the wheat-rate of interest. He defines such commodity rates as "own-rates" and notes that "there is no reason why their rates of interest should be the same for different commodities," since the relations of spot and future prices for different commodities are "notoriously different" (p. 223). Thus, in the most general context of the own-rates conception, "the money rate of interest has no uniqueness compared with other rates of interest, but is on precisely the same footing" (p. 225).

Yet, although as a record of the terms of an intertemporal market trade – or as a relative price – there is no difference between a money-denominated transaction and a wheat-denominated transaction, Keynes states that the money rate is unique for two interrelated reasons. The money rate is the standard in which all other future values are contracted for and estimated, and there are peculiar reasons why the money rate may be less flexible downward than other rates. If we can show why these two properties adhere to money rather than other assets, we will have some justification for using money as the standard in which to measure the marginal efficiency of capital, and for using the money rate as the marginal efficiency which "rules the roost" in the sense of providing a rate which other assets must attain to be newly produced. In other words, it is the fact that money is held in asset portfolios for unique reasons that warrants attention on the money rate as the regulator of investment.

In order to get to the rest of the differences and similarities between the range of observed assets and their own-rates of interest, Keynes introduces a scheme of attributes which defines the relative desirability of different assets, essentially a demand equation for assets. This scheme addresses Adarkar's comments (based on the *Treatise*) on the specific failings of the commodity rates in a monetary economy as well as illustrating Keynes's liquidity preference theory. It is through this abstraction that Keynes relocates the own-rates from the Wicksellian world to his own.

Taking "various commodity-rates of interest over a period of (say) a year" and measuring each rate "in terms of itself" as the standard of intertemporal value, Keynes finds "three attributes which different types of assets possess in different degrees." These are:

(i) Some assets produce a yield or output q, measured in terms of themselves, by assisting some process of production or supplying services to a consumer.

(ii) Most assets, except money, suffer some wastage or involve some cost through the mere passage of time (apart from any change in their relative value), irrespective of their being used to produce a yield; i. e., they involve a carrying cost c measured in terms of themselves . . .

(iii) Finally, the power of disposal over an asset during a period may offer a potential convenience or security, which is not equal for assets of different kinds, though the assets themselves are of equal initial value. There is, so to speak, nothing to show for this at the end of the period in the shape of output; yet it is something for which people are ready to pay something. The amount (measured in terms of itself) which they are willing to pay for the potential convenience or security given by this power of disposal (exclusive of the yield or carrying cost attaching to the asset), we shall call it liquidity – premium l. (*GT*, pp. 225–6)

In Keynes's scheme, an asset's own-rate of interest will be defined by "its yield *minus* its carrying cost plus its liquidity premium." Recalling Adarkar's specific complaints about commodity rates, we can now see that in Keynes's definition, we have so far taken account of "costs of the stocks held over" with c, "current ideas and expectations of businessmen as to the probable course of future production" with q (and to some extent l), and "the speculative element" with l. But Adarkar's further concern with the relation of pure commodity rates to the Fisher effect is also addressed by Keynes. It is worthwhile to look at this relationship a bit more closely since it sheds light on the important and interesting question of the relation of interest rates and inflation in the own-rates framework.

Keynes claims that in so far as the relationship between spot and future prices on different commodities reveals a multitude of own-rates, any of these commodities, which are held for investment purposes, could conceivably be used as the standard in which to measure the marginal efficiency of capital assets (recalling that his concern is with explaining investment demand):

> For we can take any commodity we choose, e.g. wheat; calculate the wheat-value of the prospective yields of any capital asset; and the rate of discount which makes the present value of this series of wheat annuities equal to the present supply price of the asset in terms of wheat gives us the marginal efficiency of the asset in terms of wheat.
>
> (p. 224)

According to Keynes, the choice of standard is arbitrary so long as "no change is expected in the relative value of two alternative standards." We are very close here to the Fisherian doctrine of the effect of expected inflation on current interest rates. The relative value of two alternative standards is just Fisher's "appreciation of money" where we are, as Keynes says (p. 227), "taking money (which need only be a money of account for this purpose, and we could equally well take wheat) as our standard of measurement . . ." In this situation, it is possible to correct for differences in both different standards over time or in relative changes with respect to one particular standard. In the case of choosing a standard, the whole structure of "own-rates" moves up and down "when one of the alternative standards is expected to change in value in terms of the other." The influence of Sraffa is echoed in this context by the concern over variant and invariant standards of value. Basically, there are two problems involved. First, there is the question of which good to use as the standard in which to measure all relative own-rates (including the all important marginal efficiency of capital) today. As Keynes said above, this choice is arbitrary in the sense that we can value any expected stream and current price in terms of any standard we choose, for example wheat. "If no change is expected in the relative value of two alternative standards, then the marginal efficiency of a capital-asset will be the same in whichever of the two standards it is measured, since the numerator and denominator of the fraction which leads up to the marginal efficiency will be change in the same proportion" (*GT*, p. 224).

But, secondly, if one of the standards is expected to change in value (appreciate), "the marginal efficiencies of capital-assets will be changed by the same percentage, according to which standard they are measured in." Keynes illustrates his conception of the effect such an appreciating standard will have on the structure of own-rates by a simple example where "wheat, one of the alternative standards, is expected to appreciate at a steady rate of a percent, per annum in terms of money." According to Keynes, in this simple case a will provide an additive adjustment factor to the marginal efficiency of an asset to distinguish rates determined in one standard or another with the ranking of asset values remaining unaffected:

> The marginal efficiency of an asset, which is x percent, in terms of money, will then be $x{-}a$ percent, in terms of wheat. Since the marginal efficiencies of all capital-assets will be altered by the same amount, it follows that their order of magnitude will be the same irrespective of the standard which is selected.

In other words, relative rates of appreciation are not all to be expected to be the same in terms of different standards. Fisher was well aware of this problem when he noted: "There are, therefore, theoretically just as many rates of interest expressed in terms of goods as there are kinds of goods diverging from one another in value" (Fisher, 1930, p. 42). Fisher's solution – not surprisingly, coming from a master of the theory of index numbers – was to express his "real rate" of interest by adjusting the money rate with *ex post* changes in these prices.

Keynes himself had already dealt with index numbers in relation to his investigation of stabilizing the price level in the *Treatise* (*CW* 5, Book II). This experience, and his collaboration with Sraffa, seems to have made him wary of aggregate indices. This wariness shows up in the present context in his comment on defining a standard:

> If there were some composite commodity which could be regarded strictly speaking as representative, we could regard the rate of interest and the marginal efficiency of capital in terms of this commodity as being, in a sense, uniquely *the* rate of interest and *the* marginal efficiency of capital. But there are, of course, the same obstacles in the way of this as there are to setting up a unique standard of value.

In accordance with this rejection of a composite standard, Keynes includes an appreciation factor "a" in his equations for own rates which take into account "what the changes in relative values during the year are expected to be" in order to "determine the expected returns on different types of assets which are consistent with equilibrium" (p. 227). Thus, where

$$q_i - c_i + l_i$$

defines the commodity own rate in real terms for commodity i, the same rate measured in money terms will yield the "money rate" of commodity i,

$$q_i - c_i + l_i + a_i$$

V. The structure of own rates in asset market equilibrium

Returning to the development of the own-rates framework of asset market equilibrium, it is useful to digress a bit and consolidate the argument so far. What we have seen is that the bare concept of a commodity rate introduced by Sraffa implies that, from the most general standpoint, a money rate of interest is not unique. A set of intertemporal prices implies an own-rate of exchange between spot and future quantities. But Keynes opposed his analysis to the "real-exchange" approach which he saw as counterproductively assimilating money to a barter state of nature – examples we analyzed in the last chapter include the Hayekian scheme in *Prices and Production* and the Walrasian conception of intertemporal equilibrium. We have also seen that each of these also exhibit own rates of interest. To begin to differentiate Keynes's version of this concept, it is well to remember what he stressed were the characteristics of a monetary economy.

His very choice of assets in Chapter 17, suggest that Keynes's case of a monetary economy is dependent on his accumulated observations of such an economy's qualities. To begin with, there are fundamental reasons that actual futures markets are rare, and so opportunities to trade over time are limited. One actual way is organized commodity markets. But such futures markets are confined to widely known and traded monetary instruments and to those gradable "commodities" for which there are large supplies and demands. Both are examples of institutions developed in capitalist economies to meet the needs of end users, we know. Yet we have also seen that such markets endow the formal monetary contracts in which they trade – contracts to deliver specified future amounts of money or goods to the end users – with the quality of "assets" to the dealers and speculators on these exchanges. Indeed this was widely known at least as far back as Emery's analysis in 1896 – information to which Keynes later added much practical experience. The asset "wheat" abstractly represents this type of opportunity here.

Second, Keynes's conception of asset holding envisions opportunities to hold real assets, which are expected to be "productive" over time. These assets imply holding for use and also imply calculating a peculiar "user cost"[5] that will vary with the capital's rate of use in providing employment and output versus the cost of waiting to so use it. There are envisioned secondhand markets for such assets, but capital goods lack the formal "grading" qualities of commodities,[6] and so capital goods secondhand markets are less organized. In terms of the stock equilibrium of asset balances, the paradigm case of this is Marshall's "horse" from 1870. Like Keynes's more modern "house," this is an example of an asset that can yield consumption services and/or capital services. This might explain the otherwise puzzling choice by Keynes of "houses" to represent productive assets in Chapter 17. One of Marshall's "appliances" or a "machine" might seemingly have been a better choice. But like in the case of "horses" in Marshall's day, maybe Keynes was confining himself to assets with well-defined existing second-hand markets. It matters little, however, for when he is not pointing to examples, he notes that the qualities of most assets are a combination of its yield, carrying costs and liquidity premium. And in the case of "instrumental capital (*e.g.* a machine) or of consumption capital (*e.g.* a house)" it is characteristic "that its yield should normally exceed its carrying cost, whilst its liquidity-premium is probably negligible" (p. 226). In the end, Keynes chose "houses" to serve as an example of an asset that represents productive assets, which have a yield greater than their carrying cost.

Then there is also the possibility of holding wealth in the form of money as an asset. Marshall ascribed this to money's convenience as a medium of exchange, and thought this was the beginning of the integration of the theory of value with the quantity theory of money. Keynes is surely including all of Marshall's, Pigou's and Lavington's ideas on the value of a stock of money as the media of exchange and as an asset. But he emphasizes, as they did not, that what gives money its value as an asset is the peculiar quality of liquidity, l. This liquidity value will be irrespective of the details one desires to include of the actual financial returns that the evolution of various instruments by financial markets make available. In other words, it is only a matter of institutional detail as to what types of financial instruments the market has made available to savers, say time deposits or bonds. What is crucial is that each is an opportunity to hold money over time. One can part with spot cash or deposits in various ways, but in the process the supplier of spot money must be paid at *least* the liquidity premium. Anything in excess of this depends on such details as the term to maturity, the credit-worthiness of the borrower and how much extra security is available to secure against estimates of default. These details were better covered in the *Treatise* than in the *General Theory*.[7] We are now at such an abstract level that the money asset is only represented by l,[8] its liquidity premium.

But there is another aspect of a monetary economy represented in Chapter 17. That is that all of the various ways of holding an asset are linked in equilibrium. That makes the equilibrium idea here a more generalized version of the covered interest parity relationship that we earlier saw Keynes had developed to analyze currency forward markets in *A Tract on Monetary Reform* (*CW* 4). There he was concerned with the balancing of expectations about future appreciation or depreciation of any one currency and the interest obtainable on money deposits at different financial centers. Here we are dealing in only one numeraire commodity, not a set of international monies. Therefore it matters in Keynes's world – whereas it does not matter in a moneyless world like that of intertemporal equilibrium – that the money asset is a *current* numeraire, so that all prices in all time periods are fixed in relation to today's value of money. It can then, given the stability of this relationship in the past, only be *expected* to be the most stable way to hold wealth into future periods. Note that in this way the very existence of money is tied to the incomplete nature of futures markets noted above. Money in these markets serves as the *general* link between the present and the future.

This is the difference between a generalized own-rates view of the economy and the *Tract* and *Treatise* "theory of the forward market" from which it is derived. There arbitrageurs could hedge themselves by a number of simultaneous spot and future trades, given current interest rates and expectations as represented by the difference between spot and forward prices. That was a complete hedge for arbitrageurs, and resulted in a position of prices such that trade in any direction yielded equal trading profit. In other words, they could not better their positions. In Keynes's analysis in the *Tract*, as well as in Marshall's previous analysis of commodity markets, it was only uncovered trades that were considered speculative. In a monetary economy, Keynes says in Chapter 17, there are certain risks that cannot be hedged, except perhaps by avoiding risk as much as possible by holding money and avoiding investment in productive activity. This is because there are no guarantees as to how the passage of time will treat values denominated in money terms. We cannot contract for productive capital goods that will deliver determinate sums of money in the future. Hence all assets held through time must deal with the uncertain expectation of future money value compared to known present money value. All commodity own-rates for assets other than money can thus only be put in comparable form to the money rate by their translation into *conventionally accepted money terms.*[9]

That is to say, for assets outside formally traded commodities,[10] assets holders have to form an expectation of that good's future price relative to its spot price – the appreciation of that good in terms of money. Defining this latter expectation is the function of the "*a*" terms, which Keynes (*GT*, p. 227) defines as "the percentage appreciation (or depreciation)" of each good in terms of that standard in which prices are reckoned. In practice there are various combinations of spot, future and option transactions that can be used by arbitrageurs to hedge their positions. But outside of commodities, and despite what modern-day hedge-funds may claim about their ability to lock in returns, this generally only results in equality for the marginal bull and bear of *expected* returns from a market configuration of prices. It is not a perfect hedge. In any case, at this high level of abstraction, it should be emphasized that this arbitrage equilibrium is an expectational construct. And because expectation may disappoint in Keynes's world, complete hedging will never be possible for all asset holders.

To be absolutely clear about this deceptively simple idea, it is convenient to resort to some algebra. In this framework, for any asset i "real" or "commodity" own rates are designated as r_c^i Denominated in money terms, the same rate becomes a "money-own-rate," which we will write as r_m^i

Keynes's "*a*" terms are the difference between real own rates and money own rates for all goods except money itself,

$$a^i = r^i_m - r^i_c$$

We can use this formulation to clarify a number of issues. First, recall that Sraffa (1932a, p. 50) had defined the commodity rate as being equal to the money rate "plus the excess (or minus the deficiency) of the spot over the forward price." This is the definition referenced to Sraffa by Keynes that he used in working out his wheat example. It provides a clear link between the abstract concept and market phenomena. We can specify this link more clearly. The relationship postulated by Sraffa is

$$r^i_c = r_m - \left(\frac{P^i_f - P^i_f}{P^i_s} \right)$$

where:
r^i_c = the commodity own-rate
r^i_m = the money-denominated commodity rate for commodity i
r_m = the money own-rate
P^i_f = the future price of commodity i
P^i_s = the spot price of commodity i

Operating on a long-period interpretation, Sraffa saw the future price as anchored, in good Marshallian fashion, by the "normal" price that would correspond to cost of production. But Keynes had already put forward in the *Treatise* an argument about the short period relationship of spot and future prices. His view there, like that in the *Tract*, was informed by extensive personal experience in trading commodities and his resulting construction of a theory of forward market prices. A short detour to this *Treatise* analysis will shed valuable light on the market mechanism that Keynes is proposing in Chapter 17 as an explanation for the possibility that an economy may get stuck in an unemployment equilibrium.[11]

Keynes was originally spurred to think about this issue by Hawtrey's writings about the importance of stocks of working and liquid capital over the course of the cycle (*CW* 6, Chapter 29, especially pp. 125–31). Keynes claimed that Hawtrey's failing was that he had not fully understood "the mechanism of short-period organization" (p. 125). It is significant that though he bases his analysis in the behavior of organized speculative markets – for Keynes exemplified by organized commodity exchanges – he also suggests that his theory is more generally applicable to "less organized markets" (p. 128).

Keynes's argument turns on the high implicit "carrying costs" that are associated with the ability of organized markets to hold significant stocks of commodities over the course of a downturn. Important aspects of carrying costs are reproduced from that discussion in the *Treatise* to Chapter 17 of the *General Theory*. These include two things that especially inhibit the likelihood that markets can carry significant stocks of liquid good during a slump, which Hawtrey had suggested would be the source of subsequent expansions. One is "[a]llowance for deterioration in quality or in suitability through the unpredictability of the precise specifications which will be required when demand recovers" The other is "[r]emuneration against the risk of changes in the money value of the commodity during the time through which it has to be carried." (*CW* 6, p. 121)

The reader will recognize that this discussion is similar to the specification of the "*c*" and "*a*" terms from Chapter 17. The point of discussion in the *Treatise* was that Keynes thought that these costs had important implications for what he considered a much-neglected topic: "the theory of short period prices" (*CW* 6, p. 126). In the *Treatise* he was concerned to show that the unexpected appearance of "liquid capital" on speculative markets – for instance, that which would occur during an unexpected downturn of demand – would result in a significant fall in spot prices. Recall that a backwardation, whereby the future price lies above the spot, exists to compensate speculators for the risk and cost of carrying even normal volumes of "working capital." When this normal trade is interrupted in a downturn, redundant "liquid," stocks arise. The question Hawtrey had raised is whether the carrying of these stocks during the downturn would act to smooth the return to a long-period position by providing the eventual means out of which the recovery would be ignited. Keynes attacked Hawtrey's assumption that this would occur.

His reasoning is as follows. Stocks come about because of the lag between production of output and consumption. Where this lag is most regular – as in crops for commodity use by manufacturers, farmers and producers – it results in the creation of markets and specialists who will take on the risk of providing certainty about input and output prices. This comes at the cost of normal backwardation, based on normal carrying costs. In the *Treatise* Keynes defined the normal backwardation as "the amount which the producer is ready to sacrifice in order to 'hedge' himself "(*CW* 6, p. 128). Now, let an unanticipated slump arise which results in an excess stock of "liquid" commodities. Will these same speculators and markets carry the normal volume of output? Keynes says no, the speculators react by demanding even higher carrying costs, especially because there is now an increase in the "*a*" category of uncertainty about the future price, due to the length of the recession being unknown – but also because "*c*" increases as the anticipated time for carrying the stock increases.

Speculators will now only hold redundant liquid stocks – which now suffer the higher-than-normal, slump-induced carrying costs of deterioration and risk of depreciation – if they are compensated for doing so. They can be by the appearance on markets of a situation where the forward price rises above the spot (a "contango"). But as we saw in the case of currency markets in our discussion of the *Tract*, this is achieved by the fact that the forward price falls below the normal expected spot price in the future. And if this forward price falls so far as to be below the cost of production it will curtail new output, until the excess stock is absorbed. One cannot improve on Keynes's (*CW* 6, p. 129) original description:

> In this case there cannot exist a backwardation; for if there was one, it would always pay to sell the stocks spot and buy them back forward rather than incur the warehousing and interest charges for carrying them during the intervening period. Indeed the existence of surplus stocks must cause the forward price to rise *above* the spot price, i.e. to establish, in the language of the market, a 'contango'; and this contango must equal to the cost of warehouse, depreciation and interest charges of carrying the stocks. But the existence of a contango does not mean that a producer can hedge himself without paying the usual insurance against price changes. On the contrary, the additional element of uncertainty introduced by the existence of stocks and additional supply of risk bearing which they require mean that he must pay more than usual. In other words, the quoted forward price, though above the present spot price, must fall below the anticipated future spot price by at least the amount of the normal backwardation; and the present spot price, since it is lower that the quoted forward price, must be much lower than the anticipated future spot price. If the stocks are expected to be absorbed within a year, the present spot price must fall (say) 20 per cent below the anticipated future spot price; but if the stocks look like lasting for two years, then the present spot price must fall (say) 40 per cent.

In the *Treatise* Keynes was concerned to show that this short-period behavior of prices would exacerbate cycles. Instead of anchoring the future price to cost of production, he saw the method by which exchanges carry risk as amplifying output changes in a crisis – the deviation from long-term normal values by which the *Treatise* characterized the cycle. They do so because the commodity markets so swiftly react to a surplus of liquid accumulations. This was Keynes's complaint about Hawtrey. Liquid stocks, he said, are absorbed by the commodity market through dramatic falls in the spot price. This is an attempt to lower stocks to the new level of demand. Moreover, the appearance of a contango discourages new production until the supply and demand for stocks balance at the new lower level of activity.

Thus organized exchanges do not operate by Marshallian rules, and actually might operate in the opposite direction during a crisis in output. But now, in the *General Theory*, Keynes is proposing that something like this operation is more general to all asset markets, organized or not, and that it can account for the persistent existence of states of involuntary unemployment. What modifications of his *Treatise* arguments are needed for this generalization? I am arguing here that Keynes, in Chapter 17, restated for a monetary economy the traditional fundamental forces that determine assets values. In so doing he was elaborating on Marshall's long-standing stock theory of asset equilibrium. Keynes was thereby fashioning a general theory of asset equilibrium – and not one just for those assets traded on the most developed asset exchanges, such as commodity markets. One indication of this is his expression of all asset qualities as inherent in themselves, as we can see from the definitions he gave for q, c and l. Thus, for example, when he identifies carrying charges on commodities as normally being greater than their yield, that carrying cost is not reckoned in financial values as such and in "interest and warehousing" costs, as it was in the *Treatise*, but in terms of its own inherent – one might say "natural" – characteristics. Actual traders may pay interest and warehouse bills, but the fundamental reason they do so is because of the inherent costs of holding a good that wastes in value with time and that must be adequately stored. Likewise some assets inherently have a yield and some have a liquidity premium.

Also important from Keynes's discussion in the *Treatise* is the point that what is true of assets for which there are organized exchanges is less visibly, but no less fundamentally, true of all assets. Thus on less formal markets, for which there is not an organized exchange on which to unload trading risk, there will only be an expectation of what a future price will be. In this case there is extra uncertainty about the c and a terms, and they are not distinguishable in the expectations that are held of the "spot" relative to the "future" price. But both types of uncertainty and risk are still present and must be born by entrepreneurs – producers and the purchasers of productive assets. Moreover, this type of asset holding may require even more "insurance" than that required by commodity traders to hold stocks in uncertain times against expected fluctuations in value – so much so that there may be no sufficient fall in price that will induce holders of productive assets to use them. Instead, just like commodity traders, they seek safety and liquidity for their wealth. Idleness and unemployment may be a natural counterpart to this flight to safety.

It is noteworthy in this respect that Keynes (CW 6, p. 121) maintains that it is due to the extremely high carrying cost of most goods other than those traded on commodity markets – perhaps due to changing fashion or changing technology making future appreciation or depreciation unpredictable – that organized exchanges have not developed in these goods. Thus when demand for these products slump, there is also a fall in their current (spot) price. But if this drop in spot price is not enough to rid the market of excess stocks, there may also be a fall in the expected future price. If this fall is great enough relative to cost of production, output will be curtailed. The result will be involuntary unemployment. How long can it last? It lasts as long as it takes expectations of price to recover. Thus when Keynes concludes in the

Treatise that stocks of commodities are not able to smooth business cycles, he adds that this is even more so in the context of "less organized markets" (*CW* 6, p 128). This is what Keynes meant in the *Treatise* when he stated that "the present economic system abhors a stock of liquid goods" (*CW* 6, p. 130). Only in Chapter 17 of the *General Theory* did he generalize this into an argument for why this quality of a monetary economy may lead to unemployment equilibria.

Therefore, in Chapter 17 of the *General Theory* we see the *Treatise* analysis of commodity markets and their role in the cycle amplified into a theoretical reason to define short-period equilibria on asset markets as a point where arbitrageurs are satisfied, given expectations, that they can make no extra profit by reallocating to any other position. This will not be either the short- or the long- period equilibrium of Sraffa's and Marshall's real-exchange economics. Stability of such equilibria will correspond to the stability of the conventional basis of those expectations. Whether one calls this a short-period or long-period affair based is a matter of taste.[12] But "long period" has many connotations of the very type of economics Keynes was working to escape from. Thus he called it a theory of "shifting-equilibrium."

Returning to our comparison with Sraffa's long-period analysis provides additional insight into this change. Keynes defines equilibrium in the asset market as the situation where all own-rates, defined in a common standard, are equal. "Thus in equilibrium the demand-prices of houses and wheat in terms of money will be such that there is nothing to choose in the way of advantage between the alternatives" (p. 227). Using money as the standard, this means that all money own rates and the money rate itself will be equal in equilibrium; or, for all commodities i,

$$r_c^i + a^i = r_m$$

Compare this with the above definition of commodity rates in Sraffa's long-period disequilibrium example,

$$r_c^i = r_m - \left(\frac{P_f^i - P_s^i}{P_s^i} \right)$$

This not only confirms the Sraffian link with Keynes's concept, but it also makes clear that Keynes's definition of equilibrium in this context is strictly a current, expected affair. To see this, recall that Sraffa, using the long period as his definition, defined "'equilibrium' rates as the situation where spot and forward prices coincide . . . and all the 'natural' or commodity rates are equal to one another, and to the money rate" (Sraffa, 1932a, p. 50). But here, Keynes has defined his "equilibrium" as equality between all own rates measured in money terms, which, as the above formula makes clear, could easily be disequilibrium in the long-period sense. But, as we have said, it is in fact a completely different type of system that Keynes is defining the equilibrium for when compared to Marshall. This may be one way of understanding Keynes's insistence that the difference between a monetary and a real economics entails a specification of the "line of division between the theory of stationary equilibrium and the theory of shifting equilibrium – meaning by the latter the theory of a system in which changing views about the future are capable of influencing the present situation. *For the importance of money essentially flows from its being a link between the present and future"* (*GT* p. 293).

In this view, Keynes's "shifting equilibrium" is defined by a monetary equilibrium on the asset market where all own rates *consistently measured* are equal, but spot and forward prices still diverge according to current expectations of productivity, carrying costs and liquidity. Alternatively, Sraffa's equilibrium commodity rates are part of the theory of "stationary equilibrium." In a formal sense, this is captured by Sraffa's view that equilibrium requires all own rates *measured in quantity terms* to be equal, and all spot and future prices to coincide. This is why the details of Keynes's "*a*" terms are so important. It is the movements of the prices on spot and future markets which guarantee that his equilibrium position will exhibit a market configuration of equal *expected* money-denominated own-rates for every asset. But to see why Keynes's equilibrium *shifts* with "changing views about the future," we need to investigate Keynes's second question of Chapter 17. What is it about money as an asset that makes it unique?

In terms of his schema of attributes of assets, Keynes distinguishes money by its high liquidity premium and low carrying cost;

> . . . it is an essential difference between money and all (or most) other assets that in the case of money its liquidity-premium much exceeds its carrying cost, whereas in the case of other assets their carrying cost much exceeds their liquidity premium.

(p. 227)

The full implications of the special character of money, however, only become apparent in terms of Keynes's argument about the relationship between his shifting equilibrium on the asset market and the level of employment. His argument focuses on the level of interest rates as the determinant of new investment spending. In the own-rates context, investment is disaggregated into individual capital assets, which are both newly produced and traded on secondhand markets. At any given time, the outstanding stocks of both physical and pecuniary assets will be valued by the market in accordance with the demand for each asset's individual attributes of productivity, carrying cost and liquidity. Given that the stocks are slowly adjusted, the price established on the secondhand market will determine, when compared with the "normal supply price," in what directions and amounts investment flows proceed.

The definitions of equilibrium and the movements implied between equilibrium positions are very poorly specified by Keynes. At some junctures, his argument involves defining instantaneous stock equilibria and at others discussing flows of production of investment goods. In fact, to make sense of his argument, it is necessary to bring in a number of elements that define a very complicated picture only hastily sketched by Keynes. A broader analytical interpretation of this framework is possible if we center our attention on Keynes's equilibrium own-rates as a market phenomenon around which his complicated macroeconomic story revolves. By this interpretation, a stock equilibrium configuration of asset returns can serve as a focus of both liquidity preference theory and discussion of money.

To begin, we have Keynes's assertion that equilibrium in the asset market will be characterized by a state where all own rates, measured in a single standard, will equal each other (*GT*, pp. 227–8). In the context of asset market equilibrium, the "*a*" terms can be seen as the *necessary* positions of supply and demand equilibrium in spot and forward markets that ensure that all assets yield an equal return when consistently measured. This is clearly shown in the form given to the *a*s above where they are defined by the difference between spot and future prices:

$$a^i = \frac{P_f^i - P_s^i}{P_s^i}$$

It is Keynes's scheme of motives for holding different assets that provides the underlying economic forces, which drive the demands for various commodities. Productivity, costs and liquidity considerations shift these demands between the various stocks of assets. This appears on the market as the price configuration between the money rate and the spot and forward money prices that is established by arbitrageurs. Conard (1959, pp. 120–34) provides clear examples of this in the form of a variety of assets, each of which has different commodity own rates, but all of which yield an equal rate when measured consistently in any of the standards. Abba Lerner (1952, pp. 173–9) provides a similar analysis in his insightful interpretation of the own-rates theory and concludes:

> The wheat rate of interest and the money rate of interest are not automatically equal by definition: they are only brought into approximate equality in equilibrium by arbitrage in perfectly competitive markets.

To use Keynes's example where there are three assets – money, houses and wheat – we get three individual money rates of own interest all measured in money as the standard. The wheat rate is due to its predominant physical characteristic of high carrying cost and is primarily held for an expected rise in its price:

$$r_{w,m} = a_1 - c_1$$

The house rate is due primarily to its productive capacity to generate services q:

$$r_{h,m} = a_2 + q_2$$

The money rate is defined by the unique character of money that "its yield is *nil*, and its carrying cost negligible, but its liquidity premium substantial" (p. 226).

$$r_{m,m} = l_3$$

Using this framework, the asset market equilibrium condition is defined by

$$r_{w,m} = r_{h,m} = r_{m,m}$$

or

$$a_1 - c_1 = a_2 + q_2 = l_3$$

VI. Stocks of assets and flows of activity: The *General Theory* viewed through the own-rates equilibrium construct

Many writers have commented on the stock equilibrium quality of Keynes's analysis, by which we mean that equilibrium is defined for a market evaluation of an existing quantity of capital, money, bonds and so on. Kenneth Boulding was so taken with this aspect of Keynes's approach that he proposed *A Reconstruction of Economics* (1950) based on the sole use of stock rather than flow equilibrium theory. G. L. S. Shackle (1967, p. 145) has commented that this use of stock analysis is particularly evident in Keynes's interest-rate theory:

> One more of the great changes in outlook of economic theoreticians stands largely to Keynes's credit, and again it is largely a case where an idea or practice of Marshall's was radically deepened and enlarged. Marshall had compared the existing with the desired total stock of money, and proposed to regard the latter as proportional to national income. This was perhaps the first turning of the tide against the neoclassical emphasis on flows in contrast with stocks. Keynes's theory of the interest-rate fused method and meaning inseparably in a purely "stocks" analysis. It is the essence of the liquidity-preference theory that stocks and not flow are in command, and in stating this theory Keynes showed a "stocks" analysis at work.

It is interesting that Shackle mentions Marshall in this context since, as we have seen above, the very definition of "equilibrium" own rates by Sraffa and Keynes, respectively, hinges on the choice of defining them in the Marshallian long period (for Sraffa) or short period (for Keynes). Consequently, Sraffa looked to flows of resources between industries to eventually equalize all own rates and the money rate by equalizing the spot and future prices of every commodity in a long-period equilibrium. But Keynes, more alive to the financial realities of a complex money economy, relies on the arbitraging of wealth owners and speculators to drive the relation of spot and future prices of the outstanding stocks of assets into a configuration today that reflects current expectations about the desirability of each in the never realized *future*. As we will see, the importance of money in this scheme will revolve around its use as the link between these current expectations and the level of own-rates on the market today. It will be through the own-rate on money defined by its liquidity premium, along with the expected return on capital, that Keynes's fascinating discussion of long-term expectations[13] will enter into the framework of the asset-holding equilibrium of Chapter 17. Two more elements of the framework of analysis must first be dealt with.

Although Keynes defines asset-market equilibrium by price configurations on spot and forward markets, this is in a sense only the observable surface phenomenon beneath which the really interesting aspects of his story are centered. In fact, the major virtue of the own-rates analysis of Keynes's interest-rate theory may be that it does provide such a manageable focusing device for the complex considerations he wanted to discuss in his interest-rate theory, the very complexities that we have argued are ignored in the "Keynesian" version of macroeconomics. It is not idle to speak of the market equilibrium rates as a "centering" device in this context since Keynes's vision encompasses movements that occur both beneath this market equilibrium, in the form of individual decisions about expected asset values, and above this equilibrium in the form of flows of newly produced assets that respond to the market-determined prices. Before continuing, it is necessary to briefly specify each.

Keynes's analysis of the interest rate in Chapters 13 and 15 of the *General Theory* is addressed to the determination of the rate of interest on money in modern financial conditions. At the root of the argument is the question of how a given level of savings out of income (the determination of which Keynes had already distinguished from financial markets *per se*, by his aggregate demand analysis) will be held. In the simplest terms, Keynes formulates an asset holder's decision as one between holding savings in the form of "immediate, liquid command" over goods and services versus being "prepared to part with immediate command for a specified or indefinite period, leaving it to future market conditions to determine on what terms he can, if necessary, convert deferred commands over specific goods into immediate command over goods in general" (*GT*, p. 166). The extent to which wealth holders prefer one type of asset over another is the definition of their current state of *liquidity preference*. Defining this preference as a demand for *money* (in excess of that required for active circulation)[14] and the rate of interest on money as the price of parting with this liquidity, money interest becomes the "'price' which equilibrates the desire to hold wealth in the form of cash with the available quantity of cash."

But a further question remains. Why is it that anyone would want to hold wealth in a form that yields a rate of return less than other financial instruments? Why does such a thing as liquidity preference exist? Keynes argues that the fundamental condition giving rise to a liquidity preference is "the existence of *uncertainty* as to the future of the rate of interest." This, of course, is the source of the famous "bootstrap" critique of Keynes whereby it is uncertainty over the future rate that determines the current rate of interest (Robertson, 1940; Hicks, 1946, pp. 163–4). From the standpoint of the own-rates structure, this is shown to be a specious critique in that all of the multifarious elements of productivity, costs and time preference – that is, the elements that are left out, according to the "bootstrap" critique – are present here. Yet, in another sense, the "bootstrap" formulation goes to the heart of Keynes's view of the fundamental nature of a world in which there is interest on money to hold as an asset: uncertainty over future prices.[15] But this should not be a criticism in the world Keynes was interested in describing. As Keynes repeatedly emphasizes, in his world actors *are* uncertain about the future, and the expectations that they hold about the future are just what the bootstrap critique implies: "hoist by their own petard."

What we are driving at is the central theme that Keynes emphasized as the distinguishing feature of his *General Theory* in his 1937 *Quarterly Journal of Economics* article, "The General Theory of Employment," (*CW* 14, pp. 109–23), namely the "conventionality" of expectations in an uncertain environment. As Keynes emphasized in that article, this conventional quality of expectations enters into the economic scheme with particular force through asset valuations, both financial and real capital. In terms of the own-rates structure, expectations about both the profitability of investments and movements of financial prices will influence the equilibrium configuration through various qs, as and ls. But expectations will be especially relevant to the discussion of the peculiarities of money since ". . . *uncertainty* as to the future course of the rate of interest is the sole intelligible explanation of the type of liquidity preference . . . which leads to the holding of cash" (p. 201).

Since our emphasis is on the use of the own-rates theory as a tool in understanding the liquidity preference theory, two elements that are laid out in Chapters 12, 13 and 15 of the *General Theory* are worth emphasizing for the insight they lend to our understanding of Chapter 17. Keynes emphasized in these discussions that the interest on money, arising as it does out of a desire for liquidity in the face of uncertain expectations about the future course of capital asset values, rests on a *conventional* judgment of what the future course of interest will be. For this reason, financial markets: (1) are "made" by the simultaneous existence of a variety of opinions; and (2) are subject to precipitous swings when the fabric of the conventional judgment is weakened. A few lengthy quotations from Keynes demonstrate the importance of these points:

. . . the rate of interest and the price of bonds have to be fixed at the level at which the desire on the part of certain individuals to hold cash (because at that level they feel "bearish" of the future of bonds) is exactly equal to the amount of cash available for the speculative motive. Thus, each increase in the quantity of money must raise the price of bonds sufficiently to exceed the expectations of some "bull" and so influence him to sell his bonds for cash and join the "bear" brigade.

(*GT*, p. 171)

. . . It is interesting that the stability of the system and its sensitiveness to changes in the quantity of money should be so dependent on the existence of a *variety* of opinion about what is uncertain.

(*GT*, p. 172)

. . . Changes in the liquidity function itself, due to a change in the news which causes revision of expectations, will often be discontinuous, and will, therefore, give rise to a corresponding discontinuity of change in the rate of interest. Only, indeed, in so far as the change in the news is differently interpreted by different individuals or affects individual interests differently will there be room for any increased activity of dealing in the bond market.

(*GT*, p. 198)

Now the tie-in between these two crucial aspects of liquidity preference theory – the necessity of a diversity of opinions and the liability of reevaluations in conventional judgments to effect sea changes in interest rates – and the own-rates theory has two consequences. First, the argument about the diversity of opinions provides the link between the equilibrium market structure of the own rates when measured in a common standard with the scheme of individual judgments as to the expected productivity, liquidity and appreciation of various assets. In other words, in order to "make a market" for the variety of individual assets, it is necessary that individual estimates of the qs, as, and ls differ among individual investors. This is what we meant earlier by the individual decisions that go on *beneath* the structure of the equilibrium market configuration of asset prices.

Thus, by this argument the asset market equilibrium configuration implied by the own-rates structure is "built up" from a sophisticated microfoundation.

The sophistication lies in the explicit recognition of the social level influences on individual behavior, in the form of the market opportunities available to wealth holders and the social conventions underlying their future expectations. Further elaboration of this kind of (neglected) microfoundations would involve the role of different classes or "ideal types" of transactors on the markets, each with different goals and constraints. Two strong-type examples of this are evident in the Cambridge tradition of dividing bondholders up into two groups: widows and orphans and freewheeling speculators. R. F. Kahn (1954) makes much of this in his view of liquidity preference theory and notes that it links up the Keynes of the *General Theory* with the "two views" of the *Treatise*. More recently, work on the social foundations of the idea of rational expectations has come back to this point (Frydman, 1982; Frydman et al., 1982). Interestingly for us, the focus has been on the possible *instability* of a rational expectations equilibrium in its resemblance to the "Holmes--Moriarty problem" which is formally the same problem as Keynes's famous "beauty contest" (see O'Driscoll and Rizzo, 1985, pp. 84–5). In the own-rates equations for asset demand, this underlying conception of individual evaluations would actually imply a different equation for each different asset for each different agent. With n assets and m traders, we would get mn own-rate equations in the most general case. The market equilibrium rates would be equivalent to evaluations of the marginal traders only.

The second implication of these views of Keynes is that this underlying variety of opinion, making up both sides of the market for the total stock of existing assets, can move rapidly between various evaluations of the future ("bearishness and bullishness") because of alterations in the skein of conventional judgments upon which such evaluations exist. Keynes goes so far as to suggest that if all opinions about the future course of prices were unanimous and held with certainty, a complete revaluation of assets could occur without any change in holdings whatsoever:

> If the change in the news affects the judgment and requirements of everyone in precisely the same way, the rate of interest (as indicated by the price of bonds and debts) will be adjusted forthwith to the new situation without any market transactions being necessary.
>
> (*GT*, p. 198)

The confluence of these two points is the determination of the shifts in Keynes's "theory of shifting equilibrium" to which we previously equated the "own-rates" theory. Assets are held in expectation of gain based on conventional judgments of the future by different individuals. This precarious equilibrium is liable at any time to "shift" when the foundation of current opinion about the future is disturbed. The magnitude of the shift will depend on the extent to which it is shared and the length of time it takes for a new convention to be established. Thus, our asset market "equilibrium" is seen to be simultaneously a fragile balancing of individual opinions, and one firmly based in the economic motives of personal gain (here, though, only personally defined) by investors and speculators seeking their own advantage.

The macroeconomic importance of this asset equilibrium, now shown to constitute a market element with an underlying microstructure, is the effect that the level of the shifting stock equilibrium has on "flows" of investment and hence on employment. It is here that the last element of Keynes's "vision" of Chapter 17 comes in. These flows are the other side of the spectrum of which the own-rates form the center. For the result of the "highly conventional" phenomenon of asset market equilibrium has a very real effect in governing the desirability of investments in labor-employing projects. As Harrod's statement implied, it is for perfectly natural reasons that the rate of interest is "wrong." If in an uncertain world there is no reason to expect asset prices to reflect purely real employment opportunities, then the interest rate:

. . . may fluctuate for decades about a level which is chronically too high for full employment: particularly if it is the prevailing opinion that the level established by convention is thought to be rooted in objective grounds much stronger than convention, the failure of employment to attain an optimum level being in no way associated, in the minds either of the public or of authority, with the prevalence of an inappropriate range of rates of interest.

(*GT*, p. 204)

This was the conclusion of Keynes's basic theoretical model of employment developed in the *General Theory* of which the liquidity preference function was an integral part. In Chapter 17, with the use of the "own-rates" theory, Keynes shows that it may be that it is the very nature of money that causes this situation. In so doing, he addresses the further points of discussion in our Wicksellian theme: the nature of money, what a non-monetary economy would look like, and whether there is such a thing as a "natural" rate of interest, which would avoid this problem altogether.

VII. Keynes's views of capital

With our notion of asset market equilibrium in mind, we can follow Keynes into his discussion of the uniqueness of money in Sections II and III of Chapter 17. It is interesting to note that he addresses himself to a situation that was firmly established as the starting point of business cycle theory in the Wicksellian literature of his time. In particular, recall that Hayek (and Mises before him) wanted to discuss the natural rate in the context of an economy in which accumulation was going forward. Likewise, for Wicksell the goal was to try to use the marginalist method to explain this situation, using the tools of a long-period value theory where factors were accumulating, but all earned an equal rate of return. Keynes's innovation was to bring the financial side into this scheme and let his asset market equilibrium configuration determine equal "financial" rates of return at any given time. This is consistent with his severing of the savings–investment link that formed the basis of the Wicksellian story, where the interest rate equated *real* flows of savings with *real* flows of investment at the natural rate. Starting from this conception, the Wicksellian and loanable funds theorists would investigate the consequences of an upward shift in the investment schedule, which set off new investment at the existing market rate of interest. In Wicksell, Mises and Hayek the result of such a shift depended on whether the market rate was allowed to move to a new higher "natural rate" that would equilibrate saving and investment. According to this story, it was because the banking system could hold the rate beneath the natural rate, that we get "forced savings," an intertemporal misallocation of resources and an eventual crisis (see Leijonhufvud, 1981, pp. 151–60).

Keynes bases his analysis of the employment-generating effects of the own-rates equilibrium on a similar situation. He asks what would be the limiting factor that brings an increased production of new capital goods to a standstill? In his scheme, where the secondhand markets for goods continually revalue the entire stock of assets, the flow of new capital goods is determined by a comparison of the market-established rate of return on the existing stock with the expected marginal efficiency of new projects. In price terms, Keynes describes the comparison in terms of a "demand price" for capital goods which is fixed by discounting expected future streams of income from an investment back to the present using the market rate of interest (determined by the own-rates equilibrium). This demand price is then compared to a supply price, which represents the marginal cost of producing that asset. If the demand price exceeds the supply price, new capital goods will be produced:

> Now those assets of which the normal supply-price is less than the demand-price will be newly produced; and these will be those assets of which the marginal efficiency would be greater (on the basis of their normal supply-price) than the rate of interest (both being measured in the same standard of value whatever it is).
>
> (*GT*, p. 228)

Once in this Wicksellian situation of accumulation, where does the process stop? For Keynes, it stops when some assets' own-rate refuses to decline as accumulation goes forward and so holds up the market equilibrium rate of interest. The importance of *declining* own rates is impressed upon Keynes by his capital theory. Basically, he assumed a declining marginal efficiency of capital assets as production of them continued over the course of an economic expansion. The best discussion of this process is found in Chapter 11 where the "Marginal Efficiency of Capital" is explicitly addressed:

> If there is an increased investment in any given type of capital during any period of time, the marginal efficiency of that type of capital will diminish as the investment in it is increased, partly because the prospective yield will fall as the supply of that type of capital is increased, and partly because, as a rule, pressure on the facilities for producing that type of capital will cause its supply price to increase.
>
> (*GT*, p. 136)

To link this disaggregated, expectations-based view of capital with the asset market that the own-rates represent, Keynes further emphasizes in Chapter 16 that the failing of technical capital theory lies in ignoring the fact that a capital asset is just another potential rate of return to investors in a modern economy. The classical argument that it is the physical productivity of capital that sets the pace of investment,

> . . . overlooks the fact that there is always an alternative to the ownership of real capital-assets, namely the ownership of money and debts; so that the prospective yield with which the producers of new investment have to be content cannot fall below the standard set by the current rate of interest.
>
> (*GT*, pp. 212–13)

This reasoning is the basis of Keynes's contention that the source of the return on capital is not that it is productive but that it is scarce:

> . . . the only reason why an asset offers a prospect of yielding during its life services having an aggregate value greater than its initial supply price is because it is *scarce*; and it is kept scarce because of the competition of the rate of interest on money.
>
> (*GT*, p. 213)

All of this attention to Keynes's theories of money interest and capital serves not only to link up the own-rates framework with the larger work of which it is a part, but also prepares our way toward understanding Keynes's attribution of uniqueness to money as an asset. In a way that Keynes does not explicitly point out (but that is implied by the grouping of chapters in Book IV in the *General Theory*),[16] his argument for the uniqueness of money assets is an integral combination of his capital theory and liquidity preference theory. As we will see, the uniqueness of money is that it is only a very imperfect capital asset; but that its peculiarities from a capital theory standpoint are just those qualities which make it desirable as a *liquid* asset. Perfectly in accordance with Keynes's views on money and capital, then, the own-rates theory brings the analysis of financial and real assets under one framework.[17]

In the simplest terms, the marginal efficiency of each capital asset, d, will be defined by that rate of interest which, when used to discount a future stream of expected returns from an investment, will just equal the current supply price of that capital asset. If P^{s^i} is the present supply price of capital asset i, then solving the following for d will yield the marginal efficiency of that capital asset.

$$P^{s^i} = \sum_{j=1}^{n} \frac{R_j^i}{(1+d)^j}$$

where:
P^{s^i} = the present supply price of capital asset i;
R_j^i = the expected future stream of returns for each period j;
d = the unvarying rate of discount that brings the supply price into equality with expected returns.

For each capital asset, in own-rates terms, this d will equal the expected own rate, in money terms, for capital asset i:

$$d_i = q_i - c_i + l_i + a$$

Then in equilibrium, those traders at the margin of preference between the different assets will determine an equilibrium value of r where for all assets $(i = 1, \ldots, n)$

$$r_m = q_i - c_i + l_i + a$$

By Keynes's simplified example, we can reduce this to our three assets (wheat, houses and money) where the equilibrium interest rate (measured in money terms) becomes

$$r = a_1 - c_1 = q_2 + a_2 = l_3$$

In this context, the importance of the declining own rates as accumulation proceeds revolves around which rate will hold up the decline of the others. Since they must be "necessarily equal" on the market, the downwardly rigid rate will provide the level to which the others fall:[18]

> As the stock of the assets, which begin by having a marginal efficiency at least equal to the rate of interest, is increased, their marginal efficiency (for reasons, sufficiently obvious, already given) tends to fall. Thus, a point will come at which it no longer pays to produce them, *unless the rate of interest falls* pari passu. When there is *no* asset of which the marginal efficiency reaches the rate of interest, the further production of capital assets will come to a standstill.

(*GT*, p. 228)

VIII. The essential properties of money

The question Keynes is led to consider by this reasoning is, which of the own-rates will be the stubborn one that holds up the decline? Keynes thought there were certain "peculiarities" of the money rate which made it the own-rate that is reluctant to fall as output increases. The uniqueness of money as an asset revolves around the employment-generating effects that we have ascribed to the own-rates market equilibrium, and which we have seen to flow from Keynes's views on capital. It is because capital assets can be produced that they ultimately fall in value (their own-rates decline) as accumulation proceeds. The first unique characteristic of money is that it cannot be so produced in response to changes in its price:

> Thus, the characteristic that money cannot be readily produced by labour gives at once some *prima facie* presumption for the view that its own-rate of interest will be relatively reluctant to fall; whereas if money could be grown like a crop or manufactured like a motor car, depressions would be avoided or mitigated because, if the price of other assets was tending to fall in terms of money, more labour would be directed into the production of money.
>
> (*GT*, pp. 230–1)

But since this zero elasticity of production is also satisfied by any other pure rent factor fixed in supply, this cannot be the sole uniqueness of money. "The second *differentia* of money is that it has an elasticity of substitution equal, or nearly equal, to zero; which means that as the exchange value of money rises, there is no tendency to substitute some other factor for it." Keynes's argument here is that since the only reason that money is held as an asset is for its liquidity value, a change in the relative value of money will not have an adverse effect on its desirability as an asset. This is because the liquidity premium of a unit of money is only *increased* by an increase in its relative value (a decrease in prices). "This follows from the peculiarity of money that its utility is solely derived from its exchange value, so that the two rise and fall *pari passu*, with the result that as the exchange value of money rises, there is no motive or tendency, as in the case of rent-factors, to substitute some other factor for it." If, like other rent factors, the desirability of the money asset falls as its price rises, then an increased demand for it would "slop over into a demand for other things." Then the demand for money as an asset would at least indirectly reach a point of calling forth new employment. Since this is not the case, there is the possibility that money could become "a bottomless sink for purchasing power" (*GT*, p. 231).

From the standpoint of capital theory, then, the two peculiar qualities of money are that demand for it cannot call forth new production directly as in the case of capital goods proper, or even indirectly through substitution of other factors as in the case of pure rental items. For these two reasons, the avenues by which movement in capital-asset own-rates is accomplished, by new production, are closed off to the money asset.

But what of other liquid goods (for example, wheat) of which it may not be possible to immediately increase the supply in response to an increased demand? Why could not the wheat rate of interest hold up all the other rates? This is where Keynes's second attribute of assets to hold, carrying costs, comes in. Recall that Keynes had earlier defined money by its quality of possessing the highest excess of liquidity premium over carrying cost. The importance of the low carrying cost of money is that it sharply distinguishes money from all other potentially liquid assets (as opposed now to productive ones). Here, the distinction rests not on the supply side but on the demand side. In the case of all other liquid assets, the advantages offered through holding increased stocks of them are sharply limited by the cost of holding them for any appreciable time. Thus, "although a larger stock might have some attractions as representing a store of wealth of stable value, this would be offset by its carrying costs in the shape of storage, wastage etc." But this is not so in the case of money where "the readiness of the public to increase their stock of money in response to a comparatively small stimulus is due to the advantages of liquidity (real or supposed) having no offset to contend with in the shape of carrying costs mounting steeply with the lapse of time" (*GT*, p. 233).

Keynes uses this argument to explain why he thinks the effect of falling prices on the "effective supply" of money will not offset the position of money as a bottomless sink of purchasing power. In essence, he is anticipating what would become the "real balances" effect made so much of by Patinkin. He asks if it might not be the case that the stagnating influence of the high money rate would be offset by an "effective" increase in the supply of cash? The increased cash that resulted from falling prices (a reduction in the wage unit) would operate via two avenues:

> A reduction in the wage unit will release cash from its other uses for the satisfaction of the liquidity motive; whilst, in addition to this, as money-values fall, the stock of money will bear a higher proportion to the total wealth of the community.
>
> (*GT*, p. 232)

Keynes disputes the argument that these effects would satisfy the increased demand for liquidity and thus negate the dominant position of the money rate in setting the pace of investment. We are now back on the terrain of the discussion of wages at the end of Part I. First, he claims that the important reaction to a fall in the wage unit concerns "the *difference* between these [capital assets' own-rates] and the money rate of interest." It could be that the decline in wages would be even worse in creating an expectation of further declines and thus in decreasing the marginal efficiency of capital. Second, he cites his frequent point that "the fact that wages tend to be sticky in terms of money, the money-wage being more stable than the real wage, tends to limit the readiness of the wage unit to fall in terms of money." And in fact, due to the major place of wages in the expectations of future demand that hold up the marginal efficiency of capital, this stickiness is beneficial on the whole. Third, "the most fundamental consideration in this context" is the characteristic of money's high liquidity premium over carrying cost which makes it possible to absorb extra quantities of money without facing extra costs. As we will see, these qualities of wage stickiness and low carrying cost are Keynes's explanation for money's liquidity. Thus, both the capital theory aspects and the liquidity characteristics of money combine to give the money rate its "sting":

> The significance of the money-rate of interest arises, therefore, out of the combination of the characteristics that, through the workings of the liquidity-motive, this rate of interest may be somewhat unresponsive to a change in the proportion which the quantity of money bears to other forms of wealth measured in money, and that money has (or may have) zero (or negligible) elasticities both of production and of substitution.
>
> (*GT*, p. 234)

The effect on employment, then, operates through the level of equilibrium set by the necessary equality of the money rate and all other own rates, and the pace of investment demand this rate calls forth. When the money rate is reluctant to fall, all other own-rates fall to its level and no further. "The money-rate of interest, by setting the pace for all the other commodity-rates of interest, holds back investment in the production of these other commodities without being capable of stimulating investment in the production of money, which by hypothesis cannot be produced." From the asset market view, the very existence of the social convention of money becomes Keynes's culprit for unemployment: "Thus in the absence of money . . . the rates of interest would only reach equilibrium when there is full employment" (*GT*, p. 235).

Ultimately, Keynes's attribution of importance to the money rate rests on the qualities of money as an asset, "which constitutes money as being in the estimation of the public, *par excellence* 'liquid'." In Section IV of Chapter 17, Keynes brings the argument full circle by considering "how far those characteristics of money as we know it, which make the money rate of interest the significant rate, are bound up with money being the standard in which debts and wages are usually fixed" (*GT*, p. 236).

His consideration proceeds in two steps. "In the first place, the fact that contracts are fixed and wages are usually somewhat stable in terms of money unquestionably plays a large part in attracting to money so high a liquidity premium." It is because future debts and costs will be payable in money that money can perform its liquidity function, by definition. If the future standard of payments were not expected to be stable (say because of a psychologically unsustainable inflation rate), then money would not be liquid.[19] But this very stability is dependent upon the low elasticity of production of the money asset, which caused the trouble with its rate of interest. It is also true, Keynes claims, that the low carrying cost of money is important to its role as the standard of deferred payments. "For what matters is the *difference* between the liquidity premium and the carrying costs." Even if the public attached as high a liquidity premium to wheat by fixing contracts in terms of wheat the carrying costs would nevertheless be so high that "the wheat rate of interest would still be unlikely to rise above zero" (*GT*, p. 237).

The importance of the low carrying cost on money is the link between this consideration of money as the medium of exchange and a standard of deferred payments and its function as a store of value. Consequently, Keynes considers the "subtle" fact that:

> The normal expectation that the value of output will be more stable in terms of money than in terms of any other commodity, depends of course, not on wages being arranged in terms of money, but on wages being relatively *sticky* in terms of money.
>
> (*GT*, p. 237)

If this was not the case, and wages were "expected to be more sticky in terms of some one or other commodities other than money," then two requirements would have to be met by those commodities if they were to take our money's place as the dominant own rate. First, they would have to have a constant cost relative to real wages for any scale of output. Second, they would have to have a sufficiently low carrying cost to allow any "surplus over the current demand at cost-price . . . [to be] taken into stock without cost." The first requirement guarantees that the good's relative value would remain stable over the short and the long run as production ebbs and flows. The second requirement ensures that any old stock of the commodity would not affect its value. If such a commodity could be found, it "might be set up as a rival to money" in its role as the most stable of all stores of value (*GT*, p. 238).

Keynes did not think it was "probable that any such commodity exists," but from our theoretical vantage point it is interesting to note that these very requirements could be met by a managed fiat standard which Keynes had in mind in the *General Theory* when he spoke of money. In that case, the cost of production is fixed (at nearly zero) and invariant to scale and the costs of holding are as close to zero as possible (in its own terms). But such expert management as would be necessary to keep employment stable, as we know from the history of central banking, is difficult to achieve. Keynes saw a duality of meaning between the predominating fact that money is the standard of payment and that it has peculiar qualities as an asset:[20]

I conclude, therefore, that the commodity, in terms of which wages are expected to be most sticky, cannot be one whose elasticity of production is not least, and for which the excess of carrying-costs over liquidity-premium is not least. In other words, the expectation of a relative stickiness of wages in terms of money is a corollary of the excess of liquidity-premium over carrying-costs being greater for money than for any other asset.

(*GT*, p. 238)

IX. Money, prices and conventions: The social context for monetary analysis

As Keynes says, "thus we see that the various characteristics, which combine to make the money rate of interest significant, interact with one another in a cumulative fashion." All of the qualities of money can now be seen as dependent on each other. Moreover, the centrality of the money rate, resting as it does on the very properties which make money liquid, illustrates the essential unity of Keynes's monetary, capital and investment theory. Even further, the fact that the liquidity function of money ensures that wages and payments will be most stable in money terms provides a theoretical justification to the traditional "Keynesian" concern with the fixed money wage case. In recent years, this assumption has become the very symbol of ad hoc theorizing with which economics should have no truck. While, in fact, Keynes's theory of unemployment does not rest on rigid money wages, as we should have made clear by now, his discussion of money shows why he thought it was such an important case to treat.

The stickiness of money wages is an assumption much closer to the reality of a money economy than the opposite assumption of Pigou effects and real-balance effects where money prices freely adjust to keep relative prices the same. Keynes emphasized this point in Chapter 17 with reference specifically to Pigou and his "presumption in favour of real wages being more stable than money-wages." Keynes point out that with change in employment (scale of output) and the high carrying cost of wage goods, the stickiness of real wages would

> . . . cause a violent oscillation of money prices. For every small fluctuation in the propensity to consume and the inducement to invest would cause money-prices to rush violently between zero and infinity. That money-wages should be more stable than real wages is a condition of the system possessing inherent stability.

(*GT*, p. 239)

In terms of our setup of the own-rates market equilibrium, Keynes is emphasizing that the "a" terms would have to fluctuate wildly if prices were assumed to be the sole adjustment factor that equated own-rates to a fixed liquidity premium.[21] In other words Pigou's mistake ("in fact experience . . . and logic") is in assuming the operation of a "real-balance" effect that would automatically readjust the nominal stock of money to provide the desired liquidity without affecting interest rates. Such a rapid and complete adjustment to changing conditions of money demand would imply much less price stability than we in fact observe or than is compatible with the stability of the system. This argument clarifies Keynes's frequent assertion that even if wages and prices were perfectly flexible in a depression, that the effect on expectations of such instability (operating through expected qs of capital asset's own-rates) would make matters even worse.

But if real relative values are not the source of stability to the system, we are led to ask what does the amount of observed stability in the interest rate depend upon? This question is not taken up by Keynes, but its fascination led one of Keynes's students, Hugh Townshend,[22] to call for an amendment to the theory of value based on Keynes's analysis of a money economy. Townshend thought that Chapter 17 represented "the most general theory" of Keynes's book (CW 29, p. 258). "Thus, it would seem that Mr. Keynes's doctrine of liquidity-preference really involves a generalization of the classical (marginal) theory of value" (Townshend, 1937, p. 160). Specifically, the generalization that Townshend envisioned depended on extending value theory into the determination of short period "money prices" in an economy where goods are not just produced for immediate consumption but are also held for future security. In this context, the structure of relative prices will not be strictly determined "at the margin of production" but will depend to some extent (depending on the degree of "moneyness" or liquidity of a good) on the psychologically determined liquidity premiums that attach to monetary assets. The psychological impacts of these liquidity premiums are explicitly referred to by Townshend as involving the distinction between the "exchange of existing assets (at the margin of exchange) and the production of new assets (at the margin of production)" (GT, p. 160).

Emphasizing the role of expectations in this generalized theory of value, Townshend sees the stability of the system of money prices so determined to depend on the existence of a stable *convention*. Here is the answer we are seeking to the necessary practical role of sticky money prices in lending stability to the system. Townshend shows us the extent to which Keynes followed out that subtle method of basing even his most highly abstract conclusions on an observed reality of the economy rather than a purely hypothetical system:

> Since in fact money-values do not fluctuate wildly in the short period (save in abnormal conditions with which we are not here concerned), they must be kept reasonably stable by some characteristic of our real world of which a realistic theory of prices must take account. It would seem that this characteristic must be either a *conventionality* of outlook

causing stability of expectations as to the money-prices of durable assets of certain kinds, or else *conventional* maintenance of some degree of stability of the money-price of the only other exchangeable value, viz. labour – that is to say a conventionally stable wage-unit.

(Townshend, 1937, pp. 161–2)

Townshend dismisses the contention that the quantity of money along with its velocity of circulation can stabilize prices since to a greater or lesser extent any money stock can support any price level. But since such upheavals of prices do not continuously occur, the stability of general prices means there must generally be a fairly stable convention (except in the case of pure asset markets for which the convention of future value may be fragile and so their prices subject to more or less wide swings):

. . . since the quantity of money does not determine "the" – or, rather, any – price level, no prices would be determinate at all, unless at least one money-value – the price of *something* – were determined by habit or convention.

(Townshend, 1937, p. 162)

The implications for economic theory are that no prices are strictly determinate since nothing is "*absolutely* determined by convention" (except perhaps in a command economy) and that economic theory can only provide "*approximately* true" propositions about relative prices "which is the best we can hope for in an undetermined and shifting price-world" (Townshend, 1937, p. 162). For Townshend, this casts a pall over any attempts at "dynamic theorizing." If we can only base our value theory on the shifting sands of a liquidity convention, then our theory can only be specified for the duration of each individual convention and no longer.[23] This notion provides some rationale for Keynes's simplest model where money wages are fixed and only the shortest short-period equilibrium is investigated.

Townshend's fascinating writings extend Keynes's views on interest and money in novel directions. But for our purposes, they also bring us back to the extent to which the own-rates theory represents a challenge to the Wicksellian framework for monetary theory. First, the emphasis on the conventional basis of interest and prices serves to illustrate that Sraffa's injunction on the use of barter theory as the starting point of monetary economics was much more than just polemical tactics. As Townshend makes clear, the very notion of a structure of prices in a world where expectations of the future influence actions today has to start from some basis in the facts of the situation:

All exchange values are relative (ratios). If all possible sets of values in a community are to be comparable numerically, there must be a money of account – a common denominator to which the ratios are reducible. In a capitalist community – that is to say, one in which some people employ hired labor for future profit – people will also hold durable assets for future security. Even if there is no legal tender money, assets so held – whether goods or paper claims – will possess liquidity-premiums; and some claims and/or other assets will come to oust other assets . . . for the purpose of liquid holdings. We then have, in *all* essentials for the purpose of a theory of value, a monetary economy . . . The generally accepted claims or goods will modify the values which they are used to measure and are already real money for the purposes of the theory of value. Thus the textbook conception of a barter as non-monetary economy has no place in a discussion of value. *The theory of value in a capitalist economy is the theory of money-prices.*

(Townshend, 1937, pp. 166–7, emphasis added)

In other words, if the essence of money involves its role as a link between the present and the future, a link that grows out of its acceptance as the social numeraire, then money can only fulfill its role if it is assumed that money will be worth something at that future date. Keynes has shown us that this sort of expectation, which the money rate of interest is based upon, ultimately rests on an agreed upon convention of the stability of money prices. In the Wicksellian framework, where the operative forces of the case are looked for in a strictly "real" side of the economy, all of this is ignored. For Wicksell and Hayek, the barter-like "natural" rate of interest is the starting point of investigation. But if Keynes is right about money, there is nothing at all natural about such a barter rate in a money economy.

X. The "Keynes Connection" versus the "Wicksell Connection"

This friction between Keynes's theory and the whole natural-rate, loanable funds framework is finally drawn out in the last two sections of Chapter 17. In these, he explicitly addresses himself to the question of what a nonmonetary economy would resemble and what meaning can be given to the idea of a *natural* rate of interest.

Recall that Sraffa had shown, and Adarkar had recognized, that the nonmonetary state in which the "natural" rate was supposed to rule could not really be conceived of in barter terms. As Sraffa commented in his review of Hayek, "It may be doubted whether under a system of barter the decisions of individuals would have their full effects" (1932a, p. 43). What the Wicksellians really wanted to define was a hypothetical state in which the social contrivance of a medium of exchange existed, but where none of the accompanying intertemporal allocation problems that follow from the use of money in an uncertain environment encumber the decisions of individuals. To the natural-rate theorists, this could be accomplished by simply controlling the money supply.

Starting from a much richer conception of the social functions of money, Keynes conceived of such a "so-called 'non-monetary economy'" in a much different way. The only meaning he could give to the idea was a situation in which no asset possessed that fundamental quality of possessing a liquidity premium in excess of its carrying cost:

> There exists nothing, that is to say, but particular consumables and particular capital equipments more or less differentiated according to the character of the consumable which they can yield up, or assist to yield up, over a greater or shorter period of time: all of which, unlike cash, deteriorate or involve expense, if they are kept in stock, to a value in excess of any liquidity premium which may attach to them.
>
> (*GT*, p. 239)

Even in this case, Keynes's liquidity motive would enter in the relative evaluation of assets by wealth holders. Here, the liquidity would depend on the variety, stability and marketability of the goods, which each asset is capable of assisting in the production.[24] The rate of interest, then, would still be dependent upon the liquidity preferences of the public, illustrating the fact that money is a purely social-specific device:

> There is, clearly, no absolute standard of "liquidity" but merely a scale of liquidity – a varying premium of which account has to be taken . . . The conception of what contributes to "liquidity" is a partly vague one, changing from time to time and depending on social practices and institutions.
>
> (*GT*, p. 240)

But if no exclusively liquid good exists, would interest rates be low enough to ensure full employment growth and accumulation? Keynes does not specifically say, but implies that if such money-to-hold did not officially exist, that one would have to be invented! It is as if liquidity preference is a human desire so strong that it creates its own object. As an example, Keynes mentions "that in certain historic environments the possession of land has been characterized by a high liquidity-premium in the minds of owners of wealth." In the absence of a good money, land might become a suitable liquidity standard because of its low elasticities of production and substitution and because of the fact that its output is at least as stable and marketable as any other. Keynes speculates that this might account for the unusually high mortgage rates, in excess of the net productivity of yields, found in many agricultural economies.

If it were the case that some readily marketable good is socially "set up" as the liquidity standard in a non-monetary economy, this answers the question of the efficiency of such a natural state. For land in these situations can be every bit as inhibiting of production and accumulation as money is today:

That the world after several millennia of steady individual saving, is so poor as it is in accumulated capital assets, is to be explained, in my opinion, neither by the improvident propensities of mankind, nor even by the destruction of war, but by the high liquidity premium formerly attaching to the ownership of land and now attaching to money.

(GT, p. 242)

It was this very conception of a liquidity premium being a *necessary* social convention where wealth holding is a private matter, which Joan Robinson focused her attention upon when she came to discuss "Own-Rates of Interest" (Robinson, 1961). Thinking along Marxian lines, this former close colleague of Keynes conceived of the problem of liquidity premiums keeping up the rate of interest as a class-distribution issue. Defending Keynes against Kaldor's (Kaldor, 1962) argument that land could not serve such a purpose because "the rise in the purchase price of land can lower its yield to any extent," and thus diminish its attractiveness, Robinson makes the important point that this ignores the fact that the liquidity premium is altogether different from a mere explicit return. As Keynes emphasizes, liquidity premiums are of the nature of his long-term expectations in the sense that they reflect uncertainty, not risk.[25] This is why he defines them as a "potential convenience or security . . . " for which there is ". . . nothing to show . . . at the end of the period in the shape of output; yet it is something for which people are ready to pay something" (GT, p. 226). Robinson takes up the idea of non-pecuniary yields from land as the liquid asset and fashions it into a historical explanation of the transition from a feudal state, represented by landed wealth, to a capitalist one, represented by capital wealth. Her argument adds "the pleasure of gentleman-likeness derived from owning land" to the argument, but essentially applies Keynes's idea that some asset will always be set up as the liquidity standard by social convention. In an interesting twist on Keynes's main premise that the interest rate on money holds up the pace of investment, Robinson speculates that, in the transition to capitalism, the traditional attribution of liquidity (and social distinction) to land holding may serve to hold up (primitive?) accumulation.

What she has in mind is a "'historic environment' when the capitalist wealth owners exist side by side with gentlemen, whose extravagance and misfortune from time to time forces to pledge their ancestral estates." In this example, which corresponds closely to Keynes's hypothetical non-monetary economy, the dissavings of the gentlemen will provide the original finance for industrial investment:

Now, so long as land is known to be safe and sound while all industrial investment has a high risk premium, and when, as Keynes assumed, the return to be expected in each round of I [investment] is less than the last, lending to a gentleman will be a formidable rival to financing industry.

(Robinson, 1961, p. 590)

Robinson notes that this situation will be even worse in a social environment in which capitalists derive a further non-pecuniary "pleasure of gentleman-likeness . . . from owning land." Also echoing Keynes, she thinks the problem could be long lasting if "capitalist wealth is diverted to purchasing land at second hand which . . . [if land yielded no non-pecuniary returns] would be more readily available to find an outlet in financing new investment." Besides providing an interesting theoretical explanation for the classical political economists' marked antagonism to the profligate ways of the landed aristocracy, Robinson shows that Keynes' framework is malleable enough to fit many social and historic environments. She even speculates that the role of takeover bids (in 1961 and now it would seem) provide a similar example of the basic phenomenon of liquidity premiums holding up productive investment.

XI. Conclusion

In order to bring our discussion back to our original starting point of the antagonism of Keynes's monetary views with the Wicksellian natural-rate tradition, it is appropriate to point out that Keynes ends his own chapter on "The Essential Properties of Interest and Money" by explicitly dissenting from that view. Attributing the idea to Wicksell, Keynes notes that his own *Treatise on Money* used the idea of a natural rate "which preserved equality between the rate of savings . . . and the rate of investment." In doing so he had, "however, overlooked the fact that in any given society there is, on this definition, a *different* natural rate of interest for each hypothetical level of employment." In other words, savings always equals investment and the rate of interest, by determining the level of investment, just determines the level of employment for which the equality of saving and investment is defined:

> Thus it was a mistake to speak of *the* natural rate of interest or to suggest that the above definition would yield a unique value for the rate of interest irrespective of the level of employment. *I had not then understood that, in certain conditions, the system could be in equilibrium with less than full employment.*
>
> (*GT*, pp. 242–3, emphasis added)

Keynes identifies the old Wicksellian concept as "merely the rate of interest which preserve the *status quo*," a rate which we really have no interest in defending. Declaring that it is not even a useful analytic category, he proposes to replace it with a *neutral* or *optimum* rate of interest. This more general concept would identify the rate of interest ". . . which is consistent with *full* employment, given the other parameters of the system" (*GT*, p. 243).

With this concept in mind, we can see that Keynes's difference with the Wicksellian framework is not a mere choice over analytical frameworks (as

Hicks, 1937 suggested), but it is every bit as fundamental to his innovations on classical theory as the theory of aggregate demand. Just as in that case, the ultimate significance of Keynes's interest rate theory is its allowance for *equilibria* consistent with both full and less-than-full employment. Rejecting the idea of a "natural" rate which would equilibrate the system at full employment is just a corollary to rejecting the full employment assumptions built into Say's Law. By his analysis of the social role of money as the liquidity standard, Keynes has shown that money as a social institution (whether a free money or a state money) has important (negative) externality effects. Harrod's comment about a "wrong" rate of interest that is "natural, durable, and in a certain sense, in the free system inevitable," can now be seen as an insight stemming directly from Keynes's essential properties of interest and money.

By channeling the richness of Keynes's vision of the financial aspects of a modern money economy into a framework which identifies these equilibriums, the own-rates theory provides another angle on Keynes's theoretical revolution. And from the standpoint of further work in macroeconomics, the lesson of this view is that trying to recast Keynes into a Wicksellian world is a graft that will not take. Keynes's monetary theory is not a simple afterthought, or appendage that can easily be thrown overboard. That is, not unless we are willing to revert to a full-employment paradigm where unemployment can only arise from a friction or rigidity, incompatibly thrust into an otherwise smoothly operating system. This is the error we have seen that led the "Keynesian Revolution" to the impasse it faces today. Such a full-employment framework is just the sort of propaedeutic world that Keynes was warning us against when he wrote:

> Or we can pass from this simplified propaedeutic to the problems of the real world in which our previous expectations are liable to disappointment and expectations concerning the future affect what we do today. It is when we have made this transition that the peculiar properties of money as a link between the present and the future must enter into our calculations. But, although the theory of shifting equilibrium must necessarily be pursued in terms of a monetary economy, it remains a theory of value and distribution and not a separate "theory of money." Money in its significant attributes is, above all, a subtle device for linking the present to the future; and we cannot even begin to discuss the effects of changing expectations on current activities except in monetary terms. We cannot get rid of money even by abolishing gold and silver and legal instruments. So long as there exists any durable asset, it is capable of possessing monetary attributes and, therefore, of giving rise to the characteristic problems of a monetary economy.
>
> (*GT*, pp. 293–4)

Conclusion: A Theory of a Monetary Economy

A Keynesian equilibrium is therefore always different from a classical or new classical equilibrium, because the latter equilibria are always fundamentally non-monetary whereas the Keynesian equilibria are more general, having all the attributes of the latter but having also the liquidity premiums associated with the private and collective determination of nominal and 'real' magnitudes.

C. Rogers and T. K. Rymes (1997)

15
"Natural Rate" Mutations: Keynes, Leijonhufvud and the Wicksell Connection[1]

> I have given in another work a long list of "sporting
> plants," as they are called by gardeners; – that is, of plants
> which have suddenly produced a single bud with a new
> and sometimes widely different character from that of
> other buds on the same plant.
>
> Charles Darwin (1859)

I. Introduction

In this chapter we make good on a promise from the introductory materi-al and project the own-rates framework into familiar macroeconomic contexts, including its implications for IS/LM analysis. We do so by way of an implicit critique of Leijonhufvud's "The Wicksell Connection." This will also serve as a conclusion to our book in the sense that it demonstrates a main theme which was argued throughout this work and which culmi-nated in Chapter 14. The own-rates of interest analysis offers an impor-tant avenue by which to demonstrate Keynes's claim for the existence of unemployment equilibria. Keynes based his argument in this area on forces integral to an economy faced with uncertainty, where asset holders might choose to fly to safety. In such an economy he suggested there would be (at least) one asset exhibiting a liquidity premia in excess of its carrying cost. This is how he defined a monetary economy. This existence did not make the attainment of full-employment impossible, though, as Leijonhufvud argues. It does mean, however, that – given institutions, expectations and the propensities to save and to consume – it is possible for new investment activity to get hung up at a level lower than the full-employment level of savings. What would happen then? One possibility is that output adjusts to this new lower level of demand and settles into a less-than-full employment equilibrium. This is the possibility we explore in this chapter.

II. "The Wicksell Connection"

Axel Leijonhufvud's "The Wicksell Connection: Variations on a Theme" (1981, Chapter 7) is a masterpiece of its kind, the historical essay with contemporary relevance. Leijonhufvud sets out to clarify some of the major modern schools of macroeconomics by examining them in light of their treatment of the interest-rate mechanism. Specifically he notes that almost all macroeconomic theory outside of strict monetarism somehow deals with the complexities of the interest-rate-savings-investment nexus.

According to Leijonhufvud the history of the subject reveals a major role for Wicksell's conception of the potential maladjustment of the interest rate – expressed in his distinction between a natural (or equilibrium) rate and the money (or market) rate. This is the central connection of Wicksell's work to subsequent (non-monetarist) macroeconomics, for "the use of the saving–investment approach to income fluctuations is predicated on the hypothesis that the interest rate mechanism fails to coordinate saving and investment decisions appropriately" (Leijonhufvud, 1981, p. 132). The puzzle for Leijonhufvud is to explain how, from being the central organizing principle of all macroeconomic theory down to the 1930s,[2] this essential connection was lost sight of in post-war macro debates (so much so that it becomes necessary for a "historian" to unearth the tradition). His answer to the puzzle, in short, is that the theme was so "obfuscated" by Keynes that all mainstream neoclassical Keynesians lost sight of the issue, and the other dominant school, monetarism, simply assumed the issue away.

Our goal is to criticize and redefine Leijonhufvud's view of the Wicksell connection as it applies to Keynes. To start from common ground, we stress our agreement with Leijonhufvud over the importance of this issue. The interest-rate mechanism is crucial in understanding the development of Keynes's position from the *Treatise on Money* to the *General Theory*, yet it is the most commonly misunderstood or neglected aspect of Keynes's work. Nonetheless we wish to raise the following points of disagreement:

(1) Leijonhufvud strenuously objects to the liquidity preference hypothesis, but he does not seriously address Keynes's reasons for explicitly rejecting Wicksell's "natural rate." We agree that *The General Theory* changed the terms of the debate over interest-rate theory, and that just how it did so it little understood, but we argue that this can be seen as a positive advance and not a retrograde move.

(2) The only way to gain a full understanding of the basis for Keynes's rejection of the Wicksellian theme is to emphasize the parts of *The General Theory* that Leijonhufvud's interpretation downplays. Of particular importance in this regard are Keynes's views on "the essential properties of interest and money" in Chapter 17.

(3) Utilizing the theoretical *framework* of Keynes's argument in Chapter 17 (as opposed to his specific use of that framework), we are able to recast the terms on which Leijonhufvud's critique rests. The view from this "own-rates" standpoint then provides a different angle on the loanable funds versus liquidity preference debate, which Leijonhufvud's history restages.

III. Leijonhufvud and Keynes on liquidity preference

Leijonhufvud makes it quite clear that his objection to Keynes's *General Theory* centers on the liquidity preference theory of the rate of interest.[3] It is clear that his distaste for the liquidity preference theory stems from its rejection of the Wicksellian "natural rate" concept that had been so important to all previous interest-rate theory, including Keynes's own *Treatise*. What issues are at stake in the transition from Wicksell himself, to the Keynes of the *Treatise*, to the *General Theory*? From Leijonhufvud's excellent account we can summarize the main points.

Wicksell's theory involved the possibility of the banking system inhibiting the adjustment of the observed market rate to the "natural" equilibrium rate. For Wicksell the latter was governed by underlying real factors of technology and preferences ("productivity and thrift"). From time to time these forces might shift, altering the natural rate, yet there was no guarantee that the bankers would perceive this shift immediately. The market rate of interest might therefore be held at an inappropriate level for some time during which the banks would bridge the gap between the flow rates of saving and investment either lending in the form of new money creation or allowing a monetary contraction due to net loan repayment, depending on the case. Wicksell's is a flow analysis: in the course of readjustment to equilibrium, it is the excess flow demand for loans, which eventually forces the banks to move market rate toward the natural rate.

Keynes of the *Treatise*, being more impressed with the powers of the Exchange than the powers of the banks, saw this as a *stock-flow* problem. The interest rate must clear the market for the existing stock of outstanding securities, even if the ultimate position of equilibrium is governed by the flow excess demand for new issues (or loanable funds). If the market rate differs from the natural rate, it is due to the speculators on the exchange offsetting the flow excess demand or supply for new issues by either absorbing or releasing "idle" cash.[4] Again, though, the "natural" reference point remains stable, processes are set in motion which will eventually restore the equilibrium rate; whether this occurs via a Wicksellian cumulative process or a Keynesian realignment of bears and bulls. Importantly, as Leijonhufvud notes, in the *Treatise* these forces of self-correction are cast as readjustments of *expectations* back to security prices consistent with the natural rate.

As for the *General Theory* and its treatment of the Wicksellian theme, Leijonhufvud has it that Keynes takes one step forward (recognizing the possibility of quantity adjustments in response to a fall in investment), and one large step back, by positing a pure stock analysis (in which the excess stock demand for money is the regulator of the rate of interest). Keynes's "obfuscation" of the Wicksellian theme is rooted in his misplaced emphasis on the necessary identity of realized savings and investment, and the net result is – note the emerging Robertsonian voice – to "gut" the loan-fund theory in favor of a "bootstrap" approach (Leijonhufvud, 1981, p. 171). The reference path given by underlying real forces is replaced by self-fulfilling speculative expectations.

As is well known, Keynes expressed his disagreement with classical economics in these terms: whereas in the classical system the supply and demand for money determine (nominal) income, and saving and investment determine the interest rate, in his own system income, is governed by the interplay of saving and investment while the supply and demand for money determine the interest rate. This neat reversal is somewhat weakened in the Hicksian IS/LM version of Keynes (here money supply and demand, as embodied in the LM curve, and saving and investment, as embodied in IS, simultaneously determine both income and the rate of interest). But even thus adulterated, the Keynesian "switch" is anathema to Leijonhufvud. In his view the classical ordering is an accurate account of the fully coordinated or "full information" state of affairs. In such an economy shocks to the marginal efficiency of capital or the propensity to consume should indeed be absorbed by movement in the rate of interest, while monetary disturbances should spend themselves in the rescaling of nominal magnitudes alone. Of course Leijonhufvud does not insist that we live in such a world. But he does insist that macroeconomics take such a world as their benchmark – if we wish to argue that real economies do not (always) behave in the classical mode, we must be ready to explain the precise form of information problem that is responsible for that failure. From this perspective Keynes himself, and even the standard IS/LM version, surreptitiously build in the tacit assumption that certain kinds of information failure are universal and irremediable.

Leijonhufvud's own contribution to the Wicksell connection, his neo-Robertsonian "Z-theory" attempts to supply this lack, reconnecting Keynes to Wicksell. According to Z-theory it is neither guaranteed nor impossible that a market, monetary economy smoothly absorbs, say, a downshift in the marginal efficiency of capital, traversing to a slower growth path with a lesser fraction of GNP devoted to investment without, however, suffering a recession along the way. The nature of the transition – whether or not a recession occurs – depends crucially on the information possessed by operators in the financial markets. If everyone realizes that a long-term shift in marginal efficiency of capital (MEC) has taken place, then all will be well. The excess flow supply of loanable funds, implied by a reduction in the rate of new issues, will result in a lowering of the rate of interest, which will in turn damp the fall in investment and/or stimulate the propensity to consume, thus preserving aggregate demand while its component parts are reshuffled. But if, on the other hand, the fall in MEC goes unrecognized by (some) agents in the financial markets, the incipient fall in the rate of interest will be stalled. As new issues are reduced and the interest rate begins to fall – and so bond prices rise – these agents will perceive an opportunity for capital gains through selling bonds out of their portfolios. Expecting a reversion to the original ruling rate of interest, these speculators aim to exploit a temporary fall; in the process they bridge the gap between the rate of new issues and the flow supply of savings onto the asset markets (in much the same way as Wicksell's bankers) and prevent an adequate fall in interest rates from taking place.

In this context, as was noted above, Leijonhufvud accepts one theoretical innovation of the *General Theory*, namely a systematic treatment of the effects of quantity adjustments in the face of changes in aggregate demand. If aggregate demand falls, as in the second version above, and if this causes a fall in real income, then the flow supply of saving onto the loanable funds market will shrink too. Once the speculators stop selling bonds, this will not of itself put things to rights, for now the demand and supply for loanable funds will be equal again – equality having been achieved via a reduction in supply, out of a lower income, to match the reduced demand. A proper appreciation of this point was missing both in Wicksell and in Keynes's *Treatise*, so that these earlier versions overestimated the forces pushing the market rate toward the natural rate of interest. So long as the economy remains at full employment, these forces are operative, but once the multiplier has done its work the loanable funds market will clear at the "wrong" interest rate (see Figure 1).[5]

From this point on, automatic adjustment back to full employment, if it is to occur at all, must rest on the effects of failing wages in response to unemployment. Whether or not this works, Leijonhufvud regards it as a symptom of an initial failure: in a full-information context, a shift in the MEC should not call for any adjustment of nominal wages or the general price level.

This, then, is Leijonhufvud's side of the story. The *General Theory* is in some respects an advance over previous variants on the Wicksellian theme, yet this advance is overshadowed by the enormity of the liquidity preference theory, which obscures the key issues to which the interpolated Z-theory is addressed. Leijonhufvud's argument against the liquidity preference theory has two interrelated aspects. First, he claims that a pure stock analysis must necessarily be inferior to a stock-flow analysis. Second, he claims that the liquidity preference theory makes it in principle impossible for a capitalist economy ever to traverse smoothly from one full-employment equilibrium growth-path to another in the face of a shift in the MEC. At some points it seems as if the possibility of the latter type of traverse is being asserted as self-evident on a priori grounds, so that any theory which denies it must *ipso facto* be false.

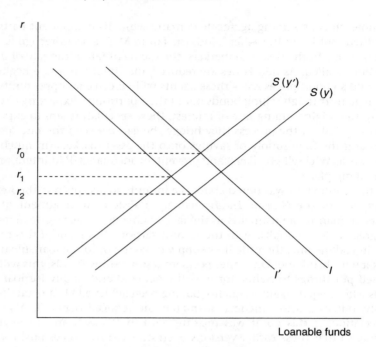

Figure 15.1 The interest rate and the amount of loanable funds

We argue against both these claims. Stock analysis of asset-market equilibrium is entirely defensible, and acceptance of Keynes's liquidity preference theory in its most sophisticated version – as in Chapter 17 – need not actually rule out the type of traverse Leijonhufvud discusses, although the theory clearly assigns it a low probability. The following section prepares the ground through an exposition and extension of Chapter 17.

IV. Chapter 17: Stock equilibrium and "own-rates" of interest

Let us review the outcome of our investigations in this final chapter. In opposition to the traditional capital-theoretic approach, Keynes begins his investigation of the essential properties of interest quite literally. First of all, we note that the money rate of interest is defined as "the percentage excess of a sum of money contracted for forward delivery, *e.g.* a year hence, over what we may call the 'spot' or cash price of the sum thus contracted for forward delivery" (*GT*, p. 222), so that if £100 spot will "buy" £105 for forward delivery this corresponds to a "money-rate of interest" of 5 percent. It is then argued that any commodity which may be traded "forward" has its own analog to the rate of interest, this simply being the percentage excess of the quantity available for forward delivery over the quantity available "spot" with the same exchange value. Calculating, say, the wheat rate of interest is, however, complicated if the money rate itself is non-zero. Keynes asks, "Let us suppose that the spot price of wheat is £100 per 100 quarters, that the price of the future contract for wheat for delivery a year hence is £107 per 100 quarters, and that the money-rate of interest is 5 percent; what is the wheat-rate of interest?" The answer is as follows. My alternatives are (a) to pay out £100 now for 100 quarters of wheat, or (b) to "invest" the £100 at 5 percent money interest for a year, yielding £105 at the end of the year. If I contract now to pay this £105 for wheat in one year, the quantity I can command is (£105/£107) × 100 = (approximately) 98 quarters, since £107 will buy 100 quarters forward. Therefore the future equivalent of 100 quarters of wheat is 98 quarters a year, giving a wheat rate of interest minus 2 percent.

Keynes then states that "there is no reason why their rates of interest should be the same for different commodities" and suggests that the special significance of the money rate of interest may be that among all the various "own-rates," it is the most reluctant to fall as asset stocks generally expand in the long run. It is, of course, the *greatest* of the own rates, which serves as the benchmark against which the marginal efficiency of prospective investment projects must be judged, and there is reason to believe that the money rate may occupy that place.

Exactly what reason? "Why should the volume of output and employment be more intimately bound up with the money-rate of interest than with the wheat-rate of interest or the house-rate of interest?" (*GT*, p. 225). Keynes approaches an answer via an investigation of the underlying attributes of the various commodities which govern their own commodity rates of interest. In a very general way these attributes account for Keynes's twist on the underlying "real" forces, which, in the traditional Wicksellian approach, govern the natural rate. Yet the addition of liquidity as one of these fundamental attributes of an asset clearly places Keynes's analysis in a monetary setting from the start.

The three relevant attributes, according to Keynes, are (1) the ability of an asset to produce a yield or output q, "by assisting some process of production or supplying services to a consumer"; (2) the carrying cost, c, incurred by holding the asset for a given period; and (3) the "potential convenience or security" yielded by the "power of disposal" of an asset. The payment which asset holders are willing to make for this "potential" Keynes labels the liquidity premium, l. In each case (1–3) the yield or cost is to be thought of as expressed in terms of the given commodity itself. Within this framework the overall return expected on holding any given assets is $q - c + l$.

Keynes's next task is to investigate the nature of the equilibrium relationships which hold between the returns on different assets. To do this, own rates must be made commensurable, and it is convenient to reduce them all to a monetary base (although in principle any base would do equally well). To move from the own rate *in natura* to the rate expressed in monetary terms, the expected rate of appreciation in terms of money, a, of the given commodity must be added to its "intrinsic" return.[6] So the "commodity-rate of money-interest," as Keynes puts it, for any commodity i, is then

$$R_{i,m} = q_i - c_i + l_i + a_i$$

Keynes goes on to illustrate the properties of this system by reference to a three-asset example, the assets being money, wheat, and houses. But as we find the lack of an explicit paper debt instrument in Keynes's highly abstract example problematic in interpreting the "Wicksellian theme," which requires a setting of financial intermediation between saving and investment, we propose a modified example. We proceed by reference to a simple model with three assets: houses, money, and a long-term zero-coupon bond; as will become clear, the money and bonds are not really independent assets. Thus, we now depart from simple exegesis and offer our own exposition of the matter.

The in-kind return on holding houses is defined as $q_h - c_h + l_h$, but following Keynes we shall assume that the latter two components are negligible, so that the sum reduces to just q_h. The house rate of money interest (the rate of return in money on holding houses) is then $R_{h,m} = q_h + a_h$. As for money (conceived of as interest-free bank deposits), we follow Keynes in assuming that both q and c are negligible, so that the in-kind return on money itself is simply l_m, the liquidity premium on money. (Here, of course, the appreciation term is zero by definition).

The paper instrument offers no inherent yield ($q = 0$) and has negligible carrying cost, and while it may offer some degree of liquidity, its liquidity premium is bound to be less than that on money. It therefore must be sold at a discount relative to its face value, generating an expectation of appreciation at a rate of a_b.[7] The total return on the bond in terms of money (the "bond rate of money interest," if you will) is then given by

$$R_{b,m} = l_b + a_b$$

For short-run stock equilibrium to obtain, the bears and the bulls trade the outstanding assets until the prospective returns to asset holders are equalized at the margin for houses, money, and bonds, that is,

$$q_h + a_h = l_m = l_b + a_b$$

Suppose in long-run equilibrium the price of houses is equal to their cost of production, and is not expected to change. The equilibrium relationship between money and houses is then $q_h = l_m$, that is, the real yield from a house is equal to the liquidity premium on money. With house prices constant, trading in houses does not provide a means of translating a given sum of present money into a larger future sum. But the paper asset offers this opportunity: since it has no "real" yield and is less liquid than money, it must offer some combination of coupon yield and expected appreciation if it is to be held at all. Thus, as Keynes states at the start of the chapter, the existence of the money rate of interest is explicitly tied to the forward trading in money that the bonds represent. In this framework, the "rate of interest" in the ordinary sense is given by:

$$l_m - l_b = a_b,$$

to the extent that bonds are seen as less liquid than money, they must offer a positive yield in terms of money (in our simple case, expected appreciation between a current discounted price and a future face value payable).

We now have in view a particular example of the stock equilibrium Leijonhufvud rightly ascribes to Keynes. Various underlying properties of assets in conjunction with expectations of the future determine the portfolio demands of wealth holders. The outstanding stocks of assets, including bank deposits, bonds and real assets *must* be held by someone. To ensure that these stocks are willingly held, the current prices of assets must move until prospective returns are equalized across the board.[8] Note that the element of expected appreciation, built into asset returns via the a_i terms, means that expectations exert their influence on asset prices and rates of interest today.

To reinforce this last point, consider a simple example where we focus on money and houses alone. Suppose we happen to "start out" from a situation where q_h is greater than l_m, that is, where the services rendered by housing exceed the liquidity premium on money. It follows from the equilibrium concept above that a_h must be negative – that house prices must be expected to fall. Suppose that expectations of the future price of housing are anchored, so to speak, by the cost of production of housing: agents expect that the demand price of housing must, over time, move in line with the supply price. Then the equilibration above means that the current price of houses must be greater than their cost of production, by a margin sufficient to ensure that an expected depreciation at a rate $q_h - l_m$ will lead down to the cost of production at the appropriate time (very much in the manner of Dornbusch's 1976 analysis of exchange rate "overshooting"). This similarity is not a surprise if we recall that Keynes's own-rates analysis began, as we showed above, with his experience on exchange markets.

So in the short run, equilibration is achieved via movements ("jumps") in the prices of assets. In the long run, however, any divergence thus opened up between demand and supply price will lead to differential flow production rates for the assets and hence to differential changes in asset stocks. To continue the house example, the situation where the current price stands above the cost of production will lead to the construction of new houses, and as the housing stock expands, it is reasonable to assume, the yield q_h will fall. Under the conditions of stable expectations, and thus of a stable liquidity premium, long-run equilibrium will be attained when q_h has fallen to equal l_m, at which point, of course, a_h will be zero; house price stability will be expected.

V. Liquidity preference, saving, and investment

The general concern toward which Keynes's exposition leads is the way in which the money rate of interest may "rule the roost" and, in particular, may cause the economy to settle into a state of less than full employment. That is, the money rate may get "stuck" at such a level that the resulting volume of investment is insufficient to absorb the amount of saving which people wish to carry out at the full-employment level of income.

Why should this be? In the case of any real capital asset, j, if its own commodity rate of interest, $q_j - c_j + l_j$, is highest of all the rates in the system, this will raise its demand price and encourage production of that asset. This in turn will depress its q value, hence moving its commodity rate back in line with the others. But suppose it is money which has the greatest own rate of interest. If the (nominal) money supply is fixed exogenously, the possibility of transferring labor into the production of money is not open. Furthermore, Keynes argues, money has a very low elasticity of substitution – no other factor is "capable, if it is sufficiently cheap, of doing money's duty equally well" (1936, p. 234). It therefore appears that, rather than the equilibration taking place on the side of money, the adjustment will be forced onto the other assets. Investment in real capital assets must be scaled back, such that the qs increase to the point where they equal the more or less fixed liquidity premium on money.

The next question, then, is how we arrive in the situation where the money rate of interest is the highest in the system. In the discussion of Chapter 17, Keynes's answer has a long-run cast: essentially it is a matter of the "capital saturation" syndrome which appears from time to time throughout the *General Theory*. The picture is of a technologically static economy, gradually accumulating stocks of real assets whose real marginal yield is gradually falling. For the reasons given above, money is exempt from this general tendency to falling yield, and so we inevitably arrive at a kind of "Keynesian stationary state." As output increases, own rates of interest decline to levels at which one asset after another falls below the standard of profitable production" (p. 229).

While there is no doubt that the capital saturation issue is at play in the *General Theory*, most of the time Keynes seems concerned with a rather different issue, namely, how monetary economics with substantial real investment opportunities still available can nonetheless get themselves into persistent underemployment states. In this context the alleged long-run tendency toward declining marginal yield as net investment proceeds is irrelevant. What matters is the conjunctural interplay between the rate of interest on monetary debt instruments on the one hand, and the marginal efficiency of capital on the other, where both magnitudes depend crucially on the state of expectations (influenced in turn by conjunctural changes in technological opportunities and product markets, along with less "rational" factors), rather than on a universal supposition of secular diminishing returns to capital. And, of course, this is also explicitly the terrain of the Wicksell connection.

Does the Chapter 17 framework aid in the analysis of the latter issue? Let us examine in this light the thought experiment which Leijonhufvud treats as the touchstone for the different theories of the interest-rate mechanism. Suppose we start out in a situation of reasonably full employment, and then for some reason the perceived marginal efficiency of capital falls. If the rate of interest payable on monetary debt instruments does not fall (sufficiently), then the flow of investment will shrink and output and employment will fall until the flow of saving has shrunk to match the reduced investment. Keynes wants to argue that the rate of interest will *not* fall sufficiently, barring appropriate action on the part of the monetary authority (and maybe not even then).

What maters directly for the level of investment is the relation between the marginal efficiency of capital and the rate payable on the debt instruments issued to finance investment. But as we have shown, the argument of Chapter 17 establishes a firm connection between the rate payable on debt and money's intrinsic liquidity premium. In this view the equilibrium bond rate can fall, at a point in time, only if bonds are perceived as more liquid than before, or if the liquidity premium on money itself is reduced. Yet according to Keynes there is no reason to believe that either of these conditions will result from a fall in the perceived marginal efficiency of capital. Debt instruments are tethered to money as alternative assets, and so long as money itself sets an inflexible standard for the required rate of return (by virtue of its attribute of liquidity), the rate payable on debt instruments is not free to decline in the face of a decline in the MEC.

Keynes does recognize a potential mitigating factor here. Once output and employment start to fall in response to the decline in the MEC, nominal wages and goods prices may begin to fall too, raising the real value of the fixed nominal money stock. As the existing money stock therefore comes to supply a greater amount of "liquidity service," so to speak, the premium which asset-holders are willing to pay for this attribute at the margin is likely to decline. (And at the same time, money will be released from transaction balances, so that even the nominal stock of money available for holding "as an asset" will rise, compounding the effect.) Therefore the rate payable on debt instruments will tend to fall correspondingly. But this type of adjustment cannot stave off the fall in real output in advance; it can only, at best, mitigate it once it is under way.

So here is Keynes's side of the case. Asset markets must be in continuous stock equilibrium, and this requirement appears to rule out any immediate adjustment of the interest rate in face of a decline in the MEC. What do we make of the contradiction between this position and Leijonhufvud's Z-theory? Leijonhufvud would have us believe (1) that Keynes's conclusion is false, and (2) that it is a correct deduction from his liquidity preference theory, implying (3) that the theory is flawed, for the reason (4) that it ignores flows, especially the flow excess demand for bonds.[9]

Leijonhufvud argues that if there is anything valid in Keynes's account of the failure of a market economy to self-adjust in the face of saving–investment disturbances, this ought to be expressible within the framework of a sophisticated, Robertsonian loadable funds theory. We argue that the boot is on the other foot: if there is anything valid in Leijonhufvud's own Z-theory, this must be consistent with, and expressible in terms of, continuous stock equilibrium in the markets for financial assets.

Keynes's analysis in terms of stock equilibrium has sometimes been defended with the claim that the stock of existing securities is "very large" relative to the flows adding to or subtracting from that stock over time.[10] In our view this statement is not strong enough. Even more so, since Keynes's day, asset markets display continuous trading and almost instantaneous arbitrage, so that the relevant "period" over which Keynes's equilibrium conditions must be established is vanishingly short. It becomes quite reasonable to think in terms of continuous time, in which case the magnitude of the flows becomes irrelevant: the time integral of *any* flow goes to zero as the period goes to zero. To prevent misunderstanding, we emphasize here that we are not suggesting that flows can be ignored; and neither is Keynes. Over time, non-zero flows obviously change the relevant stocks and hence shift the instantaneous stock equilibrium; furthermore, *expectations* regarding the effects of future flows can have a bearing on the stock equilibrium at a point in time. Nonetheless, any account of a "loanable funds" adjustment mechanism must be subject to a certain discipline – that of explaining just how stock equilibrium is maintained at every point.

Let us return to the situation where a fall in the MEC has generated a virtual fall in the flow rates of both real investment and debt issues. Insofar as we are dealing with a point in time, there is no question of any actual change in the stocks of money and bonds; that too is merely virtual. If the interest rate is to fall – and hence stave off an *actual* fall in aggregate demand – it must be because these virtual changes acquire some leverage on the current situation through the medium of *expectations*. Suppose forward-looking asset holders *expect* the loanable-funds mechanism to come into play, leading to a future fall in the rate of interest. While such an expected fall may be gradual, the analysis is simplified if we assume an expectation of a step fall. An expectation of a step fall in the rate of interest at some future date $t + k$ implies an expectation of a step appreciation of bonds at $t + k$. But this raises the total expected return on bonds between t and $t + k$, above the original equilibrium appreciation rate a_b. So the total expected appreciation on bonds exceeds the liquidity premium on money, and the preservation of current stock equilibrium requires that bonds undergo a step appreciation at time t. But this in turn means that the long rate, with which new long issues must compete, falls without delay.

This is shown in Figure 2, where a represents the original equilibrium bond rate, a' represents the rate expected to rule from $t + k$, P_t is the original bond price at time t, and P_t' the level to which the price must jump to preserve equilibrium, given the expectation of a future fall in interest rates. F is the face value payable on the existing long-term zero-coupon bonds, at time $t + n$. The new long rate is a geometric average of a and a'; if k is small and n is large, this will be close to a'. Keynes's analysis in terms of stock equilibrium would appear, therefore, to be compatible with a "smooth transition" of the type envisaged by Leijonhufvud, given especially favorable expectations. Keynes clearly accepts the idea that speculators can *prevent* a fall in interest if they do not believe the interest rate can stay below its current level for long; by symmetry, we recognize the polar possibility that speculators *force* a fall in the interest rate, if they get the idea that it cannot continue for long at its past level.

At this point, however, an issue which has been left in the background must be brought forward: Is the "steady-state demand for money" (for

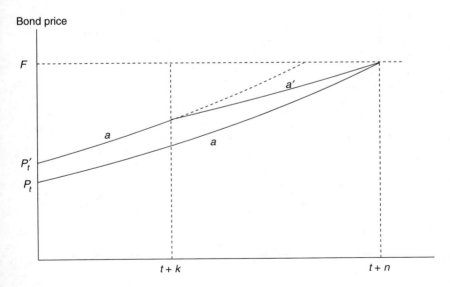

Figure 15.2 A bond price and time

transactions and precautionary, as opposed to speculative, purposes) sensitive to the rate of interest? Leijonhufvud asserts that the answer is no, but he is well aware that many macroeconomists would disagree (Leijonhufvud, pp. 138–39) with him. Suppose there is a definite non-zero interest elasticity of the demand for money for other than speculative purposes. In that case, as the interest rate falls from its original natural level toward the new natural rate there will occur a definite increase in the demand for money that has nothing to do with speculative bond sales. But this will hang up the interest rate at a level above the new natural rate, failing either an increase in the nominal money supply or a general deflation.

Here the much-maligned IS/LM diagram is useful, if handled with care. Figure 3 shows the effect of a fall in the MEC, represented by a shift of the IS curve from IS to IS'; correspondingly, the natural rate of interest, in Leijonhufvud's sense, falls from r_0 to r_2. The actual market rate is free to fall to r_2, at unchanged values of money stock and price level, only if the upward slope of LM is a *purely* speculative effect. In that case, if r_2 is widely and confidently expected to rule in future, the LM curve will shift to LM' and all will be well. If, at the other extreme, the upward slope of LM has nothing to do with speculation, then the interest rate is free to fall only to r_1 (along with a fall in output to y_1) unless deflation occurs. One then requires the "Keynes

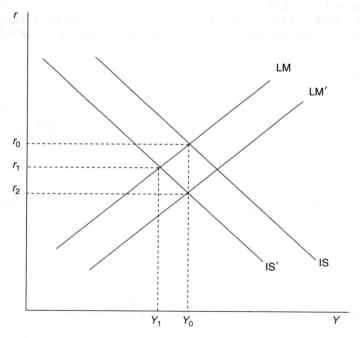

Figure 15.3 IS/LM with Keynes's marginal efficiency of capital

effect" of wage and price deflation to shift the LM curve down to LM' (a process which Keynes and Leijonhufvud both take to be slow and unreliable). That leaves the intermediate possibility – that the sensitivity of money demand is partly speculative, that is, concerned with the difference between the current and expected normal rate, and partly a steady–state phenomenon, concerned with the absolute level of the interest rate. In this case, a confident expectation that the normal rate of interest has moved down will induce *some* downward shift of the LM schedule, but not enough to lower the rate to r_2. The schedule moves to an intermediate position between LM and LM', and the "smooth transition" does not go through. To verify this contention, suppose because of forward-looking expectations of a continuing fall, the rate of interest goes straight to r_2. Then, given the location of the IS curve, real output remains unchanged. The excess unemployment, required in order to generate the deflation that would reduce the transactions demand for money and validate the fall to r_2, does not then materialize. Far from being self-fulfilling, the speculative expectation of a prompt fall to r_2 is self-defeating.

We are not convinced by Leijonhufvud's case for zero steady-state interest elasticity of the demand for money, but suppose we accept it for the sake of argument. Our basic criticism of Z-theory remains. We concede the possibility that faced with a decline in the MEC, asset holders expect a future fall in interest and their pursuit of the associated capital gains pushes this fall into the present. Clearly this is not a *necessary* sequence. Leijonhufvud's Z-theory also makes the response to a fall in MEC a contingent matter; but note the difference between the two stories. Leijonhufvud has a fall in the MEC leading automatically to a fall in the interest rate (via an emergent excess supply of loanable funds, or excess demand for bonds, as firms scale back their investment plan) *unless* asset holders are speculating against the permanence of any such fall. In our version a virtual reduction in the flow demand for loanable funds, or even an actual reduction over a short-time interval, can have a significant effect on the interest rate *only* through the mediation of forward-looking expectations, for it is only in this way that the present stock equilibrium can be shifted. If we allow enough time to elapse for an *actual* change in new issues to shift the stock equilibrium significantly, we also allow enough time for the Keynesian mechanisms to come into play: reduction in aggregate expenditure and income, reduction in saving, and/or unintended inventory accumulation. If the reduction of investment leads to an accumulation of unsold capital goods, that will itself require financing, hence mopping up at least part of the emergent excess supply of loanable funds; as Leijonhufvud stresses, the *sequence* is crucial.

Leijonhufvud admits the possibility of "wrong" expectations' derailing an otherwise "natural" adjustment; we admit the (theoretical) possibility of a particular benign type of expectation's stalling the otherwise "natural" Keynesian process of recession following a fall in the MEC. In sum, for Leijonhufvud it is sufficient that agents do not speculate *against* the loanable-funds mechanism, while for us it is required that agents speculate *in its favor*, if a fall in MES is to be neutral in its effect on real output.

VI. Conclusion: Wicksell revisited

Where do the above arguments leave us, on the Wicksellian theme of the natural rate of interest? One has to agree with Leijonhufvud that Keynes does not have much to say explicitly on this issue in the *General Theory*. The one place in which Wicksell's natural rate is mentioned at all is at the end of Chapter 17:

> I am no longer of the opinion that the concept of a "natural" rate of Interest, which previously seemed to me a most promising idea, has anything very useful or significant to contribute to our analysis. It is merely the rate of interest which will preserve the *status quo*; and in general, we have no predominant interest in the *status quo* as such.
>
> (*GT*, p. 243)

Leijonhufvud dismisses this as a trivial terminological cover-up (Leijonhufvud, 1981, p. 172): having obscured the underlying concept, Keynes finishes the job by throwing away the label. What has our investigation to say to this issue?

The obvious point is that for Keynes an own-rates equilibrium may clearly occur at a level inconsistent with a full-employment level of investment. Thus follows his comment (*GT*, p. 242) that there is a "different natural rate of interest for each hypothetical level of employment" and that the only one of these with any special significance is the full-employment natural rate (for Keynes the "neutral" or "optimum rate"). While the "optimum rate" might well be a target for monetary policy, it does not, within the *General Theory*, have the status of an attractor for the actual market rate of interest.

This is surely the key point: the "natural rate" concept has real force only if one can argue that there are definite tendencies pulling the market rate toward its natural level. When the MEC shifts, so does the interest rate which would preserve the original level of income and employment. In our view it is *conceivable* that the market rate adjusts to the new natural level, but only under rather special assumptions. And if income and employment move, the interest rate that *would* have preserved the original equilibrium immediately loses its attractive force. If the economy moves into a depressed state, there is now a new "natural rate" which will preserve the depression. As Keynes suggests, this rate is of little concern; what we should be aiming at is the "optimal" rate which equates investment and full-employment saving, whether or not that was the rate ruling "yesterday."

In Leijonhufvud's view, as we have seen, Keynes's *General Theory* assumes the inevitability of a certain kind of information failure while suppressing and obscuring the precise nature of that failure. In conclusion, it may be useful that we return to this point. For Leijonhufvud, maladjustment of the interest rate stems from incorrect perceptions of the marginal efficiency of capital; if only these perceptions were correct, the Keynesian problem would not arise. This conception derives some of its force from an analogy with certain well-known monetarist arguments. In the latter views the disturbance to the system which is treated as "typical" is, of course, quite different from the Wicksellian variants: variations in the size or growth rate of an exogenous stock of money, as opposed to shifts in the MEC or the propensity to consume. Nonetheless there is a formal similarity concerning the key role of "misperceptions." For the monetarists, monetary changes call for nominal re-scalings as a full-equilibrium response, yet misperceptions may result in incomplete adjustment in the short run, with the result that the monetary change has a (temporary) real impact. Friedman and Lucas each has his own way of explaining how the relevant misperceptions may arise.[11]

To make sense of the idea of "misperception" we surely must be able to imagine what a *correct* perception would be like. In the case of the monetarist theories, this condition is clearly met. It is not too hard to imagine agents having a correct perception of the rate of money growth or general price inflation. Indeed one of the *problems* these theories face as explanations of actual income fluctuations is that it is hard to see why agents should make the kind of mistakes the theories posit, if reasonably accurate and up-to-date statistics are available on money and prices. But the case is quite different for Leijonhufvud's argument. We do not receive monthly MEC statistics from the Federal Reserve or the Bureau of Labor Statistics. It is not at all clear that there is a sound sense to the phrase "correct perception of the MEC" in the midst of a period of uncertainty and disagreement over the long-term profitability of current investment projects. It may be possible to say, with the benefit of hindsight, that such-and-such shifts in the MEC took place at certain historical junctures, but that is not enough to justify Leijonhufvud's distinction between "correct" and "incorrect" current perceptions – certainly not enough to support the idea that incorrect perception is the pathological case, the "failure" that requires explanation.[12]

Thus at bottom, as is perhaps not surprising, the key to the Wicksellian issue lies in the description of expectations formation that one finds acceptable. Clearly Keynes saw nothing "natural" in the idea of such expectations being readily grounded in ascertainable fact. In the end he may be said to embody just the opposite viewpoint. After all, for Keynes, it is fundamental *uncertainty* over the future which makes the liquidity motive so basic to his outlook. It is worth repeating from Chapter 14 that Harrod sums it up nicely as follows:

The theory of interest is, I think, the central point in his scheme. He departs from old orthodoxy in holding that the failure of the system to move to a position of full activity is not primarily due to friction, rigidity, immobility or to phenomena essentially connected with the trade cycle. If a certain level of interest is established which is inconsistent with full activity, no flexibility or mobility in the other parts of the system will get the system to move to full activity. *But this wrong rate of interest, as we may call it, is not itself a rigidity or inflexibility. It is natural, durable, and in a certain sense in the free system inevitable.* That is why he lays what may seem an undue emphasis on the doctrine that interest is essentially the reward not for saving but for parting with liquidity. Given the complex forces affecting liquidity preference, such-and-such is the rate of interest that will naturally and necessarily and, so long as underlying forces remain unchanged, permanently obtain. Yet that rate of interest may be inconsistent with the full activity of the system.

(1947, pp. 69–70, emphasis added)

Notes

1 Motivation: Approaching the *General Theory* historically

1. Perhaps it is worth stating at the start that I do not want to be slotted into the familiar species of an interpretation of Keynes's book that favors one chapter over another, thereby becoming perhaps the first "Chapter 17 Keynesian." My explorations below range over many "chapters" of Keynes's intellectual output. Yet I do find the framework set out in Chapter 17 of the *General Theory* particularly useful as a way of centering many of Keynes's concerns into an equilibrium framework.

2. The work of these two important figures has, however, been given very good treatments by Presley (1978), Bridel (1987) and Laidler (1999).

3. Mabel Timlin's early book (1942), written in relative isolation and at the age of 51, is perhaps the most remarkable of these. Her analysis of Keynes's "shifting equilibrium" has much in common with the interpretation of the *General Theory* I will develop in Part III of this book. So too have I learned greatly from Victoria Chick's path breaking rediscovery of many of these same themes in Chick (1983).

4. Perhaps the most egregiously ahistorical of this lot was Alvin Hansen's highly influential *A Guide to Keynes* (1953). A useful recent study of this literature on the varieties of Keynesian macroeconomics is Littleboy (1990). An earlier essay that provides a more concise catalogue is Coddington (1983). Another attempt of note, much more archly drawn, opinionated and controversial, was Patinkin (1990).

5. Moggridge's biography, written by an economist explicitly for economists, focuses most intensely on Keynes as a policy advisor. Sometimes this leads to the neglect of a full-scale treatment of his theoretical development. This is particularly true of Moggridge's treatment of the *General Theory*. Skidelsky, a historian, ranges much more widely in what is bound to be the definitive Keynes's biography for some time. Yet his short and impressionistic treatment of the *General Theory*'s contents (Skidelsky, 1992, pp. 537–71.) is, it seems to me, mostly on the mark.

6. Leijonhufvud's theoretical outlook was heavily influenced by R. W. Clower's (1965) attempt to revise the micro foundations of Keynesian economics.

7. See Lawlor 1997a, pp. 353–7, for a detailed rebuttal of this stance by Shackle toward Keynes. Keynes own comments can be consulted at Keynes (1937d).

8. "In its reliance on an equilibrium method, the *General Theory* suffers from a basic handicap. For its formal method obliges it to discuss only equilibria, and these equilibria are of a kind whose occurrence is *purely accidental*, and can in no way claim to be the natural and inevitable result of a self-operating adjustment process" (Shackle, 1967, p. 240, emphasis in original).

9. Perhaps the tension of playing this dual role as a prominent macroeconomic theorist with a particular model to defend, and also an interpreter of Keynes, is the reason for the bitter and overlong controversy between Patinkin (1983, 1990, 1993) and Meltzer (1983, 1992) that followed upon the publication of the latter's article (Meltzer, 1981) and book (Meltzer, 1988). Besides providing examples of the banality of competitive quotation jujitsu in general, and the inadvisability of the slash-and-burn style of controversy to which Patinkin was especially prone,

the most telling lesson for Keynes scholarship of this spectacle was that the attempt to find the one and only "central message" of the *General Theory* – especially in a model – is not a wise activity to begin with.

10. To be fair, Patinkin (1976, pp. 98–101) doubts that Keynes ever thought in Walrasian terms himself. Instead, his view seems to be that Keynes's work nevertheless requires adoption of a Walrasian conception to be logically coherent – *on Patinkin's Keynesian grounds*. Thus, having expressed this doubt, he states (p. 101): "From this viewpoint, then, I return to my original contention that the analysis of the *General Theory* is in effect a Walrasian, general-equilibrium one."

2 Methodological stance: The Marshallian structure of the *General Theory*

1. Whether or not his new methodological stance has implication for relative price formation also, is a very underdeveloped question in the literature. One of Keynes's early interpreters, Hugh Towshend, suggested that the *General Theory* called for a complete rethinking of this question. We will briefly explore his suggestion in Chapter 14.

2. After the *General Theory* Keynes went so far as to remark, "I now feel that if I were writing the book again I should begin by setting forth my theory on the assumption that short period expectations were always fulfilled" (*CW* 14, p. 181).

3. Perhaps it is worth noting here that this is the most direct textual evidence against G.L.S. Shackle's view, noted above, that only by a reliance on the Swedish *ex ante-ex post* method can one make sense of Keynes's theory. Perhaps if one is concerned to present a non-equilibrium interpretation of the *General Theory* – as I conceive was the case with the Swedish analysts of Wicksell's economics – this is true. But if we take Keynes seriously in his profession to be presenting an equilibrium theory, and we recognize how he protested against interpreting him as relying on the *ex ante* analysis, then this problem does not arise. It is also the case that even the meanings of the notion of *ex ante* savings presented a particular problem for the Swedish theory to Keynes (see Keynes, 1937d; Lawlor, 1997a and Bibow, 2000).

4. It is an interesting indication of Keynes's vision that consumers are not depicted so much as "choosing," in the demand curve sense, a level of consumption. Rather societies imbue their consumers with a habitual psychological "propensity" to consume. Investors, on the other hand, always somewhat skittish and reluctant Nellies in Keynes's world, have to be "induced" to invest (presumably because they might otherwise "prefer" liquidity). Both of these attitudes bear a strong family resemblance to the English Political Economy tradition emanating from Smith, rather than the Walrasian tradition. Recall that Smith saw labor's consumption as largely governed by a fixed "natural" wage, and that capitalist's profit in his view was a necessary payment to induce the capitalist to pre-accumulate enough stock to make time-consuming production, and so the division of labor, possible. This same profit he thought would always be saved by "parsimonious" capitalists. His now odd-sounding stress on "unproductive" labor was really a comment on the consumption and saving habits of the one class who he thought had a choice in the matter, land-owning aristocrats. Today, when the majority of all household consumption is of services, a different set of habits apply.

5. The best summary of this work in the context of a discussion of the *General Theory* is Clower, 1997. A more theoretical statement, focusing on Marshall, is presented

in Clower, 1989. Yet the issue has long fascinated him, for instance, his well-known contributions to monetary theory are implicitly part of the same theoretical problem (Clower, 1965, 1967). He explicitly puzzled over the issue as early as Clower 1975. Finally, his neglected, but very intriguing, Micro textbook with J. Due (Clower and Due, 1972, especially Chapters 2 and 3) is explicitly cast as a Marshallian exercise.

6. Extensive historical and theoretical work on the differences for the Marshallian–Walrasian distinction for the meaning of involuntary unemployment can be found in De Vroey (2004a,b).

7. Keynes's comment to Harrod, quoted in the last chapter (*CW* 14, p. 296–7), on "choosing models which are appropriate to the contemporary world," and which develop a logical way of treating time sequences in particular cases, is relevant at this point.

8. Importantly, by "partial" Clower does not mean just the notion of one market equilibrium considered in isolation from all others, but more generally the very notion of "*ceteris paribus.*" Again recall the letter from Keynes to Harrod, quoted above, where Keynes states that "the object of a model is to segregate the semi-permanent or relatively constant factors from those which are transitory or fluctuating . . ."

3 Overview

1. In Chapters 9–12 and 14 we will dispute Patinkin's claim, referred to above, that there is no such complete theory of asset holding in the Cambridge tradition before Keynes.

2. I am aware that various scholars have also found an influence from Walras on Hayek's work in the thirties. I will discuss this in Chapter 13. I can only say here that I think this is a mistake. Lawlor and Horn (1992) explicate this point further.

4 Introduction: Keynes, the *General Theory* and the labor market

1. Strictly speaking, Pigou meant this to describe the unemployment that already existed in Britain by 1925. His factual statement of that case, however, would have accorded well with Keynes's observations both of this period, and that which followed it in the thirties (Pigou, 1947, p. 42): "The Doldrums was a period of relative stability and quasi-equilibrium. But the equilibrium was not a healthy one, because it was characterized throughout by a very large amount of involuntary idleness." Pigou wrote the 1947 book during the war in 1941–42 at the request of the British government. He was charged with reporting the facts that could be learned about the interwar-period slump up to the return to gold in 1925, with the hope of avoiding a similar post-World War II slump. It is an interesting book and shows that when constrained by facts, Pigou's style of writing improved – compared to his theoretical writings. In his theoretical works, unfortunately, as will be noted in Chapter 6, Pigou was often bound up by arid and mechanical abstractions and was thus sometimes led into unreality. Another sidelight of interest is that, in the preface Pigou (1947, p. vi.) thanks Maurice Dobb for the use of a memorandum the latter had written on labor conditions in Britain after World War I. This is interesting in light of a demonstration we will later make in Chapter 6 that Dobb's style of Marshallian labor analysis – which

was rich in institutional and historic fact and accorded those facts a large theoretical role in determining wages – contrasts sharply with Pigou's.

2. Robert Skidelsky (2002, pp. 99–100): "The incomplete recovery from the depression was the factual background to Keynes's logical demonstration of the possibility of equilibrium at less than full employment."

3. In early correspondence concerning his "new" book, written after he had become dissatisfied with the *Treatise*, Keynes referred to it as "my new book on monetary theory" (to his mother, September 18, 1931, *CW* 13, p. 380) and "my next contribution to monetary theory" (to his publisher, Daniel Macmillan, August 17, 1933, *CW* 12, p. 420).

4. There is an enormous literature on Keynes's labor market analysis and the attendant confusions over his definitions of involuntary unemployment. See Darity and Horn (1983) and Hoover (1988) for different interpretations and surveys. My own view is summarized in Lawlor (1991).

5. In Lawlor (1993) I have explicitly treated the issue of the "Pigovian" roots of *New Keynesian* labor market analysis – which is the most recent manifestation of the equating of Keynesian results and labor market rigidities.

5 The "Late Victorian" intellectual context of Marshall's labor market views

1. There is an interesting contrast between Keynes's carelessness toward the history of labor-market analysis and his much more careful attitude toward the history of monetary and interest-rate theory. In the latter case he often went to great lengths to distinguish classicals of the old school (up to Marshall) from a "neoclassical" (in his terminology someone like Robertson and Hawtrey), who was more recent and who broke with the tradition of assuming the identity of savings and investment in equilibrium. This contrast is explained by his own personal involvement in the monetary debates, and which led to his staking of his claim for involuntary unemployment on non-labor market causes and fits well with the view that this led him essentially to do away with the labor market in the beginning of his book. It is, of course, also tied up with his highly effective rhetorical skill and the need to debate with monetary theorists. On the other hand, there is little evidence of anyone rising to defend Pigou's unemployment theory in the immediate post-*General Theory* era. We are arguing here that this end position in 1936 was the product of a long evolution, and that it was one that was deeply aided by Keynes's innate Marshallian habits of thought.

2. 'The economic depression of the mid-1880s led to the so-called "discovery of unemployment." The political events of that time – especially the 1886 clashes in Hyde Park and Trafalgar Square and the 1889 dock strike – provoked a re-conceptualization of the problem . . . Within this framework, social investigators like Booth and Rowntree organized new kinds of investigation into casual labour and urban poverty, which provided evidence of problems of irregular work and low wages. By the 1900s, the economists were being outflanked by a new breed of freelance social investigators who defined unemployment as a social problem in a policy-oriented discourse.' (Williams and Williams, 1987, p. 102)

3. See Groenewegen (1995a, pp. 454–8) for Marshall's lifelong interest and involvement with the Victorian cooperative movement. His views provide an example of his political position; one we will see was endemic to his thought in many areas. In general Marshall was a gradualist and was repelled by "violent" social change.

He also tended to favor voluntary reforms and private educational efforts, which he hoped would form viable alternatives to state action and socialism. Thus in the case of cooperation in production Marshall's enthusiasm wavered, and his natural tendency to endlessly qualify arguments into a conservative stance reared.

4. The influence of rising rents, way beyond what was happening to wages, on the working-class standards of living is also recounted by Jones (1971, Part II). This helps to explain the sudden surge of interest in England in the 1880s in the work of Henry George, and in his theory of poverty caused by rising "location" rents. Both of these issues played a role in Alfred Marshall's career. Marshall debated George at Oxford in 1884 (Groenewegen, 1995a, pp. 581–7). Also, he was a lifelong proponent of the "Garden Cities Movement," designed to improve working-class life by moving families to the fresh air of the suburbs (Groenewegen, 1995a, p. 452).

5. Where this residuum was to go was a problem that had confronted other writers on the casual laborer before Beveridge. There were various suggestions for removing them, to prevent them from further spreading degeneration to the deserving working poor. This was said to occur both by baleful associations and by competing wages down to a level that only degenerates could endure. Schemes ranged from forced resettlement in domestically isolated, low-skill industrial labor camps (Alfred Marshall's recommendation) and/or "farm colonies," to forced emigration to suitable colonial lands abroad. This was also a period of high interest in eugenics. (Marshall and Keynes were both enthusiastic enough to become charter members of the Cambridge branch of the Eugenics Society). For Marshall, eugenics offered the potential to explain the hereditary transmission of poverty. The great importance of this theme to Marshall is emphasized by Groenewegen (1995a, pp. 486) who emphasizes its result in Marshall's involvement with the young J. M. Keynes in 1910 in a controversy with Pearson over the inherited effect of parental alcoholism on children. On the wider issue of the elimination of the working-class residuum see Jones (1971, pp. 303–12), who offers on p. 304 the following chilling quote from Samuel Barnett's "A Scheme for the Unemployed" (1888): "It is a shocking thing to say of men created in God's image, but it is true that the extinction of the unemployed would add to the wealth of the country . . . the existence of the unemployed is a fact and this fact constitutes a danger to the wealth and well-being of the community."

6. Of the many statements of Hobson's underconsumptionist position, his early collaboration with Mummery (Hobson and Mummery, 1889) is usually considered the best. Keynes was certainly of this opinion when he publicly reversed his early (orthodox Cambridge) view of Hobson and resurrected him as one of the "underworld" predecessors to the *General Theory*. See (CW 13, p. 634) for his more grudging private opinion, where he in fact attributes most of Hobson and Mummery to Mummery.

7. Peter Groenewegen has also written a valuable paper that compares Marshall's and Keynes's social and political outlooks (Groenewegen, 1995b). In both this paper and his biography he offers many points that have been useful to this author in explicating the relationship of Keynes's economics to Marshall's.

8. The original portrait, now hanging in the Marshall Library in Cambridge, is displayed in Plate 14 of Groenewegen (1995a), and placed in the context of Marshall's education on p. 130.

9. Himmelfarb (1991, p. 285) notes (and defends) the fact that, unlike the case in the pure utilitarianism that has often marked economics, Marshall's social philosophy did not shy from strong categorical rankings of the moral and social

good of different types of consumption. Thus he is often taunted as looking forward to the day when all workers could enjoy the leisure and pleasures of a chivalric gentleman or a Cambridge don. As she notes, other economists, notably Schumpeter, have faulted this aspect of Marshall as the *obiter dicta* of a priggish moralizer. I am arguing here that, whether one agrees with his values or not, these moral judgments cannot be separated from his more technical economics without misunderstanding both.

10. One of Marshall's first public lectures on economics in 1873 was titled "The Future of the Working Classes." About this essay Groenewegen (1995a, p. 175) remarks: "Many of the propositions contained in this lecture, on the influences of work on character, the economy of high wages and shorter hours, the economic benefits of investing in human capital, the rationale for shift work as a method to raise productivity, can be found in the *Principles.*"

11. America's importance for Marshall from the mid-seventies onward, which we will see also emphasized below in Chapter 9, on speculation and finance, is summed up in a phrase quoted by Groenewegen (1995a, p. 201) from an essay by Marshall on Hegel, where he describes America as "the land of the future, where, in the ages that lie before us, the Burden of the world's history shall reveal itself." See Whitaker, 1975, Volume II, pp. 352–77 for a discussion by Marshall of the virtues of American labor, its relative mobility in place and rank, its subsequent tendency to democracy and the role of America's example in a theory of social evolution.

12. Many Marshall scholars, including Keynes and Groenewegen, have seen this constant search for industrial and social details as an unfortunate obsession on Marshall's part. It was futile, in that such knowledge tended to date before he actually used it in his meticulously written treatises; misleading, given Marshall's weakness for induction from flimsy evidence; and counterproductive, given the time it took away from his writing. Marshall's extreme fear of being less than what he saw as exactly correct seems as responsible in this regard as any more scientific ideals were. On the other hand, his fondness for "facts" and relevancy represent an admirable spirit of realism, one that is a sadly distant memory for much of the economics profession today.

13. See Groenewegen (1995a, Chapter 11) for a detailed discussion on Marshall's contribution to this commission and the events surrounding it. See Groenewegen (1996) for a reproduction of the testimony and parts of the final report that Marshall specifically participated in.

14. But see Groenewegen (1995a, p. 371) for a more jaundiced view of the educative value for Marshall of the commission work. It does not appear, for instance, to have entered materially in any of his later books and papers.

15. See the summary "notes on social influences and conclusion" contained in Booth's last volume of his 17-volume, 17-year-long project *Life and Labour of the People in London* (Booth, 1902). It offers a catalog of such working-class woes, interestingly empirical and moralistic at once.

16. But there were more "radical" solutions offered also, mostly to deal with what were seen as the "outcasts" of the working classes, particularly the East London dockworkers and others who were only "casually" employed. Hysteria over both the moral degeneration of this class and what later Victorian reformers in the 1880s saw as the likelihood that they would infect the more respectable working classes with their immorality, led to a social crisis that is well described by Jones's *Outcast London* (1971). The most radical analysts of this period argued that such "outcasts" were far beyond the pale of reform to be helped, that they destroyed cooperative self-help efforts by essentially drinking away in gin any aid offered to

the poor, that they were reproducing at a rapid rate, and that they thus constituted a eugenics threat to the English "race." In Chapter 16, Jones describes how this led to frequent calls to segregate, forcefully resettle or even imprison this "residuum" for the good of society.

17. One theoretical point worth making that *may* distinguish Marshall from the classical economists who were relied upon by Manchester Liberals, lies in Marshall's view that economically sanctioned interference with the labor market need not be limited to the case of classes of people who were at a bargaining disadvantage and so could not be considered "free agents." The Factory Acts (of 1833, 1844 and 1847) for example, attempts to outlaw the most egregious and unsanitary working conditions, were often justified from within even the most otherwise *laissez-faire* economics of the day by the argument that woman and children were not able to adequately represent their own interests against employers' demands (see Blaug, 1958 (1971) for instance). Marshall, on the other hand, sometimes seemed to have recommended (however weakly) general policy that would alter *all* labor practices that led to unjust social inequities that he saw as rectifiable, despite the "bargaining status" of the individuals involved. A. W. Coats (1971a, editor's introduction) reminds us that there was much variety and complexity among the classical economists on policy issues. His essay (Coats, 1971b) in the same volume is a clear demonstration of this complexity on labor issues. On the other hand, Marshall becomes harder to pin down on this argument in instances when his lofty suggestions for economic chivalry came up against actual policy choices, in which case his fear of state bureaucracy rose to prominence. Then Marshall at times seems to be holding to this very same classical principal of protection of non-free agents, for instance in his questioning of Henry Hyndman during the Labour Commission hearings (see particularly Question 8668, p. 274 in Groenewegen 1996.) More broadly, this theoretical quibble is perhaps not as relevant to the kind of "popular" *laissez-faire* conception that the Manchester School represented in Victorian times, and its strong hold on popular opinion in Britain as an underlying preconception of public policy debate, through the 1870s at least. On this broader view see the essay in Coats' volume by H. S. Gordon (1971), and the even more extensive investigations of A. J. P. Taylor (1965). When liberalism is considered in this sense, defined as an automatic *presumption against* state action until proved otherwise, Marshall was always a liberal.

18. See Moss (2003), for instance.

19. See, for example, his questioning of the socialist leader Hyndman at the Labour Commission (Groenewegen, 1996, p. 274) where Marshall asks: "Is not your proposal or others of the same kind suggestive of burning down a house in order to roast a pig?"

20. See Groenewegen, (1995a, Chapter 13) for a general account of his career as an "advocate and controversialist." Particularly documented there is his enthusiastic support for better housing for the poor and his somewhat ambiguous support for the then very popular "cooperative movement," by which workers were to help themselves and improve their morals. This is covered in a wider context in Jones (1971). Groenewegen (1995a, Chapter 16) puts this in the context of Marshall's politics and, especially emphasizes his strong aversion to the more radical socialist proposals of his day. See Himmelfarb (1991, pp. 245–80) for a favorable view of Marshall's "economics of chivalry," emphasizing his views as a unique "third way" in the catalog of Victorian social philosophy and reform. Groenewegen makes the important point that it was socialists and labor "leaders" that drew most of Marshall's ire, not laborers in their more traditional role.

21. See the discussion of Marshall's behavior there and of Beatrice Webb's (irritated) published and (outraged) private accounts of the commission, recounted in Groenewegen (1995a, pp. 362–71).

22. In the case of Hyndman and Webb, however, it is not apparent that Marshall had his intended effect of muting their arguments by his hostile, and often pedantic, behavior toward them and their ideas. Both Hyndman and Webb were more than capable of defending themselves with both wit and sarcasm. See for instance the Labour Commission testimony recently collected by Peter Groenewegen (Marshall, 1996) again, for both Webb (pp. 172–14) and Hyndman (pp. 266–75). Groenewegen quotes Hyndman as later summing up his impression of the overall attitude of the commissioners as "eager to help the workers *in* their poverty but not *out* of it"(1995a, p. 592, n. *, emphasis added).

6   The treatment of labor markets in Marshallian economics

1. It is no surprise that Keynes's biography of Marshall first established this point (Keynes, 1926 [*CW* 10, pp. 199–200]). It was to mark perhaps the biggest departure Keynes's own life as an economist was to make from Marshall's. This is particularly true with regard to their respective views on unemployment. See, also, Groenewegan, 1995b.

2. Other examples of Marshall's moralizing, to name only a few, include his treatment of: women and work (*Principles*, eighth edition, p. 695), racial superiority (*Principles*, Chapters IV and V of Book IV, and Appendix A) and trade unions (*Principles*, pp. 702–22). For extensive accounts of this characteristic of Marshall as regards trade unions, see Petridis, 1973 and 1990.

3. That the issue of high wages and its relation to the future character of the working class was of high importance to Marshall is a theme highlighted by Peter Groenewegen's biography. See Groenewegen 1995a, pp. 172–9 on the role of this theme both in interesting Marshall in economics to begin with, and on his early writings on high wages in the 1870s. Commenting on an 1873 lecture by Marshall titled "The Future of the Working Classes," Groenewegen (1995a, p. 175) writes:

> Many of the propositions contained in this lecture, on the influences of work on character, the economy of high wages and shorter hours, the economic benefits of investing in human capital, the rationale for shift work as a method to raise productivity, can be found in the *Principles*. The lecture is therefore important as a link between the ideals which brought Marshall to economics and the mature work of the *Principles* . . .

4. The one issue on which he rose above his timidity was education (see Matthews, 1990, p. 29), where Marshall saw a strong role for the state.

5. See for example, Book VI, Chapter XIII, especially pp. 702–22.

6. See Marshall, 1962, Book VI, Chapter III.

7. This popular theme of the Victorian era was taken up by Marshall from contemporary sources. The senior Thomas Brassey (1805–70) was a well-known Victorian public figure – a builder of railways and public works of all kinds. Starting in England from humble roots, he grew to great prominence in his field, eventually building large projects on most continents. At one point his firm was estimated

to have 80,000 hands under hire as navies, machinists, tunnel miners and engineers. In a celebrated episode of 1854 he built a railway from the coast at Balaclava to the besieged garrison in Sevastopol in the Crimea in just six weeks. His extensive experience with hiring men of many nationalities and organizing them for maximum work efficiency was recounted in an influential volume by his then knighted son, Lord Thomas Brassey, Jr., MP (1836–1918), titled *Work and Wages* (1872). It proclaimed his father's evidence in support of "Brassey's Law," that work efficiency increased with higher wages. This book was extensively cited by F. A. Walker in *The Wages Question* (1876 [1891]), a book well know to Alfred Marshall. Lord Brassey was identified with advocacy for the benefits of higher wages in Parliament throughout his career. He further explored this theme in *Lectures on the Labour Question* (1878) Groenewegen (1995a, p. 186, n. 179) cites Marshall's references to Brassey and Walker as early as 1879 in the *Economics of Industry*, co-authored with Mary Paley Marshall. He also cites a personal visit to Walker at Yale during Marshall's visit to the United States. Additionally Marshall served on the Industrial Remuneration Commission with Lord Brassey in 1885 (Groenewegen, 1995a, p. 587).

8. The extent, to which Brassey's views also influenced Hobson, is interestingly detailed by Petridis. It is another in a series of points at which the work of the economists of the academy – especially those of the Cambridge school – intertwined with the work of that maligned but prescient outsider, J. A. Hobson. It is then fitting that Keynes finally felt it necessary to say something positive about him in print in 1936. On this side of the Atlantic, also well-known to Marshall, Brassey importantly influenced the wage analysis of Francis Amasa Walker.

9. See Petridis (1996) for the details of the changes in Marshall's terminology from the 1870s to 1880s. Generally after the third edition of the *Principles*, through the eighth and final from which we are quoting, he used the "efficiency" language.

10. As Keynes's original preface to the series states:

> Generally speaking, the writers of these volumes believe themselves to be orthodox members of the Cambridge School of Economics. At any rate, most of their ideas about the subject, and even their prejudices, are traceable to the contact they have enjoyed with the writings and lectures of the two econo-mists who chiefly influenced Cambridge thought for the past fifty years, Dr. Marshall and Professor Pigou. (Dobb, 1928, p. vi)

11. Since our argument here is that Keynes's views in the 1920s were firmly within the Cambridge tradition of his day, it is worth noting that the correspondence over planning the Handbook series shows him fully involved at every level. Thus Keynes argues with the publisher in February of 1927 that there is "no need to go outside the Cambridge circle" for authors. On June 9, 1927, he writes to Dobb concerning the manuscript, "I think it is an excellent synopsis and I really have no criticism to make." And on January 2, 1929, he complains to the publisher, Nisbet, that he has yet to receive a copy of Dobb's book: "Since I am not only the General Editor of the series, but spent considerable time over the proofs of these volumes, this seems to me something of a discourtesy." (KCKP, file CEB/1)

Other evidence of this influence on Keynes from Dobb's view of wages is found in Keynes's direct use of Dobb's paper "A Skeptical View of the Theory of Wages" (Dobb, 1929) in an essay titled "The Question of High Wages" in the *Political Quarterly* in 1930 (Keynes, 1930). There Keynes puts Dobb's theory this way: "Accordingly there is a large arbitrary element in the relative rates of remuneration and the factors of production get what they do, not because in any strict economic sense they precisely earn it, but because past events have led to these rates being customary and usual." (Keynes, 1930, p. 114) Though he uses it for an argument about the dangers of capital flight in a too-high-wage economy, Keynes in passing says of Dobb's theory of wages: "To a large extent I sympathize with these attacks [on orthodox wage doctrine]. I believe the best working theories of the future will own these assailants as their parents." (Keynes 1930, p. 114)

Also there is Robert Skidelsky's view that Keynes contended that there was a lack of money-wage-flexibility in England over the course of the 1920s and 1930s. In fact, Keynes felt that history showed wages always to have been relatively inflexible in money terms for long periods – in good times and bad – and that labor in the twenties was then not surprisingly resistant to downward pressure on money wages. Consequently he championed in this period the theoretical views of Dobb to which we have referred. Skidelsky also details Keynes's invocation of this "Dobbian" view to the Macmillan Committee proceedings. See Skidelsky, 1992, pp. 346–9 and n. 30.

12. Examination of later editions reveals that he continually updated this section as institutions changed.

13. This is a movement, which Dobb elsewhere in the book traces to the 1860s and the schemes of Lord Brassey. See Note 4, above.

14. In the second edition (Dobb, 1938, pp. 54–60) Dobb shows an even more elaborate Marshallian approach to this issue, with a discussion of the general social externalities of a high wage economy and the generational time span involved. He also notes this as an argument for a minimum wage law.

15. For an even more extensive discussion of the role of unions, compacts and bargaining in this context see the discussion in the third edition (Dobb, 1948, pp. 72–95).

16. This point was similarly made by Marshall (1962, pp. 418–23) when he elegantly and succinctly summed up the history of wage theory from the Physiocrats through to 1890 in just 5 pages.

17. If there is any doubt that this refers to Marshall in the first edition, it is cleared up in the second. The discussion here appears in two sections of Chapter 3 of the first edition (Dobb, 1928) titled "The Theory of Marginal Productivity" and "Demand for Labor." These are replaced in the second edition (Dobb, 1938) with much the same argument and as "The Theory of Marginal Productivity" and "Marshall and Supply and Demand." Also, in this latter section of the second edition is the glowing tribute to Marshall, which appears in the epigraph in Part I of this book.

18. See Chapter 4.

19. As for causes of the trade cycle itself, though subject to much debate, Pigou neatly categorizes them into "variations in the seasons, the climate and the mood of business men (Pigou, 1913, p. 146)." See Part III for a complete account of Cambridge cycle theory at this date.

20. How he defines the term in Chapter 1 is of interest in itself in that it clearly marks out unemployment as a phenomenon of "wage-earners," Pigou thus rules out of

hand the currently popular interest in defining unemployment as a preference for leisure or non-market employment:

> If a wage-earner happens to possess an allotment on which he can work when discharged for his ordinary trade, or if he is able, on these occasions, to run his hand to wood-carving or some other domestic industry, we shall not, for that reason, decline to class him among the unemployed. (Pigou, 1913, p. 14)

It is to then further clarify his *subject* that he introduces the involuntary aspect of unemployment:

> Even, however, when this is understood, it does not become possible to pass directly to a definition of unemployment. For unemployment clearly does not include all the idleness of wage-earners, but only *that part of it which is, from their point of view and in their existing condition at the time, involuntary.* (Pigou, 1913, p. 14, emphasis in original)

21. It is obvious, since he goes out of his way to attack it, that he was familiar with the heterodox underconsumptionist views of Hobson.
22. In the preface Pigou makes clear that his book is designed to correct what he saw as the excesses of the profession in "advocating policy" and devoting too exclusive an attention to the "monetary side" of the problem and so neglecting what he wanted to account for on the "real side." To compare this preface with that of Keynes's *General Theory* provides a one distinction between the two books. Although both were written as an economist tract *of* the time, *for* fellow economists, Pigou's comes off as sterile and defensive in the extreme, whereas Keynes's is optimistic, full of the excitement of socially relevant theoretical progress and clearly aggressive. One cannot but help thinking that Pigou had regressed from the theoretically pedestrian, but practically sensible views of his 1913 book.

7 Keynes and the labor market

1. This is exemplified in the lifelong contempt he expressed for the over-use of mathematics in economics. As twelfth wrangler in mathematics and a student of Whitehead and Russell's work, it is clear that he was no fool when it came to mathematics. Yet from the beginning to the end of his career he held to Marshall's dictum that such mathematics as was useful in working out a problem was to be thrown and disguised in expressing the idea. He explicitly "agrees with Marshall" on this topic in his early lecture notes (file UA/6 of the Keynes Papers at King's College). See also his comments in the *General Theory*, pp. 275, 297–8.
2. This quote is from a paper presented in the "Apostles" on February 20, 1909. It lies in the Keynes papers at King's college in file no UA/32.
3. This note in Marshall's hand is appended to set questions done by Keynes in 1905 and deposited in the Keynes papers in file UA/3/1 at the King's College Modern Archive.
4. This and all of the quotations to follow from Keynes's lecture notes on "Principles of Economics" are part of an un-paginated file in the Keynes collection at King's College, UA/6/9.
5. The extent to which Keynes at this young period was a slavish Marshallian is indicated by the fact that most of these "examples" can be found in the *Principles* (see Book VI, Chapter III).

6. On Marshall's attitude toward unions see Petridis (1990).
7. For an insightful and detailed analysis of Keynes's changing thoughts on wages throughout his career, see Millmow (1985).
8. In fact this concern with social justice is probably a holdover form his basic Moorite outlook on ethics, with its call to achieve the greatest good for the greatest number. It is interesting that he refers to the issue as early as his pre-war lecture notes cited above. For a more thorough discussion, including the argument that Pigou's *Wealth and Welfare* (1912) also bears the stamp of Moore's (1903) ethics, see O'Donnell (1989, 164–73).
9. This is from a letter to H. N. Brailsford, author of *Socialism for Today*, dated December 3, 1925, *KCKP* file CO/1.
10. It is worth noting that this position is even more free of the classical postulates than Keynes's position in the *General Theory*. There real wages also were not a causal factor in the level of employment, coming in at the end once aggregate demand had determined output and employment. But there was postulated a *unique* correspondence between the level of real wages and employment.
11. Once again reference to his views on useful economic models, discussed above in our opening chapter, is both relevant to his state of mind in the *General Theory* and to his continuing Marshallian outlook.
12. Davis (1968, 1971) is an early expression of this point with regard to U.S. economists. Bleaney (1987) makes the point more widely. Laidler (2003) has more recently elaborated upon it.
13. I should quickly add, to avoid misunderstanding, that I know Pigou also opposed a wage policy in the thirties.
14. Notice again the Marshallian heritage of Keynes's method that is implicit in the very fact of ranking influences according to their causal importance. To say a factor was an inconsequential "byproduct" of other outcomes of the economic system would be unintelligible from a Walrasian general equilibrium standpoint, where since all causes are considered simultaneously, everything causes everything.
15. Later, in Chapter 14, we will see this proposition repeated and given broader support in the *General Theory* discussion of the essential properties of a monetary system.

8   Looking backward from the *General Theory*: On the historical origins of Keynes's financial market views

1. For the analysis of the macroeconomic viewpoint that is lurking behind this essay, see Part III and Chapter 15.
2. I am not suggesting that Marshall's and Sraffa's ideas about the proper theoretical treatment of the firm and industry were the same. Sraffa had a theoretical agenda of his own, only darkly seen it appears in the 1930s. I am suggesting, alternative to Sraffa, that Marshall's own writings implicitly showed a way forward to Keynes by following out the logic of the later Marshall's own work and its contradiction with his own *Principles* framework. Moreover that this was toward a fruitful path that I think the more tightly logical, but less practical, theoretical strictures of Sraffa did not lead. This same contradiction in Marshall's thought can be said to have influenced Allyn Young (1928) in his own influential contribution to the theory of competition and of industrial organization.

3. An early awareness of the neglect of these issues is found in Liebhafsky (1955). See Arena and Quere (2003) for various modern commentary on the the incompatibility between the early and late Marshallian programs.
4. Kahn's thesis on the short period and work on the marginal cost curve, were his previous work to the more famous "multiplier" of the *General Theory*.
5. See the forward to the original edition of 1933 and a wiser, more complete, statement of the intellectual currents that led to this book in the preface to the second edition of 1969.
6. Especially in Book II, devoted to "Dominant Tendencies of Business Organization," but actually in the whole of the book.
7. Sraffa's criticism of the Marshallian theory of the firm does not seem to have ever addressed *Industry and Trade*. It may be that by 1930 his more immediate targets were Pigou and Robertson.
8. We will see in Part III and in Chapter 15, this own-rates framework can be used to illustrate the Wicksellian versus the Keynesian views of the dynamic relation of interest and output.
9. A more complete analysis of this framework will be found in Chapter 14.
10. The attitude Keynes expresses here is in conformity with a continuing theme of his post-*General Theory* correspondence – that he should have written the book under the assumption that *short-period expectations*, those concerning forecasts of required short period output levels, were always, by definition, met – "for the theory of effective demand is substantially the same if we assume that the short-period expectations are always fulfilled (*CW* 14, p. 181)." This, it is worth emphasizing, leaves "long-period expectations" – those relating to forecasts of the real return to investment projects – in an entirely different analytical category. They, by necessity in an uncertain world, are liable to disappointment. But also, as they (unlike short-period expectations) are rarely checked by reality, they can assume a life of their own. Long-period expectations thus become one of the three "ultimate independent variables" of his system (*GT*, pp. 246–7).

9 Stock equilibrium in asset markets and "The Folly of Amateur Speculators": The Marshallian setting

1. Our reading fully supports Keynes's view that the later expositions of this aspect of Marshall's monetary thought that did appear in press were extremely inferior to this early expression. For this publication see *Official Papers* (Marshall, 1926), pp. 176–8, 267–8; and *Money, Credit and Commerce* (Marshall, 1923), Book 1, Chapter 4 and Appendix C.
2. As we will show below in Chapters 12, 13 and 14, intermediate uses of the same framework show up in the *Tract* (*CW* 4) and also in the *Treatise* (*CW* 5 and 6).
3. In essence Fisher also always saw assets as being valued in expectational terms.
4. Exemplified by Mill (see Mill, 1871, pp. 541–3).
5. As we are about to show, Emery had already provided such a "modern" view in 1896.
6. Note the contrast with the quotation above from *Money, Credit and Commerce*. It is not the inaccuracy of the forecasts compared to fundamental values, which is of concern to the shrewdest traders, but the most popular opinions in the market about these values.
7. Marshall's unpublished essay and its striking resemblance to Emery and Keynes's later views, raises the question of the path of transmission of these ideas. Dardi

and Gallegati offer no direct evidence that Keynes actually ever saw Marshall's essay. Neither can we, but the larger view of the context of the then contemporary state of the discussion of speculation offered in this paper opens up some indirectly supported hypotheses.

First, as so much of Marshall's essay is in fact contained in Emery's book – and, as we will show for the first time below, in Chapter 10, Section I, Keynes was quite well versed in Emery's work as early as 1909 – it is possible that Keynes and Marshall could both be seen as developing Emery independently. Partial support for this view comes from the fact that Marshall in 1896 was actually much more critical of speculation than Keynes ever was before the mid-twenties.

But an alternative hypothesis is just as likely on current evidence. It is probable that if Keynes ever did see Marshall's essay, it would have been in 1924. It was then that Keynes wrote his memorial essay (Keynes, 1925) on Marshall in which the glowing tribute to his theory of money that we quote on the title page of Part II, above, is contained. I mention this because in the preparation of his Marshall essay Keynes utilized a number of Marshall's unpublished papers provided by Mary Marshall (*CW* 10, p. 161). In fact we have emphasized above Keynes's use in his Marshall piece of the essay "Money." We do not have any similar documentation for the "Folly" essay. The year 1924 was also the year when Keynes started working in earnest on his *Treatise on Money*, which contains the first extended discussions of the type of analysis of the stock market Marshall had made in his essay. One last piece of this puzzle is Keynes's contention in the memorial essay (1925, 34–5), that Marshall's failure to produce his later works was partly due to his insecurity over his grasp of "the progress of events in the 'seventies and 'eighties, particularly in America." It was, of course, just these developments, which Emery first analyzed and with which Marshall was grappling in 1899.

8. He confines his discussion of these aspects to a short afterthought in Chapter 5.
9. Though the same sort of notions with regard to banking institutions were also clearly laid out by Bagehot (1873) in the nineteenth century and by Vera Smith (1936) in the thirties. See (Goodhart, 1988) for a discussion of this literature.
10. In this as in other respects, Emery is in concurrence with the modern historian of the Chicago grain trade, William Cronon, whose *Nature's Metropolis* (1992, 97–147) contains a fascinating account of the development of future trading in grain between 1800 and 1870.
11. The practice is in many ways unchanged today. See Wood and Wood (1985, pp. 353–61).
12. He also notes an intermediate step in this historical evolution in which the "trading" risks were taken over from the producers by merchants. In the later evolution the strictly trading risks associated with the profitability of any line of commerce are separated off from speculative risks of price fluctuations over time.
13. But which is not really so new at all in a larger historical time frame. De Marchi and Harrison (1994) show, for instance, that seventeenth-century Dutch traders had a clear idea of many of these issues. Both Neil De Marchi and John Wood have suggested to me that De la Vega should be considered the real originator in this literature. He is not, however, Keynes's source.
14. Again, a view usually traced to Keynes's elegant rendering of this view in Chapter 12 of the *General Theory*.
15. This theme had earlier been investigated by Geoff Harcourt (1983).

10 The evolution of Keynes's views on asset markets and seculation

1. The complete notes from this set of lectures lie in the King's College Keynes papers file UA/3/2. This material was most likely part of a two-section course on "Modern Business Methods" which has two parts: Part I: "Trusts and Railways"; and, Part II: "Company Finance and the Stock Exchange." Moggridge (*CW* 12, p. 689) lists "Company Finance and the Stock Exchange" as having been given in the years 1910–13. In the text of the notes, Keynes indicates these stock exchange lectures are to follow from Part I on "Trusts and Railways."

   The titles themselves are interesting evidence of turn-of-the-century preoccupations. Then current attitudes naturally considered the cutting edge of "Modern Business Methods," to be the practices on the "Stock Exchange" and the management of "Trusts and Railways." As Emery makes clear, the beginning of the modern American developments on the stock exchange grew out of the creative financing arrangements used to cover America with railroads after the Civil War. It is also worth noting that, besides Emery on *Speculation*, Keynes assigned Veblen's *Theory of Business Enterprise* in this course. The heart of Veblen's theory was that Stock Market speculation had come to dominate the activities of the large industrial enterprises of the day, beginning with the railroads. Veblen's analysis of financial markets bears some very striking resemblances to that of Keynes's in the *General Theory*.

2. These are contained in the unpaginated file KCKP, UA/6/3–4.

3. This is a direct quotation of Keynes's own outline in KCKP UA/6/3.

4. This outline is interpolated by lifting the headings Keynes gives to his lecture notes in KCKP, UA/3/2.

5. In fact the questions turn out to be ones that Marshall had set for Keynes on November 9, 1905, when Keynes was his student.

6. "Few things have called forth greater extremes of praise and blame than modern organized speculation. On one side it is strongly denounced, either as being morally wrong in itself, or as being in addition to this a disastrous influence in business. This view is, perhaps that of a large majority of respectable persons outside of business life, and of the greater part of the newspaper press" (Emery 1896, p. 96). Contemporary fiction was also full of villains who made their living by speculation. Frank Norris's *The Pit* is an interesting example.

7. On the *Treatise on Probability*, see O'Donnell 1989 and Davis 1994. It will become increasingly obvious as our discussion proceeds through the rest of the book that we consider Keynes to have been concerned with "uncertainty" from a very early period, and not to have newly struck upon this notion in the 1930s as he was formulating the *General Theory*. This puts our analysis at odds with some authors, such as Bateman (1996). I think, however, that we are much closer to O'Donnel (1989) and Davis (1994) in seeing this concern as a continuous one of Keynes's throughout his career.

8. To repeat from above: "We do not mean by the risk of an investment its actual future yield – we mean the degree of probability of the yield we expect."

9. Moggridge (*CW* 11, p. 5, n. 5) notes: "At the time margin requirements were 10 per cent. Thus the fund could take up forward positions up to an amount equal to ten times their capital and realized capital gains."

10. The resulting relationship between spot currency exchange rates, forward prices and the relative rates of interest in two countries is still a one of the the basic parts of the international finance literature under the heading of the "covered interest parity theorem."

11. Skidelsky (1992, p. 27) argues that his extensive journalistic efforts in the early twenties, at least partly fueled by the desire to make money, largely explain why he produced no major work of theory until 1930.

12. He repeats (*CW* 4, p. 103) a line that can be found in his 1910 lecture notes and in other places in Keynes's (and Marshall's) writings, and is also almost a verbatim quote from Emery (1896, p. 162) to the effect that among large dealers and millers, *not* to hedge in the future market is considered the most dangerous kind of speculation.

13. That is both his professional interests and his personal interests. By this period Keynes had begun to speculate in commodities as well as currencies on quite a large scale. In fact in 1923 and 1924 profits on commodity speculation of £13,702 and £15,245 dominated his investment income (see Moggridge's table (Table 4) *CW* 12, p. 12). In 1928 large losses in commodities, particularly rubber, cut his net assets from £44,000 to £13,060 (*CW* 12, p. 11, Table 3, p. 15).

14. By this date Keynes had become a director of the National Mutual Life Insurance Company.

15. For an excellent short summary description in non-technical language of what Keynes of the *Treatise* saw as the normal course of the cycle see *CW* 5, pp. 271–3. We will return to the *Tract* and the *Treatise* and Keynes's aims for monetary theory, in a more extended discussion in Chapter 12.

16. In fact he refers the reader back to the *Tract* discussion we have already covered for the full details, see *CW* 6, 291, 298.

17. In the form of: "1. Allowance for deterioration . . .; 2. warehouse and insurance charges; 3. Interest charges; 4. Remuneration against the risk of changes in the money value of the commodity during the time through which it has to be carried by means of borrowed money" (*CW* 6, p. 121).

18. One can find a description by Keynes very similar to the "fashion" model of stock prices going back as far as 1910. See his article "Great Britain's Foreign Investments" (*CW* 15, p. 46).

19. It is interesting to note that the distinction Emery made between the method of speculation by fortnightly account in England versus the method of borrowing and lending stock characteristic of the Wall Street clearinghouses, shows up in the *Treatise* as an explanation of how much easier it is to ignite a speculative boom on Wall Street compared to the City (*CW* 5, p. 225; 6, pp. 175–7). The major reason for this is that the U.S. system may free speculation from running into a lending constraint from the banking system much more than the British case.

20. One might say his other "General Theory" self eventually provided this judgment.

21. Keynes did have his own troubles with investments during these years. First, his commodity losses in 1928 and 1929 necessitated the sale of English securities during a bear market to rectify growing inadequacies in his commodity cover. He also eventually got into the U.S. market in a big way in 1932 and thereafter continued large American dealings until his death (see *CW* 12, p. 13, Table 5). Like all those active in the U.S. market during this period he suffered some ups and downs. But on average he seems to have actually done quite well once he adopted his policy of "faithfulness" to a small selection of stocks. Thus Moggridge reports (*CW* 12, p. 9) "in the years after 1929, his investments outperformed the market in 21 of 30 accounting years and did so cumulatively by a large margin."

22. To an investment partner, F. C. Scott, Keynes writes in 1942: "I am quite incapable of having adequate knowledge of more than a very limited range of investments. Time and opportunity do not allow more. Therefore, as the investible sums increase, the size of the unit must increase. I am in favour of having as large a unit as market conditions will allow" (*CW* 12, 82). Interestingly, just as in the definition of speculation advanced in his 1910 lectures, this strategy implies that Keynes still thought he knew better than the market, to hold such a concentrated portfolio. On the other hand, opportunities to cheaply diversify – as are commonly found in index funds and other products today – were not easily available in Keynes's day.

23. Skidelsky (1992, p. 343) appears to date this change in Keynes's strategy to 1928 while Moggridge (*CW* 12, pp. 9–15) appears to date it to 1929. In any case it was evident by 1930, both in his portfolio and in his writings (see *CW* 12, pp. 57, 78, 82–3, 97–9,102–7). An interesting deep background source for this is a book review Keynes wrote for the *Nation and Athenaeum* in 1925 of *Common Stocks as Long-Term Investments* by Edgar L. Smith (*CW* 12, pp. 247–52). It reports the "striking" results of a long-term comparison of the return to investing in Wall Street shares versus bonds over a fifty-year period. Using various selections of stocks, Smith found that the "common stocks have turned out best in the long run, indeed, markedly so" (*CW* 12, pp. 247). This is an early report of what is now a commonplace verity of modern financial lore.

11 The development of Cambridge monetary thought (1870–1935)

1. I list what I read and consider to be the standard secondary references – those, besides the primary readings that have influenced my knowledge of this period of monetary theory's history. Also, the complete primary references are all to be found in these fine books. Many of these will be cited in this Part of the book. I apologize if I have left any major contributors out due to ignorance.

2. See Bibow (1998, 2000) on the history of the torturous loanable funds debate and its history in pre-*General Theory* Cambridge monetary theory. My contribution (Lawlor, 1997a) to this literature attempts to reformulate Keynes's contribution and to account for Keynes's ambivalent attitude toward his predecessors in the post-*General Theory* period. In Chapters 13 and 14, we will give an account of what I think Keynes was emphasizing in differentiating his theory of the rate of interest from the loanable funds theory.

3. Laidler (1999, pp. 53–5) has demonstrated that these faults were known much earlier by the Stockholm school, Irving Fisher in America and Wicksell himself. Kaldor (1942) presents this "Hayek Story" as seen through the eyes of a graduate student who actively participated in its drama. For a modern and objective account of the capital-theoretic aspect of Hayek's argument see Cottrell (1994b).

4. We have already dealt with this charge in Chapter 2 and in Lawlor (1997a).

5. Patinkin (1982, Chapter 6) also briefly covers this question, dealing mostly with the issue of stock and flows in the demand for money work of various Cambridge authors. Generally it can be said that Eshag and Bridel find the elements of Keynes's liquidity preference well represented in these authors, while Patinkin does not. Laidler is focused on determining the outlines of a wider orthodoxy in

each of his books (that of the 1870–1914 period in Laidler, 1991; and that of the IS/LM model as fashioned out of interwar business cycle theory in Laidler, 1999). For our purposes, Bridel's strict focus on Marshall's monetary thought is the most useful of these and we will rely on it especially and on the original texts of Marshall in what follows, noting any deviations from Bridel's view. Bridel's Marshall discussion (Bridel, 1987, Chapters 2 and 3) is particularly informative. As will be seen, our major deviation has to do with his insistence on a long-period interpretation of the *General Theory*. Laidler's (1999, Part II) treatment of interwar Cambridge theorists is also excellent. It will be of good value to us below. If I fail to refer at every point to both these sources, this should not hide my debt to them.

6. Marshall and his followers did not, thereby, consider themselves quantity theorists, giving a behavioral twist to velocity and recognizing that an influx of money does not necessarily result in a proportionate increase in the price level. See Laidler (1991, Chapter 3) for a discussion on this.

7. On Marshall's "money wage stickiness" argument, see Laidler (1999, pp. 95–100). His illuminating discussion also links this tradition to Pigou's (1913) *Unemployment*, and its "plasticity of wage rates" argument that we discussed in Chapter 6. On Marshall's work on indexation see Laidler (1999, pp. 172–8).

8. Our reference refers to different pages than the one Bridel inserts here since we are quoting the eighth edition of the *Principles* where this quote appears in a footnote, and a very interesting one at that, at the bottom of p. 592. Note also that here Bridel is merging a quotation from the *Economics of Industry* (Marshall and Marshall, 1879) with a quotation from a footnote in the *Principles*. This fact in itself gives some evidence of the scattered and mysterious aspect of Marshall's monetary theory of the interest rate, a quality that Keynes comments on in the appendix to Chapter 14 of the *General Theory*.

9. Although Keynes tells us in his biographical essay that Marshall was frustrated by the increasing difficulty he had in collecting "facts" on developments after 1870.

10. Groenewegen footnotes a reference to Marshall's *Economics of Industry* and to Marshall's unpublished 1899 essay "The Folly of Amateur Speculators." We have already analyzed the role of this essay in Marshall's economics, above in Part II, Chapter 9, Section III.

11. Sticklers for detail will note that these two bodies of work actually overlapped. Whether we count Keynes (1911) in his review of Fisher, or Pigou (1917) in his classic statement of the Cambridge *k* account of money demand, each occurred before the publication of Marshall (1923). Yet we know that both Keynes and Pigou had seen some of this work of Marshall in unpublished or little-published forms earlier.

12. Patinkin (1982, p. 171, n. 8) provides an interesting précis of Lavington's career and Bridel (1987, p. 96) refers to his seeming invisibility to other members of the Cambridge school. As he says "neither Keynes, nor Hawtrey, nor indeed Marshall make a single reference to Lavington's writings." Patinkin ascribes at least part of this oblivion to Lavington's "self-effacing" manner. It remains something of a mystery still. See also Footnote 14.

13. See Lawlor (1997a, Part 2) for an attempt to explain this neglect by Keynes.

14. This terminology is to distinguish it from the then "new" work of Hawtrey, Robertson and Keynes. It also further establishes the seeming invisibility of Lavington's cycle book to those other authors, who may have felt that Lavington's extremely humble attitude to Marshall was old hat. Pigou (as we

know from Pigou, 1929), on the other hand, perhaps playing his role as "The Professor," combined all the cycle authors of the Cambridge School of this period. He was in a sense representing to the world a synthetic account of the work of these younger economists.

15. The ubiquity of this terminology in Cambridge economics – we saw it in Pigou (1913), here by Lavington and we will encounter its early use by Hawtrey (1913) – establishes the fact that it was standard fare. The concept denoted by this term, however, seemed to be quite variable until Keynes's put his stamp on it in 1936. Laidler (1999, p. 116, n. 12, and p. 254 n. 4), alternatively, makes much of Keynes's denial of the use of this term by the "classicals" and claims that Hawtrey invented it.

16. Bridel (1987, p. 199, n. 6) reports that in the 1920s Hawtrey's *Currency and Credit* was "the standard textbook on money and banking on the Cambridge Economics Tripos Reading Lists together with Fisher's *Purchasing Power of Money*." He goes on to report evidence on Keynes's enthusiasm for Hawtrey's work at that period. Reading much of Hawtrey (1913, 1919, 1923, 1927 and 1932) one sees, depending on your view, much repetition or an enduring consistency.

17. See the books referenced at the point in the text of Footnote 1, at the start of this chapter.

18. Labordere's essay is attached as an appendix to the reprint in 1948 of Robertson's 1915 *A Study of Industrial Fluctuations*, according to Robertson's wishes. Robertson recounts that it was passed on to him by Keynes, who later introduced the two men. A series of amusing letters between Keynes and the (colorful and eccentric) Labordere can be found in his King's College Keynes Papers. Presley (1979) is the standard account of Robertson's economics. He makes a case for Robertson as a virtual coauthor of much of Keynes's work in the 1920s period. The fact that they worked closely together is undisputed, as is the fact that they parted ways over the *General Theory*. The other early influence on Robertson was Pigou.

19. Only on p. 206 of a 250 page book do we finally see "the wage and money systems" appear. On p. 211 can be found the following: "The influence of a money, especially of a credit money, economy upon the course of trade is of such obvious importance that it has more or less completely hypnotized all but a very few of those who have contributed to the discussion of the problem. The fact that our long, complicated and perhaps not unfruitful discussion has been conducted so far almost entirely without reference to specifically monetary phenomena relieves us of the necessity of a formal refutation of those who, like Clement Juglar and Mr. Hawtrey, find in monetary influences the sole and sufficient explanation of industrial fluctuation." His further discussion of inflexible wages in this section, is perfectly in keeping with what we saw as the orthodox view of sticky-wage-unemployment in Part I, and in our discussion of Marshall's cycle theory.

20. Who as we saw above was rapidly increasing his own first-hand and theoretical knowledge of monetary phenomena in the 1920s.

21. This book introduced a plethora of such new and unfortunate terminologies. For instance besides "lacking," it defines saving in multiple modes – in its "spontaneous," "automatic," and "induced" varieties. There are also complementary varieties of "stinting," "hoarding," and "splashing." Moreover there are negatives – as in "dis-lacking" – to contend with. As Laidler (1999, p. 95) gently puts it "it was fortunate that Robertson (1928) was soon to set out his basic results in more accessible terms." One wonders how much fun Lewis Carroll, Robertson's favorite aphorist, would have had with Robertson's own 1926 book.

22. As Laidler also shows was contained in Robertson's testimony to the Macmillan Commission (Robertson, 1931).
23. See Robertson (1926 [1949], pp. x, 5).
24. That Robertson's sequence of balance sheets is a useful way to look at bank lending we can see from any modern money and banking text. That it is useful more generally for macroeconomics, in pinpointing exactly what various assumptions about fiscal and monetary policy changes mean for lending and real-balance holdings between the stages of a multiplier analysis, see Cottrell (1986).

12 Keynes's development as a Cambridge monetary theorist

1. Recall, however, that the position that Keynes spent much of his time in the early twenties on journalism and on making money was not original with us, but is also the view of Keynes's most meticulous biographer, Skidelsky (1992).
2. Readers interested in the details of this material can consult Laidler (1991, Chapter 2) for a concise discussion.
3. An overall impression of these early lectures can be seen in the titles and dates for all of Keynes's courses contained in a table constructed by Moggridge (*CW* 12, p. 689).
4. Included in this supply treatment is an interesting digression on the history, geography and geology of gold mining (pp. 741–6).
5. As we hypothesized in Chapter 9, note 7, he more likely was given this work by Mary Paley Marshall when preparing his biographical essay after Marshall's death in 1924.
6. This status is usually attributed to his *Tract on Monetary Reform*.
7. This would make some sense of Keynes's *obiter dicta*, looking back after the *General Theory* (*CW* 14, pp. 202–3) where he says: "I regard Mr. Hawtrey as my grandparent and Mr. Robertson as my parent in the paths of errancy, and I have been greatly influenced by them . . . As it is, so far as I am concerned, I find looking back, that it was Professor Irving Fisher who was the great-grandparent who first influenced me strongly toward regarding money as a 'real' factor."
8. Authorities differ on the degree to which various ideas originated with Keynes or Robertson and which, if either, dominated the collaboration. Presley (1979) marks one extreme of this spectrum, which sees them as virtual co-authors of everything they both wrote in the period 1920–30. A much more nuanced argument is found in Bridel (1987, Chapter 6) where their ultimate parting of the ways, theoretically speaking, is also discussed in detail. Laidler (1999, Chapter 4) stresses the degree to which Robertson grew into a monetary complement to his real theory in the twenties, at least partly under Keynes's influence, and coalescing of his views with the writings of Marshall, Pigou, Hawtrey and the earlier Keynes, under a type of Cambridge orthodoxy, particularly as enunciated by Pigou (1927a, 1929). In all of these valid viewpoints there are imbedded our main points. First, whoever influenced the other, Keynes only briefly flirted with a "forced savings" style explanation of the cycle. Second, Keynes and Robertson, at the latest, grew apart with the publication of *A Treatise on Money* (1930) and made a decisive break over the *General Theory*. Thus Robertson's influence on the form of the *General Theory* was insignificant. Except as deep background, that is, as providing an example of what Keynes called "neoclassical" interest-rate theorists, those he characterized as persisting in modeling the savings–investment process as being unequal and out of equilibrium (see Lawlor 1997a).

9. This last detail sounds like a reference to Hawtrey.
10. Perhaps this is an early instance of Keynes's sloppiness with attribution, or perhaps it is evidence of what would ultimately prove to be a greater influence in the direction Keynes-to-Robertson, than Robertson-to-Keynes. Could that be what Robertson refers to in his remark on this paper by Keynes (Robertson, 1915 [1948], p. 171, n. 2) when he says: "To this paper I am much indebted, though Mr. Keynes is I believe good enough to acknowledge a reciprocal obligation"? Against this there is also Austin Robinson's opinion of the very high regard in which Keynes held Robertson's opinion (Patinkin and Leith, 1978, pp. 31–2.).
11. This may imply that Keynes at this stage did not fully understand creation of credit by banks and the money multiplier. Robertson (1928b) and Robertson's Cambridge handbook *Money* (1928) later provided a complete discussion of that process, implying it was known in Cambridge by at least the twenties.
12. One fascinating aspect of this argument is the resemblance it bears to Keynes's post-*General Theory* "finance" motive for the demand for money (Keynes 1937a,b, 1938). Consider how familiar the following quote sounds when viewed from the standpoint of this early 1913 paper: "This means that, in general, the banks hold the key position in the transition from a lower to a higher scale of activity" (Keynes 1937b, p. 222) Besides the intervening development of a liquidity view of the banks' role in determining the rate of interest, the crucial difference, of course, is that this transition is seen as necessarily temporary in 1913, but could be more or less permanent in Keynes's view of 1936.
13. In terms of rendering monetary policy ineffective, this is the same argument as the "liquidity trap." This is consistent with the argument that nothing new was likely to be sought by Keynes in defining this relationship in 1936.
14. See for example Patinkin (1976, pp. 26–8); or more recently, Laidler (1999, pp. 106–12).
15. It is a method much like Irving Fisher's use of the equation of exchange.
16. An even earlier form of this argument could be seen in Keynes's *Economic Consequence of the Peace*.
17. And indeed is still the basis of mainstream microeconomics.
18. The parallel metaphysics in Keynes would be those "forces" involved in the knowledge content of forecasts and of economically meaningful psychological propensities.
19. "Nevertheless it is easy at all times, as a result of the way we use money in daily life, to forget all this and to look on money as itself the absolute standard of value; and when, besides, the actual events of a hundred years have not disturbed his illusions, the average man regards what has been normal for three generations as a part of the permanent social fabric" (*CW* 4, p. 10).
20. I am aware that many economists today would point to this fact as an endogenous response of investment in mines to the price of gold. I do not however think that either the facts of mining or price changes completely bear this out, both activities being much more random and their successful co-occurrences more coincidental phenomena than such a simple explanation will submit to.
21. The complication to this statement is that, for traders, double-entry bookkeeping allows the marrying of different clients' supplies and demands so that no funds need move in either direction. Thus Keynes claims that the forward market will be most sensitive and fluctuating "according as buyers or sellers predominate" (p. 106). This looks forward to the liquidity preference theory of the *Treatise on Money* and the *General Theory* where it is emphasized that even drastic fluctuations

in bond prices and interest rates need not necessitate much trading of stocks of monetary assets if opinions are all on one side.

22. As I said in the last chapter, one is not sure how much of this obscurity was Wicksell's and how much was due to Keynes's limited German. At any rate, we will see that there is not a lot of Wicksell in the *Treatise*. See Keynes's Footnote #2 (*CW* 5, p. 178) where he admits, "In German I can only clearly understand what I know already."

23. Surely output adjustments are considered there by Keynes. But the amount, motivation and resulting expenditure changes that this adjustment involves, are not clearly defined and unemployment ends up, as we have seen was usual for his time, as a deviation from the natural full-employment equilibrium path over the cycle.

24. Today, it is the second volume that reads the best. This is for two reasons. One is that Keynes is there unencumbered by the need to discuss a theoretical model, and so the brilliance of his prose style and the inherent interest of the historical material shines through clearly. Also, a modern economist is not as tempted, as he naturally is in the first volume, to interpret Keynes through the prism of the *General Theory*, by which standard the *Treatise* model suffers in comparison.

25. An earlier stage of economics as Keynes saw it. Later, after much of this monetary detail failed to survive the "Keynesian Revolution," the re-appearance, in the form of "monetarism," of what for him would have been the familiar old simplistic quantity theory, seemed novel.

26. As we saw earlier, the young Keynes was making the same point in regard to the equation of exchange in his lectures prior to World War I.

27. He also enjoyed ridiculing the Victorian assumption that savings was by definition a moral act. As Skidelsky (1992, p. 447) puts it, "Keynes's delight in this analogy was not lessened by the Biblical authority he could invoke on behalf of 'riotous living.'"

28. Hawtrey provided Keynes with extensive comments, which were eventually published, on the cycle theory of the *Treatise*. His understanding of expenditure levels, which we have seen were always part of his theory, led him to stress (correctly) that Keynes was neglecting them in the *Treatise* disequilibrium analysis. He thus was influential in pushing Keynes to consider defining short-period equilibrium. Yet he persisted in considering these states – which on his own account were continuously occurring in a monetary economy – as anything other than temporary disturbances to Marshall's, evidently unaffected, long-period positions. Skidelsky (1992, pp. 444–6) is particularly clear on this.

13   Sraffa and Hayek on "Own Rates of Interest"

1. This chapter contains a substantially revised version of Lawlor and Horn (1992). Permission to quote from the original provided by Taylor and Francis Publishers.

2. Hicks's claim has been partially borne out by the literature. His comment just preceded an avalanche of scholarship on Hayek's early work in economics that has attempted to rehabilitate Hayek as an economic theorist. In no small part, this revival of interest is evidenced (and has been aided) by the emergence of a loyal group of self-proclaimed "Austrian" followers of Hayek and things Hayekian. It is important to note, however, that the essay from which this passage is quoted is in fact an attempt to explain the fatal flaw that Hicks saw as the source of the eventual abandonment of Hayek's program in those years of high theory. (See, Hicks, 1967, p. ix, 203–5).

3. For two ends of this spectrum see Caldwell (1986, 1995, 2003) and Hoover (2003).
4. We will quote from the now generally used second edition of *Prices and Production* first published in 1935. Sraffa's review, of course, was of the original 1931 edition. But a side-by-side perusal of these two editions reveals no substantive change beyond the addition of a few extra footnotes. It would seem that Hayek did not find Sraffa's criticism convincing enough to change his argument when the opportunity arose; although see Hayek (1941, p. 35, n. 1) in this context.
5. "Hayek constructed his monetary theory upon the foundations laid by early British monetary theorists and Knut Wicksell and Ludwig von Mises" (O'Driscoll, 1977, p. 37).
6. It is interesting that this is the one aspect of Hayek's work that Sraffa completely agrees with in principle. "Its one definite contribution is the emphasis it puts on the study of the effects of monetary changes on the relative prices of commodities, rather than on the general price level on which attention has almost exclusively been focused by the old quantity theory" (Sraffa 1932a, p.42). Hence one supposes the *Treatise* was also unsatisfactory in this way for Sraffa. In fact, if anything it seems that Sraffa applied his infamous critical facilities uniformly to almost any person or work he came up against. (As an example of this see the comment by Joan Robinson to Keynes (*CW* 13, p. 378).
7. J. R. Hicks was one of the young economists at the London School of Economics when Hayek arrived. Commenting on the comparison of Keynes of the *Treatise* and Hayek, a comparison which formed the burning question of the day, Hicks also refers to the greater abstraction of Hayek's argument. "The pattern of Hayek's thought, at a first impression, looked more coherent. The obstacle which confronted one on his side was his Bohm-Bawerkian model; an analytical framework that had become familiar, even orthodox, in some continental countries, but was unfamiliar in England." Hicks also notes that the unfamiliarity of the analysis led to many attempts at "translation" into more familiar language. "But what emerged, when we tried to put the Hayek theory into our own words, was not Hayek. *There was some inner mystery to which we failed to penetrate*" (Hicks, 1967, pp. 204–5, emphasis added).
8. There is a case to be made that this is Sraffa's basic mode of analysis – it is something very similar to both Marx's method of dialectical critique, and to the "immanent" criticism carried on by the Swedes. Another instance where Sraffa employs this method is his famous critique of the Marshallian supply curve. It is also perhaps this method of analysis that was at the heart of Sraffa's influence on Wittgenstein (Coates, 1996).
9. The problems concern the following issues:

    (1) Hayek's definitions of income, net income and savings.
    (2) His neglect of the issue recently dubbed "the time to build" (Kydland and Prescott, 1985). This issue, also similar to Robertson's concern with the "lumpiness of capital," revolves around determining the effect of forced saving on capital accumulation by analyzing whether the monetary expansion lasts long enough to complete a project and have it start "earning its keep." Time to build is particularly important in discussing the "permanence" and "destruction" of capital. Cottrell (1994) offers excellent insight into this issue in Hayek's theory of the cycle, emphasizing the importance of time lags in the production process.
    (3) Hayek's view that it is the barter-like natural state that would give full expression to the "the voluntary decisions of individuals."

(4) A cavalier treatment of the relationship between the velocity of circulation and changes in the supply of money. This is certainly something Keynes's *Treatise* made much of.

(5) The most obvious objection when viewed from the post-*General Theory* vantage point, that Hayek's argument assumes full employment throughout.

10. Notice here the issue of the relation of the distribution of income to monetary changes is very much in evidence. It was a continual theme of Keynes's work we have seen in the last chapter. Thus there is a strong element of a "widow's cruse" type of issue present in this passage. It also appears to grope toward the notion of consumption and savings functions. That perhaps is evidence of Sraffa's participation in the "Cambridge Circus" discussing Keynes's *Treatise* at this point. But Sraffa's early work and dissertation had also been on the distributive effects of inflation, so it would not have been a theme unfamiliar to him. Additionally, Sraffa had been the translator of the Italian edition of Keynes's *Tract on Monetary Reform*, where this issue was paramount.

11. Our comment in the preceding footnote about Sraffa's detailed knowledge of Keynes's *Tract*, which as we saw contains a detailed "theory of the forward market," should not be forgotten here.

12. I have offered some verbal examples and discussion of such changes in Lawlor (1997a). See also Kurz, (2000, pp. 288–98) for an insightful discussion of this issue.

13. The notion that Hayek and Sraffa were debating on the unstated basis of different types of equilibrium is untenable. See Lawlor and Horn (1992, pp. 325–30. especially notes 9 and 10) for a refutation of this. See also Kurz (2000, p. 290–3).

14. Bliss (1975, 1987) and Hahn (1982) contain discussions of the issues of interest rates and equal rates of return within the framework of Walrasian intertemporal equilibrium. A criticism of Keynes Chapter 17 analysis, which seems to me to miss Keynes's whole point by conducting its critique within the intertemporal equilibrium construct, is presented in Barens and Caspari (1997).

15. I am consciously avoiding the terms "supply and demand" here because that term is so conceptually rife with assumptions about its theoretical form and function – for example, whether the classicals held a utility theory, how and why such an analysis was introduced and so on. It matters little for the general characterization of market and natural states of equilibrium. Notice, though, that the "psychic analysis" of expectations, uncertainty and of the motives to liquidity, must assume some sort of "psychological" theory to define the demand for assets in Keynes's analysis. This may explain Sraffa's evident uneasiness with Keynes's *liquidity preference* asset market theory and the – I think wrong – assertion by later day Sraffians that such views are not "fundamental" and so inappropriate to a long-period setting. Perhaps they are not appropriate to the almost strictly materialist long-period setting envisioned by Sraffa. But if a monetary economy is one where such forces as expectations and liquidity preference are manifestly "fundamental" to changes in output and employment, then the equilibrium they eventuate in must be appropriate to the study of such economies and changes. On the "long-period" view of Sraffa on money see Panico (1988, 2001). On the role of the Sraffa-Hayek exchange for *Walrasian* monetary theory see Desai (1982).

16. By a stable distribution of rates of return, I mean to refer to the path-breaking work of Emmanuel Farjoun and Moshe Machover (1983), on a probabilistic interpretation of economic order. My point is not that I think anything like their work was suggested by Keynes in the *General Theory*, but to show the wide range of

opinion about the basic structure of economic theories that all feel it necessary to somehow deal with notion of rates of return converging.

17. Whether the necessary means of keeping an economy operating at close to full employment could inhibit savings habits, and if this would lead to slower economic growth, was not an issue that Keynes explored. The United States may be empirically experimenting with this issue as its household savings rate falls to zero, if it can stay at full-employment for long. But even here we discount the enormous influence of retained earnings by corporations in financing non-housing business investment in the U.S. in the post-war era. Also the now more freely adjustable international capital flows available to fund one country's lack of savings, means that the rest of the world might fund any one country's investment from world savings. What would happen to standards of living if – a far fetched "if" – the entire world was operating at full employment, is a question that has hardly been explored. Perhaps then, Keynes's point of view would no longer be relevant and the classical scheme would come into its own. But then there would still remain the issue of the relative contribution to growth of technology and savings. If technology, as seems possible, is determined to be the major driver of standards of living, then Keynes's *Treatise* point would still be applicable: "Thus the rate at which the world's wealth has accumulated has been far more variable than the habits of thrift have been. Indeed, it is not certain that the average individual has been of a much more saving disposition during the sixteenth and seventeenth centuries, when the foundations of the modern world were being laid, than in the Middle Ages . . ." (*CW* 6, p. 133).

14 Keynes: "The Essential Properties of Interest and Money"

1. We have shown in Part I of this work that the history of New-Keynesian ideas more accurately relates them to a pre-*General Theory* stage of thought. By virtue of this, a better historical grounding, for which the term seems to be aiming, would be provided by a name such as "New-Pigovian."

2. We have analyzed their message in Chapter 8. I have attempted to synthesize these post-*General Theory* articles in Lawlor (1997a).

3. Given our analysis of the Cambridge monetary theorists above, along with our discussion in the last section of Chapter 13 of Keynes's position of the essentially barter-like quality of much of traditional monetary economics, and finally in accord with the quotation that heads this chapter and the one over this section, we would substitute the term "real-exchange" economics for Leijonhufvud's "Wicksell Connection." But Leijonhufvud's term is designed to invoke a "back to Wicksell" movement, and as such is probably more appropriate to his purposes.

4. In fact, many interpreters of Keynes's *General Theory*, both hostile and sympathetic, have found the argument of Chapter 17 to be not only highly abstract – *but unintelligible*. For instance, the man generally credited with "bringing Keynes to America," Alvin Hansen, had this to say in his famous *Guide to Keynes* (Hansen, 1953, p. 159):

> Chapter 17, on the properties of interest and money, ties in with the subject matter of money and liquidity preference . . . But the topic is elevated to a very abstract plane. Immediately after the appearance of the *General Theory* there was a certain fascination about Chap. 17, due partly no doubt to its obscurity. Digging in this area, however, soon ceased after it was found that the chapter

contained no gold mines . . . in general, not much would have been lost had it never been written.

With expositors like this, it is no wonder Keynes's monetary views suffered such eclipse. This attitude carried over to Hansen's most famous student, P. A. Samuelson, who also must be credited with a large part of the "Keynesian" version of Keynes. In an evaluation of Keynes as an economist (Samuelson, 1947) in which Samuelson relegates the own-rates theory to the category of "Mares' nests or confusions" (p. 149), and in which he explains why "liquidity preference . . . cannot be of crucial significance," he draws the following remarkable conclusion about Keynes as an economic theorist:

> . . . Keynes seems never to have had any genuine interest in the theory of value and distribution. It is remarkable that so active a brain would have failed to make any contribution to economic theory. (p. 155)

One supposes this view of Keynes's contribution, obviously erroneous on the evidence displayed throughout this book of his long interest in these matters, goes a long way toward explaining the easy cooptation of "Keynesianism" by neoclassical theory.

Turning to hostile reviews, one that takes a particularly venomous line on Chapter 17 is H. Hazlitt's (1959) "The Failure of the 'New Economics.'" Hazlitt's volume has much to recommend itself as a curative to anyone considering putting a vituperative attack into print. It reserved a large quota of its venom (and exclamation points!) for Chapter 17:

> Chapter 17 of the *General Theory*, "The Essential Properties of Interest and Money," is dull, implausible, and full of obscurities, non sequiturs, and other fallacies (p. 236).

5. "User Cost" was important to Keynes's re-thinking of Marshallian value theory during the composition of the *General Theory*. He developed it in the context of rethinking how his now "expectational" sense of "income" would be appropriately linked to the short-period decisions by entrepreneurs to offer employment. See the discussion in the *General Theory*, Chapter 6 and its appendix, devoted to this topic.

6. An interesting intermediate case, not treated by Keynes, falls somewhere between secondhand markets for individual capital goods and full-blown commodity trading: this is the stock exchange. Stock markets trade the right to the expected future receipts from using (or not) such capital. Keynes felt there were forces in such markets that often caused them to price these expectations, not on long-term enterprise, but on short-term speculative grounds. This meant that stock prices might be dominated by the price that average opinion expects these rights to trade at. "And there are some, I believe, who practice the fourth, fifth and higher degrees" (*GT*, p. 156). In pre-*General Theory* correspondence with Ralph Hawtrey, Keynes rejected Hawtrey's criticism that the *General Theory* and the own-rates analysis did not sufficiently distinguish between trading in shares of enterprises that use capital and the capital goods themselves. Keynes replied: "A good deal of your criticism is based upon alleged ambiguity as to whether I mean marginal efficiency to apply to instruments or enterprises. My intention is to apply to both indifferently. I do not see that, at the level of abstraction in which I am writing any different treatment is required" (*CW* 13, p. 629). It must be said that this has continued to be a problem for interpreters of the *General Theory*, and more generally for economists concerned with the links between the level of the interest rates, firm share

prices and new investment flows. But it is not apparent that modern finance or macro-economics has made much of an advance over Keynes in this respect.

7. See Keynes's discussion in (*GT*, Chapter 13, especially p. 167, n. 1 and n. 2).

8. Modern macroeconomics most commonly represents this by the necessary inverse relationship of the market rate of interest and bond prices, where bonds are traded on a secondhand market. We will follow this modern taste when we adapt Keynes's theory to discuss the traditional macro-model in Chapter 15.

9. Any asset could perform this function of a common unit of account, but there are special reasons, we shall see, for choosing to express all own rates in money terms.

10. For which the future price is a datum of the market, although the "*a*" term of any individual trader may differ from this. In fact for there to exist bulls and bears at the same time, the actual backwardation or contango must just balance trading between members of these camps in such a way that the marginal trade reflects the expectations of a marginal member of each camp.

11. The reader is urged to consult the original (*CW* 6, Chapter 29) for the details, some of the historical examples of which were drawn from a number of memoranda that Keynes had regularly produced (*CW* 12, pp. 253–659) throughout the twenties. Significantly we saw in Part II how much he was personally involved in such speculation himself in this period.

12. Colin Rogers (1994, 1997) criticizes me for not nearly escaping enough, or as much as I could do, from the traditional notions of equilibria in a previous analysis of Keynes's own-rates theory. He is correct if I have left the impression, as I think here I have not, that Keynes's monetary theory in 1936 fits well into either the long-period or the short-period analyses that preceded him – for instance of the kind that Marshall envisioned. Neither, I am arguing, does it fit into the Walrasian scheme. I hope I am clear that the term "long-period" does not seem to capture what Keynes is after either. Keynes was proposing a monetary theory that starts from the conventional basis of asset valuation. For me, "shifting equilibria" captures his message best. Moreover, it does so without re-casting old terminologies, and retaining with them unfortunate connotations of older analytical schemes. This seems clear in comparing Sraffa's (long-period) use of own-rates with Keynes's monetary conception of them. Other than over this issue of terminology, I agree in substance with Rogers's writings on Keynes.

13. Discussed in detail in Part II, and especially in Chapter 10.

14. We discussed in Chapter 12 the role of Keynes's intricate analysis of the circulatory route of cash in different uses in the economy as it was laid out in the *Treatise* (1930, Book 1, Chapter 3). Although it is suppressed in the *General Theory*, this analysis is essential to a complete understanding of liquidity preference theory. See Shackle (1967, ch. 15) for an insightful blending of the two strands of the theory of cash balances.

15. In the context of a demand for money function, Tobin (1958, pp. 65–86), shows that there is a further distinction to be made over a definite expectation of a changed future rate (that is held with "certainty") versus a situation of no certain expectation of a change, but a general subjective "uncertainty" over its future value. He is able to show that both situations can lead to a typically shaped liquidity preference function. I am grateful to Allin Cottrell for this point, whose analysis (Cottrell, 1993) of this work of Tobin in light of Keynes's own theory of probability is very enlightening.

16. Book IV of the *General Theory*, titled "The Inducement to Investment," includes the following chapters (in order): "The Marginal Efficiency of Capital, The State of Long-Term Expectations, The General Theory of the Rate of Interest, The

Classical Theory of the Rate of Interest, The Psychological and Business Incentives to Liquidity, Sundry Observations on the Nature of Capital, The Essential Properties of Interest and Money, and, The General Theory of Employment Restated." The implication is that investment is explained by the interaction of money, capital and interest, all bound together in an expectational framework. We are arguing that Chapter 17 provides just such a framework.

17. This intricate fusion of capital theory and monetary theory is the core of Shackle's (1967, Chapter 11) unique blending of Keynes's views on money and uncertainty in the *General Theory* with his crucial restatement in "The General Theory of Employment" (1937c). Shackle makes no use of the own-rates paradigm, but I think our discussion to this point might clarify his argument for some readers. For instance, the following eloquent passage nicely complements our view with that grace of expression that was G. L. S. Shackle's hallmark:

> Writers on Keynes's theory of investment incentive give all their attention to the concepts of the marginal efficiency of capital and the interaction of a quantity so named with the interest-rate on loans of money. To do so is to study the formal configuration of the engine without asking about its thermal source of power. The marginal efficiency of capital is nothing but a formal sum waiting for the insertion of numerical values in place of its algebraic symbols. The essential problem of why at any time the investment flow has the size it has is contained in the question what is the source of these numerical values, by which psychic alchemy is the list of incongruous ingredients chosen and fused into an answer to the unanswerable. Keynes's whole theory of unemployment is ultimately the simple statement that, rational expectation being unattainable, we substitute for it first one and then another kind of irrational expectation: and the shift from one arbitrary basis to another gives us from time to time a moment of truth, when our artificial confidence is for the time being dissolved, and we, as businessmen, are afraid to invest, and so fail to provide enough demand to match our society's desire to produce. Keynes in the *General Theory* attempted a rational theory of a field of conduct, which by the nature of its terms, could only be semi-rational. But sober economists gravely upholding a faith in the calculability of human affairs could not bring themselves to acknowledge that this could be his purpose. They sought to interpret the *General Theory* as just one more manual of political arithmetic. In so far as it failed this test, they found it wrong, or obscure, or perverse. The same fate had overtaken his *Treatise on Probability*. (G. L. S. Shackle, 1967, p. 129)

18. It will be immediately clear from this that Keynes's whole argument about the importance of the money rate of interest in determining investment flows depends on the assumption that the own-rate on capital goods, or the marginal efficiency of capital will eventually *decline* as production increases during an expansion of activity. The question arises in this context (see, for instance, Eatwell, 1983 and Eatwell and Milgate, 1983): is the own-rates analysis as Keynes uses it subject to the capital critique? Would the well-known possibility of capital reswitching and reversal undercut Keynes's argument just as they have the typical neoclassical parables about "productive" capital accumulation?

I do not think so for a number of reasons. One is that Keynes's rankings of the capital assets that make up the MEC schedule are more along the lines of Ricardo's extensive margin of production than the inverse productivity relations of the neoclassical marginal product of capital. Second, Keynes makes it clear in statements like the following that he was fully aware of the pitfalls of trying to define aggregate notions of value capital:

> There is, to begin with, the ambiguity whether we are concerned with the increment of physical product per unit of time due to the employment of one more physical unity of capital, or with the increment of value due to the employment of one more value unit of capital. The former involves difficulties as to the definition of the physical unit of capital, which I believe to be both insoluble and unnecessary. (*GT*, p. 138)

His alternative to productivity theory was to fall back on the notion of "scarcity" of capital as the fundamental reason that the produced means of production can earn a rate of return over cost. Additionally it should be emphasized that Keynes's emphasis on expectations meant that he viewed the major shift between periods of high and low output and employment as associated with changes in the conventional basis of the MEC (see *GT*, p. 145). Thus his discussion of "long-period" expectations in Chapter 12 was aimed at explaining how precarious such a convention could be. For more elaboration on the status of Keynes's investment demand theory see Eisner (1997) and Pasinetti (1974, 1997).

19. In fact, Irving Fisher found an actual example of the effect on interest rates of uncertainty – not just over the stability of the monetary unit, but over its *existence*. He analyzes an example in his *Rate of Interest* (1907, pp. 258–261) where two types of U.S. bonds existed simultaneously that were payable in gold and paper notes, respectively. The variations in the spread between the two over the years 1870 to 1896 are attributed by Fisher to the changing expectations of the future form of the standard of payment caused by the then active public debate over the various proposals of the "money doctors."

20. The extension to a monetary economy of this quality of the liquidity premium to a short period theory of value – that of a monetary economy – was first broached by Hugh Townshend (1937), whose work is discussed below in Chapter 14, section IX. J. A. Kregel (1973, 1983, 1997) and Colin Rogers and T. K. Rymes (1997) build on Townshend's early insight. Rymes and Rogers argue persuasively that Keynes's analysis call for a new "monetary theory of value and modern banking." I have learned greatly from reading these papers. I view what I am saying in this chapter to be in fundamental agreement with these authors' work.

21. Keynes seems to have thought that most of the adjustment in the "*a*" terms would be accomplished by movements in the present spot prices. See the discussion in Chapter 17 (*GT*, p. 228) for an example in the context of the equilibrium of own rates. In a protracted pre-publication correspondence with R. C. Hawtrey, Keynes defended his own-rate theory as valid in the face of excess stocks of liquid commodities, against Hawtrey's criticism (on both theoretical and practical grounds as we argue in the text). In the process, he makes the same point about the adjustment factor "normally" being the spot price (*CW* 13, p. 629).

22. In Keynes's collected works (*CW* 29, p. 235), Townshend is identified as follows: "Another discussant was Hugh Townshend (1890–1974), who, after taking a first in mathematics in Cambridge in 1912, had been a pupil of Keynes while preparing for Civil Service examinations in 1914. He had then entered the Post Office." Besides the note referred to in the text and a few scattered reviews in the *Economic Journal* in the late thirties, the only other work of his I have found is a co-authored book (Curtis and Townshend, 1938). This book is interesting in that it is an attempt to provide a layman's guide to the workings of a "monetary economy" via

the views of two authors who "belong to the school of thought associated with the name of J. M. Keynes" (p. vi). That this self-identification is not idle (at least for Townshend) is attested to by Keynes's surviving correspondence with Townshend in which he credits him with even *more* than a complete understanding of his theory. For example, consider the following fragments from Keynes's letters to Townshend (*CW* 29, pp. 235–47 and 255–59):

> "It is evident that you have a perfect comprehension of the matter: and indeed it may prove to be the case that, whilst the book is chiefly meant for my academic friends, it may sometimes get easier reception from those outside academic circles, whose ideas are not so crystallized." (*CW* 29, p. 238)
>
> "Once more you have shown a complete comprehension of what I am driving at, and I am very grateful." (*CW* 29, p. 239)
>
> "Once again I have to thank you for an acute and understanding criticism, with the whole of which, I may say, I agree." (*CW* 29, p. 245)
>
> "Criticisms like yours are mainly useful in helping me to get more fully emancipated from what one has emerged out of." (*CW* 29, p. 247)

This last fragment reinforces the view of Shackle – who we must presume had not seen Keynes's comments quoted here when he wrote in 1967 as these papers were not found in the famous "Tilton hamper" until later – that Towshend saw earlier and deeper than most writers into the depths of the departure from orthodoxy that Keynes's views on money and interest represent:

> "Townshend's brilliant paper, although thirteen pages long, appeared only under *Notes and Memoranda*. It leapt too far ahead for the mass of Keynes's critics, still tapping the wheels of his theory to see whether it would clank decently round like the sort of thing they were used to, and Townshend attracted no attention." (Shackle, 1967, p. 228)

23. Moreover, it would seem to follow that there can be no such thing as long-period dynamic economic theory, failing the (most unlikely) discovery of a plausible long-term convention of price-stability. It is perhaps now being generally realized that such long-term dynamic theories as these are considered implausible ones. It is not unnatural that those who forecast the future in algebra or geometry should be chastened by hard fact more slowly than those who have to forecast it in arithmetic. Nor is the conclusion that the search for laws to enable us to predict economic events far ahead, like eclipses, must be given up, so surprising – not to say nihilistic – as it may seem (to some economists) at first sight. For in the past, in long periods prices have in fact moved all over the place. The inference that there is no reason to believe in the probable indefinite recurrence of a *regular* cycle of price-fluctuations is less generally accepted, but seems to follow from Mr. Keynes' conclusions. (Townshend, 1937, p. 166)

24. There is an interesting parallel between Keynes's discussion of a liquidity standard in a non-monetary economy and Menger's (1871, Chapter 8) hypothetical-historical account of the origin of a medium of exchange. Both revolve around the concept of "marketability." I think a comparison of them would show strong complementarities between the discussions. Menger explains the process and reasons for the evolution of a generally accepted means of payment. Keynes shows that this spontaneously evolved social institution has important externality effects – even in the most primitive monetary systems.

25. "The liquidity premium, it will be observed, is partly similar to the risk-premium, but partly different; the difference corresponding to the difference between the best estimates we can make of probabilities and the confidence with which we can make them" (*GT*, p. 240).

15 "Natural Rate" mutations: Keynes, Leijonhufvud and the Wicksell connection

1. This is a slightly revised version of Cottrell and Lawlor, 1991. Permission to quote from the original provided by Duke University Press.
2. Leijonhufvud provides a "family tree" of major twentieth-century macroeconomists to illustrate this point (1981, p. 133). Although all emanate from the quantity-theory tradition originally, two parallel lines of descent are traced. The first is strict monetarism that evolves through Fisher (1898) and Friedman. The other descends from Wicksell and branches into the various mutations associated with the Austrian, Swedish, and Cambridge schools.
3. "[T]he LP hypothesis should have been rejected from the start; and . . . failing this, propositions derivative from it ought systematically, if belatedly, to be rooted out of macroeconomics" (Leijonhufvud, 1981, pp. 134–35). Leijonhufvud contends that a theory interpolated between the *Treatise* and the *General Theory*, a genetic sport he labels the Z-theory and identifies as "the *Treatise* plus quantity adjustments," is the contribution of Keynes that should be "preserved and developed." Z-theory is further discussed in Chapter 15, Section V.
4. In interpreting Keynes's monetary analysis it is once again important to remind the reader of his complex and important views on bank deposits and monetary circulation as developed in the *Treatise* (*CW* 5, Chapter 11). For discussions of the relevance of these views to the *General Theory* see Shackle (1967, Chapter 11), and Miller (1984). For present purposes it is sufficient to distinguish between "active balances" which circulate as income deposits in the traditional quantity theory sense, and "idle balances" which represent the financial deposits of money as an asset.
5. For the geometrically inclined, Figure 1 displays the argument discussed in the text. The fall in MEC is represented by the fall in the investment demand schedule from I to I'. The "desired result" is a fall in interest to r_2, but speculation against such a fall may hold the interest rate at r_1. In Wicksell and in Keynes's *Treatise* this situation can persist only so long as bankers or speculators are bridging the horizontal gap between I' and the saving function $S(y)$, at r_1; in Z-theory this gap disappears when aggregate income falls to y' and the saving function shifts to $S(y')$.
6. Conard (1959, Chapter 10) provides a complete algebraic derivation of the a terms, showing that Keynes's presentation is an approximation to the exact result.
7. We choose a zero-coupon bond for simplicity. The inclusion of a coupon payment would complicate the analysis without changing its substance.
8. Consider how closely this accords with the following passage from R. F. Kahn, a man well-placed to possess insight on Keynes's outlook on such matters: "the total wealth of the community (together with the National Debt) is represented by the total amounts of securities in existence and by physical assets held directly. Part of the securities are held by the banks themselves; part of the securities held by the public is financed by the banks; and banks finance the holding of physical assets by businesses, thus reducing the supply of securities. The extent to which the banks hold securities, finance the holders of securities, and finance the

holding of physical assets, is equal to the quantity of money. The quantity of money is the means by which the public hold that part of their wealth which is looked after by the banking system. The prices of securities are such as to secure a home for all of them with the public, apart from what the banking system looks after itself. *That is the essence of the Keynes's liquidity preference theory of the rate of interest,* the supply and demand for money being the obverse of the supply of securities in the hands of the public and the demand for securities by the public" (1954, pp. 237–38, emphasis ours).

9. Compare Harry Johnson's account of the matter: "The use of a loanable funds approach does not necessarily carry with it the belief that real forces determine the supply of and demand for loanable funds; nor does the use of a liquidity preference approach necessarily carry with it the opposite belief . . . [T]he relative importance of productivity and thrift in determining the rate of interest is a different question entirely from the emphasis to be placed on stocks as compared with flows; both issues, of course, are questions of fact or judgment" (1951, p. 93). As will be apparent, we end up closer to Johnson's view.

10. George Horwich (1964, p. 416), who produced one of the most detailed studies of the stock-flow problem in monetary economics, claims that this notion originates in Volume 1 of the *Treatise on Money*. As this aspect of the *Treatise* carries over to the *General Theory*'s discussion of the interest-rate mechanism, a fairly extensive quote (drawn from Horwich's discussion) is appropriate: "But the volume of trading in financial instruments, i.e., the *activity* of financial business, is not only highly variable but has no close connection with the volume of output whether of capital-goods or of consumption-goods; for the current output of fixed capital is small compared with the existing stock of wealth, which in the present context we will call the volume of *securities* (excluding liquid claims on cash); and the activity with which these securities are being passed around from hand to hand does not depend on the rate at which they are being added to. Thus in a modern Stock-Exchange-equipped community the turnover of currently produced fixed capital is quite a small proportion of the total turnover of securities" (*CW* 5, pp. 248–9).

11. Leijonhufvud adverts to this comparison himself (1981, p. 141).

12. From this point of view Leijonhufvud's argument might be seen as applying more naturally not to the case of a fall in the MEC, but to a pre-announced change in fiscal policy. He might be on stronger ground if he were to argue, against the standard Keynesian position, that a well-understood cut in government deficit spending "ought" to produce a fall in the rate of interest sufficient to leave aggregate demand unchanged, rather than a recession – still assuming, of course, that the steady-state demand for money is not sensitive to the interest rate.

Sources and Bibliography

1. The General Theory (*GT*)

John Maynard Keynes. 1936. *The General Theory of Employment, Interest and Money.* London: Macmillan.

2. The collected writings of John Maynard Keynes (*CW*)

Volumes 1–30, published for the Royal Economic Society, London: Macmillan, St. Martin's and Cambridge University Presses, Elizabeth Johnson, Donald Moggridge and E. A. G. Robinson, editors.

Volumes used, title, collected writing publication date, (original date of publication, if applicable):

2. *The Economic Consequences of the Peace,* 1971, (1919).
4. *A Tract on Monetary Reform,* 1971, (1923).
5. *A Treatise on Money, 1, The Pure Theory of Money,* 1971, (1930).
6. *A Treatise on Money, 2, The Applied Theory of Money,* 1971, (1930).
8. *A Treatise on Probability,* 1973, (1921).
9. *Essays in Persuasion,* 1972, (1931).
10. *Essays in Biography,* 1972, (1933).
11. *Economic Articles and Correspondence,* 1983.
12. *Economic Articles and Correspondence: Investment and Editorial,* 1983.
13. *The General Theory and After: Part I, Preparation,* 1973.
14. *The General Theory and After: Part II, Defense and Development,* 1973.
20. *Activities 1929–31: Rethinking Employment and Unemployment Policies,* 1981.
28. *Social, Political and Literary Writings,* 1982.
29. *The General Theory and After: A Supplement to Volumes 13 and 14.* 1979.

3. Unpublished writings of John Maynard Keynes (*KCKP*)

Copyright the Provost and Scholars of King's College Cambridge, 2006. These are deposited in the King's College Library, Cambridge. These are quoted as: KCKP, File Designation/file number/page.

4. Secondary sources

Adarkar, B. P. 1935. *The Theory of Monetary Policy.* London: P. S. King & Sons.
Aftatalion, A., 1909, La re'alite' des surproduction ge'nerales 3me installment,' *Revue d'Economie Politique,* vol. 23, pp. 201–9.
Aftatalion, A., 1913. *Les crises périodiques du surproduction.* Paris: L. Marcel Riviere.
Arena, R. and M. Quere. 2003. *The Economics of Alfred Marshall: Revisiting Marshall's Legacy.* Houndmills, Basingstoke: Palgrave Macmillan.

Arrow, K. J. and G. Debreu. 1954. "Existence of an Equilibrium for a Competitive Economy," *Econometrica*, vol. 22, pp. 265–90.

Arrow, K. J. and F. H. Hahn. 1971. *General Competitive Analysis*. San Francisco: Holden-Day.

Bagehot, W. 1873. *Lombard Street: A Description of the Money Market*. London: P. S. King.

Barens, I, and V. Caspari. 1997. "The Own-Rates of Interest and the Relevance for the Existence of Underemployment Equilibrium Positions," in G. Harcourt and P. Riach, eds., 1997, pp. 283–303.

Barnett, S. 1888. "A Scheme for the Unemployed," *Nineteenth Century*, vol. 24, pp. 753–54.

Bateman, B. 1996. *Keynes Uncertain Revolution*. Ann Arbor: The University of Michigan Press.

Beveridge, W. 1909. *Unemployment, a Problem of Industry*. London: Longman.

Bibow, J. 1998. "On Keynesian Theories of Liquidity Preference," *The Manchester School*, vol. 66, pp. 238–73.

———. 2000. "The Loanable Funds Fallacy in Retrospect," *History of Political Economy*, vol. 32, pp. 789–831.

Blaug, M. 1958. "The Classical Economists and the Factory Acts – A Re-examination," *Quarterly Journal of Economics*, vol. 72, May. Reprinted in Coats, 1971a, pp. 104–22.

Bleaney, M. 1987. "Macroeconomic Theory and the Great Depression Revisited," *Scottish Journal of Political Economy*, 1987, vol. 34, pp. 105–19.

Bliss, C. J. 1975. *Capital Theory and the Distribution of Income*. Amsterdam: North Holland.

———. 1987. "Equal Rates and Profits," in J. Eatwell and M. Milgate and P. Newman, eds., *New Palgrave Dictionary of Economics*. London: Macmillan.

Booth, C. 1902. *Life and Labor of the People in London* (17 volumes). London: Macmillan.

Boulding, K. E. 1950. *A Reconstruction of Economics*. New York: John Wiley & Sons.

Brassey, T. 1872. *Work and Wages*. London: Bell and Daldy.

———. 1878. *Lecture on the Labour Question*. London: Longmans, Green.

Bridel, P. 1987. *Cambridge Monetary Thought: The Development of Saving-Investment Analysis from Marshall to Keynes*. London: Macmillan.

Brothwell, J. F. 1997. "The Relation of *The General Theory* to the Classical Theory," in G. C. Harcourt and P. A. Riach, eds., 1997.

Caldwell, B. 1986. "Hayek's Transformation," *History of Political Economy*, vol. 20, pp. 513–41.

———. 1995. "Introduction," in Hayek F. A., *The Collected Works of F. A. Hayek*, vol. 9, *Contra Keynes and Cambridge, Essays, Correspondence*, edited by B. Caldwell. London: Routledge.

———. 2003. *Hayek's Challenge: An Intellectual Biography of F. A. Hayek*. Chicago: University of Chicago Press.

Cassel, G. 1922. *Money and the Foreign Exchange after 1914*. New York: Macmillan.

Chick, V. 1983. *Macroeconomics After Keynes*. Deddington, UK: Phillip Allan.

Clapham, J. H. 1922. "Of Empty Economic Boxes," *Economic Journal*, vol. 32, pp. 305–14.

Clarke, P. 1988. *The Keynesian Revolution in the Making*. Oxford: Clarendon Press.

Clower, R. W. 1965. "The Keynesian Counter-revolution – A Theoretical Appraisal," *The Theory of Interest Rates*, F. H. Hahn and F. R. P. Brechling, eds., pp. 103–25. London: Macmillan.

———. 1967. "A Reconsideration of the Microfoundations of Monetary Theory," *Western Economic Journal*, vol. 6, pp. 1–33.

Clower, R. W. 1975. "Reflections on the Keynesian Perplex," *Zeitschrift fur Nationaleconomie*, vol. 35, pp. 1–24.

———. 1989. "Keynes's *General Theory:* The Marshall Connection," in D. A. Walker, ed., *Perspectives in the History of Economic Thought*, vol. II. Upleadon, Gloucestershire: Edward Elgar.

———. 1997. "The Principle of Effective Demand Revisited," in G. C. Harcourt and P. A. Riach, eds., *A 'Second Edition' of the* General Theory, vol. I. London and New York: Routledge.

Clower, R. W., and J. F. Due, 1972. *Microeconomics*, 6th ed. Homewood, Illinois: Richard D. Irwin, 1972.

Coates, J. 1996. *The Claims of Common Sense: Cambridge Philosophy and the Social Sciences.* Cambridge: Cambridge University Press.

Coats, A. W. 1967. "Sociological Aspects of British Economic Thought," *Journal of Political Economy*, vol. 75, pp. 706–29.

———. 1971a. *The Classical Economists and Economic Policy.* London: Methuen.

———.1971b. "The Classical Economists and the Labourer," in Coates, 1971a, pp. 144–79.

Cockshut, A. O. 1964. *The Unbelievers: English Agnostic Thought 1840–1890.* London: Collins.

Coddington, A. 1983. *Keynesian Economics: The Search for First Principles.* London: George Allen and Unwin.

Collard, D. 1990. "Cambridge After Marshall," in *Centenary Essays on Alfred Marshall*, J. Whitaker ed., pp. 164–92. Cambridge: Cambridge University Press.

Conard, J. W. 1959. *An Introduction to the Theory of Interest Rates.* Berkeley and Los Angeles: University of California Press.

Cottrell, A. 1986. "The Endogeneity of Money and Money-Income Causality," *Scottish Journal of Political Economy*, vol. 33, pp. 2–27.

———. 1993. "Keynes's Theory of Probability and Its Relevance to His Economics," *Economics and Philosophy*, vol. 9, pp. 25–51.

———. 1994a. "Keynes's Appendix to Chapter 19: A Reader's Guide," *History of Political Economy*, vol. 26, pp. 681–95.

———. 1994b. "Hayeks's Early Cycle Theory Re-examined," *Cambridge Journal of Economics*, vol. 18, pp. 197–212.

Cottrell, A. C. and M. S. Lawlor. 1991. "'Natural Rate' Mutations: Keynes, Leijonhufvud and the 'Wicksell Connection.'" *History of Political Economy*, vol. 23, pp. 625–43.

Cournot, A. 1838. *Recherches sur les Principes Mathematiques de la Theorie des Richesses*, Paris, France: L. Hachette; English translation by N. T. Bacon in *Economic Classics*, New York, NY: Macmillan, 1897; reprinted by Augustus M. Kelly, 1960.

Cronon, W. 1992. *Nature's Metropolis: Chicago and the Great West.* New York: Norton.

Curtis, M and Townshend, H. 1938. *Modern Money.* New York: Harcourt, Brace and Co.

Dardi, M. and M. Gallegati. 1992. "Marshall on Speculation," *History of Political Economy*, vol. 24, no. 3, pp. 586–93.

Darity, W. A. and B. L. Horn. 1983. "Involuntary Unemployment Reconsidered," *outhern Economic Journal*, vol. 49, pp. 717–33.

———. 1988. "Involuntary Unemployment Independent of the Labor Market," *Journal of Post Keynesian Economics*, vol. 10, pp. 216–24.

Darwin, C. 1859. *The Origin of Species.* Republished in 1958. New York: New American Library.

Davidson, P. 1972. *Money and the Real World*. 1978 edition, New York: Halstead.

Davidson, P and E. Smolensky. 1964. *Aggregate Supply and Demand Analysis*. New York: Harper and Row.

Davis, J. 1994a. *Keynes's Philosophical Development*. Cambridge: Cambridge University Press.

———. 1994b, ed. *Keynes: The State of the Debate*. London: Routledge.

Davis, J. R. 1968. "Chicago Economists, Deficit Budgets, and the Early 1930s," *American Economic Review*, vol. 58, June, pp. 476–82.

———. 1971. *The New Economics and the Old Economists*. Ames: Iowa State University Press.

Debreu, G. 1959. *The Theory of Value*. New Haven: Yale University Press.

De Marchi, N. and P. Harrison. 1994. "Trading 'in the Wind' and with Guile: The Troublesome Matter of the Short Selling of Shares in Seventeenth-Century Holland," in *Higgling: Transactors and Their Markets in the History of Economics*, edited by N. De Marchi and M. S. Morgan, *History of Political Economy*, vol. 26, special supplement. Durham: Duke University Press.

Desai, M. 1982. "The Task of Monetary Theory: The Hayek–Sraffa Debate in a Modern Perspective," in Baranzini, Mauro *Advances in Economic Theory*, Oxford: Blackwell.

De Vroey, M. 2004a. "The History of Macroeconomics Viewed Against the Background of the Marshall–Walras Divide", in M. De Vroey and K. Hoover, eds., *The IS-LM Model. Its Rise, Fall and Strange Persistence*, Annual Supplement to Volume 36, History of Political Economy, Duke University Press, Durham and London, 2004, pp. 57–91.

———. 2004b. *Involuntary Unemployment: The Elusive Quest for A Theory*. London: Routledge.

Dicey, A. V. 1905. *Law and Public Opinion in England During the Nineteenth Century*. London: Macmillan. 2nd edition, 1914, reprinted in 1924.

Dillard, D. 1948. *The Economics of John Maynard Keynes: The Theory of a Monetary Economy*. New York: Prentice Hall.

Dobb, M. 1928. *Wages*. London: Nisbet and Company.

———. 1929. "A Skeptical View of the Theory of Wages" in *Economic Journal*, December, pp. 506–19.

———. 1938. *Wages*. 2nd rev. ed. London: Nisbet and Company.

———. 1948. *Wages*. 3rd rev. ed. London: Nisbet and Company.

Dornbusch, R. 1976. "Expectations and Exchange Rate Dynamics," *Journal of Political Economy*, vol. 84, pp. 1161–76.

Dunlop, J. T. 1939. "The Movement of Real and Money Wage Rates," *Economic Journal*, vol. 48, pp. 413–34.

Eatwell, J. 1983. "The Long Period Theory of Employment," *Cambridge Journal of Economics*, vol. 7, pp. 269–85.

Eatwell, J. and M. Milgate. 1983. *Keynes's Economics and the Theory of Value and Distribution*. London: Duckworth.

Edgeworth, F. Y. 1925. *Papers Relating to Political Economy*. New York: Burt Franklin.

Eisner, R. 1997. "The Marginal Efficiency of Capital and Investment," in G. C. Harcourt and P. A. Riach, eds., 1997, pp. 185–97.

Emery, H. C. 1896. *Speculation on the Stock and Produce Exchanges of the United States*, New York: Columbia University Press.

Eshag, E. 1963. *From Marshall to Keynes: An Essay on the Monetary Theory of the Cambridge School*. Oxford: Basil Blackwell.

Farjoun, E. and M. Machover. 1983. *Laws of Chaos, A Probabilistic Approach to Political Economy*. Norfolk: Thetford Press.

Sources and Bibliography 337

Fisher, I. 1898. *Appreciation and Interest*. Reprinted in 1991. New York: Augustus M. Kelly.

———. 1907. *The Rate of Interest: Its Nature, Determination and Relation to Economic Phenomena*. New York: Macmillan.

———. 1930. *The Theory of Interest: As Determined by Impatience to Spend Income and Opportunity to Invest it*. Reprinted in 1954, New York: Kelley and Millman.

Frydman, R. 1982. "Towards an Understanding of Market Processes: Individual Expectations, Learning and Convergence to Rational Expectations Equilibrium," *American Economic Review*, vol. 72, pp. 652–88.

Frydman, R., G. P. O'Driscoll, Jr. and A. Schotter. 1982. "Rational Expectations of Government Policy: An Application of Newcomb's Problem," *Southern Economic Journal*, vol. 49, pp. 311–19.

Garraty, J. 1978. *Unemployment in History: Economic Thought and Public Policy*. New York: Harper Colophon Books.

Goodhart, C. A. E. 1988. *The Evolution of Central Banks*. Cambridge: The MIT Press.

Gordon, H. S. 1971. "The Ideology of Laissez-Faire," in Coats, 1971, pp. 180–205.

Groenewegen, P. 1995a. *A Soaring Eagle: Alfred Marshall 1842–1924*. Aldershot: Edward Elgar.

———. 1995b. "Keynes and Marshall: Methodology, Society, and Politics," in A. Cottrell and M. Lawlor, eds., *New Perspectives on Keynes, History of Political Economy*, annual supplement to vol. 27, pp. 129–56. Durham: Duke University Press.

———. 1996, ed. *Official Papers of Alfred Marshall, A Supplement*. Cambridge: Cambridge University Press.

Haberler, G. 1937. *Prosperity and Depression*. Geneva: League of Nations.

Hahn, F. 1982. "The Neo-Ricardians," *Cambridge Journal of Economics*, vol. 6, pp. 353–74.

Hansen, A. H. 1953. *A Guide to Keynes*. New York: McGraw-Hill.

Harcourt, G. C. 1972. *Some Cambridge Controversies in the Theory of Capital*. Cambridge: Cambridge University Press.

———. 1983. "Keynes's College Bursar View of Investment," in *Distribution Effective Demand and International Economic Relations*, edited by J. A. Kregel, New York: St. Martin's.

Harcourt, G. C. and P. A. Riach, eds., 1997. *A 'Second Edition' of* The General Theory. London and New York: Routledge.

Harrod, R. F. 1947. "Keynes the Economist," in S. E. Harris, ed., *The New Economics*. New York: Alfred A. Knopf.

———. 1951. *The Life of John Maynard Keynes*. London: Macmillan.

Hart, N. 1991. "Returns to Scale and Marshallian Economics," *History of Economics Review*, vol. 16, pp. 31–79.

———. 1995. "Marshall's Theory of Value: The Role of External Economies," *Cambridge Journal of Economics*, vol. 20, pp. 353–69.

———. 2003. "From the Representative to the Equilibrium Firm: Why Marshall was not a Marshallian," in R. Arena and M. Quere, 2003, pp. 158–81.

Hayek, F. A. 1931. *Prices and Production*. London: Routledge and Kegan Paul.

———. 1932. "Money and Capital: A Reply to Mr. Sraffa" *Economic Journal*, vol. 42, pp. 237–49

———. 1935a. *Prices and Production*. 2nd rev. ed., London: Routledge and Kegan Paul.

———. 1935b. *Monetary Theory and the Trade Cycle*. London: Routledge and Kegan Paul.

———. 1941. *The Pure Theory of Capital*. Chicago: University of Chicago Press.

Hawtrey, R. G. 1913. *Good and Bad Trade*. London: Constable.

———. 1919. *Currency and Credit*. London: Longmans.

Hawtrey, R. G. 1923. *Currency and Credit,* 2nd ed. London: Longmans.

———. 1927. *Currency and Credit,* 3rd ed. London: Longmans.

———. 1932. *The Art of Central Banking.* London: Longmans.

Hazlitt, H. 1959. *The Failure of the "New Economics."* Princeton, N J: D. Van Nostrand.

Hession, C. H. 1983. *John Maynard Keynes: A Personal Biography of the Man who Revolutionized Capitalism and the Way We Live.* New York: Macmillan.

Hicks, J. R. 1937. Mr. Keynes and the Classics – A Suggested Interpretation. *Econometrica,* vol. 5, April, pp. 147– 59.

———. 1939. *Value and Capital.* Oxford: Clarendon.

———. 1946. *Value and Capital,* 2nd ed. Oxford: Clarendon.

———. 1967. "The Hayek Story," in J. Hicks, *Critical Essays in Monetary Theory,* Oxford: Clarendon Press, 203–15.

———. 1982. *Money, Interest, and Wages: Collected Essays on Economic Theory,* vol. 2. Oxford: Basil Blackwell.

Himmelfarb, G. 1991. *Poverty and Compassion: The Moral Imagination of the Late Victorians.* New York: Knopf.

Hobson, J. 1896. *The Problem of the Unemployed: An Inquiry and an Economic Policy.* London: Methuen and Co.

Hobson J. and A. F. Mummery. 1889. *The Physiology of Industry.* London: Murray.

Hoover, K. 1988. *New Classical Macroeconomics: A Skeptical Inquiry.* New York: Basil Blackwell.

Hoover, K. 2003. *Economics as Ideology: Keynes, Laski, Hayek, and the Creation of Contemporary Politics.* Lanham, MD: Rowman and Littlefield,

Horwich, G. 1964. *Money, Capital and Prices,* Homewood Illinois: Richard D. Irwin.

Johnson, H. 1951. Some Cambridge Controversies in Monetary Theory: *Review of Economic Studies,* vol. 19, pp. 90–104.

Jones, G. S. 1971. *Outcast London.* Oxford: Clarendon Press.

Kahn, R. F. 1954. "Some Notes on Liquidity Preference," *Manchester School of Economics and Social Studies,* vol. 22, pp. 229–57.

———. 1976. "Unemployment as Seen by the Keynesians," in *The Concept and Measurement of Involuntary Unemployment,* G. D. N. Worswick, ed. London: George Allen and Unwin.

———. 1990. *The Economics of the Short Period.* London: St. Martin's Press. "Professor Hayek and the concertina effect'" *Economica,* vol. 14, pp. 359–93.

———. 1962. "Keynes's Theory of Own Rates of Interest," *Essays on Economic Stability and Growth,* pp. 59–74. London: Duckworth.

Keynes, J. M. 1911. "Review of Irving Fisher: *The Purchasing Power of Money*" *Economic Journal,* vol. 21, September. Reprinted in *CW* 11, pp. 275–81.

———. 1923. *A Tract on Monetary Reform.* Reprinted in *CW* 4.

———. 1925. "Alfred Marshall, 1842–1924," in A. C. Pigou, ed., *Memorial of Alfred Marshall.* Reprinted in *CW* 10.

———, ed. 1926. *Official Papers of Alfred Marshall.* London: Macmillan. Reprinted in *The Collected Works of Alfred Marshall,* P. Groenewegen, ed., vol. 8. Bristol: Overstone Press.

———. 1930. "The Question of High Wages," Political Quarterly, vol. 1, pp. 110–124. Reprinted in *CW* 20, pp. 3–16.

———. 1933. "A Monetary Theory of Production," in Der Stand und die Nächste Zundkunft der Konjuncturforschung: *Festschrift für Arthur Spiethoff.* Reprinted in *CW* 13, pp. 408–11.

———. 1936. *The General Theory of Employment, Interest and Money.* New York: Harcourt, Brace and World.

Keynes, J. M. 1937a. "The Theory of the Rate of Interest" in *The Lessons of Monetary Experience: Essays in Honour of Irving Fisher*. Reprinted in *CW* 14, pp. 101–8.

———. 1937b. "Alternative Theories of the Rate of Interest," *Economic Journal* 47:241– 52. Reprinted in *CW* 14, pp. 201–15.

———. 1937c. "The General Theory of Employment," *Quarterly Journal of Economics*, vol. 51, pp. 209–23. Reprinted in *CW* 14, pp. 109–23.

———. 1937d. "The 'Ex Ante' Theory of the Rate of Interest," *Economic Journal*, vol. 47, pp. 663–669. Reprinted in *CW* 14, pp. 215–223.

———. 1938. "Mr. Keynes and 'Finance,'" *Economic Journal*, vol. 48. Reprinted in *CW* 14, pp. 229–33.

———. 1939. "The Process of Capital Formation," *Economic Journal*, vol. 49. Reprinted in the *CW* 14, pp. 278–85.

Klein, L. 1947. *The Keynesian Revolution*. New York: Macmillan.

Kneiser, T. and A. Goldsmith. 1987. "A Survey of Alternative Models of the Aggregate U.S. Labor Market," *Journal of Economic Literature*, vol. 24, no. 4, pp. 1241–80.

Koot, G. 1987. *English Historical Economics: The Rise of History and Neo-Mercantilism*. Cambridge and New York: Cambridge University Press.

Kregel, J. A. 1973. *The Reconstruction of Political Economy*. New York: Halsted Press.

———. 1976. "Economic Methodology in the Face of Uncertainty: The Modelling Methods of Keynes and the Post-Keynesians." *Economic Journal*, vol. 86, pp. 209–25.

———. 1982. "Money, Expectations and Relative Prices in Keynes' Monetary Equilibrium," *Economie appliqué*, vol. 35, pp. 449–65

———. 1997. "The Theory of Value, Expectations and Chapter 17 of the *General Theory*, in G. C. Harcourt and P. A. Riach, 1997, pp. 261–82.

Kurz, H. D. 2000. "The Hayek-Keynes-Sraffa controversy reconsidered," in H. D. Kurz, ed., *Critical Essays on Piero Sraffa's Legacy in Economics*, pp. 257–301. Cambridge: Cambridge University Press.

Kydland F. and E. Prescott. 1982. "Time to Build and Aggregate Fluctuation," *Econometrica*, vol. 50, pp. 1345–70.

Labordere, M. 1908. "Crise Ame'ricaine de 1907 ou Capitaux-reels et Capitaux-apparents," *Revue de Paris*, fevrier. Reprinted in D. H. Robertson 1915 [1948].

Lachmann, L. 1986. "Austrian Economics under fire: the Hayek–Sraffa duel in retrospect," in W. Grassl and B. Smith, eds., *Austrian Economics: historical and philosophical background*. New York: New York University Press.

Laidler, D. 1991. *The Golden Age of the Quantity Theory*. Princeton, NJ: Princeton University Press.

———. 1999. *Fabricating the Keynesian Revolution: Studies of the Inter-war Literature on Money, the Cycle, and Unemployment*. Cambridge and New York: Cambridge University Press.

———. 2003. "The Price Level, Relative Price, and Economic Stability: Aspects of the Inter-War Debate," paper delivered at the conference on "Monetary Stability, Financial Stability and the Business Cycle." Basel: Bank for International Settlements.

Lavington, F. 1921. *The English Capital Market*. London: Methuen.

———. 1922. *The Trade Cycle*. London: P. S. King & Son.

Lawlor, M. S. 1991. "Keynes, Meltzer and Involuntary Unemployment: On the Intensional and Extensional Logic of Definitions," *Review of Social Economy*, vol. 49, pp. 317–38.

———. 1993. "Keynes, Cambridge and the New Keynesian Economics." *Labor Economics: Problems in Analyzing Labor Markets*, W. A. Darity, ed., pp. 11–58. Boston: Kluwer Academic Press.

————. 1994a. "On the Historical Origin of Keynes's Views on Financial Markets." *Higgling: Transactors and Their Markets in the History of Economics*, N. De Marchi and M. Morgan, eds., *History of Political Economy*, vol. 26, supplement, pp. 184–225. Durham: Duke University Press.

————. 1994b "The Own-Rates Framework as an Interpretation of the *General Theory*: A Suggestion for Complicating the Keynesian Theory of Money." John Davis, ed., pp. 39–102, *Keynes: The State of the Debate*, London: Routledge.

————. 1997a. "The Classical Theory of the Rate of Interest," in G. C. Harcourt and P. A. Riach, eds., pp. 343–67.

————. 1997b. "Keynes and Financial Market Processes in Historical Context: From the *Treatise* to the *General Theory*." P. Arestis and M. Sawyer, ed. *Capital Controversy, Post-Keynesian Economics and the History of Economics: Essays in Honour of Geoff Harcourt*, pp. 233–48, London: Routledge.

Lawlor, M. and B. Horn. 1992. "Notes on the Sraffa-Hayek Exchange." *Review of Political Economy*, vol. 4, pp. 317–40.

Leijonhufvud, A. 1968. *On Keynesian Economics and the Economics of Keynes: A Study in Monetary Theory*. London: Oxford University Press.

————. 1981. "The Wicksell Connection: Variations on a Theme," in *Information and Coordination*, Oxford: Oxford University Press.

Lerner, A. P. 1952. "The Essential Properties of Interest and Money," *Quarterly Journal of Economics*, vol. 66, pp. 172–93.

Liebhafsky, H. H. 1955. "A Curious Case of Neglect: Marshall's *Industry and Trade*," *Canadian Journal of Economics*, vol. 21, pp. 339–53.

Littleboy, B. 1990. *On Interpreting Keynes: A Study in Reconciliation*. London: Routledge.

Marshall, A. 1871. "Money," in *The Early Writings of Alfred Marshall*, 2 vols, edited by J. Whitaker, pp. 164–77. London: Macmillan.

————. 1875. "Some Features of American Industry," in *The Early Writings of Alfred Marshall*, 2 vols, edited by J. Whitaker, pp. 352–77, London: Macmillan.

————. 1879. *The Pure Theory of Foreign Trade. The Pure Theory of Domestic Values*. Series of Reprints of Scarce Tracts in Economic and Political Science, No. 1. London: London School of Economics and Political Science.

————. 1886. "Answers to Questions on the Subject of Currency and Prices Circulated By the Royal Commission on the Depression of Trade and Industry." Reprinted in Keynes, 1926, pp. 1–16.

————. 1887a. "Memoranda and Evidence Before the Gold and Silver Commission." Reprinted in Keynes, 1926, pp. 17–196.

————. 1887b. "Remedies for Fluctuations of General Prices," *Contemporary Review*, March. Reprinted in *Memorials To Alfred Marshall*, A. C. Pigou, ed., pp. 188– 211. London: Macmillan, 1925.

————. 1899a. "The Folly of Amateur Speculators Makes the Fortunes of Professionals, The Wiles of Some Professionals," reprinted in M. Dardi and M. Gallegati, 1992.

————. 1899b. "Evidence Before the Indian Currency Committee." Reprinted in Keynes, 1926, pp. 263–326.

————. 1919. *Industry and Trade*. London: Macmillan.

————. 1923. *Money, Credit and Commerce*. London: Macmillan.

————. 1926. *Official Papers of Alfred Marshall*, ed. J. M. Keynes. London: Macmillan.

————. 1961. *Principles of Economics*, 9th variorum edition, edited by C. Guillebaud. London: Macmillan.

————. 1962 [1920]. *Principles of Economics*, 8th ed. London: Macmillan.

————. 1996. *Official Papers of Alfred Marshall, A Supplement*, edited by P. Groenewegen. Cambridge: Cambridge University Press.

Marshall, A and M. P. Marshall, 1879, *Economics of Industry*. London: Macmillan.

Marx, K. 1867. *Capital*. Translated by S. Moore and E. Aveling. Moscow: Foreign Languages Publishing House, 1961.

Matthews, R. C. O. 1990. "Marshall and the Labour Market," in *Centenary Essays on Alfred Marshall*, ed. J. Whitaker. Cambridge: Cambridge University Press.

Meltzer, A. H. 1981. "Keynes's General Theory: A Different Perspective," *Journal of Economic Literature*, vol. 19, no. 1, pp. 34–64.

———. 1983. "Interpreting Keynes," *Journal of Economic Literature*, vol. 21, no. 1, pp. 66–78.

———. 1988. *Keynes's Monetary Theory: A Different Interpretation*. Cambridge: Cambridge University Press.

———. 1992. "Patinkin on Keynes and Meltzer," *Journal of Monetary Economics*, vol. 29, February, 1992, pp. 151–62.

Menger, C. 1871 [1981]. *Principles of Economics*, New York: New York University Press.

Mill, J. S. 1871, 8th ed. [1st ed. 1848, reprint, 1965] *The Principles of Political Economy with Some of Their Applications to Social Philosophy*, J. M. Robson, ed. Toronto: University of Toronto Press.

Miller, E. M. 1984. Bank Deposits in the Monetary Theory of Keynes. *Journal of Money, Credit and Banking*, vol. 16, pp. 242–46.

Millmow, A. 1985. "The Evolution of J. M. Keynes's Wage and Employment Theory 1920–1946." Unpublished graduate diploma thesis, Department of Economic History, Australian National University.

Moggridge, D. E. 1992. *Maynard Keynes: An Economist's Biography*. London and New York: Routledge.

Moore, G. E. 1903. *Principia Ethica*. Cambridge: Cambridge University Press.

Moss, L. S. 2003. "Marshall's Objective: Making Orthodox Economics Intelligible the Business Leader," in R. Arena and M. Quere, 2003, pp. 67–83.

Napolitano, G. 1978. "The Unknown Sraffa," *New Left Review*, vol. 112, pp. 67–80.

O'Donnell, R. M. 1989. *Keynes: Philosophy, Economics and Politics: The Philosophic Foundations of Keynes's Thought and their Influence on his Economics and Politics*. New York: St. Martin.

O'Driscoll, G. 1977. Economics as a Coordination Problem: The Contributions of Friedrich A. Hayek, Kansas City: Sheed Andrews and McMeel.

O'Driscoll, G. and Rizzo M. 1985. *The Economics of Time and Ignorance*, Oxford: Basis Blackwell.

Panico, C. 1988. *Interest and Profit in the Theories of Value and Distribution*, London: Macmillan Press.

———. 2001. "Monetary Analyses in Sraffa's writings," pp. 362–76 in *Piero Sraffa's Political Economy: A Centenary Estimate*, edited by Terenzio Cozzi and Roberto Marchionatti. London: Routledge.

Pasinetti, L. L. 1974. *Growth and Income Distribution: Essays in Economic Theory*. Oxford: Basil Blackwell.

———. 1997. "The Principle of Effective Demand," in G. C. Harcourt and P. Riach, eds., 1997, pp. 93–106.

Patinkin, D. 1948. "Price Flexibility and Full Employment," *American Economic Review*, vol. 38, pp. 534–64.

———. 1956. *Money, Interest, and Prices*. Rev. ed., 1965. New York: Harper and Row.

———. 1976. *Keynes's Monetary Thought: A Study of Its Development*. Durham: Duke University Press.

———. 1982. *Anticipations of the General Theory? And other Essays on Keynes*. Chicago: University of Chicago Press.

Patinkin, D. 1983. "New Perspectives or Old Pitfalls? Some Comments on Allan Meltzer's Interpretation of the *General Theory*," *Journal of Economic Literature*, vol. 21, pp. 47–51.

———. 1990. "On Different Interpretations of *The General Theory*," *Journal of Monetary Economics*, vol. 26, pp. 205–43.

———. 1993. "Meltzer on Keynes" *Journal of Monetary Economics*, vol. 32, pp. 347–56.

Patinkin, D. and J. C. Leith, eds., 1978. *Keynes, Cambridge and the General Theory*. London: Macmillan.

Petridis, R. 1973. "Alfred Marshall's Attitude to the Economic Analysis of Trade Unions," *History of Political Economy*, vol. 5, pp. 165–98.

———. 1990. "The Trade Unions in the Principles: The Ethical Versus the Practical in Marshall's Economics." *Economie Applique*, vol. 42, pp. 165–98.

———. 1996. "Brassey's Law and the Economy of High Wage in Nineteenth- Century Economics," *History of Political Economy*, vol. 28, pp. 583–606.

Pigou, A. C. 1912. *Wealth and Welfare*. London: Macmillan.

———. 1913. *Unemployment*. London: Williams and Norgate.

———. 1917. "The Value of Money," *Quarterly Journal of Economics*, vol. 32, pp. 38–65.

———. 1920. *The Economics of Welfare*. London: Macmillan.

———. 1925. *Memorials of Alfred Marshall*. London: Macmillan.

———. 1927a. *Industrial Fluctuations*. London: Macmillan.

———.1927b. "The Laws of Diminishing and Increasing Cost," *Economic Journal*, vol. 37, pp. 188–97.

———. 1928. "An analysis of supply," *Economic Journal*, vol. 38, pp. 238–57.

———. 1929. *Industrial Fluctuations*, 2nd ed. London: Macmillan.

———. 1933. *The Theory of Unemployment*. London: Macmillan.

———. 1943. "The Classical Stationary State," *Economic Journal*, Vol. 53, pp. 343–351.

———. 1947. *Aspects of British Economic History, 1918–1925*. London: Frank Cass and Co.

Presley, J. R. 1979. *Robertsonian Economics*. New York: Holmes and Meier Publishers, Inc.

Robertson, D. H. 1915 [1948]. *A Study of Industrial Fluctuations*. London: P. S. King. Reprinted,1948, London School of Economics.

———. 1922. *Money*. London: Nisbet

———. 1926 [1949]. *Banking Policy and the Price Level*. London: Macmillan.

———. 1928a. *Money*, 3rd ed. London: Nisbet.

———. 1928b. "Theories of Banking Policy," *Economica*, vol. 8, pp. 131 –46.

———. 1930. "The Trees of the Forest," *Economic Journal*, vol. 40, pp. 80–9.

———. 1931. *Minutes of Evidence Take Before the Committee on Finance and Industry*, vol. I, London: HMSO.

———. 1934. "Industrial Fluctuation and the Natural Rate of Interest," *Economic Journal*, vol. 44 pp. 650–6.

———. 1940. "Mr. Keynes and the Rate of Interest," in *Essays in Monetary Theory*.London: Staples Press.

Robinson, J. 1933. *The Economics of Imperfect Competition*. London: Macmillan. 2nd edition, 1969.

———. 1953. *On Re-Reading Marx*. Cambridge: Students' Bookshop.

———. 1961. "Own Rates of Interest," *Economic Journal*, vol. 71. Reprinted in *Collected Economic Papers of Joan Robinson*, Oxford: Basil Blackwell, pp. 132–8.

———. 1962. "The General Theory after Twenty-Five Years," a review of H. G. Johnson, *Money Trade and Economic Growth*, in the *Economic Journal*, vol. 71. Reprinted in *Collected Economic Papers of Joan Robinson*, Oxford: Basil Blackwell, pp. 100–2.

———. 1969. "Preface to the Second Edition" of the *The Economics of Imperfect Competition*. London: Macmillan.

Rogers, C. 1989. *Money, Interest and Capital, A Study in the Foundations of Monetary Theory*. Cambridge: Cambridge University Press.

———. 1994. "Michael Lawlor's Own-Rates Interpretation of The *General Theory*," in J. B. Davis, ed., *The State of the Interpretation of Keynes*, Dordecht: Kluwer.

———. 1997. "The General Theory, Existence of a monetary long-period unemployment equilibrium," in G. C. Harcourt and P. A. Riach, eds, *A 'Second Edition' of the General Theory*, vol. 1, pp. 324–42. London and New York: Routledge.

Roger C. and T. K. Rymes. 1997. "Keynes's Monetary Theory of Value and Modern Banking," in G. C. Harcourt and P. A. Riach, 1997, pp. 304–23.

Rowntree, B. S. 1902. *Poverty: A Study of Town Life*. London: Longmans.

Samuelson, P. A. 1947. "The General Theory," in S. E. Harris, ed., *The New Economics*. New York: Alfred A. Knopf.

Saulnier, R. J. 1938. *Contemporary Monetary theory*. New York: Columbia University Press.

Schiller, R. J. 1991. *Market Volatility*. Cambridge: The MIT Press.

Shackle, G. L. S. 1967. *The Years of High Theory*. Cambridge: Cambridge University Press.

———. 1972. *Epistemics and Economics*. Cambridge: Cambridge University Press.

———. 1974. *Keynesian Kaleidics*. Cambridge: Cambridge University Press.

Shove, Gerald. 1930. "The Representative Firm and Increasing Returns," *Economic Journal*, vol. 40. pp. 94–116.

Skidelsky, R. 1983. *John Maynard Keynes. Volume One: Hopes Betrayed, 1883–1920*. London: Macmillan.

———. 1992. *John Maynard Keynes. Volume Two: The Economist as Saviour 1920– 1937*. London: Macmillan.

———. 2000. *John Maynard Keynes: Volume Three: Fighting for Britain* London: Macmillan.

———. 2002. "The Great Depression from Keynes's Perspective," in H. James, ed., *The Interwar Depression in an International Context*, pp. 99–112. Munich: Oldenbourg.

Smith, A. 1776 [1937] *An Inquiry into the Nature and Causes of the Wealth of Nations*, New York: Modern Library.

Smith, V. 1936. *The Rationale of Central Banking*. London: P. S. King & Son.

Sraffa, P. 1926. "The Laws of Return under Competitive Conditions," *Economic Journal*, vol. 36, pp. 335–50.

———. 1930. "Increasing Returns and the Representative Firm: A Criticism," and "A Rejoinder," *Economic Journal*, vol. 40, pp. 89–92, 93.

———. 1932a. "Dr. Hayek on Money and Capital," *Economic Journal*, vol. 42, pp. 42–53.

———. 1932b. "A rejoinder," *Economic Journal*, vol. 42, pp. 249–51.

———. 1960. *Production of Commodities by Means of Commodities*. Cambridge: Cambridge University Press.

Stone, R. 1978. *Keynes, Political Arithmetic and Econometrics*, Proceedings of the British Academy, vol. 64. Oxford: Oxford University Press.

Tarshis, L. 1939. "Changes in Real and Money Wages," *Economic Journal*, vol. 49, pp. 150–4.

Taussig, F. W. 1911. *Principles of Economics*. New York: Macmillan.

Taylor, A. J. P. 1965. *English History 1914–1945* (Volume XV of the Oxford History of England). Oxford: Oxford University Press.

Thomas, B. 1991. "Alfred Marshall on Economic Biology," *Review of Political Economy*, vol. 3, pp. 1–14.

Timlin, M. 1942. *Keynesian Economics*. Toronto: University of Toronto Press.

Tobin, J. 1958. "Liquidity Preference as Behavior Toward Risk," *Review of Economic Studies*, vol. 25, pp. 65–86.

Townshend, H. 1937. "Liquidity Premium and the Theory of Value," *Economic Journal*, vol. 47, pp. 197–205.

Veblen, T. B. 1904. *The Theory of Business Enterprise*. New York: Scribners. Reprinted, New Brunswick NJ: Transactions Books, 1978.

Viner, J. 1941. "Marshall's Economics in Relation to the Man and to his Times," *American Economic Review*, vol. 31, June, pp. 22–35.

Walker, F. A. 1876 (1891). *The Wages Question*. New York: Henry Holt & Co.

Warming, J. 1932. "International Difficulties Arising out of the Financing of Public Works during Depression," *Economic Journal*, vol. 42, June, pp. 211–24.

Weintraub E. R. 1979, *Microfoundations: The Compatibility of Microeconomics and Macroeconomics*, Cambridge: Cambridge University Press.

Weintraub, S. 1958. *Approach to the Theory of Income Distribution*. Philadelphia: Chilton.

Whitaker, J. ed. 1975. *The Early Writings of Alfred Marshall*, 2 vols. London: Macmillan.

———. 1990. "What Happened to the Second Volume of Principles? The Thorny Path to Marshall's Last Books," J. K. Whitaker, ed., *Centenary Essays on Alfred Marshall*, pp. 193–222. Cambridge: Cambridge University Press.

———. 2003. "Alfred Marshall's *Principles* and *Industry and Trade*: Two Books or One? Marshall and the Joint Stock Company," in R. Arena and M. Quere, 2003, pp. 137–57.

Wicksell, K. 1893. *Value, Capital and Rent*. Translated to English, S. H. Frowein. London: Allen and Unwin, 1965.

———. 1898. *Interest and Prices*. Translated to English, R. F. Kahn, 1936. London: Macmillan.

———. 1901. *Lectures on Political Economy, Vol. I: General theory*. 1967 reprint of 1934 translation, New York: Augustus M. Kelley.

———. 1907. "The Influence of the Rate of Interest on Prices," *Economic Journal*, vol. 17, June, pp. 213–20.

———. 1915. *Lectures in Political Economy*. Translated to English, E. Classen. London: Routledge & Kegan Paul, 1935.

Williams K. and J. Williams. 1987. *A Beveridge Reader*. London: Unwin Hyman.

Wood, J. and N. Wood. 1985. *Financial Markets*. New York: Harcourt Brace Jovanovich.

Young, A. 1928. "Increasing Returns and Economic Progress," *Economic Journal*, vol. 38, pp. 527–55.

Young, W. 1987. *Interpreting Mr. Keynes: The IS-LM Enigma*. Oxford: Blackwell-Polity.

Author Index

Adarkar, B. P., 217, 240–3
Aftatalion, A., 173
Arena, R., 313
Arrow, K. J., 231

Bagehot, W., 314
Barens, I., 324
Barnett, S., 305
Bateman, B., 7, 315
Beveridge, W., 40, 43,
Bibow, J., 302, 317
Blaug, M., 307
Bleaney, M., 312
Bliss, C. J., 324
Booth, C., 40, 306
Boulding, K. E., 259
Brassey, T., 57, 309
Bridel, P., 155–6, 159–60, 162–5, 169,
    172, 176, 301, 318–20
Brothwell, J. F., 90

Caldwell, B., 160, 187, 323
Caspari, V., 324
Cassel, G., 197
Chick, V., 301
Clapham. J. H., 97
Clarke, P., 7
Clower, R. W., 23, 301–3
Coates, J., 7, 323
Coats, A. W., 53, 307
Cockshut, A. O., 46
Coddington, A., 301
Collard, D., 53, 61
Conard, J. W., 258, 331
Cottrell, A., 91, 317, 320, 323, 327, 331
Cournot, A, 96
Cronon, W., 314
Curtis, M.,

Dardi, M., 28, 108, 115
Darity, W. A., 304
Darwin, C., 283
Davidson, P., 11, 239
Davis, J., 7, 71, 124, 315
Davis, J. R., 312

Debreu, G., 231
De Marchi, N., 314
Desai, M., 324
De Vroey, M., 303
Dicey, A. V., 40
Dillard, D., 7
Dobb, M., 26, 33, 36, 38, 63–6, 70,
    309–10
Dornbusch, R., 291
Dunlop, J. T., 90
Due, J. F., 303

Eatwell, J., 328
Edgeworth, F. Y.,
Eisner. R., 329
Emery, H. C., 28, 93, 116–22, 128, 132,
    315–6
Eshag, E., 155–6, 160, 168

Farjoun, E., 324
Fisher, I., 12, 248, 329, 331
Frydman, R., 263

Gallegati, M., 28, 108, 115
Garraty, J., 40
Goldsmith, A., 90
Goodhart, C. A. E., 314
Gordon, H. S., 307
Groenewegen, P., 31, 44–46, 48–9, 51,
    53, 56, 167, 304–9

Haberler, G., 155,
Hahn, F., 231, 324
Hansen, A. H., 301, 325–6
Harcourt, G. C., 314
Harrison, P., 314
Harrod, R. F., 7, 237, 245, 300
Hart, N., 96–7, 100
Hawtrey, R. G., 141, 173, 319
Hayek, F. A., 31, 214–8, 222–4, 324
Hazlitt, H., 325
Hession, C. H., 7
Hicks, J. R., 16, 160, 213, 222, 261,
    322–3
Himmelfarb, G., 305, 307

Hobson, J., 44, 305
Hoover, K., 304
Hoover, K. R., 160, 323
Horn, B. L., 303–4, 322, 324
Horwich, G., 143, 332
Hyndman, H., 307–8

Johnson, H., 332
Jones, G. S., 42–3, 305–7

Kahn, R. F., 68, 159, 212, 263, 331–2
Kaldor, N., 277, 317
Keynes, J. M., (*see subject index*)
Klein, L., 7
Kneiser, T., 90
Koot, G., 61
Kregel, J. A., 25, 239, 329
Kurz, H. D., 215, 324
Kydland, F., 323

Labordere, M., 174, 319
Lachmann, L., 215
Laidler, D., 8, 13–15, 16, 108, 110,
    155–6, 159–60, 163–4, 166, 168,
    170, 175, 233, 301, 312, 317–21
Lavington, F., 168–71
Lawlor, M. S., 301–4, 317–8, 320, 322,
    324–5, 331
Leijonhufvud, A., 7, 155, 158–9, 174,
    239, 265, 284, 286, 296, 298, 331–2
Lerner, A. P., 258
Leith, J., 98, 321
Liebhafsky. H. H., 313
Littleboy, B., 301

Machover, M., 324
Marshall, A., (*see also subject index*), 28,
    48, 54–5, 58–61, 98–102, 108–116,
    160–7, 169, 182, 308, 310–11, 313,
    318
Marshall, M. P., 48, 164, 166, 309, 318
Marx, K., 40
Matthews, R. C. O., 54–5, 61–2, 308
Meltzer, A. H., 8, 10, 301
Menger, C., 330
Milgate, M., 328
Mill, J. S., 115, 164, 166, 313
Miller, E. M., 331
Millmow, A., 312
Moggridge, D. E., 7, 124, 133, 148, 201,
    315–7, 320

Moore, G. E., 312
Moss, L. S., 307
Mummery, A. F., 305

Napolitano, G., 213

O'Donnell, R. M., 7, 71, 124, 128–9,
    312, 315
O'Driscoll, G. P., 263, 323
Ohlin, B., 21

Panico, C., 230, 324
Pasinetti, L. L., 329
Patinkin, D., 8–12, 98, 155–6, 169,
    301–2, 317–8, 321
Petridis, R., 57–9, 308–9, 312
Pigou, A. C., 9, 35, 38, 45, 67–9, 97,
    100, 111, 168, 170, 303, 310–12,
    318–20
Prescott, E., 323
Presley, J. R., 155–6, 173, 184, 301, 319

Quere, M., 313

Rizzo, M., 263
Robertson, D. H., 97, 155, 168, 173–5,
    184–7, 261, 319–21
Robinson, J., 1, 31, 59. 98, 100, 277–8
Rogers, C., 10, 19, 239, 281, 327, 329
Rymes, T. K., 281, 329
Rowntree, B. S., 40

Samuelson, P. A.,
Saulnier, R. J., 155,
Schiller, R. J., 122
Schotter, A.,
Shackle, G. L. S., 6, 7, 8, 155, 157, 160,
    239, 259, 301, 327–8, 331
Shove, G., 97
Skidelsky, R., 7, 27, 93, 124, 132, 133,
    139, 197, 212, 301, 304, 310, 316–7,
    320, 322
Smith, A., 40, 232
Smith, V., 314
Smolensky. E., 11
Sraffa, P., 97–8, 100, 156, 214–5, 219–29,
    252, 256, 275, 323
Stone, R., 72

Tarshis, L., 90
Taussig, F. W., 76

Taylor, A. J. P., 307
Thomas, B., 96
Timlin, M., 7, 301,
Tobin, J., 327
Townshend, H., 273–5, 329–30

Veblen, T. B., 117, 123, 315
Viner, J., 45, 49

Walker, F. A., 309
Warming, J., 212
Webb, B., 308

Webb, S., 308
Weintraub, E. R., 16,
Weintraub, S., 11
Whitaker, J., 45–7, 73, 98–102, 306
Wicksell, K., 159
Williams, J., 304
Williams, K., 304
Wood, J., 314
Wood, N., 314

Young, A., 312
Young., W., 16

Subject Index

Austrian Economics
  influence on Cambridge School, 255
  political role in Britain during the
    1930s and today, 214–5

backwardation
  definition of normal size in the *Tract*
    198–9
  in Sraffa's review of Hayek, 257–9
  in the *General Theory*, 254–7
  in the *Treastise*, 242–3, 251–4
banking system
  in Hayek's theory, 216–8
  in Keynes 1913 view, 184–7 role in
    Hawtrey's theory, 172
  role in Keynes's view in the *General
    Theory*, 285
  role in Keynes view in the *Treatise*
    207–10
  role in Marshall, 162–3
barter economics
  criticism of by Sraffa, 224–9
  Keynes view of in 1930's, 237, 240–3
bond
  rate of interest and price, 292–6
  relation to liquidity preference theory,
    262–4
business cycle, *see* cycle theory; credit
    cycle theory

Cambridge School of Monetary
    Economics, 153–77, 178–212
Cannan, E., on supply and demand for
    labor, 65
capital (*see also*, investment)
  'free' (Marshall), 162
  Hayek's use of Bohm-Bawerk's theory
    of, 216–8
  Keynes's theory of, 264–8
capital assets
  characteristics of in Keynes's own-rate
    theory (1936) 249–55
  characteristics of in Marshall's stock
    equilibrium (1870), 108–11

carrying costs
  in Keynes theory of commodity
    markets in the *Treatise* and *General
    Theory*, 140–2, 252–7
  role in the dominance of money's
    own-rate, 268–72
classical economics
  and unemployment, 40
  in Marshall's cycle theory, 158, 164
contago
  definition in the *Treatise*, 254
conventions; role in defining liquidity
    preference, 261–4
  role is determining relative prices of
    uncertain goods, 273–5
coordination, intertemporal, 232–3
'Cournot problem' (Marshall), 196–8
credit
  role in Hawtrey's theory, 172–3, role
    in Hayek's theory, 217–8, 221–4
  role in the Robertson-Keynes forced
    saving theory (1913–26), 184–8
credit cycle theory
  in the early twentieth century, 158–60
  Keynes's attempt at explaining in
    relation to speculation, 139–47
  Marshall's theory of, 169–4
  view of on Cambridge interwar
    theoretical scene, 170–6
cumulative process
  Hawtrey's version of, 172–3
  Keynes's version of in the *Treatise*,
    203–4
  Marshall's version of, 162–4
  Wicksell's version of, 158–9
cycle theory
  of Hawtrey, 172–3, of Hayek and
    Mises, 215–218
  of Keynes and Robertson (1913–1926),
    183–8
  of Keynes in the *Treatise*,203–12
  of Marshall, 160–4
  of Pigou and Lavington, 170–2
  of Robertson, 173–5

Danaid jar analogy, 210
demand for money (*see also*, liquidity
    preference theory)
  basis in Marshall's treatment of
    demand for a stock of assets, 103–6,
    108–11
  distinction between Cambridge
    tradition of and the quantity
    theory, 182
  Keynes's *General Theory* discussion of,
    260–4
  Lavington and Pigou discussion of,
    168–170
distribution theory
  Marshall's comments on lack of
    analogy to output-price theory,
    54–5
  Marshall's theory of, 53–62
Dobb, M.
  as a Marshallian, 63
  on classical wage theory and
    marginalist revolution, 64–5
  on 'economy of high wages,' 63
  on 'indeterminacy' on the labor
    market, 66
  on supply and demand for labor, 65–6

'Economics of Keynes'
  Leijonhufvud focuses attention on, 7
  Meltzer on, 8–9
efficiency wage
  in Keynes's early lectures at
    Cambridge, 75–9
  in Marshall, 57–9
  in modern Keynesians, 66, 70
Emery, H. C.
  Keynes use of in early lectures, 126–32
  *Speculation on the Stock and Produce
    Exchanges of the United States*,
    116–23
employment (*see also*, labor market
    analysis, unemployment)
  and rigid wages, 67–8
  as motivating the *General Theory*,
    35–6
  Beveridge's theory of, 43
  in Keynes's shorter writings of the
    twenties and thirties, 79–84
  in the *General Theory*, 36–9
  and rigid wages, 67–8

in the *Treatise*, 84–6
  Hobson's theory of, 43–4
  Marshall's theory of, 61–2
  Pigou's theory of, 66–70
  problem for Victorian Britain, 40–52
  'essential properties of money,' 431–438
equalization of rates of return
  in Keynes's post-*General Theory*
    defense, 103–6
  in Keynes's short-period equilibrium
    versus Marshall's and Sraffa's long-
    period notion, 249–59
  in Marshall's stock asset market
    equilibrium, 108–11
  versus the Walrasian conception of
    equilibrium, 230–5
equilibrium
  at less-than-full employment, 4–5
  Keynes uses of, 22–4, 235–6
  long-period versus short-period, 17–8,
    255–6
  Walrasian versus traditional notions
    229–36
ex ante-ex post distinction
  Keynes's denial of, 22
  Ohlin's criticism of the *General Theory*
    on the basis of, 21–2, 160
  Shackle's reliance on, 8
exchange-rate system
  Keynes analysis of in *Tract*, 134–6,
    185–201
  basis of Keynes's own-rate analysis,
    251
expectations (*see also*, uncertainty;
    speculation)
  as determining output, 17–8
  in Keynes of the *General Theory*, 16–24
  in Marshall, 18
  how treated by Leijonhufvud,
    292–298
  how treated in own-rates framework,
    249–59
  in the marginal efficiency of capital,
    256–68
  long-term versus short-term in the
    General Theory, 17–8

forced savings
  Hayek's conception of, 215–8
  in Robertson's cycle theory, 174–5

forced savings – *continued*
   Keynes's (1913–1926) brief flirtation
     with Robertson's analysis of,
     183–188
   Sraffa's critique of Hayek's argument
     for, 221–4
   well-known in Cambridge before the
     arrival of Hayek, 159
foreign exchange (*see* exchange-rate
   system)
'fundamental equations"
   defined in Keynes's *Treatise*, 205–9
   relation to quantity equation, 209

general equilibrium (*see also*, Walrasian)
   compared to economic tradition of
     equalized rate of return, 229–32
   compared to Marshallian analysis,
     16–18
   on Hayek's purported use of, 303, 324
   on influence on post-World War II
     macroeconomics, 16
George, Henry
   socialism of in relationship to economic
     doctrines of A. Marshall, 305
gold
   in Keynes early monetary lectures,
     182–3
   in Marshall, 162–4
   mining of in Keynes, 320
gold standard
   Britain's return to, 81–3, 201–2
   Keynes view of in pre-World War I
     period, 181–2
   Keynes's view of in inter-war period,
     81–3
   Marshall's view of, 162–3

Hawtrey, R.
   theory of commodity stocks attacked
     by Keynes, 141–2, 252–4
   theory of the business cycle, 172–3
Hicks, J. R.
   role in instituting a Walrasian view of
     Keynes, 16
   temporary equilibrium, 160
   view of Hayek, 213, 322–3
hoarding (*see also*, demand for money,
   liquidity preference theory)
   in Keynes's early monetary lectures, 182

   in Marshall, 163
Hyndman, H., socialism of in relationship
   to economic doctrines of A. Marshall,
   51, 307–8
hyperinflation; in the *Tract*, 192–5

income distribution
   in Keynes's *Economic Consequences of*
     Peace, 80
   in Keynes's social theory of wage
     developed in interwar years, 81–6
   in Keynes's *Tract*, 188–95 in Keynes's
     Treatise, 207–8
inflation tax
   Keynes treatment of in *Tract*, 186
interest, rate of (*see* rate of interest)
intertemporal allocation
   common framework to all cycle
     theorists before World War II, 232–3
   in the inter-war Cambridge theorists,
     177
intertemporal equilibrium, 229–36
investment (*see also*, rate of interest,
   marginal efficiency of capital,
   savings)
   demand for as function of the rate of
     interest (Marshall), 161–2
   in Hawtrey's cycle theory, 217
   in Keynes of the *General Theory*, 264–8
   in Keynes of the *Tract*, 193–5
   in Keynes of the *Treatise*, 206–9
   in Robertson's cycle theory, 173–4
   in the own-rates framework, 259–64
IS-LM model
   as an interpretation of the *General*
     Theory, 6, 14–5
   its comparison to a Marshallian
     interpretation of the *General Theory*,
     16–24
   its Walrasian formulation, 16
   Laidler's history of, 14–5

Kant, I, Marshall's reading of, 46, 306
Keynesian Economics
   its dependence on wage rigidity or on
     interest inflexibility, 238
   its dominance in post-World War II
     era macroeconomics, 16
   its 'New Keynesian' form, 26–7, 39,
     66–70, 157–7,238

its Pigovian roots, 39
Leijonhufvud's critique of, 7–8
Patinkin's version of, 9–12
own-rates framework one way to view
  Keynes's alternative theory, 283–302
Keynes, J. M.
ambitions for the *Treatise*, 203–5
analysis of essential properties of
  interest in a monetary economy,
  244–8
analysis of speculation as he becomes
  personally involved in speculating
  (1919–1923), 132–40
analysis of speculation in early
  lectures (1909–1915), 126–32
analysis of speculation in relation to
  the 'credit cycle,' 139–47
analysis of speculation in the 1930's,
  147–51
and 'a piece of financial machinery'
  (the foreign exchange market in the
  Tract), 195–205
and definition of 'own-rate of
  interest,' 244–6
and D. H. Robertson, 183–8, 218
and 'faithful' theory of stock
  investing, 147–51
and *General Theory* viewed through his
  own-rates of equilibrium construct,
  259–64
and Marshallian monetary theory,
  176–7
and Marshall's monetary theory as a
  precursor to the *General Theory*,
  165–8
and Marshall's stock theory of
  interest, 110–1
and monetary theory in writings
  between the *Tract* and *Treatise*,
  201–3
and the historical literature on
  speculation, 123–5
and the root of the *General Theory* in
  the crisis in later Marshallian
  economics, 105–6, 166–8
and *Tract* on a monetary economy,
  188–95
and *Treatise*, 139–147, 203–212
and use of the concept of 'efficiency
  wage' in early lectures (1911), 77–8

and "Wicksell Connection,' 275–8
as a lecturer, 75
as a Marshallian economist, 71–5, 91,
  178–212
as a 'moral scientist,' 71–2
assumption of the Marshallian stock
  equilibrium approach to asset
  markets, 103–106
commitment to Dobb's theory of the
  labor market, 309–10
comparison of analysis of stock
  market in *Treatise* and *General
  Theory*, 144–7
comparison to Sraffa as an economist,
  229–30
contrast of his view of a monetary
  society vs. a real exchange one in
  Marshall, 189–95
emerging social theory of wage in the
  1920s, 79–86
estimate of his personal 'velocity of
  money' in pre-WWI lectures, 181
his 'activism,' 180
investment experience in the 1930s,
  148
labor market view in the *General
  Theory*, 35–9, 86–91
origin of asset market meta-theory in
  Marshall, 103–6
pre-World War I monetary lectures,
  181–3
relation of analysis of 'forward
  markets' in *Tract* and *Treatise* to
  'own rates of interest' in *General
  Theory*, 251–7
review of I. Fisher (1911), 183
role of the rate of interest in the
  General Theory, 243–4
strategy in opening the *General Theory*
  with a labor market experiment,
  89–90
the 'fundamental equations' of the
  Treatise, 205–9
the historical context for monetary
  theory of, 179–81
the orthodox Marshallian labor market
  views of as a young don, 75–9
the 'widows-cruse' analogy of the
  Treatise, 210–2
view of A. Marshall, 72–5

Keynes, J. M. – *continued*
  view of speculation on currency and
    commodity exchanges, 140–2,
    195–201
  view of capital in the *General Theory*,
    264–7
  view of speculation on stock
    exchange, 142—7
  view of the early interpretations of
    the *General Theory*, 103–5
  view of the 'essential properties of
    money,' 268–72
  view of the social context for
    monetary analysis, 272–5
  view that Marshall was not good at
    discovering concrete facts, 61
'Keynes literature,' 7–15
Keynes's question in the *General Theory*,
    4–6, 156, 235

labor leaders
  Marshall's private ambiguous relation
    to, 47–8
  Marshall's questioning of, 50–2
  opinion of Marshall, 307–8
labor market analysis
  in Marshallian tradition, 53–70
  in neoclassical thought, 40–1, in the
    tradition of Pigou, 66–70, its lack of
    a role in the *General Theory*, 35, 86
  of Beveridge, 43
  of Dobb and an inter-war Cambridge
    orthodoxy, 636
  of Hobson; 43–4
  of Keynes in his early lectures, 75–9
  of Keynes in the *General Theory*, 17,
    36–9, 86–91
  of Keynes in the twenties, 79–86
labor supply
  Keynes's critique of the classical
    account of, 57
Labordere, M., 73–4, 319
Lacking, abortive, spontaneous, etc., in
    Robertson, 175
'late Victorian' context of Marshall and
    the British labor question, 40–52
Lavington, F., 169–72
Leijonhufvud, A. (*see also author index*)
  on the 'economics of Keynes,' 7, on
    the Wicksell Connection, 239,
    283–300

liquidity preference theory
  and role of conventionality of
    expectations in state of uncertainty,
    261–2
  basis in Marshall's stock theory of
    demand for money, 103–6, 108–11
  comparison of treatment by Keynes's
    Treatise and *General Theory*, 142–7
  critique of Leijonhufvud's criticism of,
    285–8
  translation into own-rates framework,
    261–4, 288–92
  used to illustrate 'Wicksell
    Connection,' 292–298
liquidity premium
  definition in Keynes's *General Theory*,
    246, 268–72
  role of conventional social analysis in,
    272–5
  possibility of attaching to land,
    277–8
liquidity trap
  in Keynesian macroeconomics, 238,
long-period equilibrium
  compared to Keynes's short period
    economics, 19–21, 167
  focus of Marshall's efforts, 101–2
  role in Marshallian cycle theory,
    165–6
  role in Marshall's analysis of
    speculation, 11–6
  Sraffa's interest in compared to
    Keynes's, 229–30
London School of Economics
  Hayek's Lectures to, 215–6
  ideology compared to Cambridge,
    159–60, 214–5
  Lionel Robbins's view of Hayek's
    lectures there, 216

Macmillan Committee
  Keynes's testimony to, 85–6
  Robertson's testimony to, 320
Mann, T
  relationship to Marshalls, 47
marginal efficiency of capital, 149–50,
    265–7
marginal product of labor
  in Dobb, 65–6
  in Keynes, 75–9, 309–10
  in Marshall, 56–60

market or money rate of interest (*see also*, rate of interest)
  in Hawtrey, 172
  in Hayek, 215–8
  in Keynes's *General Theory*, 268–72, 278–9, 292–8
  in Keynes's *Treatise*, 203–5
  in Marshall, 161–3
  in Wicksell, 158–9
Marshall A.
  as a curious Victorian, 84
  as a social theorist, 83
  attitude toward truth and controversy, 86–7
  hunger for influence on business and policy, 82
  public persona relative to Victorian labor reform movement, 50–2
  view of Keynes, 74–5
Marshall, A. and M. P.
  as 'late Victorians,' 44–52
  educational vacations of, 52
  relationship with labor leaders, 50–2
Marshallian Economics
  and capital, 161–2
  and 'ceterus paribus' conditions, 60, 99
  and *Economics of Imperfect Competition*, 100
  and essay 'Money' (1871), 108–111
  and *Industry and Trade*, 98–102, 111–3, 161, 166–8
  and later attempts at monetary analysis, 160–1, 166–8
  and later crisis in with respect to the 'joint stock company,' increasing returns, and 'representative firm,' 96–102, 166–8
  and later essay on "Stock Speculation" (1899), 115–6, 166–7
  and long period normal values, 11–6, 98–9, 165–6
  and major revision of the *Principles* in 1907, 98
  and *Money, Credit and Commerce*, 113–5, 160, 162, 167, 182
  and *Principles*, 45, 53–62, 96–102
  and Royal Commission on Labour (1891–4), 48, 51–2
  and speculation, 111–16
  and static-hypothetical theory versus evolutionary history, 100–2

  and 'symposium on representative firm,' 97
  and the cycle, 162–4
  and *The Economics of Industry* (with M. P. Marshall), 164, 166
  and the joint stock company, 100, 167–8
  and the 'reconciliation problem,' 96
  and unemployment, 61–2
  and view of America, 46
  and Whitaker's comment on the conflict between the *Principles* and *Industry and Trade*, 101–2
  as a "late Victorian" British intellectual, 49–52
  'Brassey's Law' and, 57–8
  extension by Dobb, 63–6
  intended to influence policy and businessmen, 50–1, 55
  his economics versus Walrasian economics, 16–24
  'oral tradition' in monetary economics, 108
  vision of the economy compared to Keynes's, 189–95
  Sraffa's critique of, 97–8, 100
  and theory of interest, 161–3
  on 'indexation' of loans and wages, 164
  later program of pupils of Marshall and, 100, 102, 168–75
  role of "facts" and, 47–8, 72–3
  ethnology and, 46–7, 53–5
  penchant for making "an astounding observation with no basis in fact," 61
  on 'price-stability' as a sufficient remedy for cycles, 164
  on 'foreign trade', 161
  treatment of "efficiency wages," 55, 58–60
  treatment of marginal product of labor and of distribution of national dividend, 56–62
  view of J. S. Mill, 46–50, 115, 170
  view of J. S. Mill's theory of the business cycle reiterated in Keynes's early lectures on monetary theory, 183
Marshallianism as a precursor to the *General Theory*, 165–8
  'the goals' of, 229–36
  the social context for, 272–5

"method of neutral money," (*see* neutral money tradition *and* Wicksellian tradition)

models
Keynes's view of formal models, 5
models in spirit of *General Theory*, 4–6
Marshallian versus Walrasian, 16–18, 230–232
range of that consider equalization of rates of return, 232

monetary economy
in context of Leijonhufvud's Wicksell Connection, 285–98
Keynes's view of, 152, 188–95, 207–10, 237–79
Sraffa's critique of Hayek and the Wicksellian method of neutral money on, 218–20, 227–9

monetary theory
as developed by Marshall's pupils, 168–75
historical context for that of Keynes, 179–81
in early twentieth century, 158–60
in Keynes's pre-WWI lectures, 183
Keynes and Marshallian tradition of, 176–7
Marshallian, 160–4

money, demand for
in Keynes's early lectures, 181–2
in Keynes's *General Theory*, 259–264
in Keynes's *Tract*, 188–9
in Keynes's *Treatise*, 205–9
in Marshall, 108–11, 160–3
in Pigou and Lavington, 168–70

natural rate of interest
of Hayek, 215–8
of Wicksell, 217
of "Wicksell Connection," 158–9
view of Keynes in the *General Theory*, 275–8, 298–300
view of Keynes in the *Treatise*, 203–5

neo-classical synthesis, 13–15

neutral money tradition
in Hayek, 215–8, 227–9
in Wicksell 240–3
Keynes's final view of, 278–9
Sraffa's critique of, 218–20

Ohlin, B.
in correspondence with Keynes, 21–2

own-rates of interest
general determinants of in qualities of assets (Keynes), 244–9
in real exchange economies, 225–6, 248
in Keynes's 'shifting-equilibrium' versus Sraffa, long-period conception of equilibrium value, 256–7
in Walrasian general equilibrium tradition, 230–2
Keynes's examples of, 249–51
short period conception of equilibrium value (Keynes), 256–9
Sraffa's example of, 225
relation to Marshall's stock equilibrium tradition of asset market analysis, 249–50
structure of equilibrium value of on asset markets, 249–59
the *General Theory* viewed through them, 259–64
use in the *General Theory* different related to Keynes analysis of currency and commodity markets in the *Tract* and *Treatise*, 250–9
used by Sraffa to critique Hayek, 224–7

paradox of thrift
in Robertson, 175
relation to transition from *Treatise* to *General Theory*, 210–2

Pigou, A. C.
and "mechanical Marshallianism," 66–70
and theory of money demand and of cycle, 168–71
as the author of the 'classical postulates,' 90
evidence against simplistic view of him presented in the *General Theory*, 68–9
on rigid wage explanation of unemployment as preventing the labor market from achieving equilibrium, 67–9

view of social problem of
  unemployment in the twenties and
  thirties, 35, 303
Pigou effect, 9–10
Post Keynesians, 5
'postulates of the classical economics,'
  17, 26, 36–39, 86–91
'potential' and 'actual' GDP, 234–5
price-level stability
  in Hayek, 216, in Marshall, 163–4
  in the *General* Theory, 272–275
  in the *Tract*, 195
  in the *Treatise*, 209
  Keynes's objection to Robertson on,
  188
producer's expectations, Keynes and,
  18–22

rate of interest (*see also* liquidity
    preference, 'own-rate of interest')
  Cambridge stock-equilibrium meta-
    theory, 108–11
  in Hayek 215–8
  in Hawtrey, 172–3
  in Keynes of the *General Theory*,
    237–79, 285–98
  in Keynes of the *Treatise*, 203–9
  in Robertson, 173–5
  Sraffa's critique of Hayek's conception,
    224–7
  Wicksell on, 158–6, 204, 278–9, 284
'real balance effect (Patinkin), 9–10
Robbins, Lionel, his view of Hayek's
  work, 216
Robertson, D. H.
  theory of the cycle, 173–5
Royal Commission of Inquiry on Labor
  (1891–4)
  Marshall's participation on, 48–52

saving (*see also* forced-saving, saving
    and investment)
  abortive, 175
  demand of depends on rate of
    interest, 162, 188
  depends on income,173, 176, 212
  in Hayek, 216–7
  in Hawtrey, 216–7
  in Keynes *General Theory*, 237–79
  in Keynes *Treatise*, 203–6

in Marshall, 161–3
induced,' 175
'lump-sum' of, 172
Robertson's view of, 174–5
Sraffa's criticism of Hayek's
  conception of, 221–4
'shifting equilibrium,' 8, 153, 235–6,
  249–59, 301, 327
Short-period equilibrium
  in modern macroeconomics, 234–5
  of Keynes's variety, 18–9, 235–6
Sidgwick, H.
  influence on Marshall, 46
speculation on the organized exchanges
  (*see also*, commodities, currency,
    exchange rate system, shares,
    stocks, speculation)
  analysis of in Emery, 116–123
  historical development of, 117–9
  in relation to theory of probability
    (Keynes), 128–32
  Keynes's analysis of in *General Theory*,
    147–51
  Keynes's analysis of in pre-World War
    I lectures, 126—32
  Keynes's analysis of in *Tract*, 132–9
  Keynes's analysis of in *Treatise*,
    140–7
  Keynes's investment advice and
    memoranda, 148–9
  Keynes's own participation in, 132–4,
    139, 147–8
  Marshall's analysis of 112–6
Sraffa, P. (*see also* forced-savings, own-rates
    of interest, Wicksellian tradition)
  compared to Keynes as an economist,
    229–30
  his critique of Hayek's argument for
    'forced saving,' 221–4
  his critique of Hayek's capital theory
    argument, 224–7
  his critique of the use of the
    distinction between real and money
    rates of interest, 227–9
  his use of a long-period conception of
    own-rates equilibrium compared to
    Keynes, 249, 252, 256
  his view of Hayek's use of the
    'method of neutral money,' 219,
    224–29

Sraffa, P. – *continued*
  meaning of his critiques of Hayek for
    the 'goals of monetary theory,'
    229–36
Stockholm School
  ex ante-ex post analysis, 8, 21–2
  influence on Cambridge monetary
    tradition, 159–60
stock market
  Emery's depiction of, 119–20
  historical development of, 121–2
  role in Keynes's *Treatise*, 142–7
  role in Keynes's *General Theory*, 147–51
  role in Marshall's *Principles*, 98–9
  role in later Marshall publications,
    99–102, 113–5
  role in Marshall's unpublished essay
    "The Folly of Amateur Speculators,"
    115–6
structure of production
  in Hayek's theory, 216–7
  in Robertson's theory, 174
  Sraffa's criticism of, 221–4

Tillett, Ben
  relationship to Marshalls, 47
Townshend, Hugh, and Keynes's
    monetary views, 272–5, 329–30
trade cycle (*see* credit cycle theory, cycle
    theory)
trade-unions (*see* unions)

uncertainty
  as a continual concern of Keynes's
    throughout his career, 315
  in Emery's analysis of commodity and
    stock markets, 119–21
  in Keynes's analysis of exchange-rate
    market in *Tract*, 195–201
  in Keynes analysis of stock-markets in
    the *Treatise*, 140–7
  in Keynes's analysis of rational action
    in *Treatise on Probability*, 128–9
  in Keynes's analysis of speculation in
    pre-World War 1 lectures, 126–32
  in Shackle, 8
unemployment (*see also*, employment,
    unemployment, labor demand,
    labor market analysis, labor supply)
  Beveridge on, 43

equilibrium view of (Keynes), 85–6
  extensive treatment by non-economist
    in Victorian England, 41–3
  Hobson's theory of, 43–4
  in Keynes's *General Theory* 89–91
  lack of connection with efficiency
    wages in Marshallian tradition, 70
  lack of much about in classical
    economics, 40
  Marshall's theory of, 61–2
  'New-Keynesian view not that of
    Keynes, 69–70
  Pigou's theory of, 66–9
  involuntary unemployment in Pigou,
    68
  role in motivating Keynes to write
    General Theory, 35
unions (*see also* labor leaders)
  in Dobb's labor market analysis, 66
  in Keynes's view of the Tract, 193–4
  in Keynes's view of unemployment in
    the 20s, 84
  in Marshall's labor market analysis, 55
  Keynes personal feelings toward, 84

Veblen, T.
  builds an alternative theory of a
    speculative economy to Keynes's,
    122
  uses Emery as a standard source on
    methods of speculation (1904), 123
velocity of money
  assumption about by Hayek in *Prices
    and Production*, 219
  Keynes personal estimate of in pre-
    World War I money lectures, 181
  role in Keynes's *Treatise on Money*, 207
  variability in emphasized by
    Cambridge School, 163

wages
  Dobb's theory of, 63–66
  Marshall's theory of, 53–62
wages, money
  Keynes conventional analysis of,
    36–39, 86–91, 271–3
wage inflexibility
  Keynes's view that money wages have
    been inflexible throughout history,
    309–10

New Keynesian explanations for, 69–70

not related to unemployment in Marshall and Dobb, 70

not related to unemployment in *General Theory*, 27, 86–91

related to unemployment in Keynesianism, 238

relation to unemployment in Pigou, 26–7, 66–9

wages, real

Dobb's view that they are indeterminate, 65–6, 309–10

Keynes's *General Theory* view that the don't change with every change in employment and output, 37

traditional view (Pigou) that they determine employment level, 69

Walrasian general-equilibrium analysis

abandons long-established preoccupation of economics with equalization of rates of return, 230–2

and Austrian theory, 159

becomes the standard form of macroeconomics in post-World War II period, 16, 230–3

compared to Marshallian structure of the economics of Keynes, 16–24

not the form of the *General Theory*, 17

Wicksell Connection

and 'Keynes Connection,' 275–8

as a critical juncture in the history of monetary theory, 239

critique of, 292–300

Leijonhufvud's definition of, 158–9, 284–5

translated into own-rates framework, 248–292

Wicksellian tradition

and Sraffa's critique of Hayek, 218–20

Cambridge view of in early thirties, 240–3

compared to economics of Keynes, 31, 275–80

four tests given there concerning the rate of interest and cumulative process of price-level changes, 217

from the standpoint of *General Theory*, 278–9

Hayek's use of, 217

influence on Cambridge School, 158–9

relation to own-rates framework, 264–5

windfall profits and losses

in Keynes's *Treatise*, 210

Widow's cruse analogy

Cambridge 'Circus' criticism of as a 'fallacy,' 210

definition of in Keynes's *Treatise*, 210

manner in which it looks forward to *General Theory*, 211–2

Wittgenstein, L.

Sraffa's influence on (Emma and Coates), 323